T0305281

Para Power

Para Power

THE WORKING CLASS
IN AMERICAN HISTORY

Editorial Advisors
James R. Barrett, Thavolia Glymph,
Julie Greene, William P. Jones,
and Nelson Lichtenstein

*For a list of books in the series, please see
our website at www.press.uillinois.edu.*

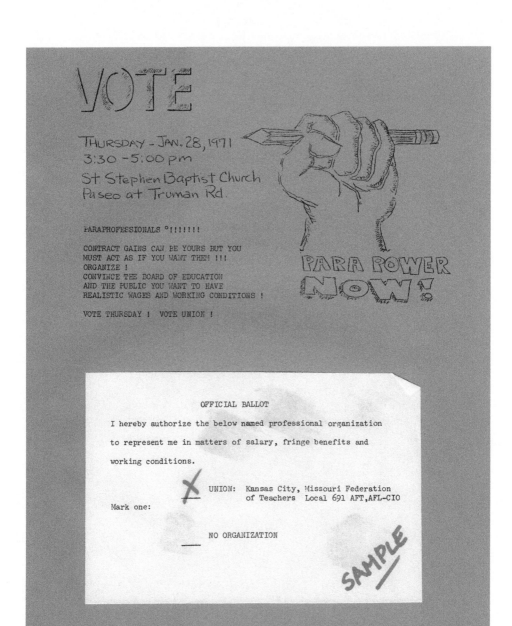

Para Power Now! Kansas City Federation of Teachers Paraprofessional Election Flyer, 1971. AFT Local 691 Kansas City Federation of Techers Collection Box 10, Folder 21. Walter P. Reuther Library, Archives of Labor and Urban Affairs, Wayne State University. This flyer inspired the cover of this book.

Para Power

How Paraprofessional Labor Changed Education

NICK JURAVICH

© 2025 by the Board of Trustees
of the University of Illinois
All rights reserved

**UNIVERSITY OF
ILLINOIS PRESS**
Urbana, Chicago, and Springfield

Cataloging data available from the Library of Congress

ISBN 978-0-252-04615-5 (hardcover)
ISBN 978-0-252-08823-0 (paperback)
ISBN 978-0-252-04741-1 (ebook)

For Jean

For Jean

Contents

Acknowledgments

It is impossible to come to the end of a research project about community-based paraprofessional educators without reflecting on my own educational community. I could not have written this book without the guidance, support, and goodwill of a great many people. I am grateful to everyone who shared their time and energy to help me along the way.

To start, I am profoundly thankful to all the narrators who shared their stories with me in oral histories, even as these recollections brought back the difficult memories that accumulate in struggle. All these individuals are listed in the bibliography. Special thanks are due to Velma Murphy Hill, Marian Thom, and Aurelia Greene, who helped me reach additional narrators, and to Shelvy Young-Abrams, Louise Burwell, Mary Dowery, and Hope Leichter, who made time to attend events, view exhibits, and read materials I produced, giving me encouragement that my analysis of their experiences rang true. Many of these individuals have told their stories in other contexts, cited herein. Mine is not the definitive narrative, but it is a product of their generosity and willingness to discuss the movements and principles to which they committed their lives.

This book began as a seminar paper for Elizabeth Blackmar at Columbia University and grew into a dissertation under the supervision of Mae M. Ngai, who introduced me to union organizers and read endless drafts while reminding me to stay focused on the big questions. Ansley T. Erickson, Ira Katznelson, Alice Kessler-Harris, and Samuel K. Roberts all served on my dissertation committee, welcomed me into scholarly communities and spaces they built, and provided invaluable guidance on the path to the defense. Natasha Lightfoot's course "Resistance and the Black Atlantic" shaped my thinking on core questions of power and organizing. The opportunity to learn from Mary Marshall Clark and everyone at the Columbia

Center for Oral History Research during its Summer Institute in 2014 proved generative on many levels.

As a graduate student, my research on this project was supported by the Jacob K. Javits Fellowship and the National Academy of Education/Spencer Dissertation Fellowship. I was also fortunate to receive a graduate travel grant from the Labor and Working-Class History Association, an Albert Shanker Fellowship for Research in Education from the American Federation of Teachers and the Walter P. Reuther Library at Wayne State University, and a Sam Fishman Travel Grant from the Walter P. Reuther Library. A History in Action grant from Columbia and the AHA/Mellon Career Diversity Initiative took me to South El Monte and El Monte, California, to work with and learn from Romeo Guzmán and Carribean Fragoza on their award-winning public history project, "East of East: Mapping Community Narratives." Support from the Columbia Center for the Study of Social Difference allowed me to take part in the "Social Rights after the Welfare State" workshop, which informed many parts of this book.

The friendship and camaraderie of fellow students in seminars, writing groups, union organizing meetings, and on runs through Central Park sustained me through graduate school. Heartfelt thanks to Wes Alcenat, Carolyn Arena, George Aumoithe, Kathleen Bachynski, Anna Danziger-Halperin, Andre Deckrow, Clay Eaton, Megan French-Marcellin, Masako Hattori, Maria John, Colin Jones, Thai Jones, Suzanne Kahn, Mookie Kideckel, Jessica Lee, Nicole Longpre, David Marcus, Daniel Morales, Keith Orejel, Allison Powers, Jason Resnikoff, Lou Dayton Resnikoff, J. T. Roane, Noah Rosenblum, Ian Shin, Mason Williams, and Michael Woodsworth.

Ansley T. Erickson and Ernest Morrell welcomed me into the Harlem Education History Project at Teachers College as a graduate student in 2013, an experience that shaped this book in countless ways. I am grateful to all the contributing authors in the *Educating Harlem* volume, as well as Teachers College graduate students with whom I had the privilege of working: Esther Cyna, Deidre Flowers, Barry Goldenberg, Viola Huang, Jean Park, and Antonia Smith.

Throughout my research, I have relied on generous archivists to light the way. American Federation of Teachers Archivist Dan Golodner went above and beyond, welcoming me to Detroit and guiding me through the immense collections he oversees. Tom Dickson, Chela Weber, Kate Donovan, Sara Moazeni, and everyone at the Tamiment Library and Robert F. Wagner Labor Archives helped me access the records of the United Federation of Teachers, while David Ment, Dwight Johnson, and Anna Ciepiela-Ioannides led me through the labyrinth of the Municipal Archives. At the Schomburg Center in Harlem, Steven Fullwood helped me think through the materials I found in the Preston Wilcox and Richard Parrish Papers. Liam Adler, then at Metropolitan College of New York (MCNY), opened the college's little-known but remarkable holdings to me.

Daniel Katz, as dean at MCNY, conferred with Liam and MCNY President Vinton Thompson and created a new scholar-in-residence position for me. Many thanks to Dan and all the MCNY faculty and staff for welcoming me into their community: Beth Dunphe, Natasha Johnson, Erica Morales, and Jinx Roosevelt, who had just completed her own history of MCNY and graciously shared research with me. Board members Alida Mesrop and Laura Pires-Houston sat for oral histories with me and shared their experiences at events we organized for the college.

I am grateful, as well, to the faculty, staff, and students of the Harry Van Arsdale Center for Labor Studies at SUNY Empire State College, which runs career ladder programs for United Federation of Teachers paraprofessionals in New York City today. Rebecca Bonanno and Brenda Henry-Offor invited Velma Murphy Hill and me to speak at their annual "Paraprofessional Symposium" at their Manhattan campus in 2014. Gina Torino invited me to give the same presentation to her Staten Island students and invited me back for a workshop the following year. These events helped me connect my historical research to the lived experience of paraprofessional educators in New York City today and shaped my understanding of their work.

The History of Education Writing Group at NYU, helmed by Jon Zimmerman, Natalia Mehlman Petrzela, and Zoe Burkholder, deserves special thanks for workshopping fully half of the chapters in this book. For their comments and camaraderie, both at NYU and at History of Education Society meetings, my thanks are due to Jon, Natalia, Zoe, Michael Glass, Dominique Jean-Louis, Brian Jones, Lauren Lefty, Erika Kitzmiller, Joan Malczewski, and Jonna Perrillo. Working as an associate editor for the blog of the Gotham Center for New York City History helped me improve my overall knowledge of New York City history and afforded me and several graduate students in the NYU workshop the chance to publish our work in a roundtable. My thanks to Peter Aigner, Tim Keogh, Brian Purnell, and Heather Lewis.

I am indebted, as well, to a great many people who took time to chair, comment on, and attend panels and roundtables in which I have participated over the past decade. Among those whose feedback has improved this project are Dawson Barrett, Rudi Batzell, Eileen Boris, Leo Casey, Mahasan Chaney, Marisa Chappell, Barry Eidlin, Elizabeth Faue, Kelly Goodman, Will Goldsmith, Christina Groeger, Jon Hale, William P. Jones, Emily Lieb, Nancy MacLean, Nikki Mandell, Adam Nelson, Diana D'Amico Pawlewicz, Dan Perlstein, Crystal Sanders, Andrew Sandoval-Strausz, Amanda Seligman, Aaron Shkuda, Joseph Slater, Sonia Song-Ha Lee, David Stein, Clarence Taylor, Will Tchakirides, John Terry, Amanda Walter, Joe Walzer, Naomi R Williams, and Gabriel Winant.

I spent two amazing years as an Andrew W. Mellon Foundation Postdoctoral Fellow at the Center for Women's History at New-York Historical Society, where I learned how to do public history from founding director Valerie Paley and the brilliant team at the center, including Jeanne Gardiner Gutierrez, Sarah Gordon, Laura Mogulescu, Linsdey King, Allison Surgeary, and Nicole Mahoney. Thanks, as well, to Mia Nagawiecki, Leslie Hayes, Allyson Schettino, Lee Boomer, and the entire Education Division for the opportunity to share this work with an audience of educators working in New York City (and beyond) today. Lana Dee Povitz, with whom I worked at New-York Historical, invited me to join a writing group led by Sarah Schulman, along with Jeannette Estruth and Amanda Ricci, that significantly improved the manuscript.

Since 2019, I have been Assistant Professor of History and Labor Studies and Associate Director of the Labor Resource Center at UMass Boston, a position in which I have enjoyed tremendous support and encouragement from colleagues and students. The faculty and staff of the History Department and the Labor Resource Center have welcomed me to UMass Boston, while graduate and undergraduate students in history and labor studies classes have continually amazed me with their energy and insights. In this role, I have had the opportunity to partner with the Boston Teachers Union (BTU) on an oral and public history project with their members, a process that has enriched this book and my understanding of educator unionism more broadly. Many thanks to Betsy Drinan, my co-director on this project, as well as BTU's supportive leadership and everyone we have interviewed and met with as part of this work. Since 2016, I have also enjoyed conversations about paraprofessional history and organizing with Jessica Wender-Shubow, who recently retired as president of the Brookline Educators Union. Being in Boston has allowed me to work more closely with Jess as both the union and our statewide federation, the Massachusetts Teachers Association (of which I am a proud member), have made paraprofessional organizing a priority.

I am extremely grateful for the support and patience that everyone at the University of Illinois Press has offered me in the years since my dissertation won the Herbert Gutman prize and, with it, an opportunity to publish in the Working Class in American History Series. James Engelhardt and Jim Barrett provided initial feedback that has structured the revision of my overlong dissertation into this book, and Alison Syring has gone above and beyond to help me push this project over the finish line. I am in debt to Jon Shelton and Lois Weiner for reviewing the manuscript blindly and then sharing further feedback with me, and to Leigh Ann Cowan for helping me organize and submit the final manuscript. Finally, thanks to Bill Nelson for his cartography and Judy Lyon Davis for her indexing.

My mother and father raised me in a house full of books and spirited debates, and it is no surprise that I grew to love both. My mother, the local historian, imbued every rock, tree, and house that we passed with a story, and made the past exciting for me. My father, a scholar of the labor movement, taught me how these histories live in the lives of working people. My brother and sister endured endless bouts of my youthful yakking but still managed to teach me a great deal. Years spent with them have made me a better and kinder thinker and person.

Finally, in the twenty years since I first met her, Jean Seestadt has brightened my days as no one else can. Her earnest generosity, mischievous sense of humor, passionate commitment to doing what's right, and total intolerance for moping and self-pity of any kind have helped me make my way through this project and continue to guide us as we make our way through the world with our two children, Alden and Russel. I dedicate this book to her.

Para Power

Para Power

INTRODUCTION

In Search of Para Power

August 1970

On Monday, August 3, 1970, paraprofessional educators in New York City ratified their first contract with the city's Board of Education. Their union, the United Federation of Teachers (UFT), had bargained a 140 percent wage increase, health care, and paid career advancement, including teacher training, for all "paras." Writing in the *New York Amsterdam News,* the city's largest Black-owned newspaper, the socialist civil rights organizer Bayard Rustin called the contract—one of the first of its kind in the nation—the "Triumph of the Paraprofessionals."[1] For comment, he turned to Velma Murphy Hill, the UFT's lead paraprofessional organizer and a protege of Rustin's in the civil rights and labor movements. "Paraprofessionals, who have already demonstrated that they can contribute greatly to the education of children," said Hill, "are now guaranteed the opportunity to make an even greater contribution" to their schools, their communities, and their new union.[2]

Hill had first encountered paraprofessional educators three years earlier. In the fall of 1967, 1,500 working-class women, nearly all Black and Latina, had started in these new roles in New York City public schools. They were part of a nationwide hiring wave that would bring 10,000 paras into New York City schools by 1970 and nearly half a million into the national educational workforce by 1975. A coalition of civil rights organizers, antipoverty programs, and teacher unionists had pushed the city's Board of Education to create these jobs with funds from the 1965 Elementary and Secondary Education Act. The board directed principals to hire local residents—93 percent women, 80 percent the mothers of schoolchildren, all receiving or eligible for welfare—to improve instruction, build links between schools and communities, and train to become teachers. It paid paras fifty dollars a week with no benefits.[3]

Hill had earned a master's degree from the Harvard Graduate School of Education after leaving the Congress of Racial Equality (CORE) in 1966, and she met a few paras while visiting a school in Manhattan. Hill struck up a conversation that revealed their low wages and decided, "I want to organize these women."[4] She talked to Rustin, who introduced her to UFT president Albert Shanker. In short order, Hill was working as a para herself, laying the groundwork for an organizing drive that would culminate the 1970 contract. As Hill recalled in 2011, she felt, "this is really the civil rights movement as far as I'm concerned."[5] She relished the opportunity to organize with working-class Black and Latina women to win living wages, respect on the job, and opportunities to become teachers who would help desegregate New York's teaching corps.

Paras started work in New York amid fierce conflicts over public education. In the fall of 1967, parents in Harlem, Brooklyn, and the Lower East Side had just launched new experiments in community control of schools, drawing ideas and practices from the Black Power movement and funding from the Ford Foundation.[6] The UFT was on strike, fighting for a new contract that included a provision allowing teachers to remove "disruptive" children from classrooms, which infuriated many parent activists.[7] One year later, in the fall of 1968, teachers across the city struck for forty-two days in response to the efforts of community control leaders in Brooklyn to remove tenured teachers from local schools. These struggles shaped every facet of paraprofessional labor, from their work in classrooms and communities to the organizing drive that the UFT launched in January of 1968. Conflict between parent activists and organized teachers made paras' charge to bridge these divides both essential and extremely difficult.

Just before the 1970 contract was finalized, Cleo Silvers penned a frank account of her experience as a para in the feminist journal *Up from Under*. Silvers, a Philadelphia native, had come to New York City to work for VISTA (Volunteers in Service to America), which posted her in a tutoring program at PS 51 in the Bronx. Along with poverty wages, Silvers wrote, "we para-professionals do not even receive any degree of respect for our work inside these agencies."[8] Silvers detailed the wide-ranging labor expected of paras: "assist the teacher inside the classroom, take attendance, make pretty bulletin boards, act as a police-woman in the hall, control the children, and go into the homes of problem children to speak to their parents." Even as she did all this, Silvers wrote, she was "refused a key to the teacher's rest room" and told by teachers "para-professionals really should not share the teacher's lounge for eating lunch."[9] Silvers explained that the combination of excessive demands and dismissive hostility that she faced from teachers—nearly all of whom were middle-class and white—was "not unique," a truth borne out by research Velma Hill's UFT team conducted at the start of its para campaign.

Some teachers' fear of, and hostility toward, paraprofessional educators presented a serious challenge to paras' ability to do their jobs, as well as to Hill's nascent organizing efforts.

In a 2016 interview with Alondra Nelson, Silvers explained that her time as a para was a radicalizing experience. After teachers told her that a group of sixth graders "couldn't learn," she taught them to read, and she learned in the process that "we couldn't work with those kids without being in contact with their families" (which teachers rarely were).[10] Silvers began traveling with her students' families to welfare offices and the emergency room at Lincoln Hospital. In all these institutions—school, welfare office, and hospital—she was "horrified to see that there was little care on the part of the system for these people . . . and that to get what you needed you had to fight."[11] After leaving VISTA, Silvers joined the Black Panther Party and then the Young Lords, whose organizing, she believed, promoted "genuine struggle and care."[12]

Analyzing her experience as a para in *Up from Under*, Silvers offered a radical critique. Schools, she wrote, hired women because administrators feared Black and Latino men, and also because "with such inadequate salaries a man could not possibly support a family (although many female paraprofessionals are the sole support of their families!)."[13] As implemented by administrators, paraprofessional programs had offered false promises "that we would be able to make effective changes within these inflexible institutions" and that paras would advance to positions of power. Instead, paras found themselves in "second-rate positions . . . expected to work in both professional and nonprofessional roles at a tiny fraction of the salaries the professionals received."[14] Administrators asked Silvers to promote the school to parents but, Silvers wrote, "we must begin to act not as representatives of our respective agencies, but as advocates and representatives of black and Puerto Rican people . . . these institutions can be of real value to our people, but only if we can control them."[15] An addendum to Silvers's piece written by para Dulcie Garcia noted that the UFT was trying to negotiate a contract, but Garcia expressed reservations about both the union's motives and its ability to deliver.[16]

Velma Murphy Hill and Cleo Silvers were not typical paraprofessional educators. They were leading organizers in movements for jobs, freedom, and self-determination. Both women recognized the exploitation paras faced on the job and urged them to organize. More broadly, they recognized the crucial role paras could play in addressing a crisis of care in public education. Each responded from her own political and institutional positions: Hill as a socialist and integrationist (her preferred word) working in the labor movement; Silvers as a member of the Black Panther Party seeking radical transformation of the control and delivery of services. Both believed paraprofessional educators could, and should, exercise power in broader struggles over public education, social welfare, and jobs in New York City and beyond.

In 1970, Hill and the UFT did deliver a contract, which Bayard Rustin called "one of the finest examples of self-determination by the poor."[17] The contract gave him hope for renewed collaboration between the labor movement and the civil rights movement, as paras could "help bring together the UFT and minority groups around the common struggle for better schools." For a decade, Rustin had been organizing to unite the civil rights and labor movements to advocate for full employment and economic justice.[18] As a coauthor of the 1966 "Freedom Budget for All Americans," he had drawn up a massive program of public-sector job creation for this purpose.[19] By "putting millions of dollars in the pockets of the poor," Rustin believed, the paras' contract did "more to combat poverty" than any other War on Poverty program. It provided living wages and job security to paraprofessional educators and empowered them in public schools and union halls. The paras' victory, Rustin wrote, was "a benefit not only to the paraprofessionals but to the entire society" and was "likely to be repeated in other cities as part of a nationwide struggle by low-income workers to achieve equality."[20]

Nonetheless, questions remained. Would paras have the opportunity and support to "learn professional skills and technology so we can use them according to the values and real needs of our people," as Silvers hoped? Would the contract truly be a step toward integrating and democratizing public schools and teacher unions, as Hill and Rustin believed? What power would paras have to shape public education and the resources it distributed in New York?

Today, paraprofessional educators continue to perform essential work in public schools, but they also continue to struggle for living wages, respect on the job, and the power to shape their work and their schools, much as they did in the late 1960s. What, then, became of this work, the women who did it, and their visions for more democratic and equitable schools, cities, and unions? What remains from this era of paraprofessional organizing and empowerment? How can the labor, experiences, and organizing of paras in these years inform ongoing struggles for educational equality, economic justice, and social rights in our schools, cities, and unions today?

Labor, Care, and Power in Public Education

This book is about paras and power: both the entrenched hierarchies of power in public schooling that created and shaped paraprofessional jobs, and the ways that paras and their allies organized to win power for themselves and to implement their visions for public education. In the first instance, this book shows how school administrators and education researchers in philanthropic foundations created a new category of low-wage jobs by redividing educational labor in response to a crisis of care in public schooling after World

War II. By stripping the care work out of teaching and passing it off to contingently hired "teacher aides," they believed they could staff overcrowded classrooms cheaply and efficiently. Across seven decades and innumerable struggles, these ideas have persisted among educational decision-makers. Nearly 1.2 million paraprofessional educators work in US public schools today, where their labor is both essential and, too often, unacknowledged.[21] Their experiences reflect the inequalities of the broader US economy, in which care work is primarily performed by working-class women of color for poverty wages and with little opportunity for advancement. This is a history, in part, of how our stratified, care-based economy took particular form in US public schools.[22]

At the same time, *Para Power* illuminates the ways these educators deemed "aides" organized to win power and transform the conditions of, and possibilities for, their own labor and urban public education more broadly in the 1960s and 1970s. Paraprofessionals, as they came to be known by the late 1960s, labored at the center of struggles for jobs and freedom, as the stories of Velma Hill and Cleo Silvers show. In working to respond to the crisis of care in public education, the first generation of paraprofessional educators fought to both create and redefine their jobs. Once hired, they organized tirelessly to realize the potential of this work. To borrow from E. P. Thompson, paras were "present at their own making."[23]

In making their work anew, paraprofessional educators joined and partnered with three interconnected movements: Black and Latinx struggles for civil rights, social justice, and self-determination; the War on Poverty in its many manifestations; and the labor movement, specifically teacher unions. Paras and their allies in these movements demanded expanded roles for paras to achieve three interlocking goals: bringing local knowledge, language, and culture into schools to improve instruction and care; making schools more responsive to the families and communities they served; and creating paths to teaching careers that would grow and diversify the teaching corps in urban school districts. With backing from civil rights and labor leaders and funding from War on Poverty legislation, paras began making changes in their schools in the late 1960s, where they improved pedagogy, curriculum, the care of students, the maintenance of learning environments, and communication with families and communities. In turn, these allies supported paras as they organized for living wages, job security, opportunities for advancement, and the power to make public schools serve their communities better. These struggles did not just reshape schools. They opened new fronts for social movements, modeled new ways to fight poverty, and expanded the organizing and membership of teacher unions. Thus, in addition to showing how people with power in public education created and defined paraprofessional labor, *Para Power* examines paras' unheralded achievements and the ideas, practices, and politics that sustained their work and organizing in these transformative years.

This book concludes by examining changes in political economy, social movements, and educational policy in the late 1970s and 1980s that undermined this expansive vision of paraprofessional labor and the coalition that supported it. Paraprofessional jobs did not disappear—indeed, they remain essential to the functioning of public schools—but without the support of the coalition that had sustained paras in preceding decades, administrators and policymakers returned to constructing hierarchical workplaces that exploited the caring labor of working-class women of color.

Today, organized paraprofessional educators are remaking their jobs once again. In local unions across the nation, paras are fighting for the same things this first generation did: living wages, respect on the job, and paths for advancement.[24] These struggles have persisted for over half a century because of the ways skill and care are defined and prescribed in capitalist economies, and how the work of each is parceled out along lines of race, class, and gender. To understand the construction of paraprofessional jobs, past and present, as well as the ways paras themselves have worked and organized to reconstruct their jobs, we must start by analyzing how hierarchies of reward, respect, and responsibility are sustained in public schools.

"Paraprofessionals," wrote *Education Week*'s Madeline Will in 2022, "are known as the backbones of the classroom for their work supporting student learning and well-being. But they report feeling underpaid and overworked—a perennial issue that's only getting more dire."[25] As a Brown University study detailed in 2021, paras "are a large and growing workforce that provides key services for schools and, importantly, diversifies the demographics of educators in schools—providing adults with knowledge of local communities and shared experiences with students." However, the study noted, "these educators receive substantially lower wages, and their contracts provide fewer protections as well as fewer supports for advancement."[26]

The tasks paras have performed since the creation of the first teacher aide positions range widely: from individualized special education to bilingual group work, classroom assistance, and community outreach. This work remains a source of unionized jobs and access to some forms of on-the-job training for working-class women and men, across the country and particularly in Black and Latinx urban neighborhoods.[27] However, as these reports make clear, para jobs continue to pay low wages and rarely offer unbroken paths to teaching careers. Why, when their work is acknowledged as essential, are these workers poorly paid and rarely acknowledged?

As Johanna S. Quinn and Maya Marx Ferree show in the most complete theorization of paraprofessional labor to date, paras' paradoxical status is no accident. "These public school employees," they explain, "are majority Black and Latina and perform essential but devalued work in US school communities," a result of the ways the public education system "draws on and reproduces class, gender and race as matters of how work is to be done, by whom and for whom."[28] Quinn and Ferree show how skill—the preserve of white, credentialed, middle-class, predominantly female teachers—is rewarded by school systems, while care, performed by working-class women of color, is poorly compensated. The work of navigating racial boundaries to promote respect among students, parents, and teachers—the active linking of schools with the communities they serve—is rarely recognized at all. "This structural difference in how race interacts with gender in credentialing, hiring, organizing work and assigning rewards," Quinn and Ferree demonstrate, "matters to the paras."[29] These hierarchies limit how paras are compensated, as well as their ability to work effectively with students, teachers, and wider school communities. Jennifer Gaddis notes a similar dynamic among school lunch workers who, like paras, "are all part of a larger political economy of care that currently depends on (mostly) women's unpaid and low-wage labor in order to function." Like paras, "school cafeteria workers care for the nation's children, yet they cannot afford to adequately care for themselves or their families on the paychecks they bring home."[30] Paraprofessional organizing, past and present, has sought to restructure hierarchies of reward, respect, and responsibility, and in so doing, to replace the racism, sexism, and class bias on which the political economy of care is currently built with solidarity, security, and opportunity for all educational workers.

The conditions of paraprofessional labor that Quinn and Ferree diagnose result from what socialist feminist scholars analyze as "capitalism's crisis of care," in Nancy Fraser's formulation. As Fraser explains, "capitalism's orientation to unlimited accumulation tends to destabilize the very processes of social reproduction on which it relies."[31] This is evidenced not just by the devaluing of paras' social reproductive labor in schools, but also by administrators' and politicians' frequent attempts to outsource, casualize, or cut their jobs entirely. As discussed in the final chapter of this book, the para workforce has grown significantly in the neoliberal era—one of near-constant fiscal crises and austerity budgets for urban public schools—precisely because paras are paid so little and enjoy less job security than teachers. In a cruel but predictable irony, paras are asked to solve ever-greater challenges of social reproduction under austerity conditions, while, at the same time, their low wages are used as evidence that their jobs are unskilled and thus either unnecessary or easily replaceable with temporary, non-union hires. While paras, their unions, and their allies among parents and teachers have fought these cuts, which prove disastrous for students and teachers when implemented, the refrain that paras' labor is unskilled or unnecessary has proved resilient among neoliberal education "reformers."[32]

While attacks on paraprofessional educators today exacerbate our present crisis of care in public education, these jobs originated in an earlier crisis of social reproduction in public schooling, one that emerged in US cities after World War II. Three overlapping factors generated this postwar crisis. The first was the "baby boom": the near-doubling of the US school-going population between 1949 and 1969.[33] As class sizes ballooned and schools held double sessions, teachers simply did not have time or space to attend to students adequately. Desperate administrators, from individual principals to philanthropic foundations, launched a range of experiments to bring more adults into classrooms, of which hiring "teacher aides" was one.

The overcrowding crisis generated by the baby boom was exacerbated by two additional factors. The first was that the population of urban schools was not just growing but changing. As white families followed jobs and federal housing incentives to suburban districts, Black and Hispanic (the term used in most demographic reporting from the era) families migrated to urban centers from the US South and the Caribbean.[34] Their children needed education attuned to their languages and cultures, and care to address the challenges of living in segregated, under-resourced neighborhoods. Public schools, led by white, middle-class administrators and staffed by teachers of the same demographic, often proved unable or unwilling to provide such care. Instead, city administrators segregated these students into overcrowded, badly maintained, poorly resourced, and mismanaged schools. In response, parents began organizing to demand high-quality education for their children.

The final factor in the postwar crisis of care in public education was a redefinition of "professionalism" in public schools, one shaped both by the baby boom and by teachers' renewed efforts to unionize. As Diana D'Amico Pawlewicz and Bethany Rogers have both shown, the postwar teacher shortage was compounded by fears that teacher quality was in decline and new efforts were necessary to attract "the right kind of teachers."[35] Union leaders rightly interpreted most administrative solutions—including emergency licensure and merit pay—as threats to organized teachers. The business elites who staffed philanthropic foundations, however, proposed a solution from the corporate management playbook that appealed to unions and administrators alike: the division of labor, specifically the decoupling of skilled, professional instruction from social-reproductive work. Teachers and administrators agreed that "non-teaching chores," including many forms of care and community-relations work, took up too much time on the job and deterred college graduates from teaching careers. While today, education reformers working within neoliberal capitalism seek to outsource care work to the ever-growing market of private, precarious labor, these earlier reformers, working in the era of Fordist capitalism, sought to promote the efficient use of educational labor from within the educational "firm," or bureaucracy, by dividing instruction from care work.

The hiring of "aides" thus moved forward. As teacher unions won collective bargaining rights and their first contracts, many bargained directly for the hiring of aides to provide relief from "non-teaching" tasks. During a period when students needed both more care and new forms of care, foundations, administrators, and teacher union leaders redefined the work of education to displace the burdens of care from "professional" teachers onto a new class of school workers.

Because the hiring of the first teacher aides in the early 1950s was a response to a crisis of care, the fifteen years of debate, experiment, struggle, and collaboration that followed in the making of paraprofessional jobs focused on the questions of who should provide care in schools, and how. The question of *who* made for contests over qualifications, credentials, training, links to students and their families, access to jobs, and more. The question of *how* this work should be done proved even thornier. Efforts to define "non-teaching" chores generated absurdly large and varied lists of custodial, care, support, and disciplinary labor that schools needed to function. Even the lines between "non-teaching" work and instruction proved fuzzy and porous, both on paper and in the practices aides and paras developed at work. Questions about paraprofessional labor thus quickly became debates about the practice and purpose of public education in an era when schooling was a key site of campaigns for opportunity, resources, and citizenship.

These are the questions that made the struggles of paraprofessional educators so important to Velma Murphy Hill, Cleo Silvers, and the movements of which they were part. Those who wielded power in public education—foundations, politicians, administrators, and (initially) some union leaders—believed "aides" could solve their problems of social reproduction cheaply and easily. However, as those first aides and the people who worked with them realized, this work is foundational to public schooling. Aides—and, later, paras—laying this foundation thus had the power to shake the hierarchies built atop their labor, especially when they organized and built coalitions and movements to support their visions for public schooling. Over two decades in the 1960s and 1970s, their organizing intersected with, energized, and drew power from wider movements for civil rights, ending poverty, and public-sector labor rights. *Para Power* analyzes the elite creation of para jobs and the rise and fall of the first movements to reimagine this work, in the belief that both are necessary to understand this work—its place and its potential—in our schools, communities, unions, and cities today and in the future.

Where Are the Paras? Rethinking Recent History with Paraprofessional Educators

In analyzing the creation of paraprofessional jobs and movements to transform them, *Para Power* shows that paras worked at the center of struggles for jobs and freedom in the 1960s and 1970s. It explores how paras' labor to respond to the crisis of care in public education transformed public schools and the relationships between schools and the neighborhoods they served. Paraprofessional programs created thousands of jobs in working-class Black and Hispanic neighborhoods facing rising unemployment and became a key pipeline for the training of Black and Hispanic teachers in the 1970s and early 1980s. Paras' organizing helped drive the expansion and integration of public-sector unions. And yet, despite their demonstrable impact, paras remain on the margins of scholarship about public education, social movements, poverty policy, and union organizing in these years, much as these workers remain essential but unacknowledged in public schools and education policy today. Their sidelining is a consequence of policy and scholarly frameworks that have obscured the work of these educators, both in the past and in the present.

Almost from their beginning, paraprofessional educators have been overshadowed by conflicts between parent activists and teacher unionists. Paras in New York had been at work for less than a year when simmering hostilities between the UFT and advocates of community control exploded in May 1968 in the Ocean Hill–Brownsville neighborhood in Brooklyn. The ensuing UFT strike has long been described as an epochal breaking point, so much that one historian's account concluded: "Ocean Hill-Brownsville sparked a cultural war between blacks and whites that would last for the rest of the twentieth century and on into the twenty-first."[36]

Narratives of failure and fracture on the path from integrationist civil rights to separatist Black Power remain all too common, particularly in the history of education in New York City.[37] Narrative arcs from the 1964 boycott for school integration to the 1968 community control struggle—and thence to decades of failed schools and hostile politics—continue to dominate scholarship and popular memory, despite some notable recent revisions.[38] What positive impact could paraprofessionals—hired from neighborhoods that supported community control to work alongside unionized teachers—make amid such devastation?

Studying paraprofessional programs reveals one major way Black and Puerto Rican organizers fought for rights and power in public education both before and after 1968. As Russell Rickford writes, the "themes of self-government, equitable integration, relevance, survival, and cultural rebirth in African American philosophies of education" that animated the struggles of the late 1960s represent neither a clean break nor direct continuity between the eras and philosophies of civil rights and Black Power. Rather, they "suggest a vision of schools as sites of entry into the democratic order, and as a mechanism for rendering that order more hospitable to black folk and others on the margins."[39] Para programs became key points of entry into public schools and new mechanisms for transforming them, before and after 1968. Campaigns for and by paraprofessional educators involved organizers from across the political and ideological spectrum of Black freedom struggles, such as Velma Murphy Hill and Cleo Silvers. Paras and their allies articulated broad goals that took many forms in practice: the incorporation of local voices and cultures into pedagogy, curricula, and school governance; a greater degree of voice and control for parents in schools; and job creation for the desegregation of the educational workforce. As Jane Berger writes of Black women working in the public sector in Baltimore, paras fought to secure the "legacies of the civil rights movement" for decades.[40]

Paraprofessional programs began within the War on Poverty, but paraprofessional educators' trajectory into permanent roles in school districts, and their unionization, was highly unusual. Critical histories have shown how most community action programs funded through the War on Poverty stood outside traditional structures of municipal governance, rendering them impermanent and alienating potential allies in urban politics. These critical histories examine how such programs focused on educational and behavioral approaches to poverty rather than job creation, and how they framed urban poverty as a product of impoverished places apart from the affluent city, thereby limiting the potential for structural change or wider political mobilization.[41] War on Poverty programs hired residents in paraprofessional roles in health care, social work, and community organizing, as well as education, but as federal funding shrank in response to conservative backlash and national recession in the 1970s, sustaining these jobs, and particularly the promise of career opportunities, became impossible.[42] Paraprofessional educators, however, worked within local educational bureaucracies. By organizing with teacher unions, they both preserved their jobs and made more progress than any other group of paraprofessionals toward living wages, job security, and career advancement opportunities.

In fighting both to create and to realize the promise of their jobs, paraprofessional educators joined working-class women around the country in fighting a "War on Poverty from the Grass Roots Up."[43] In schools, hospitals, and community centers around the nation, the objects of poverty policy—poor and working-class Black, Latinx, Asian, Native, and rural white people, particularly women and mothers—fought for employment, self-determination, and state resources.[44] Their efforts were part of a wider upsurge in organizing by poor and working-class women in tenant activism, public health, and welfare rights.[45] They deployed the language of self-determination and sought control of resources and systems that governed the lives of the poor, but they were not "separatist." As Rhonda Williams argues, "black power" in this context meant making the state realize its "responsibility to black people and communities."[46]

Paraprofessional educators in New York and across the country were nearly all women and mostly mothers, hired expressly because administrators believed they had natural caregiving abilities that could be exploited to address the crisis of care in urban schools. Gendered expectations shaped paraprofessional work and organizing at every level, from encounters with parents and local activists to debates at the contract bargaining table. As many people sought to take advantage of their status as mothers, paras engaged in the practice Black feminist thinkers have theorized as "activist mothering": women promoting youth and community survival by using "indigenous knowledges" rooted in home, kinship, and community.[47] This organizing was rooted in commitments to community that persisted even in the face of government abdication and popular condemnation in the 1970s. Paras were "local people," in Jeanne Theoharis and Komozi Woodard's definition, possessed of "a political orientation, a sense of accountability, and an ethical commitment to the community."[48] And, as they established themselves in schools, they asserted their value as what Jessica Wilkerson calls "caring citizens" whose labor sustained the civic and social bonds on which communities relied.[49]

At the same time, activist mothering proved challenging as paraprofessional educators became entangled in the expanding disciplinary and surveillance apparatus in public schools. Many paras' job descriptions included maintaining safe and supportive learning environments at a time when overcrowding, lack of resources, and fear and distrust between educators and students militated against peaceful classrooms. When discipline was meted out, paras faced difficult choices. These fraught tasks could be carried out with care or in punitive fashion, depending on the expectations of teachers and administrators, paras' relationships with students and families, and the degree to which paras had the power to act autonomously. Some embraced their roles as disciplinarians and even took jobs in the emerging world of school security. Others challenged punishments and sought to implement alternatives to harsh and police-adjacent school safety plans, though doing so became much harder as administrators, teachers, media, and the public grew increasingly alarmed by school violence and embraced punitive solutions in the 1970s.[50] Even as they tried to "fight their own War on Poverty," paras found themselves walking the path "from the War on Poverty to the War on Crime," as new state systems of surveillance and control, particularly of young people, took shape in schools and antipoverty programs.[51]

As Stuart Hall wrote, "the State in advanced industrial capitalist societies is not simply coercive . . . the State is also educative: It enlarges social and cultural possibilities; it enables people to enter new terrains" and "it is necessarily a contradictory site on which concessions have been won."[52] Nowhere is this more evident than in state-provided public education. Paraprofessional educators labored at the contradictory center of the US welfare state apparatus at a moment of great attention and investment, simultaneously winning concessions through organizing and being incorporated into unequal and coercive systems of social control.

The United States has a long history of "educationalizing" social problems, but paraprofessional educators and their allies did not separate the work of education from social welfare. Instead, they "used the American commitment to educating children in order to gain support for other state services," in Miriam Cohen's formulation.[53] These were educational programs funded by War on Poverty legislation, but they created hundreds of thousands of jobs in just over a decade and made a permanent place for community-based educators in public schools.[54] The design of these jobs and programs challenged deficit-based descriptions of paras' neighborhoods by drawing on local knowledge from these neighborhoods to improve schooling. A wave of recent scholarship has revealed the constitutive role of schools in "making the unequal metropolis," from the structuring of markets in land and labor to the formation, categorization, and legitimation of neighborhood-community units.[55] This book shows how schools shaped not just individual students through instruction, but also the distribution of employment opportunities, paths for political participation, and the process of community formation in the city.[56]

In classrooms and schools, paraprofessional educators built solidarity with teachers across lines of race, class, and metropolitan space through shared experiences as working women.[57] Paras were part of an intergenerational, cross-class variety of women's activism that flourished in New York City in the 1960s and 1970s, within and beyond what is typically considered the feminist movement in these years. Scholars have shown how women's solidarity sustained local movements for tenant rights and neighborhood restoration; in the case of paraprofessional educators, these bonds laid the groundwork for unionization drives.

The unionization of paraprofessional educators is the most contentious part of this history. By 1965, 382,000 New Yorkers worked in the public sector, a quarter-million of them on the municipal payroll.[58] The public sector's expansion particularly afforded opportunities to Black and Latina women, who had previously been segregated in the worst jobs available. In 1940, two out of three employed Black women in Brooklyn labored in domestic service;

by 1970, the number had dropped to fewer than one in ten, as former domes-
tics—including many paras—moved into new jobs in the "human services."[59]
Uptown, only about 5 percent of Harlemites worked in the public sector in
1960, but by 1980, nearly 20 percent did, and nearly 30 percent of women.[60]

As state and municipal governments grew in the postwar era, public-sector
unions became some of the most dynamic and progressive forces in the labor
movement, organizing over 2 million workers in the years between 1960 and
1976.[61] These organizing drives brought thousands of women and workers
of color into the labor movement, and connected organized labor to social
movements, including the civil rights movement.[62] In addition to the material gains they made, paraprofessional educators and their allies articulated
broad new visions for work, politics, and participation in the postindustrial
city, with what Jane Berger has termed "a new working class"—no longer
white, male, or industrial—at its center.[63]

The organizing drives of paraprofessional educators should be a major part
of this story, but they have not featured in the history of teacher or public-
sector unionism except as footnotes. A robust recent literature—focused, as
this study is, on New York City—has shown how the United Federation of
Teachers built militant teacher unionism by appealing to "teacher rights,"
in Jonna Perrillo's framing, defined in terms of autonomy from administrative and community pressures.[64] As Diana D'Amico Pawlewicz argues, this
militancy was gendered; in place of the caring image of the woman teacher,
UFT leaders promoted masculine visions of the professional teacher, possessed of credentialed skill and managerial-class leadership, like the white-
collar professionals of the private sector.[65] Professionalism—long a cudgel
wielded by administrators to critique teachers—came to be a powerful but
parochial rallying cry for unionizing teachers in the 1960s, a claim to rights
and autonomy at work rooted in credentials and capacity for leadership that,
implicitly or not, presumed professionals to be white and middle-class.[66]

Across the country, Jon Shelton shows, teachers' initial postwar organizing won wide support in cities, where their struggles aligned with those of
other unions claiming middle-class status for their members. As Pawlewicz,
Perrillo, and Shelton all argue, however, the jealous defense of teacher professionalism and teachers' rights presaged explosive clashes between unions and
Black activists in New York, Newark, and other cities. They also left teacher
unions susceptible to political attacks in the 1970s, in which political opponents argued teacher union activity, particularly strikes, constituted action
"against the public" in an era of economic crisis.[67]

Examining the complex and changing relationship between paraprofessional educators and their union is essential to understanding the trajectory of
teacher unionism from the 1970s through the present. After a decade of defining themselves as a professional union comprised exclusively of credentialed

teachers, in 1969 the American Federation of Teachers announced it would become a "vertical" union that would welcome paraprofessionals and other educational workers.[68] This shift was the product of fierce internal debates about the value of organizing paras, and it generated conflict in many locals, with some teachers opposing these organizing drives. The language of verticality also indicated the AFT leadership's intent to preserve professional hierarchies within the union as well as inside the schoolhouse.

The leading advocates of paraprofessional unionization in the UFT and AFT appealed both directly to teachers' self-interest—arguing that unionized teachers needed paras' support—and to broader visions of social unionism, arguing that paras' presence would help AFT locals build political alliances with the communities they served. In their appeals to paras, the UFT and AFT likewise married bread-and-butter concerns—living wages, job security, and career advancement—to broader promises of political and social empowerment for paraprofessional educators. Velma Hill described paraprofessional organizing as "an education in democracy" for all involved, while Cleo Silvers worried that paras allied with the UFT would remain "assistants of the oppressors" rather than "the servants of our people." Paras' experiences would run the gamut. Teacher unions were not monolithic actors but sites of contestation and engagement. At one level, paras' presence in these unions meant new access to resources and power; at another, it meant entering a new arena of struggle over what these programs meant and who would decide. Over 100,000 paraprofessional educators would join the AFT in the twenty years between 1969 and 1988, by which time paras comprised 14 percent of the union's membership.

In the same years that paraprofessional educators joined teacher unions, the political economy under these unions was shifting dramatically. In the 1960s, urban teachers had fought for contracts to make the fruits of the New Deal order their own, and they had done so with the support of what Shelton terms the "labor-liberal" voting coalition in their cities. As paras tried to do the same in the 1970s, that coalition was disintegrating. Private-sector workers enduring job loss and union busting absorbed right-wing attacks on public-sector workers that blamed them, and the increasingly non-white urban residents they served, for high taxes. As Jane Berger shows in Baltimore, these attacks mobilized racism and sexism to equate Black and Latina women workers with the demonized, "undeserving" poor Black and Latinx families they served.[69]

Attacks on the public sector grew worse as fiscal crises brought a new generation of politicians and policymakers to power in US cities. Even as paras unionized, these new regimes hastened the disappearance of progressive visions and practices of community-based educational hiring. Led by Ed Koch in New York City, these politicians ushered in an era of "austerity

politics": slashing social services, subsidizing private development, and abandoning traditional allies in the labor movement and freedom struggles.[70] In
educational and antipoverty policy, this new regime privileged cost-benefit analysis of performance, outsider expertise, and elite qualifications for
employment, and it devalued the local knowledge and commitments to educational equity that paras brought to public schools. These shifts in policy
and practice obscured paras' contributions to education and sidelined them
as sources of ideas and innovation in schools. They also set in motion the
strategies that neoliberal politicians would use to attack care workers and
public-sector unions more broadly in the decades to come.

Schools are sites of state power and state making. Efforts to transform the
work of education through paraprofessional programs were part of ongoing
struggles by working-class people "to win from the state what was owed to
them," as Stuart Hall writes, and "to enlarge that aspect of the state" that provides necessary resources and status for citizens.[71] Paraprofessional educators
won for themselves and their cities such an enlargement, even if temporarily.
The legacy of these community-based hiring programs is evident both in
the continued presence of paraprofessional educators in public schooling,
and in their continued demands for an urban politics that is simultaneously
responsive to local people and capable of building broad social movements
and coalitions to make lasting political and institutional change.

Charting the Arc of Paraprofessional
Programs and Organizing

Para Power examines the creation of para jobs and the evolution and impact
of paraprofessionals' labor and organizing in education in seven chapters. It
shifts in scale from national policy debates to school-level interventions and
back in order to analyze the interplay between local struggles and national
developments in educational and employment policy.[72] Throughout, it keeps
the stories of paraprofessional educators at the center of the narrative, while
locating them both within entrenched hierarchies of power in public education and wider social movements: parent and community organizers, the War
on Poverty, and the labor movement.

The first three chapters chart the path from the crisis of care in public
education to the signing and implementation of the landmark paraprofessional contract in New York City in 1970. Chapter 1 shows that while school
administrators used foundation funding to hire "aides" to address the need
for care in overcrowded schools in the 1950s, it was a coalition of parent
organizers, antipoverty organizations, and progressive teacher unionists
that reimagined and reworked "aide" roles into more expansive "paraprofessional" jobs over the course of the 1960s. This coalition was based in New

York City, where its efforts shaped national policy and convinced the local Board of Education to hire its first paraprofessionals in the spring of 1967.

Chapter 2 uses oral histories and local archives to illuminate the experiences of the first generation of paraprofessional educators in New York City in the late 1960s. Though educators, bureaucrats, activists, and union organizers had coalesced around a general vision for paraprofessional programs, it was paras themselves who realized this vision through their labor. Paras worked to address the crisis of care in public schools using three broad strategies: activist mothering, coalition building, and collective advancement. The UFT clashed repeatedly with Black and Puerto Rican parent activists in these years, but despite this tumult, this chapter argues that paras "made themselves essential" to students, teachers, parents, and administrators.[73] The solidarity they built in schools and communities underlaid their push for a union contract.

Chapter 3 analyzes the unionization of New York's paraprofessional educators in 1969 and their contract campaign in 1970. Both these campaigns were shaped by the most divisive teacher strike in New York City history, in which the predominantly white, middle-class UFT shut down the schools for several weeks in 1968 to protest the unilateral transfer of eighteen white educators out of an experimental Black- and Puerto Rican–led community school district in Brooklyn. Paras' 1969 unionization drive generated heated debates about who would define the terms, goals, and conditions of paraprofessional labor, and it ended with paras choosing to join the UFT in a close vote. However, the Board of Education refused to bargain with paras, believing that they would not dare risk a strike that would infuriate their neighbors and expose the unwillingness of white rank-and-file teachers to support paras. In response, paras and their union organized a two-front campaign in communities and the union, demonstrating widespread support for their cause and winning their contract in August of 1970.

Chapter 4 examines the implementation and impact of the paraprofessional contract in New York City in the early 1970s, arguing that unionization produced tangible benefits and power for paras that earlier scholarship has not recognized. The agreement the UFT brokered guaranteed living wages and job security for paras, empowering them to continue and even expand their work in schools and neighborhoods while other War on Poverty programs were shuttered or defunded. Unionization supported many paras as they took on leadership roles in schools, churches, neighborhoods, and the union itself. Most significant, the Board of Education partnered with the City University of New York to create the promised "career ladder" program for paras to become teachers, which educated thousands of paras every semester from 1971 to 1976. The gains paras made in these years did not come easily, however. New challenges emerged to para programs in the early 1970s, first through the New York City school system's restructuring, and then through the emergence of fiscal crisis in the city.

Chapters 5 and 6 examine how ideas, institutions, and practices from New York City shaped paraprofessional programs across the United States in the 1970s. Exploring the trajectories of teacher unionists, scholars of poverty, and radical Black organizers demonstrates the significance of paraprofessional work and organizing to major movements in US history. Chapter 5 shows how the American Federation of Teachers used the UFT's 1970 campaign as a model for organizing in the 1970s. Deploying organizers, materials, and ideas from New York, the AFT added tens of thousands of paraprofessional members in these years. Paras' organizing proved a dynamic and important part of the teacher union movement in the 1970s, at both the local and international level. However, the AFT's leadership promoted an assimilationist vision of para organizing focused on seamlessly incorporating paras into a teachers' union. This top-down approach limited the more robust visions of educational and social transformation articulated by local para organizers, including those who joined the AFT's organizing committee.

While the AFT blueprint was the dominant form of paraprofessional organizing in the 1970s, Chapter 6 shows how two other models from New York City also shaped national programs and policies. The first was the "New Careers" movement in antipoverty policy, which found its fullest form in the Career Opportunities Program (COP), a federally funded Office of Education initiative that supported the hiring and training of nearly 15,000 paraprofessional educators nationwide. Led by Frank Riessman, New Careerists imagined a post-capitalist public sector that would remake the welfare state and higher education through job creation and training. However, they lacked the political strategies and savvy of their fellows in the labor movement and the Black freedom struggle, and when funding ran out, the COP was shuttered.

The second model explored in Chapter 6 was created by Black radical educator and organizer Preston Wilcox. Wilcox is best known for his advocacy of community-controlled schools in New York City, but throughout his career, he fought for the hiring and empowerment of local residents. Wilcox opposed unionization and professionalization for community-based educators, but he continued to promote local hiring even after paras joined the UFT. As a coordinator for the Office of Education's "Follow Through" program for students in first, second, and third grades, Wilcox devised a program of "Parent Participation in Follow Through" that focused on local employment and empowerment. He advised dozens of projects in eight different states, and through prolific writing, traveling, and hosting an annual conference, he became a leader in the Follow Through program nationally. His self-described vision of "radical pluralism" guided a wide range of local parents in asserting their rights.

Chapter 7 returns to New York City during its 1975 fiscal crisis. New York had been the leading site of paraprofessional organizing and innovation for a decade, but in 1975, the city became the leading edge of attacks on paraprofessional educators. Both during and after the crisis, politicians and policymakers embraced critiques of para programs that combined racist and sexist tropes about the labor of working-class women with neoliberal cost-benefit analyses of education, social welfare, and the labor movement. Paraprofessionals maintained their jobs in New York City and still do to this day. But without the coalition of allies that had sustained them, they became increasingly marginalized and exploited in public schools once again.

While the rise of paraprofessional labor and organizing was a national phenomenon with innumerable local iterations, it was shaped significantly by programs, institutions, and people from New York City. New York became a center of paraprofessional innovation for two reasons: the city received an outsized share of early federal spending for antipoverty programs, and its teaching corps was highly segregated by northern standards.[74] Because of this segregation, civil rights activists sought to bring local people and perspectives into public schools. Local antipoverty programs, which later became models for the federal War on Poverty, created experimental programs of local hiring in these neighborhoods. Once the Board of Education began hiring paras, this workforce grew rapidly. By 1970, New York City employed 10,000 paraprofessional educators, more than any other school district in the country, in a wide range of roles. New York is thus an ideal setting in which to analyze the full range of this labor. In addition, the ascendance of New Yorkers to leadership roles in the AFT and programs funded by the federal Office of Education meant innovations and ideas developed in the city became national models, as discussed in Chapters 5 and 6. New York City serves both as a rich case study and as a hub of innovation with national influence.

Limits arise in choosing a case study, and despite its significance, New York City is no exception. Exploring the national programs discussed in Chapters 5 and 6 reveals the remarkable range and creativity of paraprofessionals' labor and organizing in many different local contexts. While these are noted briefly in those chapters, the lives and work of paras who rode school buses during desegregation in Boston and Minneapolis, and who delivered language education to the children of migrant workers in the rural Southwest, merit studies of their own. *Para Power* is thus one history, focused on New York and its influence. Let us hope for more.

This book focuses on paraprofessional educators in the American Federation of Teachers, which today is the smaller of the two international teacher unions in the United States. More work is needed on the organizing efforts of paraprofessional educators in National Education Association (NEA) locals, where they are known today as education support professionals, or ESPs.

NEA paras do not feature in this book because their organizing began in the mid-1970s, and only in earnest after paras were given full status in that union in 1979 (before which they were "auxiliary" members). As a union primarily representing paraprofessional educators in suburban and rural contexts, the NEA story takes place not only in a different era but also in different kinds of school districts, where future researchers hopefully will find it.

Finally, nearly half of paraprofessional educators today work with students with disabilities in various contexts, including the one-on-one work necessary to realize individual education plans, or IEPs, mandated under federal law. While paras in the 1960s and 1970s often worked in "compensatory" education programs and programs for "emotionally disturbed" or "maladjusted" youth—whose relationship to present-day "special education" has been explored by critical scholars of disability—the story of paraprofessional labor alongside students with disabilities since the 1980s demands both different frameworks and different research expertise than those found in *Para Power*.[75] I hope this study provides some groundwork for future research on paras' roles in the education of students with disabilities.

To return to our opening anecdote, paraprofessional programs and educators attracted the attention of Velma Murphy Hill and Cleo Silvers (and Bayard Rustin and Albert Shanker) because paras' work proved fertile ground for organizing and theorizing about the future of freedom struggles, public education, labor organizing, job creation, urban democracy, and the social welfare state. The political, economic, and social conditions of the mid-1960s brought organizers together to create and promote programs of local hiring. By the time New York City's paras won their first contract, key players in civil rights, labor, and anti-poverty organizing agreed on the three general goals of paraprofessional programs: improving instruction, connecting schools and communities, and creating jobs and careers in education. They disagreed—often strongly—on how best to achieve these goals, and about who should control that process, as well as how to convince their own constituencies to support them.

The coalition supporting paras did not emerge from a natural alignment of interests but through organizing. As US cities underwent drastic political and economic changes in the 1970s, this coalition began to pull apart. Paraprofessional educators continued to seek power to realize their goals in classrooms and neighborhoods, but they lost valuable allies in the struggle to sustain and expand their efforts, and the conditions under which they worked became, and remain, increasingly precarious and exploitative. Studying the creation of "teacher aide" jobs by educational elites explains the presence of paraprofessional educators in schools today. Charting the arc of paras' organizing—as well as the alliances that sustained it and the visions and practices it generated—reveals a struggle for power in public schools that remains unfinished.

Social worker Mary Dowery (second from left) with parent aides and program staff at Mobilization for Youth, 1963. Collection of Mary Dowery.

CHAPTER 1

From Aides to Paras

Creating New Forms of Educational Work

"Non-Teaching Chores"

In December of 1956, the *New York Times* interviewed Virginia Patrick of Bay City, Michigan. "A housewife with two children," Mrs. Patrick appeared in the paper of record because she worked as a "teacher aide" in a program funded by the Ford Foundation's Fund for the Advancement of Education.[1] Launched in 1952 in Bay City, the experiment for the "Better Utilization of Teacher Competencies" had expanded to twenty-five cities in Michigan and seven others in the Midwest over four years. Ford's expansive vision for the project had generated a flood of journalism and scholarship about it. As the *Journal of Teacher Education* wrote in 1956, introducing a special issue devoted to the project, Ford's Bay City plan promised "a possible new plan for 1) easing the extreme teacher shortage, and 2) improving the quality of teaching services." At the heart of this "experiment" was "the use of teacher aides" like Virginia Patrick.[2]

Patrick worked alongside a regular teacher in a class of fifty-two first graders. The *Times* introduced her leading a reading group of six children, who told the reporter "Miss Patrick helps us" and "we learn faster." Aides' duties, the article explained, included "help with blackboard work, arranging bulletin boards, help with playground at recess time, escorting sick children home, correcting papers, giving additional help to a slow learner, assisting with artwork, obtaining reference material, and helping children who have been absent." The *Times*, drawing on the language the project used, described these tasks as "non-professional duties" handled by aides so that teachers could lead large classes more effectively. Still, it was clear to everyone involved that this work was educational. Patrick reported that she was taking classes to become a teacher, as were one-third of her new coworkers. Aides earned fifty dollars a week.[3]

Reporters and scholars flocked to Bay City, as the *Journal of Teacher Education* explained, because the Ford Foundation promised a response to "the revolutionary changes which are now taking place" in public schools across the United States.[4] Demography drove this revolution. During the "baby boom" after World War II, elementary and secondary school enrollments in the United States climbed from 28.5 million students in the fall of 1949 to 40.9 million in 1959 and 51.1 million in 1969.[5] This explosion of the school-going population created a crisis of care in schools and generated massive demand for educational labor.

The "extreme teacher shortage" that resulted inspired all manner of desperate, short-term solutions, of which the hiring of teacher aides was one, at least initially. Administrators needed to get more adults into classrooms quickly and cheaply, and so they turned to local mothers, both as volunteers and in paid aide roles. However, these efforts to expand the educational workforce quickly attracted the attention of all those who wanted to transform educational work.

Education researchers in foundations, universities, and government launched experiments to make schooling more efficient and effective, of which Bay City's was one. Many of these individuals would influence the educational visions of the War on Poverty a decade later. Civil rights organizers sought to recruit, hire, and train more Black educators, both to better serve Black students and to create jobs. Teacher unionists were organizing furiously, using the demand for educators—and the demanding conditions teachers faced in overcrowded classrooms—to build a massive surge in membership, recognition, and first-time contracts for teacher unions. All these actors took an interest in the "teacher aide" idea as part of their own organizing projects.

The intersection of labor demand and incessant organizing transformed aide work from its low-wage, stopgap origins over the course of the next fifteen years. This chapter analyzes the conflicts and collaborations that brought forth "paraprofessional" jobs in education and various visions for them. While school administrators sought help haphazardly, foundations formalized teacher aide roles through research and experimentation in the 1950s. New York City's civil rights and antipoverty organizations reimagined these roles in "parent aide" programs in the early 1960s, and the movement for community control of schools expanded on their ideas after 1964. Teacher unionists, in New York and nationally, urged school districts to hire aides to alleviate burdens on teachers in the 1950s, and haltingly embraced expanded roles for aides in the 1960s. Funding, frameworks, and new organizations that sprang from War on Poverty legislation combined with all these forms of local and national organizing to push New York City's Board of Education to hire the city's first paraprofessional educators in the spring of 1967.

By the time the first official paraprofessional educators went to work in New York, a diverse and unlikely coalition of community organizers, teacher unionists, poverty warriors, and school administrators agreed on the three broad goals that would animate paraprofessional programs: improving instruction, connecting schools and communities, and creating new careers in education. They disagreed, often strongly, about how paras would be recruited, trained, deployed, and evaluated; how they would relate to students, parents, teachers, and administrators; and who would wield the power to determine the answers to these questions. The creation of these positions opened a new front in ongoing struggles for power and control in public education, both in New York City and across the nation.

At the center of these debates stood paras themselves. Many women who became paras in the late 1960s took part in the struggles to create and define these roles before they existed. This chapter introduces several of these individuals, whose personal and political commitments brought them into educational organizing and thence into paraprofessional positions. Their experiences would inform their work, as well as their organizing *as* paras, in the years to come.

Overcrowded Origins: The Rise of Teacher Aides

After World War II, the number-one challenge facing public education in the United States was overcrowding. School administrators scrambled to respond with measures that ranged from double and triple sessions for students to temporary classrooms (and, in some cases, temporary schools) assembled in trailers and military-surplus Quonset huts.[6] Once children were packed into these spaces—as many as fifty or sixty at a time, as in Bay City—principals and superintendents scrambled to staff them cheaply. They hired student and substitute teachers on temporary licenses and urged teachers out of retirement.[7] However, they rarely raised teacher wages, at least not until teachers' union organizing forced their hand.

It was in this scramble that schools hired the first "school aides" or "teacher aides." They were typically the mothers of schoolchildren, possessing no formal educational training, who worked in schools and classrooms to help overwhelmed teachers handle paperwork, maintain order, keep classrooms tidy, and manage other chores and errands. While there is no clear "first" example of teacher aide hiring in the United States, the idea quickly caught the attention of researchers and foundations, leading Ford to launch its Bay City experiment in 1952. The project was run through Central Michigan College from 1952 through 1957, and Ford's involvement ensured that it received national attention from educators, policymakers, and teacher unionists.

Ford had created the Fund for the Advancement of Education in 1951 to address what it termed "the deepening educational crisis of the postwar years."[8] The chief driver of this crisis was, of course, sheer numbers, but Ford was among the many elite institutions that believed the postwar technological and economic environment demanded not just more but better teaching.[9] The fund made $50 million in grants during its first decade (roughly half a billion 2023 dollars), half of which went to teacher education. Ten million dollars in grants went to "utilization," in which Ford argued "the shortage [of teachers] may be met by using the available teachers more efficiently and effectively."[10] This premise led them to Bay City and hiring aides.

Ford's researchers began with the idea that educational work could be subject to the detailed, hierarchical division of labor that ruled industrial production. They devoted the entire first year of the Bay City project to applying managerial Fordism to the teaching profession. Using a job analysis and time study framework adapted from Dow Chemical's Personnel Division, field researchers sat in classrooms with stopwatches and tracked 137 teachers' every move. They categorized each component of educational labor and decided that somewhere between 21 percent and 69 percent of the teacher's day was spent on "non-instructional" tasks. A comparative study in Lansing, Michigan, confirmed these numbers.[11] By atomizing and analyzing the work of education in this way, the Bay City project team believed they could devise a way to employ—and pay—credentialed teachers only for their "professional" labor, while passing the rest of the work to a new class of low-wage educational employees: aides.

However, the question of what, exactly, counted as "non-instructional" work was contested from the moment the researchers began clicking their stopwatches. Ford's definition of instruction involved standing before the class imparting information. However, the teachers and staff in Bay City designated a category of aide labor they considered "instructional," including "give additional help to the slow learner, take over the class when the teacher leaves the room . . . read to the group . . . give additional instruction to students who have been absent." As they concluded, "many of these duties could be considered almost entirely professional in nature."[12]

In 1956, a pair of curriculum specialists rolled their eyes at the arbitrary distinctions Ford applied to instruction. "If the individual development is taken seriously," they wrote, "then the concept of the teaching task must be viewed as relating to the total school experience of the child, and not primarily to assignments and recitations."[13] Bay City aides were explicitly classified as non-pedagogical employees, but their role in the learning process was undeniable.

Bay City hired its first teacher aides in 1953. Each aide worked in a classroom with over forty-five students, previously staffed by a lone teacher. Bay

City administrators sought aides "who had good personalities, poise, and pleasing appearance; who were respected in their neighborhoods; who were interested in the problems of the schools; who were willing and able to accept the position on a full time basis, and who had a good health record."[14] The project targeted mothers, and a child psychologist observed that a significant portion of aide work was of a "personal, 'mothering' type," including "tying loose shoe laces, buttoning a girl's dress, fixing a hair ribbon, admiring a child's crayoning" and other such caregiving and emotional labor.[15] The *Milwaukee Journal* reported that sixty-four mothers applied for the first eight aide positions, but "only one asked how much the pay was," presumably because mothers wanted the work out of their love for children, not their need for the wages.[16] The Bay City Project had defined caregiving and emotional labor as non-professional and expected aides to do this work out of natural, gendered desire, and not economic need or a desire for a career in education.

Administrators hoped to recruit middle-class women who had not worked before and tried to avoid attracting working women by paying the "going unskilled wage." They promoted the project in this way, describing featured aides such as Virginia Patrick as housewives. A paradox of postwar assumptions about gender, class, and motherhood quickly emerged: Ford and Bay City wanted to hire "good" mothers, but the very act of working suggested maternal failure. One project report opened by describing "an underprivileged section of Bay City" where "poverty, broken homes, *working mothers*, and other threats to stable childhood are common" (emphasis mine), before praising the work of mothers as aides.[17] In this contorted worldview, poor and working-class children suffered at school due to their lack of maternal support at home, and this could be remedied by employing a surrogate, middle-class mother at school.[18]

In reality, most aides had worked before and were attracted to the "working conditions in school, as contrasted with other means of employment."[19] As the project director noted, "Many mothers who have accepted positions as aides have done so in preference to working in factories or in offices largely because the job schedule coincides with the school schedule of their children."[20] Aide work appealed to poor and working-class women who needed to support their families precisely because it allowed them to better balance the demands of work and home.

The Bay City experiment prompted sensationalized articles about the future of education that worried teachers and their unions.[21] Reporters wondered whether local school boards would "use the aides to raise class sizes unnecessarily" or "use the aide as a spy on the teacher or as an eventual cheap replacement for her."[22] John McLean, reporting for the *Milwaukee Journal*, mused, "If untrained, lower paid aides achieve considerable success, won't

this undermine the professional status of teachers?"[23] The National Education Association's (NEA) Lucille Carroll came to Bay City to investigate this
very issue. She found the division of labor satisfactory. "If it is necessary that
the teacher be absent," she wrote, "the aide is never considered as a substitute for the regular teacher."[24] Carroll asserted that teacher professionalism
would not be threatened by this new division of labor and could, in fact, be
enhanced by it, as aides took on non-teaching "chores." Carroll's NEA had
long defined itself as a "cooperative, nonconfrontational, professional association," in the words of Wayne Urban, but Carroll's distinction also mattered
for the rising tide of teacher organizing under the banner of the NEA's rival
American Federation of Teachers.[25] As militant AFT organizers asserted a
new, "masculinized image" of the professional teacher, handing off care work
and emotional labor to aides made sense.[26]

As several observers noted, teachers and aides seemed to get along very
well in Bay City. "Teachers working with aides," noted Charles Park, "found
more time for work with individual children" (even though such work was
deemed "non-professional") and "they also enjoyed sharing their school
experiences with another adult."[27] Many of the aides that Bay City hired
expressed interest in becoming teachers themselves, and Carroll suggested,
"the teacher aide program could be regarded as a long-range recruitment
plan."[28] The idea that aides might become teachers proved a crucial element
in securing funding for "career ladder" programs in the 1960s and 1970s, and
in convincing teachers to welcome aides and paras into their unions.

The Bay City project also demonstrated the importance of locality. Finding qualified aides turned out to be "the easiest" part of the program, with
candidates "referred by teachers, administrators, PTA members, and others."[29] Hiring aides with prior formal and informal social connections to
other parents contributed to the program's success. In their final report, Bay
City staff noted parents, teachers, aides, and pupils all favored the plan over
prior classroom arrangements. "100 per cent of the parents interviewed felt
that their children enjoyed school more under the aide plan," wrote Park,
while older pupils surveyed "liked the plan and felt that they received more
personal help and attention from the teacher as well as from the aide."[30]

Ford's commitment to, and promotion of, the Bay City experiment pushed
teacher aide hiring into the educational mainstream as more than a stopgap
intervention. In Michigan, the teacher aide model spread to fifty local school
districts by 1961, and researchers affiliated with the Bay City project helped
launch programs in Utah, Colorado, Iowa, and Minnesota.[31] The foundation
also funded several additional experiments, including a joint project with
Yale University in Fairfield, Connecticut.[32] By 1961, Ford estimated that 5,000
teacher aides were at work across the United States, most of them in programs
Ford itself had helped to create.[33]

While the project's directors had narrow goals for the aides they hired, their efforts revealed that uncredentialed women could do the work of education. These women succeeded in their new roles by mobilizing their intimate connections to local communities (connections teachers often lacked); by building solidarity with teachers (despite fears that aide work would undermine teacher professionalism); and by making space for new kinds of pedagogical practices in classrooms, including individual and small-group instruction. And while administrators recruited middle-class women to take these jobs as an extension of their domestic obligations without regard for wages, aide work proved attractive to working-class women balancing home and work and seeking new opportunities to support their families. When asked about their hopes for their work, Bay City aides explained that they wanted not only better pay but also the opportunity to advance as educators and eventually become teachers themselves.

The Bay City experiment concluded in 1957. That fall, the New York City Board of Education hired its first teacher aides. The move was approved by the city's largest teacher union, the Teachers Guild, which had lobbied since 1955 for an "experimental training program for people to assist in the handling of clerical and monitoring duties in the schools" and to relieve teachers of these "burdensome chores which interfere with teaching and lesson preparation."[34] The guild's vision for this work was as narrow as the Ford Foundation's, if less explicit about modeling schools on corporations. Its focus was on making teachers' lives easier by stratifying and professionalizing the work of education. The guild was silent on questions of community interaction, job creation, and the recruitment of future teachers.

However, between 1957 and 1967, the ideas and debates that emerged in Bay City would be taken up by a diverse range of educators, activists, and unionists. New York City would become a center for new experiments in local hiring, and ultimately the place where the broad contours of paraprofessional labor emerged. Organized teachers would come to play a key role, but first, the city's burgeoning civil rights movement would reimagine this work.

From Teacher Aides to Parent Aides: Civil Rights and Antipoverty Programs in New York

In New York City's public schools, the baby boom was accompanied by the city's rapid racial and ethnic transformation. Gotham's total population held roughly constant from 1950 to 1970, at around 8 million people, but nearly 1 million white residents left the five boroughs in these years. Their movement to suburbs was facilitated by governmental subsidies and support for new housing and transportation. In the same years, the city's Black population grew from 748,000 to 1,668,000, and its Puerto Rican population grew from

187,000 to 818,000. By the 1970s, the census identified roughly 20 percent of New Yorkers as Black and 10 percent as Hispanic. The public school population changed even faster; by 1970 nearly 60 percent of students in New York City public schools were classified as Black or Hispanic.

Housing segregation and ongoing urban renewal pushed families arriving from the US South and the Caribbean into poorly maintained buildings in poorly serviced neighborhoods.[35] Administrative decisions by the Board of Education, particularly the zoning of schools and siting of new ones, exacerbated this segregation.[36] Schools serving Black and Hispanic students were among the most overcrowded and under-resourced, with metrics of student achievement among the lowest.[37] To address these inequalities and injustices, Black and Puerto Rican New Yorkers organized to demand equal educational opportunities for their children.

As Black and Puerto Rican New Yorkers got involved in their children's education, they were often incensed at what they found. Struggles for desegregated, equitable schooling in New York City date back to the early nineteenth century, but the Supreme Court's 1954 decision in *Brown v. Board of Education* spurred a new wave of organizing. Kenneth Clark, a psychologist at City College and key witness in *Brown*, turned his attention to New York, blasting the city's Board of Education for practicing "a most effective form of racial segregation" in its schools, one administered through a combination of unequal resources and the tracking of students.[38] Board officials strenuously denied the charge, but in the face of consistent pressure, they commissioned a study of school segregation in 1956. The Commission on Integration produced a series of reports in 1957 and 1958 that documented segregation in the city's schools.[39] These reports offered recommendations to address the situation, but the board was not bound by them.

Longtime civil rights organizer and educator Ella Baker responded to the release of the commission's reports by launching Parents in Action Against Educational Discrimination. The organization led weekly parent workshops and "went beyond the simple demand for racial integration, calling for greater parent and community involvement in running the schools."[40] As Baker told Mayor Robert F. Wagner at a meeting in 1957, "We parents want to know first hand from you what is or is not going to be done for our children. . . . New York City, the world's leading city, should reflect the highest degree of democracy in its public school system."[41] Baker's phrasing made clear that parents were not simply seeking numerical desegregation, but a substantive restructuring of the power relations between schools and the people they served. One way to effect this restructuring, which activists suggested regularly, was hiring more Black and Puerto Rican educators, particularly those with connections to New York City's students.

Parents in Action was one of many organizations in New York City that drew attention to disparities in the staffing of schools and the quality of instruction. Black and white teachers in the New York City Teacher's Union (TU), a rival of the Teachers Guild, "went beyond the liberal consensus that called for equal opportunity and an end to employment discrimination, making a case for the importance of taking steps to hire blacks" in New York City schools.[42] The Commission on Integration itself had highlighted the staffing problem in one if its 1957 reports, in which it recommended transferring experienced teachers into schools serving Black and Hispanic children. These schools employed a disproportionate number of the city's least experienced and lowest-rated teachers, who taught a curriculum that alternately ignored or demeaned Black and Hispanic people. In 1958, nine mothers in Harlem held their children out of school because of these terrible conditions, highlighting the lack of licensed and experienced teachers among many other issues.[43] In 1962, the Brooklyn chapter of the Congress of Racial Equality boycotted schools in Central Brooklyn for the same reasons.[44]

Throughout the 1960s, New York City's teaching corps remained over 90 percent white. This was no accident: Black and Hispanic educators were regularly disqualified from teaching jobs in the city by elaborate tests that hinged on oral examinations of "dialect," and those who did pass the city's examinations went to the back of the hiring line.[45] Black and Puerto Rican parents reported that white teachers and administrators, many of whom lived far from the schools where they worked, regularly blamed children's poor performance on parental failings and local culture. All these factors generated intense demand for new educators.[46]

President John F. Kennedy's administration turned its attention to Black and Hispanic youth in cities during the early 1960s under the rubric of "juvenile delinquency." Using the lens of criminality to analyze the challenges school-aged children faced created immediate and long-term problems. Scholars and policymakers produced an influential body of literature that explained delinquent behavior as the product of family and community pathologies rooted in matriarchal households, effectively blaming Black and Puerto Rican communities for their children's struggles.[47] Furthermore, defining the problem as crime, rather than education or social service provision, grew the size and scope of what scholars now call the "carceral state" by directing resources to law enforcement and new forms of youth surveillance.[48] As these imperatives made their way into public education, aides—and, later, paraprofessional educators—contended with and became entangled in new forms of punishment and policing in schools.[49]

Despite these problems of framing and resource allocation, presidential interest in juvenile delinquency did create opportunities for scholars

and organizers. A subset of New York's civil rights activists used this attention to advance alternative explanations and solutions for juvenile delinquency, rooted not in pathology but in structural racism and class conflict.
The Kennedy administration funded a pair of programs in New York City to
combat juvenile delinquency and, more broadly, poverty: Mobilization for
Youth (MFY) and Harlem Youth Opportunities Unlimited, Incorporated
(HARYOU). Activists, scholars, social workers, and educators working in
these new antipoverty programs created projects that hired and trained parents—primarily mothers—in new ways.

Up to this point, school administrators in New York had followed the Bay
City model, hiring women at low wages to work as teacher aides, performing
"non-teaching" tasks while supervised by teachers and administrators. Civil
rights activists working with new antipoverty organizations imagined new
roles for "parent aides," who would represent and respond to community
needs in classrooms and schools, while also working outside of school time
with students and parents. Not only would this work necessarily involve
both pedagogic and curricular labor; it was also explicitly designed to make
schools more responsive and responsible to the communities they served.
The "parent" in parent aide signaled a power shift in two ways: first, aides'
status as parents—providers of parental care—should matter in schools and,
second, these aides should be connected and responsible to other parents
amid community struggles for improved and equitable schooling.

This reimagining of aide work in the service of working-class Black and
Puerto Rican children and their families brought together a growing cadre
of highly educated Black and Puerto Rican educators, social workers, and
researchers. Mary Dowery was raised by a family of Black educators in Frank-
fort, Kentucky. She attended the Rosenwald Elementary School, a center
of African American life that hosted talks and performances by W. E. B. Du
Bois, Marian Anderson, and Roland Hayes, among others, while she was a
student. As a child, she made her spending money by selling copies of the
Chicago Defender and *Pittsburgh Courier* that her uncles brought home from
their travels as Pullman porters. Dowery graduated from Berea College in
Kentucky and went on to earn a master's in social work at Clark Atlanta
University. There, she later recalled, "we studied all aspects of social work,"
including "psychiatric information, medical information, community organization, and group work."[50] This holistic preparation was very different
from the individualized treatment that was the dominant paradigm of the
day. It served her well as a social worker in New York City, where she moved
after graduation. "We had no problem in confronting projects and going to
the community and exploring and organizing," she remembered, "getting
down with the nitty-gritty, you know."[51] After stints at the Salvation Army
and Lincoln Hospital, Dowery joined Mobilization for Youth.

Laura Pires-Hester was raised by Cape Verdean immigrants outside New Bedford, Massachusetts. She excelled in high school and won a scholarship to Smith College, upending the local hierarchies. One administrator, upon hearing the good news, wondered, "who will come back and pick the cranberries?" As Pires-Hester explained years later, it was a "life lesson" in how not to think about people. "Where you are today or what you are today," she asserted, "does not define, necessarily, what you will be." Pires, as she was then known, moved to New York City to study social work at Columbia, where she met radical practitioners including Preston Wilcox, who would later become a leader of the community control movement in Harlem, and Kenneth Marshall, a founding organizer with HARYOU who asked Pires to join after she graduated.[52]

Dowery and Pires belonged to a "new generation of Black and Puerto Rican leaders" who "creat[ed] independent spaces of political organizing" within antipoverty programs and municipal bureaucracies.[53] Joined by radical and dissident white professionals, this new generation rejected what Kenneth Clark called "social work colonialism" and sought instead to engage and empower the poor and working-class people they aimed to serve. Many of these "successful, rebellious professionals" worked for HARYOU and MFY.[54] Both organizations generated tremendous innovation in parent involvement, community action, local hiring, and community-based education. They demonstrated the value of such work and helped to spur the eventual hiring of paraprofessional educators by New York City's Board of Education.

As neighborhood-based antipoverty initiatives, MFY and HARYOU focused intensively on particular places that had been defined by their residents' poverty. Their "place-based politics" aimed to restructure relationships between residents and the institutions that governed their lives, including public schools and social welfare offices.[55] Critics have argued that such place-based politics were analytically and politically truncated, reducing the sphere of action against systemic economic inequality to neighborhood-level palliatives, foreclosing the possibility of broader solidarities, and building alternative institutional structures that ultimately lacked staying power.[56] The short-lived, star-crossed trajectories of both organizations attest to these challenges. MFY was red-baited out of existence in the late 1960s, though its legal services division survives to this day. HARYOU was taken over by Harlem Congressman Adam Clayton Powell Jr. in 1965 and lost most of its original staff and programming thereafter.

However, the rise of community-based educational programs at MFY and HARYOU demonstrates their capacity to transcend narrow definitions of place or poverty. While specific programs were rooted in place, the educators, activists, and policy scholars who created them circulated throughout the city, building a network that connected places rather than isolating them.

And when their early innovations garnered hostile responses from teachers and principals, these activists and practitioners responded by putting direct pressure on the Board of Education to hire locally, thus building their new ideas into the public schooling bureaucracy itself.

Mobilization for Youth was built on Lloyd Ohlin and Richard Cloward's theories of opportunity and delinquency, which argued that structures of opportunity, not culture or inborn traits, determined delinquent behavior.[57] The two Columbia sociologists led the "research" arm of the program. They were joined by Frank Riessman, a professor of social work and psychology at New York University, and by Dowery, who knew Riessman from Lincoln Hospital.

At MFY, Dowery led an experimental "parent aide" program designed by Riessman. Using community networks, including social work clients, PTAs, and a local Spanish-language radio show, she hired about fifteen parents of Puerto Rican, Chinese, and African American descent. She trained these aides to work with local parents to resolve issues their children were having with schools. This work included attending parent-teacher conferences and meetings with principals alongside parents, many of whom did not speak English fluently. Aides also held after-school and summer workshops to guide parents in navigating the school bureaucracy and to help them feel confident articulating their children's needs to teachers and administrators. "Don't be afraid, don't be intimidated," was their mantra. As she later explained, Dowery trained aides to "be respectful and courteous, but don't take any crap!"[58]

These parent aides helped many parents win support and services for their children. However, their presence in schools drew the ire of both teachers and administrators in the local school district. In 1964, several principals worked together to shut the program down by banning MFY aides from district schools.[59] While the program proved short-lived, the work these aides did laid the groundwork for future interventions. As Dowery noted, "they were the forerunners, there's . . . no way you can get around it." They "demonstrated the need" for community-based educators in public schools.[60] Many of the aides Dowery trained later went on to careers in education and nonprofit work, including some who became paraprofessional educators.

Welfare rights activist Beulah Sanders worked briefly as a parent organizer with MFY. While she never worked as a paraprofessional educator herself, Sanders frequently contrasted the misery of domestic work with women's willingness to work in human services. "If they want us off the welfare rolls, come up with the training program and the jobs," Sanders said in 1969. "You know, the women would be glad to take it."[61] The desire of aides to advance within human service professions impressed Frank Riessman. In short order, he became a leading advocate for career training for aides, particularly in education.

Shelvy Young-Abrams did not work directly with Mary Dowery at MFY, but she was one of those parents who started as a volunteer and took on additional responsibilities with community organizations on the Lower East Side, eventually becoming a paraprofessional educator. Born and raised on her mother's tobacco farm in North Carolina, Young-Abrams moved to the Lower East Side as an adult and labored in domestic work, a toy factory, and a chemical plant to feed and clothe her two daughters.[62] Once her children entered school, Young-Abrams began organizing. She began volunteering after school and was soon elected president of the Parent-Teacher Association, becoming "very, very involved in the schools and [speaking] to the teachers and the parents."[63] In this capacity, she conducted outreach with families to connect them with local resources, including those provided by MFY. Under Young-Abrams's direction, her PTA particularly targeted families living in homeless shelters and transient hotels in the East Village. Her work with the PTA and the wider Lower East Side community led the principal at her daughters' school to encourage her to apply to become a paraprofessional in 1967.

While Dowery and Riessman developed their parent aide program for MFY, HARYOU launched a similar aide program uptown in Harlem. HARYOU's founding in 1962 brought together a diverse team of social workers, psychologists, and educators. Their research director was Kenneth Clark, who had pioneered community-based social work and psychology with his wife and partner Mamie Phipps Clark at Harlem's Northside Center over the preceding decade.[64] HARYOU aimed to involve Harlemites, particularly youth, in a wide range of antipoverty and community-improvement efforts. Laura Pires's first role in the organization was as the director of a paid leadership training program for Harlem teenagers, which included group sessions with local leaders and activists and training at eight placement sites in the neighborhood.

In the fall of 1963, HARYOU launched an after-school enrichment program for local students. They partnered with the Community Teachers Association, an organization of Black teachers based in Harlem that was founded by Richard Parrish in 1957.[65] Parrish was a teacher and union organizer who was, at the time, the only Black vice president in the American Federation of Teachers (AFT). He had fought to desegregate the AFT's locals in the 1950s and coordinated freedom schools for the students of Prince Edward County, Virginia, in the summer of 1963 after the county closed its public schools rather than desegregate them.[66]

For HARYOU, Parrish recruited two hundred teachers to work with four hundred "especially trained teacher aides" hired from among local parents.[67] They served 2,800 students at ten after-school centers, providing one-on-one and small-group tutoring in elementary and middle-school reading and mathematics. Along with these academic goals, the program was designed to give students the opportunity to "identify and associate with adequate role models on a more personal level." Parrish believed that by pairing parents and teachers, "parent and teacher cooperation" would be "encouraged and provided for to a greater extent" in local public schools.[68] He hoped the Board of Education could be encouraged to replicate these efforts.

Jerome A. Greene, a new Black teacher in Harlem, joined Parrish in the HARYOU project and was so impressed that he replicated it when he transferred to a school in the Bronx. Greene applied for funds from the district to hire parents to work with students on Saturdays, providing basic tutoring and talking with teachers about their children and their needs. Greene found a receptive community of parents seeking greater involvement in their schools, including Oneida Davis, a Bronx native who was then working as a cashier on Fordham Road.[69] As Davis explained, once her children were in school, "I was involved in everything. I was the PA [Parent Association] president up until junior high school for both of my daughters . . . that's how I became active, that's how I became knowledgeable about what was going on in the school system."[70] She was a serving as parent association president when she joined Greene's group in 1965. By 1968, she, too, was working as a paraprofessional educator.

As they built successful programs, activists in HARYOU and MFY sought to put direct pressure on public schools to replicate them. The principals' reaction to MFY's parent aides on the Lower East Side demonstrated that experiments built outside the public-school bureaucracy could only do so much before encountering resistance from within the school system. The solution was to make parent aides a regular part of that system. In 1963, Thelma Griffith Johnson, the chair of HARYOU's Committee on Education and the Schools, met with the local superintendent in Harlem to urge him to hire locally. After the superintendent suggested hiring local college students to help walk children to and from school, Johnson proposed he look closer to home, suggesting "diverting Department of Welfare funds to pay female recipients of Welfare a stipend to transport these children, and perhaps to care for them until four or five o'clock when their parents return from work." Johnson expected that such a program "would serve the dual purpose of getting the children to school and providing the Welfare recipient with a sense of pride at being able to work for the funds she has received."[71] Out of context, such a proposal has echoes of "workfare," but the proposal should be understood in the context of HARYOU's commitment to local employment as part of a broad strategy for making Harlem's public institutions more responsible to its residents. Informed by this work, Johnson believed that these women could do the work of education and that doing so would help them assert their membership in the polity. Still, her suggestion of "diverting welfare funds" also carried an undertone of condescension, one that highlighted the class distance between some of HARYOU's leaders and the people they aimed to serve.

In 1964, HARYOU released an extensive report titled *Youth in the Ghetto: A Study of the Consequences of Powerlessness and a Blueprint for Change.* In it, they listed "parent aides" in schools as one of ten "anticipated needs" for the young people of Harlem. As they explained:

> The youth of Harlem appear to be in need of parent aides or surrogates who would demand for them what middle-class parents demand and obtain for their children from schools and other social institutions. HARYOU should seek to provide machinery whereby community groups such as fraternities, sororities, social groups, PTAs, and churches assume the responsibility of this role. It would be important that the activities of these groups do not increase the dependency of the parents, but rather stimulate and motivate them to develop an increasing sense of their own power to effect desired change.[72]

HARYOU, like MFY, reconfigured the Bay City "teacher aide" idea by redefining these workers as "parent aides," responsible to and representative of their working-class, Black and Puerto Rican neighborhood. The argument that these aides would demand "what middle-class parents demand" recognized the need for working-class mothers to be paid for the care work that middle-class women could afford to do voluntarily.[73] The call to "stimulate and motivate [parents] to develop an increasing sense of their own power" came straight from New York's long organizing tradition. HARYOU's staff believed that these "parent aides" would improve educational practices in schools, and that doing this work would empower Harlem's parents as activists and organizers for the rights of their children.

Laura Pires was one of the authors of *Youth in the Ghetto*, and during revisions, she added a broad statement about the philosophy and practice of local hiring. As she later recalled, one of HARYOU's most important interventions in the human services was addressing the problem of "people having different talents that are not necessarily recognized and/or credentialed in our systems of education or employment."[74] In her revision to *Youth in the Ghetto*, she laid out HARYOU's philosophy, as she understood it:

> In a very real way, the use of indigenous nonprofessionals in staff positions is forced by the dearth of trained professionals. At the same time, however, the use of such persons grows out of concern for a tendency of professionals to "flee from the client" and for the difficulty of communication between persons of different backgrounds and outlooks. It is HARYOU's belief that the use of persons only "one step removed" from the client will improve the giving of service as well as provide useful and meaningful employment for Harlem's residents.[75]

Pires's words proved more influential than she ever expected. They caught the eyes of scholars and policymakers just as the War on Poverty was taking off in 1964.

The War on Poverty and the Expansion of Community-Based Educational Work

President Lyndon Johnson declared "unconditional war on poverty" in his State of the Union address on January 8, 1964. Johnson's War on Poverty generated new legislation and funding to combat poverty, beginning with the Economic Opportunity Act (EOA) of 1964, passed in August. Title II, Section A of the act created the Community Action Program (CAP), which aimed to replicate many of the innovations that Kennedy, Johnson's predecessor, had supported at MFY and HARYOU. CAP created a vast new network of local antipoverty programs in areas of concentrated poverty, which were to be "developed, conducted, and administered with the maximum feasible participation of the residents of the areas."[76]

Johnson's commitment to maximum feasible participation was tenuous and convenient; as a vast body of scholarship has shown, the president and his aides were looking for a model that would engage and channel the energies of the burgeoning Black freedom struggle while avoiding expansive (and expensive) interventions in the nation's political economy.[77] Much as Kennedy's earlier investments had, however, Johnson's promise of "maximum feasible participation" was reworked and realized on the ground by community organizers, who created many new programs with the funds, including those that hired local residents as educators.

The most notable of these was the early childhood education program Head Start. Head Start programs nationwide were funded by the federal Office of Economic Opportunity (created to administer the EOA) and run by local organizations like HARYOU and MFY. By one count, over 46,000 women, mostly mothers, worked for the program in its first two years.[78] Head Start quickly became one of the most popular—and controversial—War on Poverty programs. Operating outside of traditional educational bureaucracies, Head Start programs created new curricula that celebrated local history and culture and hired activists and community organizers to teach them. The Child Development Group of Mississippi (CDGM), one of the earliest and largest Head Start programs, professed a commitment to what Crystal Sanders calls "full freedom" for children and adults that drew the ire of that state's segregationists, and Mississippi Senator John Stennis successfully pressured the Johnson administration to eventually eliminate the CDGM.[79] However, the CDGM, and Head Start more broadly, lent credence to the idea that hiring local residents in low-income communities could improve education, connect educators to communities, and create jobs.

President Johnson and the Congress that passed War on Poverty legislation believed the US economy was fundamentally sound, strong, and fair, and that those living in poverty simply needed access to it. As a consequence, the War on Poverty's commitment to "community action" was paired with a focus on training and education, which Johnson called "the only valid passport out of poverty." He made this statement at the signing of the 1965 Elementary and Secondary Education Act (ESEA), which poured over 1 billion federal dollars into K-12 schools to address educational inequality, particularly for children living in poverty.

Historians of education and poverty policy have argued that the "the belief that education was the key to winning the war on poverty" emerged because schooling "promised to do something for the poor without either antagonizing business by interfering in the labor market or alienating the middle class by redistributing income to the least advantaged."[80] This scholarship contrasts the direct job creation of the New Deal's Works Progress Administration with the job training and educational programs of the War on Poverty, and it notes the weakening of organized labor's place in the political system as a significant outcome of this shift of focus.[81] On the whole, this scholarship argues, the War on Poverty confirmed the tendency of liberal capitalist democracies, and the United States in particular, to "educationalize" social problems.[82]

In addition, the specific focus on "compensatory" education in the implementation of Title I programs reproduced two counterproductive practices in many of the local grants the ESEA funded. The first such practice was what social scientists now call the "deficit" model of intervention: essentially, many educators and researchers believed that children living in poverty were "culturally deprived" on account of their surroundings and needed to be taken out of these spaces and ways of thinking and taught mainstream, middle-class behaviors. The second practice was the "pull-out" model of pedagogy: pulling children who struggled out of their regular classrooms and into separate settings. Both of these widespread "classroom-level shortcomings," wrote Gloria Ladson-Billings on the fiftieth anniversary of the ESEA, "contributed to the reasons that compensatory education (that is, the ESEA) failed to live up to the promise of 1965."[83]

However, the use of ESEA monies to hire local residents to work in public schools allowed countervailing tendencies to develop in schools. Rather than "educationalize" social problems, the civil rights organizers and antipoverty programs who hired "parent aides" problematized the dominant view of education, in which credentialed teachers imparted skills to individual students who would then be sorted by merit into their social positions. The alternative programs they created envisioned education that was both embedded in and responsive to the needs of communities, in which parents played active, recognized roles as educators. In hiring aides, they asserted that local knowledge was an asset. And, as discussed in the following chapter, aides' work in classrooms offered an alternative to pull-out pedagogy in certain cases.

As written, the ESEA included direct measures for community action, with $75 million of its $1.3 billion allocated expressly for the hiring of aides. These aides were hired into dozens of programs, including one that the Office of Education later dubbed "Follow Through," as it was designed to build on the gains of Head Start in grades K–3.[84] Title I of the act offered an influx of $1.1 billion (the vast majority of the ESEA's initial funding) for "compensatory education" for children living in poverty, and new programs were meant to be designed with input from the communities served. One way to achieve this was through the hiring of local residents. Title III of the act, which funded independent community education centers (CECs), reiterated the Economic Opportunity Act's promise of "maximum feasible participation," making clear that these CECs were to act as incubators for the kind of educational activism and experimentation already underway in organizations like HARYOU and Head Start programs.[85]

While city school districts initially hoped to use ESEA dollars as general supplements to their existing budgets, a series of directives from the Office of Education made clear that these new funds were intended to generate new approaches to poverty-area education. Commissioner of Education Harold Howe II singled out community-based hiring in June 1966, urging school districts to use federal monies to "tap every possible source of helpers in their own communities" in a speech on the purpose of the ESEA.[86] The following year, the president himself said much the same. In a speech on February 28, 1967, President Johnson asserted, "New kinds of school personnel—such as teacher aides—are needed to help schools."[87]

Unlike the Community Action Program, whose funding streams bypassed state and local governments to directly fund poverty-area programs, the ESEA's new federal funding for education was channeled through state and local educational bureaucracies. States and localities, in turn, put out requests for grant proposals, and educators, policy scholars, social workers, and activists with antipoverty experience offered responses. This model privileged those who had worked with grant-giving government and philanthropic entities already, and thus amplified knowledge produced in those spaces in the previous decade.

How best to produce and deploy "poverty knowledge" became a contest within War on Poverty programs, as historian Alice O'Connor has shown. The "community action" model, pioneered by Sargent Shriver's team at the Office of Economic Opportunity (OEO), "transformed the very notion of demonstration research from a mechanism for small-scale experimentation into an instrument for direct, and some cases immediate and large-scale, action."[88] HARYOU and MFY were demonstrations, as was Head Start. These projects "pushed past the limits of standard social service reform ... to draw community residents more directly into school governance."[89] However, OEO's Office of Research, Plans, Programs and Evaluation (RPP&E) promoted an "analytic" approach to poverty knowledge, in which "neutral experts" deployed cost-benefit analysis to assess the "individual improvement" of each subject of antipoverty interventions.[90]

This contest over knowledge was particularly relevant in public education. Scholars, administrators, and foundations such as Ford advanced an "analytic" approach that used abstract metrics to evaluate schooling. Unionizing teachers fought hard to reject these intrusions and define themselves as the best producers and evaluators of educational success. Teacher and parent aides and those advocating for them, by contrast, espoused the "community action" model that Laura Pires-Hester outlined in *Youth in the Ghetto*. Her friend and collaborator, Frank Riessman, built on this insight as he developed a series of policy frameworks for local hiring.

Frank Riessman used new War on Poverty grant opportunities to expand his work with MFY by developing a "New Careers" framework that combined the goals of job creation and community empowerment in a vision he later described as "maximum feasible employment."[91] Riessman earned a PhD at Columbia University in 1955 and quickly joined antipoverty programs in health and education. These experiences led him to challenge the behaviorist focus and deficit models of his field. In a series of books and papers, Riessman aimed "to challenge the widely-held notion that the 'culturally deprived' child is not interested in education."[92] He was working toward a "new human services paradigm" that "turn[ed] the needs/resources ratio on its head by viewing problems as resources and those who have them as uniquely qualified problem solvers ... their indigenous, inside understanding, organized collectively in mutual aid groups, becomes a new and powerful resource."[93] Riessman's thinking was informed by the practices of his friends Mary Dowery at MFY and Laura Pires at HARYOU, both of whom he had worked with on local hiring and aide programs, and whose thinking would influence his own.

Riessman's clearest and most influential statement of this new paradigm arrived in the same year as the ESEA. The publication of 1965's *New Careers for the Poor*, coauthored with Arthur Pearl, was a watershed moment for the ideas and practices of "paraprofessional" work. The book's preface excerpted the complete paragraph Pires wrote in HARYOU's *Youth and the Ghetto* (quoted on page 37) and followed it with a simple affirmation: "This statement, taken from the HARYOU proposal, forms the basic thesis of this book."[94]

New Careers for the Poor articulated the three key components of paraprofessional programs: instructional assistance, school-community connections,
and teacher training. In addition to citing HARYOU's influence, Pearl and
Riessman quoted the Economic Opportunity Act (EOA) promise of "maximum feasible participation." They argued that the legislation "provide[d] a
tremendous opening for widespread employment of the poor themselves in
programs for the poor."[95] The authors proposed full employment through
the creation of "a sufficient number of jobs for all persons without work" in
the human services, and particularly in education. Schooling, they believed,
offered "a model for new careers," on account of the wealth of experimentation already taking place.[96] For an accounting of this work, they turned to
Henry Saltzman of the Ford Foundation, who provided an overview chapter
on "The Poor and the Schools" in which he outlined Ford's many experimental programs dating back to the Bay City experiment. Public education, Pearl
and Riessman argued, "must ultimately become the United States' largest
enterprise," citing the massive growth of enrollment in public schools.

Riessman and Pearl also drew on Kenneth Clark's book *Dark Ghetto*,
released in 1965 and based heavily on Clark's experiences as a Harlem psy-
chiatrist and HARYOU leader. As *New Careers for the Poor* asserted, citing Clark, "schools constitute a colonial imposition because nothing about
the system belongs to the poor."[97] This critique anticipated the rise of Black
Power and language that Preston Wilcox and other community activists
would deploy in community control struggles still to come. For Pearl and
Riessman, "introducing the indigenous poor into meaningful teaching roles
could be an important step toward producing a fundamental change," if, and
only if, "the poor ... become truly a part of the teaching organization." To this
end, Pearl and Riessman laid out the most detailed proposal of their book, a
five-step "career ladder" from "teacher aide" to "master teacher." By bringing
aide programs that had proved popular in antipoverty programs into public
schools in formal ways, Frank Riessman hoped to launch a transformation
of both hiring and relations of power in the human services.[98]

The contrast between *New Careers for the Poor* and reports on Bay City a
decade prior is stark. In place of fifty-dollar weeks, the authors envisioned
a full-employment program. In place of carefully maintained hierarchies,
they proposed "meaningful teaching roles" for aides or, in their language,
"indigenous nonprofessionals." Riessman quickly adopted the term "paraprofessional," and later "new careerist," to describe those he worked with
in new programs.

Though theirs was the most comprehensive of such statements, Riessman
and Pearl were far from outliers. Their ideas quickly inspired legislation.
New York City Congressman James Scheuer proposed the "Subprofessional
Careers Act" in 1966 as an amendment to the Economic Opportunity Act.

Scheuer's amendment expressly channeled tens of millions of dollars into training and hiring programs for paraprofessionals in education, health care, and social work. Reporting Scheuer's proposal, the *New York Herald-Tribune* linked it directly to Pearl and Riessman's work. The paper favorably contrasted the economic impact of direct hiring to more "conservative" proposals designed to stimulate the entire economy with fiscal policy instruments.[99] Community-based hiring in education, pioneered by activists and antipoverty professionals in New York City, had become a national model for scholars and policymakers.

The civil rights organizers and antipoverty workers who created "parent aide" programs did not seek to "educationalize" social problems. Rather, they re-imagined schools as sites for employment, training, and the distribution of state resources in neighborhoods, all of which would be negotiated through collective, democratic processes. Much as Miriam Cohen documents in the early twentieth century, "efforts to expand schooling... stimulated the growth of the programs we traditionally associate with the welfare state."[100] Once the ESEA went into effect, this influx of educational funding stimulated the growth of local hiring programs on the ground, just as the struggle for equal education in New York City entered a new phase.

Freedom Struggles after 1964: Seeking Power, Jobs, and Equality in New York City

The Civil Rights Act of 1964 is remembered as a national high-water mark for the Black freedom struggle, a major victory driven by sustained grassroots organizing across the Jim Crow South. However, as scholars have shown, the act's language around school segregation, in particular, was designed to confine remedies for inequality to states that had enshrined Jim Crow in law.[101] In the urban North, segregation flourished because of less explicit, but no less effective, administrative and popular practices in housing and schooling, which were unaffected by the landmark law. For organizers in New York City, 1964 was a bitterly disappointing year.

After years of localized struggles against segregated, unequal schooling, students and parents staged a massive one-day boycott on February 3, 1964. Some 460,000 students stayed out of school, joining tens of thousands of parents and activists in marches, freedom schools in church basements and community centers, and rallies across the five boroughs. The protest was led by Brooklyn pastor and former NAACP organizer Milton Galamison and longtime civil rights organizer Bayard Rustin, himself one year removed from the organizational triumph of the March on Washington for Jobs and Freedom. Despite massive numbers, the boycott failed to sway the Board of Education to desegregate, particularly after white parents, primarily from

Queens, launched counterprotests in March and September.[102] That summer, protests erupted into rioting in Harlem and Bedford-Stuyvesant after
a white police officer shot and killed James Powell, a Black teenager from
the Bronx, on the Upper East Side.[103] Across the city, whether in schools or
on the streets, Black and Puerto Rican New Yorkers felt that they had little
control over the systems that governed their lives.

After the 1964 School Boycott failed to force the city to desegregate, many
Black and Puerto Rican parents and activists shifted gears, demanding the
power to control jobs and schools in their communities more forcefully than
ever before. Russell Rickford has described the rise of Black Power in New
York City as producing an "educational renaissance" in thought and practice.[104] Ideas and practices of community-based hiring evolved amid this
renaissance.

In 1966, Harlem parents launched what became New York City's movement for community control of schools when they protested the design,
zoning, and staffing of Intermediate School 201 in Harlem. The Board of
Education had promised a state-of-the art integrated school. Instead, it built
what appeared to be a windowless box that was "50 percent Black and 50
percent Puerto Rican." Furious, parents demanded the right to control the
school's operations and initially focused their organizing on the hiring of a
Black principal.[105]

Preston Wilcox, a professor of social work at Columbia and a longtime
organizer in Harlem, became one of the leading theorists of this nascent
movement. In an influential article published in the *Urban Review* in 1966,
Wilcox called for a "fundamental restructuring of the relations between
school and community based on a radical redistribution of power" that
would include "training local residents as foster teachers."[106] Wilcox cited
the example of Head Start, and particularly the Child Development Group
of Mississippi, in his writing.[107] The Harlem Parents Committee, formed in
the wake of the failed integration efforts in 1964, echoed this sentiment in
their newsletter, *Views*, asserting the need to employ parent aides at IS 201 in
1966 and again in 1967 as part of their larger vision of community control.[108]
Parent frustration ran high in Harlem, and hiring local residents to improve
the school system from within seemed like one step toward the broader goal
of controlling the local public schools.

In response to the organizing around IS 201, New York City Mayor John
Lindsay recruited Ford Foundation President McGeorge Bundy to head a
commission on restructuring New York City's public school system to give
parents and community members more input. The commission's 1967 report,
Reconnection for Learning: A Community School System for New York City,
recommended decentralizing the school system. It became the basis for creating three experimental districts, funded by Ford, in the 1967–1968 school

year: one in Harlem and East Harlem centered on IS 201, one on the Lower East Side, and one in Ocean Hill–Brownsville, Brooklyn. Among its many proposals, *Reconnection for Learning* argued for the hiring and training of what its authors now termed "paraprofessionals," arguing that "community participation would [be] strengthened by a bond of direct educational participation."[109]

As New York City public schools authorized the hiring of paraprofessional educators in 1967, these experimental districts took the lead. Mercedes Figueroa had fled an unstable family situation in her native Puerto Rico by coming to New York as a teenager. By the mid-1960s she had three children at home and was working as hard as she could to give them the "security, encouragement, and inspiration" she had longed for as a child.[110] As she told an interviewer in 1976, Figueroa was aware of the injustices around her, but she felt too uncomfortable and overwhelmed as a young mother to get involved in local activism. She did, however, explain that she managed to enroll all three of her children in honors programs, navigating the labyrinthine New York City schools bureaucracy despite her limited command of English. The experience gave her the confidence to apply for a new paraprofessional training program hosted by the Women's Talent Corps, and from there, to a job at IS 201.

Across New York City, organizers seeking power and control took advantage of federal dollars available from the Community Action Program to "fight their own War on Poverty."[111] In Brownsville, Brooklyn, organizers demanded employment for residents in antipoverty programs, public housing, and youth programming. Their efforts yielded a slow but steady shift in the city's hiring policies, away from the employment of professionals and college students who lived outside the neighborhood, and toward the employment of local residents with knowledge of the area. As Wendell Pritchett has argued, these struggles anticipated the neighborhood's central role in the struggle for community control of schools from 1967 onward.[112]

Shortly after the publication of *New Careers for the Poor,* Frank Riessman became the founding director of New York University's New Careers Development Center, from which he launched attempts to realize his proposed programs of local hiring and professional development. With support from the Twentieth Century Fund, Bank Street College, and Title III of the ESEA, Riessman partnered with Preston Wilcox to design a classroom aide program that combined in-school service, educational training at NYU, and civic empowerment in East Harlem in 1967. As Riessman told evaluators, "the program was so designed to permit [aides] to develop strategies which would enable them, as auxiliary personnel trainees, as parents, and as citizens to communicate to the Board of Education."[113] Riessman hoped to see these experimental positions made permanent, and Samuel Peyer, the assistant principal of PS 171 in East Harlem, agreed, writing in the grant application that "There is a need for an enabling program to permit adults of the East Harlem Area to become trained for the skilled, semi-professional, and professional fields in which they have already demonstrated talent and or skill as a layman or volunteers."[114] The program bore a strong resemblance to the parent aide program Riessman and Mary Dowery had built at MFY four years earlier, scaled up with the backing of federal dollars.

These experimental programs using a range of newly available federal funds—from the Economic Opportunity Act as well as the ESEA—sprang up around the nation. The Bank Street College team that supported Riessman and Wilcox in East Harlem was commissioned by the Office of Education to survey eleven such programs in 1966, a number that grew to fifteen by the time they completed their study in 1968.[115] The programs served students from Head Start to high school, primarily in the summers of 1966 and 1967, though five—those in Berkeley, Detroit, Eastern Kentucky, Northeastern Maine, and New York City's Lower East Side—continued in some form during the school year. Other sites involved included the cities of Boston, East St. Louis, Jackson, Mississippi, Los Angeles, and Washington, DC, as well as rural sites in Flagstaff, Arizona (working primarily with Navajo students) and Southeastern Ohio (serving Appalachian counties in the state).[116] The New York Program surveyed by Bank Street was run jointly by the Two Bridges Neighborhood Council and the New York City Department of Education, with support from Riessman and New York University's School of Education. Much as in East Harlem, the program used ESEA Title III monies to hire and train about twenty classroom reading aides in multiracial, multilingual Lower East Side schools. While the program showed promise in the summer, the Bank Street Report noted that the aides had been hired from among the existing staff of school aides, and that their principals and teachers often relegated them to "clerical and custodial tasks" when they tried to carry their training in the teaching of reading into classrooms during the school year.[117]

Jerome Greene left teaching in the late 1960s to head the Morrisania Education Council (MEC), the educational arm of the Morrisania Community Progress Corporation, another federally funded antipoverty organization. In this capacity, he won funding from Congressman Scheuer's Subprofessional Career Act of 1966 for the hiring and training of paraprofessionals at Bronx schools.[118] In a long career as a school administrator that followed, Greene would earn the informal title "father of paraprofessionals" for his commitment to local hiring.[119] Oneida Davis, the PTA president who had joined his Saturday gatherings, was one of Greene's first hires.

Nearby in the South Bronx, Puerto Rican parent leader Evelina Lopez Antonetty discovered that public schools were giving English-language IQ tests to Spanish-speaking students and placing them in classes according to the results. Antonetty translated an IQ test into Spanish for the guidance counselor at her children's school, and the results were predictably drastic, revealing that the complete lack of Spanish-language instruction in New York City schools put Puerto Rican children at a severe disadvantage.[120] As Antonetty stayed involved in her children's school, she also found that most parents "never felt knowledgeable enough or strong enough to question and change things," and that teachers and administrators routinely kept parents in the dark about what took place in public schools in the neighborhood.[121]

Antonetty founded the United Bronx Parents (UBP) with funding from the Office of Economic Opportunity in 1966 to empower parents and address the marginalization of Spanish-speaking students. The UBP printed flyers detailing "The Use of Auxiliary Personnel (Paraprofessionals)" and encouraging parents to demand that principals hire local mothers for these positions as the board began hiring in the fall of 1967.[122] As one flyer explained, the community should "have a say in the recruitment and selection of Title I personnel" and "where possible, all jobs [should] be filled by concerned community people."[123]

UBP materials appeared across the city, used by parent and activist groups to put direct pressure on school officials and politicians to hire locally. Writing in 1968, after the first year of official board hiring, the UBP congratulated its members, noting, "more and more pressure was brought upon the Board to hire people from the community to assist the teachers in their work with the children," leading to the creation of formal paraprofessional programs.[124] The UBP's work is an important reminder that postwar struggles in New York included growing populations of Puerto Rican and Asian American activists, who frequently joined Black-led struggles to demand improved education.[125] This is not to ignore political and pedagogical tensions between African-American and Latinx educational goals in New York; the question of bilingual education became a contentious topic after national court cases required school districts to hire additional Spanish-speaking educators at the perceived expense of other groups.[126] However, the shared experiences of racism in working-class, deindustrializing neighborhoods could also generate interracial solidarity among non-white New Yorkers in these years.[127] These included shared campaigns for local hiring, a goal that could serve many local struggles.

While Black Power was the ascendant philosophy in educational activism in the late 1960s, demands for local hiring also built on long-running campaigns for jobs. Bayard Rustin strongly opposed the language and tactics of Black Power and Black nationalism. After years of working toward national legislation on civil rights, Rustin turned his attention to interracial labor and socialist organizing in the mid-1960s. He worked closely with the American Federation of Teachers and its New York City local, the UFT, as the director of the A. Philip Randolph Institute. As one of the authors of the *Freedom Budget for All Americans*, Rustin supported local hiring wholeheartedly as a step toward building full employment through public-sector job creation. A staunch integrationist, Rustin also believed that local hiring in education would help to integrate the staff of public schools and, if career ladders could be set up, serve as a path to integrating the teaching corps as well. Rustin recruited like-minded civil rights unionists to his cause, including Norman and Velma Murphy Hill, organizers who had trained with Randolph in Chicago before moving to New York to work on Congress of Racial Equality campaigns.[128]

Even as new political and philosophical differences emerged among organizers, the push for local hiring brought educators, activists, and poverty warriors together. In 1966, Preston Wilcox accepted the chairmanship of the board of the Women's Talent Corps. The corps was founded by Audrey Cohen with an Office of Economic Opportunity grant in 1964. Cohen, a graduate of the University of Pittsburgh raising her children at home on the posh Upper East Side, had founded a consultancy employing married, college-educated women in 1960 called Part-Time Research Associates. The goal of the consultancy was to give college-educated women a chance to earn money for their families while continuing to manage their households. In 1964, the civil rights movement and the War on Poverty inspired Cohen to think more expansively about the challenges working-class women faced, and how her original vision might grow to create jobs and opportunities for the people who needed them most.

After creating the "Women's Talent Corps," as she dubbed the new program, she sought out leading activists and organizers to help her build it. She recruited Wilcox to chair the board because of his connections to Harlem and East Harlem parents, and asked Evelina Lopez Antonetty to join as vice chair. Before the corps began working with women or training them for new jobs, Wilcox organized meetings with Cohen and community associations across New York City to gauge community interest and get feedback on the sorts of jobs women wanted. Alida Mesrop, who joined Cohen and Wilcox at the corps, remembered Cohen "at every community meeting in the city, it seemed to me," learning about "the kind of abilities these people had and how you put them together with the needs within our city."[129]

The Women's Talent Corps was an anomaly. Unlike most programs and organizations funded by the OEO, it was not rooted in a particular place. While MFY and HARYOU, and later the United Bronx Parents and the Morrisania Community Progress Corporation, hired local residents as part of broad programs of empowerment in specific neighborhoods, the Women's Talent Corps aimed to train women from around the city to take on these roles. As such, it was uniquely positioned to shape the kinds of training such workers would receive, and how these jobs would be conceptualized. Cohen hired Laura Pires from HARYOU to serve as the training coordinator for the corps, bringing both her ideas and her networks into the corps' service. Cohen and the Women's Talent Corps also worked to apply citywide pressure to agencies considering local hiring. Seeking to place educational aides not just in community-run after-school programs but in the public schools themselves, the corps and its trainees conducted a letter-writing campaign, and Cohen herself staged a one-woman sit-in at the Board of Education.[130]

The Women's Talent Corps was one site of collaboration among many in the city, bringing together educators, social workers, and activists from both local freedom struggles and the world of antipoverty policy and scholarship. To bring pressure on the Board of Education to institute a program of local paraprofessional hiring, however, they needed additional partners. In October of 1966, a WTC progress report noted, "meetings with top representatives of the United Federation of Teachers have produced offers of cooperation and assistance . . . interest has been expressed by the union in representing the new position of teacher assistant as the role would be 'pedagogical.'"[131] As Audrey Cohen remembered in 1973, "It became clear that we needed their cooperation," and so she "went over to Albert Shanker's citadel" to convince the president of New York City's teacher union "that this was very important for the future of the Union."[132] Antipoverty scholars and Black and Puerto Rican activists had come together around local hiring. Now they urged the teachers of the UFT to welcome a new kind of educator into their classrooms.

Replacing Teachers or Future Teachers?
Teacher Unions and Community-Based Hiring

Teacher unions expanded rapidly in urban school districts in the 1950s and 1960s as part of a broad wave of public-sector organizing. Government employment ballooned in the postwar era—over 200,000 jobs were added in New York City alone from 1950 to 1970—and public-sector unions accounted for 80 percent of union growth, jumping from 1 million to 3 million members.[133] This expansion brought new people into the labor movement; by 1960, Black workers were more likely to be unionized than any other racial or ethnic group, and thousands of women had joined unions as well.[134]

In New York City, several smaller organizations merged to form the United Federation of Teachers (UFT) in 1959. The largest of these was the Teachers Guild, which organized teachers in the 1950s. Overcrowding was a huge problem in New York City, and one the guild used to recruit members and demand improvements for teachers. New York City teacher Leonora Farber cited overcrowding as her inspiration to join the union, after struggling to teach a class of 62 students in a Brownsville junior high school in which many students "were sitting on the radiators."[135] The guild listed overcrowding as one of many features that threatened teacher professionalism, along with administrative overreach, loyalty oaths, and the "forced transfers" threatened by the Commission on Integration's 1957 report.[136] In protesting these transfers, the guild staked out different ground than the Teachers Union (TU) and its smaller, more radical membership.

This focus on teachers' status proved an effective organizing tactic and shaped much of local and national union policy. As the idea of local hiring emerged—first of aides, then paras—teachers and their union negotiated their relationship to these new workers through the lens of professionalism. As discussed above, the Teachers Guild had pushed for the hiring of school aides beginning in 1955 to relieve members of "burdensome chores."[137] The UFT included the hiring of school aides for the same purpose among the provisions of its very first contract in 1962.[138] This position proved common across the locals of the American Federation of Teachers; in 1967, the Chicago Teachers Union included a similar provision in its first contract.[139]

In bargaining for aides' labor, the union drew stark lines between their professional, pedagogical duties and the aides' work. The UFT's 1962 contract defined aides as "civil service, administrative, non-pedagogical employees," and certainly not as potential UFT members.[140] A group of aides wrote to newly elected UFT President Albert Shanker in 1964 requesting membership in the UFT, advancing many of the same arguments the UFT would make for incorporating paraprofessionals into their union four years later. Shanker, however, told the aides that as they were classified as civil service employees, they should unionize with the local public service workers' union, District Council 37 of the American Federation of State, County, and Municipal Employees (AFSCME). New York's school aides would do so in 1966.[141]

Richard Parrish, though he served as treasurer of the UFT and a national vice president of the AFT, was an outlier in supporting non-professional educators in the classroom. In 1964, amid debates about federal funding for local hiring in education, Parrish was the sole member of the AFT Executive Council to oppose a resolution that read: "Teaching is a profession and all instructional contact with children should be performed by professionally qualified teachers."[142] The programs Parrish had developed with HARYOU in Harlem suggested different possibilities.

The passage of the ESEA in 1965 raised the stakes of this debate, pouring $1.3 billion into public schools without earmarking any of this money expressly for teachers. Across the country, AFT members argued about whether and how they should support the measure.[143] One year later, the union moved its international headquarters from Chicago (where it was founded) to Washington, DC. The move signaled the union's intention to play an expanded role in federal education policy, and to do so by articulating teacher professionalism.[144]

During a tense meeting of the AFT Executive Council at its new offices inside the beltway on July 9, 1966, union leaders cited several concerns about the local hiring that the ESEA encouraged. "Bringing in various people from the community," they argued, set dangerous precedents, allowing school districts to close personnel gaps without hiring more teachers, with aides "used as teachers," and particularly as "strikebreakers."[145] Most argued for the council to pass a direct resolution demanding aides not be used as teachers or to reduce class sizes. Some went as far as to argue, "we ought to be opposed to this entirely and come out with federal aid for teacher salaries," while others noted the need to "uphold our professionalism."[146]

Only one AFT vice president argued differently: Rose Claffey of Lynn, Massachusetts, a leading organizer of the Massachusetts Federation of Teachers. After noting that the AFT had been "in direct opposition to school aides" during the Bay City experiment, Claffey cited earlier programs created by federal funds, and remarked that many teachers in her state had been pleased with them. She described one in detail:

> In the wholly segregated schools in one of our native cities there was no contact between the school personnel and the community . . . they had to go out into the community and get people who did not have high school diplomas, but who were recognized as leaders in that part of the community, and so they then became the liaison between the schools and the community. And it has worked most effectively. In fact, it has enabled many of these people again to rise out of lowly situations and to get more effective leadership roles in the city.[147]

AFT President Charles Cogen argued against Claffey, as did his trusted advisor, future AFT President David Selden. The gender politics of this internal clash reflected the AFT's larger shift in its outward presentation in these years; as Diana D'Amico Pawlewicz writes, Cogen, Selden, and Albert Shanker had risen to power in the AFT after leading the UFT's successful contract campaign in New York City. This campaign, argued a celebratory film released in 1966, had "'smashed the old stereotype' of the nurturing female teacher and replaced that with a masculinized image that conformed to popular perceptions of the professional."[148] While women comprised 80 percent of the teaching force, men made up this new generation of militant union leaders, and their masculine self-presentation made little room for organizing the women workers whose aid was intended to enhance teachers' professionalism.

Nonetheless, Claffey stood her ground. As she argued, "I think we ought to view it [federal aid] with an open mind and hope it is the way we are going to

get more funds that we can use as they best serve the needs of a community."
She repeated reports from her chapters that some teachers described Title
I programs and materials as "the most fabulous things they have ever seen."
Selden had the last word, asserting "we should put the AFT squarely out in
front as the champion of the teacher," but Claffey's understanding of paras
as future teachers would be championed by Selden himself as AFT president
in 1968, just two short years later.[149]

The AFT's change of heart was driven, as Claffey's testimony foretold,
by two factors. First, having realized that federal funding for education was
going forward regardless of whether the union approved of it, AFT leaders
decided it would be better to become involved in these programs than to fight
them. Second, the rise of demands for community control of public schools
in the late 1960s threatened much more radical changes to teaching.[150]

Nowhere were deteriorating relations with Black and Hispanic communities felt more strongly than in New York City, where long-running demands for
the recomposition of the teaching corps reached new heights in the struggle
for community control. Responding both to the directives of the international
union and the challenges brewing at home, Shanker and UFT changed their
tune on unionizing "aides" and opened discussions with the Women's Talent
Corps. The UFT's executive council approved a resolution to encourage the
Board of Education to hire paraprofessionals, and recruit them into the union,
on February 15, 1967. By March, Shanker was writing to Cohen to assure her,
"You may continue to count on us as an ally as you work for the adoption of
the program. The teachers and the community have a single goal concerning
the employment of teacher assistants. We know that teachers, children, and
the community will benefit."[151] Shanker wrote this even as the union prepared
to insist on teachers' rights to remove a "disruptive child" from the classroom
in their 1967 contract, an explosive demand that set the union on a collision
course with Black and Hispanic parent activists in that same year.

How did Shanker and the UFT come to embrace these new educators?
The key rhetorical shift was present in what the NEA's Lucille Carroll wrote
from Bay City in 1956: teacher aide and paraprofessional programs could,
and should, be considered a "long-range recruitment plan." Rose Claffey, in
her remarks to the AFT Executive Committee a decade later, made a similar
observation. Speaking of an experimental training program that had included
the opportunity to earn college credit in Lynn, she implored the AFT leadership to see themselves as benevolent guides to women in need. In her school
district, she claimed, "we were the salvation of many of these people . . . the
opportunity for them to go back to school and serve as a wholesome aspect
of society put many of them on their feet."[152]

By casting paraprofessionals as hardworking women seeking the opportunity to become teachers and "serve as a wholesome aspect of society," Claffey

provided a powerful counterweight to the image of the para as a community spy or threatening activist that many teachers feared in the context of rising demands for community control. Shanker, in describing aides as "pedagogical" employees, and by endorsing career ladder training from the outset, positioned himself and his local leadership to make a similar claim, both on UFT's membership and on paraprofessionals. Offering unionization and training to paras was not just an act of kindness; such organizing also offered new, dues-paying members and the chance to give the union the power to shape nascent paraprofessional programs as the board began hiring. In the years to come, the idea that paras were future teachers would serve both to unite and empower these new educators, and sometimes to limit their union's vision of their roles, potential, and future as community workers. In the short run, however, winning union support for paraprofessional programs was a crucial step in bringing paras into schools.

From Teacher Aides to Paraprofessional Educators

After negotiating with both the Board of Education and the UFT, seventy-five women trained by the Women's Talent Corps started work as classroom and guidance assistants in New York City schools in the spring of 1967.[153] They were the first paraprofessional educators to work in classrooms during the school day, and their labor set the stage for the board's official embrace of local hiring that fall.

The hiring of paraprofessional educators in New York City represented a convergence of ideas while also revealing ongoing tensions that would shape these programs going forward. Each set of actors involved came to community-based hiring from a different starting point, and each evolved its own logic for supporting these programs. Administrators sought cheap labor and efficient management of school-day tasks. Community organizers in local freedom struggles fought to bring local people into schools as part of a broader vision of democratic self-determination, community involvement in school governance, and integrated, equal access to resources, in the form of education for children and jobs for adults. Scholars of poverty and New Careerists believed the combination of jobs, training, and improved service delivery could radically improve the lives of the poor in urban communities. Teacher unionists, who maintained their skepticism about these other goals, developed their own reasons to incorporate paraprofessionals into their union, based on ideas of teacher training and recruitment that served both to recruit new members and settle the nerves of older ones.

Despite these clear differences, paraprofessional education programs never would have emerged in formal school settings had substantial overlap between each set of actors not led to sustained and generative collaborations in the decade between Bay City's experiment and New York's formal hiring. The imperatives of these years—overcrowding, educational inequality, and the arrival of federal dollars—demanded and fueled these collaborations. Richard Parrish was a committed unionist, but he was equally committed to empowering the students and parents of Harlem. Preston Wilcox was a self-described "radical pluralist" with a deep distrust of bureaucracies, but he was glad to lead the eclectic cast of characters from inside and outside the establishment on the Women's Talent Corps board to build paraprofessional training and push for para hiring. The idea of hiring locally predated the War on Poverty, but the outlay of new funds generated new collaborations and new ideas. Activists, educators, policymakers, and unionists came together across lines of class, race, and gender to experiment, assess, and advocate for these programs.

As the Women's Talent Corps trainees took their posts in classrooms in the spring of 1967, the story of paraprofessional labor in New York City was only just beginning. While the individuals and organizations described in this chapter watched eagerly, it was these women themselves who took on the task of realizing these programs' promise. As they did so, they articulated their own vision for their new careers as community-based educators.

Paraprofessionals at work in a classroom with students, October 16, 1969. United Federation of Teachers Hans Weissenstein Negatives; PHOTOS.019.001, Box 9, Item 12114, Tamiment Library & Robert F. Wagner Labor Archives, New York University.

CHAPTER 2

"They Made Themselves Essential"
Paraprofessional Educators Go to Work in New York City, 1967–1970

First Day Jitters

The first day of school makes everyone nervous, from wide-eyed kindergartners and their anxious parents to first-time teachers and the veteran educators supervising them. As New York City's youngest public-school students entered their classrooms on the first day of school in the fall of 1967, however, many of them were greeted by familiar faces. The city's Board of Education had used Title I funds from the Elementary and Secondary Education Act of 1965 to hire 1,500 local residents, nearly all mothers of schoolchildren, to work in kindergarten classes "in selected schools in low-income areas": Harlem, the South Bronx, and Central Brooklyn, the city's largest Black and Puerto Rican neighborhoods. Given the trepidation that accompanies the very first day of school, these kindergartners and their parents must have been thrilled to see friends and neighbors welcoming them. It was a new experience for most Black and Hispanic parents and children in a school system whose teaching corps was 91 percent white.[1]

These new paraprofessional educators had first-day jitters, too. What would they do in classrooms and schools? How would they help support the students and parents from their neighborhoods? Would teachers and principals respect them? Would they have the power to deliver on the expectations of the parent and community organizations that had fought to create their jobs? Paras had been hired to improve instruction, connect schools and communities, and prove that they could succeed as educators and, with training, future teachers. For them, the first day of school marked the beginning of their efforts to meet this triple challenge.

What was that first day like? Over half a century later, Maggie Martin's eyes widened. "Before there was a union, a bargaining unit?" she asked rhetorically in 2019. "I don't like using the word, but it was hell."[2] Of her first year in the classroom, Martin said in 2015, "it was rough, make no mistake about it." The teacher Martin worked for, one of the only Black educators at her school in Queens, was a "dynamite" pedagogue, but "teaching was her profession" and she felt Martin's presence cheapened her hard-won professional status. She barely spoke to Martin for the first several months of the year, relegating her to menial tasks at the back of the class.[3]

Shelvy Young-Abrams had the same experience on the Lower East Side, where the white teacher she worked for "did not want me to have anything to do with the children." The teacher stationed Young-Abrams at the back of the classroom, and children were told they "couldn't even come over and ask me a question." The teacher "was very protective of that classroom." Her treatment gave Young-Abrams, a former PTA president, migraine headaches for months.[4]

The Women's Talent Corps received a report that one teacher told a paraprofessional that "the idea of creating jobs for Negroes was bad" and "Negroes should earn their equality by being better than white people." In protest of the program, the teacher "refused to call [the para] anything but 'aide.'"[5] Another teacher on the Lower East Side wrote to United Federation of Teachers President Albert Shanker to complain, "It appears the primary purpose of the program has been to provide employment for poor people rather than primarily to help the children." The teacher argued all staff should be chosen through "open, competitive examinations."[6]

The first days, weeks, and months on the job were often brutal for these new paras, and many felt powerless. Administrators treated them as cheap labor to exploit in whatever way they desired. Teachers' reactions betrayed a multitude of fears and anxieties. Some teachers believed paras had been hired to spy on them for parents or community organizations, while others feared administrators would use paras as replacement teachers and strikebreakers. Still other teachers felt the presence of uncredentialed, working-class women of color in their classrooms undermined their status as professionals, which they relied on at the bargaining table. Many simply assumed that these women could not possibly contribute to the work of education.

To be sure, some paras, teachers, and administrators hit it off from the start, particularly those in programs that prepared them to work together over the summer and supported them during the year. However, like many War on Poverty programs, New York City's paraprofessional rollout was long on promise and short on specifics. It was up to teachers and paras to make this experiment work, classroom by classroom, school by school.

It did not help that the school year got off to a rocky start. The United Federation of Teachers went on strike in early September when negotiations for their second contract broke down. Like all teachers' strikes, the walkout and subsequent closure of schools wreaked havoc on the daily lives of working families. One UFT demand, a provision allowing teachers to unilaterally remove a "disruptive child" from their classrooms, made things worse. While teachers argued that maintaining sovereignty over their classrooms was paramount, Black and Puerto Rican parents saw the measure as a violation of their children's rights and evidence of teachers' racist, classist assumptions. The UFT's belief that teachers needed the power to define and punish children as "disruptive" to do their jobs cast the crisis of care that had developed in New York City's public schools in high relief.[7]

It was in response to such treatment, in part, that parent activists had sought community control of schools. That same fall, parents in Harlem, the Lower East Side, and Ocean Hill–Brownsville began sorting out what "control" would look like in three new experimental districts within the larger system. The union had initially supported the experiments but withdrew its backing as it became clear parent organizers sought control over personnel decisions.

Hanging over all these conflicts between parents and teachers was the specter of the urban uprisings of 1967, one of which had engulfed Newark, New Jersey, ten short miles away. Community-based paraprofessional educators had been hired, in part, to close the distance between schools and the neighborhoods that they served. That distance appeared to be widening rapidly. A tenuous alliance of civil rights organizers, antipoverty practitioners, and teacher unionists had pushed the Board of Education to hire paraprofessional educators. Now, paras had to meet the expectations of all these stakeholders, often in a very hostile work environment.

At the close of the school year, in May of 1968, the UFT ran an internal survey of 200 teachers and 230 paraprofessionals to assess the first year of paraprofessional work in New York City schools. The results were overwhelming and surprising: teachers loved the program. One teacher wrote, "She is essential! I could not do without her," while another teacher declared that her classroom was "so much more successful because of her [paraprofessional's] assistance, especially reaching out to parents."[8] Of 230 paras surveyed, only four reported negative experiences. Most paras believed their work was "very good for community relations" and that by giving "the people in the community a chance to take part in the education of their children," para programs were "particularly good in bettering relations between black and white in ghetto areas."[9] Reports from principals and in the press echoed this praise. Despite a rough start and everything happening in public schools and the wider city, the first year had been a success.

These glowing reviews—and the continued availability of federal funding—encouraged a tremendous expansion of para hiring in New York in the years between 1967 and 1970. The Board of Education began with seventy-five women trained by the Women's Talent Corps in the spring of 1967; by the spring of 1970, it employed over 10,000 paraprofessional educators. The board commissioned a study of paras in over 200 New York City schools that year; it opened with the line: "whatever may be wrong with the paraprofessional program in the schools of New York City, nothing could outweigh the overwhelming evidence we have found of its success."[10] In the words of Aurelia Greene, Jerome Greene's partner and a community organizer in the Bronx, the first generation of paras had "made themselves essential" in New York City schools.[11]

This chapter illuminates the ways in which paraprofessional educators—"paras"—made themselves, and their work, essential in New York City public schools. To understand this achievement, this chapter examines the lives and labor of these educators at the local level—in the classroom, the schoolhouse, and the neighborhood—where their work had the power to transform the social and institutional geography of public schooling. Scaling down to the local level brings the contributions of community-based educators into focus. It also highlights the connections and alliances paras built with students, parents, and teachers. These intimate, interpersonal solidarities laid the political and organizational foundations for paras' drive to unionize, win a contract, and expand their work and its impact in the following decade.

Paraprofessional educators made themselves essential in New York City public schools by working to address the growing crisis of care in public education. The language and practice of caring suffuses their recollections of this work, often in high contrast to the impersonality, and even brutality, of crowded classrooms, overwhelmed teachers, and the educational bureaucracy. Much like care workers in other fields, their labor was simultaneously devalued and exploited by their bosses, even as the clear impact they made became impossible to ignore.[12]

Across New York City, paras were as diverse as the communities from whence they came. Their paths to this work varied widely, and it is difficult to generalize about the "typical" politics or experiences of these educators. Nonetheless, three sets of practices and philosophies emerged in common among community-based paraprofessional educators. These practices are visible in the paths they took to their positions, the ways they conceptualized the work of education, and their everyday labor in classrooms and neighborhoods to improve instruction, connect schools and communities, and train toward careers in education.

The first way paras addressed education's crisis of care was by practicing what Black feminist thinkers have termed "activist mothering."[13] The second was by building cross-class, interracial solidarity among working women that spanned from parents to paras, teachers, and union organizers.[14] The third was seeking personal and collective advancement through education. Put simply, paras sought to rise with their communities rather than from them.[15]

These three practices helped community-based educators "make themselves essential" to the antipoverty organizations that trained and recommended them, the parents and activists who demanded their hiring, and the teachers and administrators with whom they worked. They also helped paras succeed in their new roles as community-based educators on their own terms, and to expand, enrich, and reimagine official definitions of "paraprofessional" or "teacher aide" labor.[16] These definitions often relied on racist, sexist, and classist assumptions about the knowledge and capacities of working-class women of color, particularly those engaged in care work. As Quinn and Ferree demonstrate in their study of paraprofessional labor, educational bureaucracies value credentialed, skilled knowledge work far more than the labor of social reproduction, and they often completely ignore the work of building respect that paraprofessional educators do to bring students, families, and teachers onto common ground.[17] The first generation of paras began to subvert this hierarchy by making their labor and organizing indispensable and, in doing so, building power for themselves and their communities.[18]

Many of these new paraprofessional educators made a profound impact in their schools and communities, but they did so within an educational bureaucracy that typically offered them minimal preparation and very little official support for creativity and collaboration. Some of the paras whose contributions are analyzed in this chapter worked in unique programs that provided exemplary planning and encouragement, while others showed fierce determination in making the most of difficult situations. Paras made themselves essential in New York City public schools between 1967 and 1970, but that does not mean they reformed a notoriously unequal and unresponsive bureaucracy, or that every individual paraprofessional educator had a positive and influential experience. Many found themselves marginalized and disrespected in classrooms and schools, or deeply frustrated, as Cleo Silvers was, by the pedagogies, curricula, and punishment they were expected to administer to the children of their communities. It was precisely these tensions—between the possibilities apparent in some paras' experience and the frustrations many encountered at work—that would drive paraprofessional educators to organize.

Recruiting "Indigenous Nonprofessionals": The Structure of Paraprofessional Programs

How did paras find their jobs? The city's Board of Education hired its very first paras in March of 1967: seventy-five women trained by the Women's Talent Corps. The board used this pilot to shape the system for paraprofessional hiring and training that it was preparing for the fall. It applied for an Elementary and Secondary Education Act (ESEA) planning grant to do so, asserting "the steady proliferation of jobs of all kinds for auxiliary non-professional neighborhood personnel in our schools makes it essential that we begin to plan now for the orderly and coordinated recruitment, training, and classification of such personnel." Together with the New York City Council Against Poverty, the citywide coordinating office for all federally funded community action programming, the board outlined five "ultimate objectives":

1. To liberate teachers from a wide range of mechanical chores so that they may devote themselves more intensely to teaching
2. To provide role models drawn directly from the community for the pupils
3. To give the community a more direct and meaningful stake in the school and a more practical understanding of its problems
4. To provide opportunities for increased individual attention and services for pupils
5. To provide eventually a steady and continuing source of teachers recruited from minority groups.[19]

These objectives mirrored formulations put forth by the diverse range of actors who campaigned to create these positions. They retained the hierarchical goal of "liberating teachers" from "mechanical chores," advanced both by teacher union leaders seeking benefits for their members and administrators looking for ways to divide the labor of education in the service of saving money. However, the board's new objectives also made space for the goals of improving instruction and community involvement. Finally, and most nebulously, these objectives suggested the possibility of creating a path to teaching for paras, one that would integrate the teaching corps and create "new careers" for working-class women.

In the fall of 1967, the board hired 1,500 positions to expand the kindergarten pilot program across the city. Superintendents and principals, in concert with antipoverty agencies, settlement houses, and other nonprofit entities, could now propose their own programs for community-based education, which the board would then approve. The funding for these programs now came almost entirely from Title I of the ESEA, which provided the vast majority of the resources to hire in-school paraprofessional educators across the country. Title III, which funded community education centers, also offered monies for para hiring, as did the Bilingual Education Act (Title VII of the ESEA) after President Johnson signed it into law on January 2, 1968.[20] As the Board of Education explained in a special circular sent to all principals and district superintendents in October of 1967, it hoped para programs would "improve communications with communities, improve instruction in the kindergartens, and provide opportunities for residents in disadvantaged communities, who possess the ability, to develop into teachers."[21] The tripartite structure the Board of Education outlined in this memo—classroom improvements, community coalitions, and career training—was drawn directly from works including Riessman's *New Careers for the Poor* and HARYOU's *Youth in the Ghetto*. It provided an aspirational vision, but not a direct plan of action, for educators and administrators.

The board implemented a collaborative hiring structure for all paraprofessional positions. The only formal requirements for applicants were that they demonstrate a fifth-grade reading level, pass a physical and background check, and be eligible for public assistance with a household income less than $4,000 per year. While the board did not implement a formal residency requirement, it stated, "in all cases absolute priority must be given to residents of the zoning area of the elementary school."[22] Paras were paid between $1.75 and $2.25 an hour depending on their educational credentials, numbers that barely cleared the federal minimum wage of $1.60 an hour. Working an average of six hours a day, paraprofessionals brought home roughly fifty dollars a week, the same amount Bay City aides had earned back in 1953.[23]

To be hired, applicants also needed a referral. Half of these new employees were to be referred by principals, either from "incumbent employees in other titles" or parent volunteers, including participants in parent-teacher associations. The other half were to be recommended by city-recognized, federally funded antipoverty agencies.[24] HARYOU and Mobilization for Youth, the sites of key pilot programs in community-based education, were two such agencies. Others included Bedford-Stuyvesant Youth in Action, the Morrisania Community Progress Corporation, the United Bronx Parents, and the Crown Heights Education Committee.[25] After one semester, the Board of Education amended the hiring process to allow District Council 37 of the American Federation of State, County, and Municipal Employees (DC 37)—the public-service employees union that represented school aides and cafeteria workers in schools—to refer applicants to the principal. From then on, recommendations from schools were split evenly, so that administrators and AFSCME each referred one-quarter of applications and community-based antipoverty organizations provided the balance.

The Board of Education held the purse strings, but individual schools and local sub-districts (of which New York City had thirty at the time) did the work of developing programs that hired, placed, and trained paras, often in partnership with antipoverty agencies, local universities, and philanthropic foundations. They applied for grants, funded by the ESEA, that the central Board of Education approved. Many grants and programs ran for short-term trial periods, often a single summer or semester, while others stretched across multiple years. Through this diffuse, decentralized process, the city as a whole hired paraprofessional educators—listed as "educational auxiliaries" in official records—by the hundreds, and occasionally thousands, in every month of 1968 and 1969.[26] While not all the individuals hired for each program remained employed after the trial period, many stayed on in other roles and additional programs. By 1970, the board employed over 10,000 paraprofessional educators in public schools, working with students from kindergarten through high school, as well as nontraditional and older students earning GEDs. The hiring policies outlined by the Board of Education ensured that the first generation of paras would bring intimate local knowledge of students and parents into public schools, along with personal connections to local struggles and organizations. This ensured a very different workforce from the faculty with respect to race, class, and experience.

An extensive study conducted by the Institute for Educational Development for the Board of Education in 1970 offers a statistical portrait of New York City's first paras. About half were identified as Black, and 40 percent had Spanish surnames. Ninety-three percent were women, and 80 percent were mothers. Nearly all lived within the catchment area of the school where they worked, and 80 percent lived within ten blocks.[27]

Mothers who became paraprofessionals often worked at the schools their children attended, and some programs designed by individual districts required them to do so. Across the board in 1970, 85 percent of paras reported seeing their students outside of school regularly. Sixty percent of paraprofessionals reported formal involvement in an existing community institution, and nearly all of them reported increased engagement with neighbors and local institutions in the context of their new jobs.[28] The hiring structure of para programs, combined with the fact that demands for these jobs emerged in local programs and struggles to improve education, ensured that the first generation of paraprofessional educators came into schools with extensive experience in community organizations. As Anne Cronin, the director of training for the Women's Talent Corps, observed of her organization's recruits:

> [T]he women who had the courage and initiative to make application were people who are alert and active in community affairs. There were many PTA officers, den mothers, community council members, church volunteer workers. . . . Almost all had children, for whose future they are intensely concerned. In general they were bright and verbally sophisticated, with a rich life-knowledge and wisdom about the ways of their world.[29]

Another Women's Talent Corps report noted, "most of them [paraprofessional educators] had been active in recently developed community activities in their own neighborhoods; several were officers of PTAs and similar programs, a number had worked as assistants in Head Start, as school aides, or as settlement house aides."[30] Laura Pires, who joined the Women's Talent Corps from HARYOU in 1965, lauded the "Harlem sophistication" of trainees who came to the WTC steeped in that neighborhood's organizing traditions.[31]

As Aurelia Greene recalled in 2014, paraprofessional programs created an opportunity for many women "to get some reward for the work that they were doing" in their communities already.[32] Maggie Martin volunteered to walk a small band of students, including her own children, to and from their school in Jamaica, Queens. The principal sought her out when the school began hiring paraprofessionals.[33] Oneida Davis started at PS 55 in the South Bronx in 1968 after serving as the parent association president in both of her daughters' schools.[34] On the Lower East Side, Shelvy Young-Abrams and Chinese American para Marian Thom started their careers in education as volunteer parent liaisons with community antipoverty organizations, doing outreach to parents to make them aware of resources and opportunities for their children.[35] Young-Abrams had also been PTA president in her daughters' school, where the principal recommended her for her first paraprofessional job.[36]

These first paras also recruited like-minded women to the cause. Greene, who worked with the Morrisania Education Council to push principals and superintendents to hire paraprofessionals, recalled that recruitment was facilitated by networks of "parent leaders who passed the word on to one another."[37] Martha McNear, who started with the Women's Talent Corps in 1967, noted that she was "[sought] out for advice" and "encouraged others to try for another chance at improving themsel[ves]." McNear's work as a para, she reported, led her to "become even more active in my community."[38]

For these women, commitments to community ran deep. "I've been volunteering since I was a kid," remembered Marian Thom in 2013. "My mother, bless her soul, she had these people from her village [in China], and they had kids, and they couldn't get out to shop, so they would call, and she would pick up the stuff and then I would have to drop it off on my way to school."[39] Thom mastered the subway by age twelve, accompanying pregnant women to the doctor, delivering tailored clothing to family friends, and carrying traditional remedies to far-flung relatives.

While all these women were new to paraprofessional work, they brought a wealth of organizing experience and "indigenous knowledges" (in Nancy Naples's phrase) into public education.[40] Once inside the schoolhouse door, they put this experience and knowledge to work. Day by day, they showed students, parents, teachers, and administrators that their labor could, under supportive conditions, improve the experience of public education for all parties involved.

It's More Than Watering Plants: Paraprofessional Labor in Classrooms and Schools

What did paraprofessional educators do in public schools? In 1970, the *New York Post* ran a profile of para Letty Concepcion titled "It's More Than Watering Plants." The humorous title echoed a point the article made: although the *Post*'s readers, as well as school administrators quoted in the article, might imagine "aides" doing menial labor, paras shaped every facet of the school experience, from instruction to discipline to emotional support and guidance. The *Post* emphasized that in New York, paras "are concentrated in classes making the slowest progress" and described their work as a combination of "small group instruction" and "troubleshooting" in the classroom. "Tutoring, reading aloud . . . communicating with parents—as sometimes only a resident of the same block can—these are some of the functions of a paraprofessional." A photo of Concepcion standing over a smiling student at PS 250 in Williamsburg, Brooklyn, confirmed the assessment of the teacher she worked with (invoking the rhetoric of care): "She's a very, very warm person. The children respond to her."[41]

Like many teachers, Helen Steinmetz was initially hostile to the idea of having a para in her classroom. "Here I was, a new teacher, faced with a class that had quite a discipline problem," she told the *Post*, "and suddenly here I had another adult to supervise. I was so scared when Letty walked in, I was petrified. We both looked at each other and glared." Right off the bat, however, Concepcion proved extremely useful to Steinmetz: she spoke Spanish. "If the children knew no English, I was practically helpless with them," Steinmetz explained. Concepcion "would take four or five and work with them in the back of the room." One student, a recent arrival from Puerto Rico who was placed in Steinmetz's second-grade class at age twelve, acted out constantly and "almost ruined the class" until Concepcion stepped in to work with her. "I was ready to treat Maria as a discipline problem," said Steinmetz, "but Letty made me realize she had a mind."[42] Paras' presence in classrooms, for many teachers, presented a host of alternative solutions to removal for "disruptive" children.

Concepcion connected Steinmetz to her students' parents, as well. "Through Letty," Steinmetz said, "the parents learned to trust me. She told them I was really interested in the children."[43] Concepcion's job was clearly much more than watering plants, and she knew it; as she told the *Post,* she loved working with children and hoped to become a teacher herself.

As the *Post*'s story demonstrates, neither Concepcion nor Steinmetz received much preparation for the addition of a paraprofessional educator to an elementary classroom. Their experience was very common, even though scholars including Frank Riessman at NYU and Garda Bowman and Gordon Klopf at Bank Street College urged more focused planning and training. In their 1968 report on fifteen pilot programs, Bowman and Klopf highlighted several "difficulties which might arise" and should be planned for, including unclear role definitions and limited opportunities for development for paras, and teachers' fears and anxieties about the place of these new educators.[44]

With paraprofessional hiring advancing as quickly as it did in New York City, training programs developed by the Board of Education lagged behind.

Thus, in the fall of 1967, many paras and teachers met on the first day of school, and some teachers did not realize they would have another adult in their classroom until they arrived. In a memo to principals regarding the employment of paras at the end of October, the Board of Education listed twenty-six potential duties for paras that appear to have been spitballed on the fly. They include "get milk" and "take sick children to nurse" as well as "translate for students and parents" and "explain Puerto Rican community and culture to teachers and administrators."[45] Paraprofessionals, in the board's estimation, would do work ranging from menial to anthropological in the course of a day, all for fifty dollars a week. "Role definition," as Bowman and Klopf urged districts to plan, was going to have to be sorted out on the job.

Paraprofessional programs reflected the diversity of New York City neighborhoods by design, and so did the work paraprofessionals did in their classrooms and communities. There was no "typical" day for a para, but another profile gives a sense of what one para's day looked like. In 1969, NBC New York ran a half-hour feature on the Women's Talent Corps that followed three of the corps' trainees through their work.[46] Julia Castro, a paraprofessional at PS 198 in East Harlem, lived in a public housing development near the school where she worked. Getting out of the house in the morning, she told NBC's interviewers, was a challenge; she had six children to feed and send to school. She then walked to work, greeting neighborhood children on her way through the schoolyard. In her first-grade class, as the teacher led a math lesson, NBC's cameras followed Castro making her way around the room to help individual children, particularly those who spoke Spanish (fourteen of the twenty-five students, as Castro reported). At three-thirty, NBC followed Castro home to her apartment, where she helped her own children with their homework and prepared dinner. Several evenings a week, Castro headed downtown to the Women's Talent Corps for training and coursework. The schedule, as she told NBC, was "not easy" for her or her family, but she felt her children were inspired by her new job and working harder on their own schoolwork as a result. "If mommy does this," her youngest told Castro, "we should do it too."[47]

The profiles of Concepcion and Castro capture many common elements of the paraprofessional experience. In classrooms, paras' academic labor consisted primarily of individual and small-group work, with an initial focus on reading. This focus reflected a national push to raise reading standards that had gathered steam for a decade since the Soviet launch of Sputnik provoked a panic about US educational levels. As Christine Sleeter has shown, the rush to raise reading levels made literacy a primary metric for defining new categories of ability, and thus disability, in public education, a process itself shaped by assumptions about race, class, and language.[48] In navigating the ways urban public schools explained low reading scores as the products of "cultural deprivation" and "emotional disturbance," or (more severely) "slow learning" and "mental retardation," paras became educators of children with disabilities while that field was in its infancy.[49] Teacher Leanora Nelson wrote to New York City Superintendent Bernard Donovan to praise Jean Smith of the Women's Talent Corps for "tak[ing] over a slow-reading, very active group of children for intensive direction and assistance."[50] In East Flatbush, Brooklyn, teachers described paras in an intensive reading program as "very helpful in working with small groups of children."[51]

These Brooklyn teachers singled out the impact of paras on those students who struggled with English. As the profiles of Concepcion and Castro revealed, those paras who spoke another language quickly became de facto classroom translators and bilingual educators, as programs of bilingual education were just beginning. After the passage of the Bilingual Education Act in 1968, many more would be hired in explicitly bilingual programs, as Laura J. Kaplan shows in her study of P.S. 25, the Bilingual School, in the South Bronx.[52] In 1971, principal Hernán LaFontaine of P.S. 25 explained his philosophy of local hiring: "Highest preference should be given to parents of children in the school since there is really no other group which could have a greater stake in developing the best instructional program possible."[53] At P.S. 25, Kaplan writes, Title VII funds meant that paras received "exceptional training" that prepared and empowered them to work closely with students, educators, and the wider community.[54]

Some paras worked with the same teachers and students all day and covered every elementary school subject. As Marian Thom remembered, "you helped the teacher any way you could."[55] In other instances, paras worked in focused programs in particular subjects; at different times, Thom and Shelvy Young-Abrams both did mathematics instruction with students on the Lower East Side.[56] While individualized instruction and small group work were encouraged as part of new teaching models in the mid-1960s, many paras started doing this work for the simple reason that, as Oneida Davis recalled, "overcrowded classrooms" bred a "sense of frustration" for overwhelmed teachers.[57] Paras, in many cases, had the power to relieve that frustration.

Providing individual and small-group instruction under the supervision of a teacher was part of the work administrators and teacher unionists had imagined for these "aides," "assistants," and "auxiliaries" (as paras' official titles defined them). This could be rote; in Bowman and Klopf's 1968 study, running basic drills was a commonly reported and observed task assigned to aides, in part because it seemed easier for teachers to supervise and evaluate, and in part reflecting the relatively low expectations teachers and administrators had at first.[58] Conducting such reading drills, especially when doing so involved pulling students away from the rest of the class, hardly constituted a transformative community intervention.

However, when they won teachers' trust, some paras moved well beyond these assistant roles and developed new pedagogical, curricular, and cultural experiences for students. As Oneida Davis put it, she and her fellow parent educators brought "community knowledge" into local schools to "empower" their students.[59] As part of the "Parent-Teacher Teams" program in West Harlem in 1968, paraprofessional Azalee Evans developed her school's first African American history lessons for fifth graders.[60] Doris Hunter did similar work at her school in Bedford-Stuyvesant, Brooklyn. In East Harlem, District Four's Community Education Center (CEC) launched a district-wide program, staffed primarily by paras, to provide materials on Puerto Rican history and culture to classrooms and the wider community in 1969. In Chinatown, Chinese American paras Marian Thom and Virginia Eng initiated the first celebrations of the Lunar New Year in local public schools.[61] These classroom interventions won over students, parents, and activists, as well as teachers and administrators, who saw how positively students and their communities responded to them.

Because paraprofessional educators were asked to do so much by so many different stakeholders, it can be hard to gauge their educational impact. Bilingual education, culturally responsive curriculum, and celebrations of students' cultures are now commonplace in schools. Paraprofessional educators served as early, and crucial, pioneers of these educational practices.

Another regular component of paraprofessional labor was the caring or emotional labor expected of these workers. Much as teaching became a predominantly female profession over the course of the nineteenth century due to expectations about women's natural, maternal qualities, teacher aide and paraprofessional labor was imagined as mother-work by everyone from administrators and philanthropists to community organizers to paras themselves. The key question, of course, was what appeals to maternity demanded of paras, as well as how they limited their roles. When Ford Foundation researchers in Bay City sought out mothers to work in their experimental aide program in the 1950s, they did so to keep the costs of their wages low, while describing "mothering" labor as tying shoes and admiring drawings.[62]

Paras, however, invoked very different traditions, those of activist or community mothering, in their work with students, who they knew faced a crisis of care in their schools. For many of them, the work of education included serving as relatable role models and accessible authorities to students. Oneida Davis took pride in being both a "role model" and "like mom to all these kids," both as a paraprofessional and, later, as a teacher. She noticed that, in contrast to many teachers, students found her "touchable," and could give her celebratory hugs or cry on her shoulder in school.[63] Maggie Martin felt "at that particular time, it worked, where they [African American students] could see more of their community in their school." In the years that followed, she noticed that "the ESL children" also "need[ed] to see and hear their people in that school, it makes them feel a little more comfortable."[64] While community-based educators knew that mere representation did not guarantee equity, they also saw firsthand how their presence made a positive impact on students. For students, these educators served both as evidence of educational participation and achievement in their neighborhoods, and as points of access for communicating their emotions in school settings.

Maternalist assumptions and rhetoric shaped the terrain on which paras took action. Leatrice Wilkerson, a guidance assistant in the Bronx, was described as "almost like a mother hen" in a Women's Talent Corps review of her work, which continued, "it appeared to us that she had been probably playing this role for many years."[65] The reviewer noted Wilkerson's ability in operating from this non-threatening position: "She has the ability to go into the schools with both eyes open, point out glaring injustices, but in such a way that does not make the administration mad but rather mobilizes them to do something about it."[66] The implicit contrast in this review between the effective "mother hen" and the radical agitators just offstage enraging the administration is stark, and it suggests why paraprofessional labor appealed to people who otherwise opposed efforts toward community control of public schooling. In this context, paras' own reworking of maternalism to advocate for their students and communities could be very effective, but administrators and even some community organizers would also deploy maternalist expectations to oppose paras' efforts to advance their own careers in the years that followed.

Paras' labor could also take the form of cultural brokerage—what Quinn and Ferree describe as the work of respect, particularly across racial lines—as paraprofessional educators translated elements of local culture and language for educators to foster mutual understanding. Virginia Eng explained to the teacher she worked with that several boys came to her class without the school-assigned uniform because of its similarity to funeral attire in their families' home region of China.[67] Her intervention kept the children from being punished.

Discipline and Classroom Authority

The question of how discipline should be maintained in New York City public schools generated furious debate in 1967. The UFT's early-September strike, and the union's insistence on teachers' right to remove children from their classrooms, reflected teachers' real fears and frustrations.[68] Black and

Hispanic parents, however, knew that their children bore the brunt of such policies, and they did not trust teachers to administer discipline fairly.

The "disruptive child provision" was the latest of many new disciplinary policies introduced in public schools in US cities after World War II. These policies, and their implementation, reflected racist assumptions about the capacity of Black and Hispanic students to learn and behave, as well as teachers' and administrators fears of them.[69] By the 1960s, teachers and administrators used increasingly harsh discipline to address real problems of keeping order that emerged in the understaffed, overcrowded schools in Black and Hispanic neighborhoods.[70] In doing so, they distanced themselves from the students and communities they served and drove the creation of new systems of surveillance and punishment in schools, some with formal links to the police department and thence to the courts and correctional facilities. In New York City, as Francine Almash has shown, the UFT's 1967 demand built on two decades of Board of Education policies that effected the "removal and isolation" of Black and Puerto Rican children from their neighborhood public-school classrooms "by labeling them as maladjusted, delinquent, and emotionally disturbed." The board placed these students in the city's "600" schools (named for their numerical codes) for "maladjusted" students, inaugurating a pattern of segregation through special education that persists to this day.[71]

Paraprofessional educators often were called on to resolve disciplinary issues, and doing so opened a Pandora's box of challenges. In some cases, paras were able to reduce or resolve tensions before bureaucratic punishment was set in motion. In other instances, they were called on to administer punishment that they felt was unfair or unjust. The question of what role paras, as educators and community members, would play in school disciplinary procedures has remained a major source of debate, tension, and activism across the history of this work.

Clara Blackman, the assistant director of guidance for the New York City Board of Education, told Women's Talent Corps interviewers that paraprofessional educators "really proved themselves in many cases to be invaluable," citing instances when paraprofessionals would "sit and talk to the children" struggling to control their behavior, "just to have them release some tension."[72] As she recalled, paraprofessional educators "could see the problems that were encountered with certain children in the school that they could off-set to some extent in the community. . . . They would be in a position to transmit to parents in the community some of the problems that they perceived in the school."[73] Virginia Eng's intervention kept Chinese boys from being punished for not wearing their uniforms, while Letty Concepcion's efforts allowed Helen Steinmetz to see her troubled student as more than a disciplinary issue. In these instances, paras responded to conflicts with care and cultural brokerage. In doing so, they offered an alternative to standard school disciplinary procedures in resolving these situations. Having a para in the classroom could mean keeping Black and Puerto Rican children there, too, running against the trend of removal by suspension, expulsion, or transfer to a "600" school.[74]

Marian Thom, by contrast, worked with a new teacher who she felt was too afraid of her students to maintain discipline. When one student became aggressive with Thom, she told the teacher, "Look, I live in this neighborhood, I've got to walk home, so I'm not going to let this kid diss me." Thom called the student's father, someone she knew from the neighborhood, who addressed the issue.[75] While Thom's intervention was about imposing discipline, the result was similar: a paraprofessional educator addressing a classroom disruption without recourse to suspensions, expulsions, or police that might further alienate students and parents from school.

New York City students organized in favor of hiring local residents instead of ramping up school policing. In 1969, student organizers at Franklin K. Lane High School issued demands including "Black teachers and aides proportional to the student body," while joining the Black and Puerto Rican Citywide High School Committee in demanding "No more police and police aides inside New York City high schools."[76] In paras' labor, students, parents, and teachers saw the possibility of a different path toward maintaining functional learning environments.

At the same time, paraprofessional educators often did not have the power to determine the course of disciplinary action. Cleo Silvers, who worked as a para at PS 51 in the Bronx before joining the Black Panther Party and then the Young Lords, rejected administrators' expectations that she would punish and control students and parents. In addition to being asked to administer corporal punishment, which had been outlawed in New York City years earlier, Silvers was expected to "calm down parents who had come to school to protest over a teacher's violation of their child's rights." Paras, Silvers argued, served to legitimize an oppressive system, especially when they performed discipline or acted as a "buffer" between angry parents and offending teachers. Silvers proposed that paras should serve instead as "representative community watchdogs, making sure that not one of our people is mistreated."[77] The *New York Amsterdam News* reported that many paras in Harlem agreed and "considered protection of children as primary," even when teachers accused them of being "intruders or busybodies."[78]

The accusation that paraprofessionals were "spying" reflected teachers' fears about classroom order and their mastery of it. This accusation also reflected a larger set of anxieties about to whom paras ultimately should be accountable. "Teacher aides," in the programs developed with Ford Foundation funds, clearly worked under the teacher's supervision, while the "parent aides" envisioned by HARYOU and hired for their after-school and summer programs reported to local parents through community organizations. By the time classroom paras started working in significant numbers for the Board of Education in the fall of 1967, both teachers and parents hoped paras would serve their interests, even as trust between teachers and parents—on matters of discipline and much else—had broken down severely.

Fear of losing professional authority over classroom discipline—and their classrooms overall—was one of many anxieties teachers harbored about paraprofessionals in the late 1960s. Leonora Farber, who taught in Browns-ville, Brooklyn, and later trained paras at LaGuardia Community College in Queens, recalled colleagues who worried they would soon find themselves replaced by people they described as "poorly trained," and whom they knew to be poorly paid.[79] Jacqueline Watkins remembers hearing administrators tell teachers, "they're going to spy on you, and they're going to interfere with what you're doing in the classroom." One teacher Watkins worked with told her the students' parents "were not smart enough to do this."[80] Marian Thom recalled "they were afraid that we were going to take over their jobs . . . because teachers were having a hard time as it was."[81] Thom, a stalwart unionist even before she herself became a UFT member, sympathized with educators who found themselves blamed for many of the problems plaguing the city, and nation, in the 1960s.

Gradually, the deep hostility many paras encountered in their first days gave way to respect and collegiality in the classroom. As Alida Mesrop of the Women's Talent Corps explained it, "the teachers who were the strongest welcomed anything that would help make their jobs, not easier, but their jobs more focused so that they could be more effective."[82] Jacqueline Watkins concurred, noting, "paraprofessionals did come into the schools" and "from my standpoint, and having been a teacher in the school, it seemed to work out pretty well." Watkins diagnosed a nascent solidarity in shared classroom labor. "The more you understand people, the more you understand their thoughts, and you share your thoughts and ideas, we're all the same!"[83] Board of Education hiring policies ensured that paraprofessional educators worked primarily in working-class Black and Puerto Rican neighborhoods, which typically saw high rates of teacher turnover and transfers. As a result, many of these first paras worked either with inexperienced teachers, who needed all the help they could get, or experienced teachers who had decided to commit themselves to teaching in Harlem, the South Bronx, or Central Brooklyn. Teachers in this latter category often welcomed efforts to connect to paras and their neighborhoods.

As Maggie Martin remembered, "after they got over the fear of us spying on them, it was a beautiful relationship." The teacher she worked with "finally . . . rose around to it," and the two shared a productive relationship, meeting over lunch to plan lessons, compare notes on students, and strategize together to educate the children of their community.[84] Shelvy Young-Abrams said the same of her teacher: "We ended up having the best working relationship in that classroom. . . . It took her a little while, but she came around."[85] Both Martin and Young-Abrams had faced tremendous hostility on their first days at work, but they successfully made a place for themselves. Reports around the city affirmed these conclusions. When teachers grew comfortable enough to share their authority in the classroom with paras, educators' experiences improved, as did their ability to manage classroom environments and relationships with students and parents. These incremental but visible shifts, where and when they took place, suggested the possibility that paras could make an even wider impact. They also demonstrated the need for programs of training and collaboration, like those advocated by scholars of "new careers."

"We Lived in the Community": Paraprofessional Work in New York City Neighborhoods

Paraprofessional educators had been hired to improve relationships between schools and the communities they served. Doing this required working outside of classrooms and schools. Paras collaborated with local residents and shared in local struggles, building lasting alliances while doing so. Some paraprofessional educators were employed expressly as "family aides," a role in which they made one-on-one visits to families to share resources and information, but even those who worked primarily in classrooms did outreach work. In the East Flatbush intensive reading program, paras were responsible for "communicating with the children's parents about how they can help their child at home."[86] Lillian Boyce, a guidance assistant at PS 167 in Brooklyn, organized and led families from her school in attending reading clinics at Long Island University.[87] Louise Burwell, who excelled as a student in East Harlem in the 1960s, remembers a para reaching out to her mother to guide her through the open enrollment process so that Burwell could attend a midtown school in junior high and high school.[88] Bilingual paraprofessionals were particularly important in outreach and collaborative efforts. Marian Thom's principal told her that parent attendance at parent-teacher conferences doubled after Chinese- and Spanish-speaking paraprofessionals promised to attend and translate for parents.[89]

Building links and doing outreach was one of the three overarching goals of paraprofessional programs. It was in this area of their work that paraprofessional educators' impact was most directly and immediately visible to students, parents, and local residents. Shelvy Young-Abrams put it simply: "We lived in the community." She remembers seeing parents and students while shopping at the supermarket, walking down the street, and at local community meetings.[90] In the same neighborhood, Marian Thom described herself as "a liaison between the school and the community."[91] Paras' efforts in these conduit roles earned high praise from parents across the city. In the South Bronx, the United Bronx Parents created parent-run evaluations of local schools that "called for more paraprofessionals," which they used to urge the Board of Education to hire and promote more local women.[92] LaFontaine responded at P.S. 25, hiring extensively from the South Bronx neighborhood and "fostering democratic participation in schools" among these paraprofessionals, "with the goal of creating community activists."[93]

Some paras worked in newly established Community Education Centers, run by each of New York City's thirty local subdistricts to provide a wide range of alternative, adult, and community-based educational programming. Title III of the 1965 Elementary and Secondary Education Act dedicated $100 million to "supplementary educational centers and service" designed "to stimulate and assist in the provision of vitally needed educational services not available in sufficient quantity or quality" in public schools. The long list of potential services in the act included "guidance and counseling, remedial instruction, and school health, physical education, recreation, psychological, and social work services designed to enable and encourage persons to enter, remain in, or reenter educational programs," as well as "comprehensive academic services and, where appropriate, vocational guidance and counseling, for continuing adult education." Title III also encouraged "making available modern educational equipment and specially qualified personnel, including artists and musicians, on a temporary basis to public and other nonprofit schools, organizations, and institutions."[94]

The provisions of Title III were widened even further with a series of amendments to the ESEA passed in 1966, of which the Adult Education Act was one. This new law was designed to "encourage and expand basic educational programs for adults to enable them to overcome English language limitations, to improve their basic education in preparation for occupational training and more profitable employment, and to become more productive and responsible citizens." While such programs could be in schools, they could also be located in the "supplementary centers" that were springing up with Title III money around the country. And while the Adult Education Act's language certainly contained traditional logics of education as individual skill acquisition and job training, it also suggested both citizenship and language acquisition as goals, which created opportunities for organizers and educators on the ground to imagine adult and community education programs far more expansively.[95]

In New York City, each of the city's local school districts used Title III money to create a "Community Education Center" staffed with a combination of teachers, social workers, and paraprofessional educators. These CECs served various functions loosely organized under the rubric of community education. One CEC initiative that ran across the city paired paras with teenagers from the Neighborhood Youth Corps, a citywide program that hired thousands of young people in community service roles.[96] In East Harlem's District Four, paras and youth workers tutored elementary students, raised awareness about sickle cell anemia, and shared resources for drug addiction treatment at the CEC.[97]

Paras at the District Four CEC also worked in the College Bound Program, helping high school students graduate, complete college applications, and pass entrance exams. Some helped create and staff alternative educational facilities for pregnant teenage girls, at a time when pregnant teens were barred from regular New York City high schools.[98] Still others worked in the curriculum initiative that District Four set up to promote Puerto Rican history and culture. Run by artist and educator Rafael Montañez Ortiz and staffed by local parents, the program initially ran out of a storefront. During the 1970s, the project evolved into El Museo del Barrio, a museum of Latin American diasporic art, history, and culture.[99]

Paras' work on behalf of their neighborhoods demonstrates that community-based paraprofessional work was not a minor policy intervention in education. It was part of a movement for social and economic justice in urban neighborhoods, a vision for improving the lives of children and adults by bringing resources from schools into neighborhoods. Teachers and administrators realized that this work built key connections between schools and communities. As Leonard Litwin, principal of Benjamin Franklin High School, explained in a letter to Superintendent Bernard Donovan, "these assistants, indigenous to our school neighborhood, function as receptionists, interpreters, and liaison agents between school and community."[100]

While positive evaluations of these programs abounded in these years, teachers and administrators reserved special praise for the impact that paraprofessional educators had on the relationship between schools and the surrounding community. Principal Seymour Levey of PS 45 in Manhattan wrote to the Women's Talent Corps to praise his two guidance aides, Anna Quinones and Rose Garcia, who were "doing valuable work on such matters as pupil attendance, family guidance problems, punctuality."[101] In a *New York Daily News* report, Principal Milton E. Goldenberg of PS 146 in the Bronx said, "Thanks to these women, we are reaching children we never reached before. They've also built a wonderful rapport with the community, and we have noted a definite lessening of tension between parents and schools."[102] The Board of Education wrote in 1969 that "educators are becoming increasingly aware of the *special contributions that indigenous workers* can make [emphasis original]. Research has revealed . . . [that paras can] improve communications between schools and poverty-area communities."[103] One principal wrote to the Women's Talent Corps to praise paraprofessional Sara Thomas: "She's very unusual . . . but there are others like her to be found in her community. If we had more people like her, it would be the best thing that could ever happen." Ms. Thomas, wrote the administrator, had "connected with students and parents" in ways the teacher "could not."[104]

Participant information preserved from the "Parent-Teacher Teams" program in Local School District Five—in Harlem and on the Upper West Side—offers an opportunity to visualize the ways different varieties of paraprofessional labor overlapped and reinforced one another at the neighborhood scale.[105] Created by parents, teachers, administrators, and community organizations including HARYOU (by then HARYOU-ACT) in the fall of 1967, the program's goal was "mutual understanding through teamwork in the classroom."[106] The project employed 135 local parents in their children's schools as teacher aides and offered two paid trainings a week in partnership with Teachers College. Parent aides lived within a few blocks of the school where they worked, while the teachers they were paired with came to school from across the metropolitan area. At PS 179, all five parents lived in the Frederick Douglass Houses, a public housing development that surrounded the school and housed many pupils.[107] According to a report on the program, the local knowledge these paras brought into the classroom benefited children, as a classroom aide could "understand and relate to the children whose environment she shares," particularly in classes with bilingual pupils.[108]

The program began in the summer of 1967 when a self-selected group of parents and teachers began meeting voluntarily under the aegis of the district. One parent reported that she "learned that all mothers care about their children" and that she had "become far less bigoted against those who are not of my race." A teacher echoed this sentiment, saying, "I learned that parents want the same thing that I want—each is looking out for the welfare of the child. I can't wait to have a parent in my room."[109] Unlike many thrown-together teachers and paras, District Five prepared its teachers and parents to work together, and in so doing, laid foundations on which these working women could, and did, build solidarity.

Mapping out the home addresses of some of the parent and teacher participants in this program is a revealing exercise.[110] On the following page, the lower map shows the home addresses of the parents employed as paraprofessionals in two "clusters" of schools in the spring of 1968, as well as the outlines of the schools in each cluster: four in southern Harlem (Cluster B) and three in the Manhattan Valley neighborhood (Cluster C). The upper map shows the home addresses of all the teachers who were paired with a parent/para in their classrooms.

These two maps help to visualize the impact of hiring local residents to work in public schools. Each paraprofessional address represents a new link

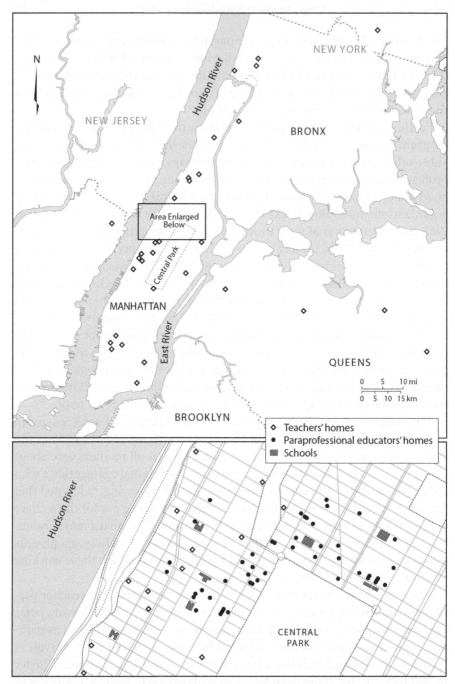

Home addresses of parent (dots) and teacher participants (diamonds) in Clusters B and C of the Parent-Teacher Teams Program, Local School District Five, New York City Board of Education, Spring 1968. Participating schools are gray. Data retrieved from participant lists digitized by the Harlem Education History Project, Teachers College, Columbia University. Source: Morningside Area Alliance Records, Box 55, Folder 16, University Archives, Rare Book & Manuscript Library, Columbia University in the City of New York. Cartography by Bill Nelson.

between school and community, as well as a new job for a mother on welfare in a neighborhood facing rising unemployment in these years. While most students in these schools, and their parents, would never have had the opportunity to encounter their teachers after school, the likelihood of encountering a paraprofessional educator was high, whether on the street, in apartment buildings, at the store, in the park, or at a place of worship. The conversations that took place between these paras and parents surely would have run the gamut, from individual student behaviors to the needs of the community at large. These maps help us see how paraprofessional programs opened new conduits for community participation and rescaled the educational bureaucracy, creating new processes for producing and sharing knowledge.

In an article in "TC Week" in 1969, the assistant principal of one participating school told the writer that the program "worked beautifully."[111] Her assessment mirrored the statements of many other administrators and teachers, many of whom initially had been quite skeptical of the idea of local hiring. Community-based paraprofessional educators had won them over. As Onedia Davis recalled, "bringing the community together" was a primary goal of her own parent organizing and, later, paraprofessional labor, "because with that connection, that's what causes education to work."[112]

An Expanding Network for Collective Advancement: Paraprofessional Educators in Training Programs and Antipoverty Organizations in New York City

As discussed in Chapter 1, parent aides hired by antipoverty organizations in the mid-1960s helped demonstrate the need for, and value of, local hiring to parent activists and practitioners and scholars of poverty policy. It was in these early programs that aides first deployed the practice of activist mothering, subverting the "culture of poverty" thesis that suffused so much antipoverty policy.[113] Before paras were formally hired by schools, these aides began building the first of many cross-class, interracial alliances among working women.

Parent aides hired by Mobilization for Youth, HARYOU, and, later, the Women's Talent Corps also demonstrated their unswerving commitment to personal and communal advancement through training and education. The success of community educators in antipoverty agencies encouraged formal hiring, and it also changed the course of antipoverty policy, as the scholar-practitioners who worked with them reformulated their theories and programs. Working with these community-based educators convinced many middle-class, professional allies that working-class Black and Latina women could, and should, be agents of positive change and political organizing in their communities—that they could serve not just as "aides" but as educators in their own right.

For paras, training programs offered the opportunity to earn the credentials and experience they needed to earn higher wages and respect from teachers and administrators on the job. They also helped paras make connections to people doing this work in neighborhoods across the city. It was in these early training programs that paras not only articulated an ethos of collective educational advancement but also began to organize themselves as a class of workers.

The faculty and staff of the Women's Talent Corps were deeply impressed by the knowledge, experience, and performance of the paraprofessionals they trained. The internal correspondence among these mostly white, middle-class women reveals a rapid change of perspective. In editing one early progress report in 1966 while trainees were still being recruited, one staff member noted in handwriting, "Do the trainees selected to date actually belong to the 'culture of poverty' or are they still striving to be middle class?"[114] This framing, typical of the time, suggested a false dichotomy between individualized striving and pathological behavior.

By the time they had placed their first trainees six months later, Director of Training Anne Cronin was emphatic about the potential of these new paraprofessional educators:

> The training program reflects a basic philosophy about the "teachability" of uneducated people. It assumes that the "culture of poverty" [quotation marks in original] does not affect the attitudes of most of the low-income groups in New York City, and specifically not of women enrolled in the Women's Talent Corps program. Rather, the Women's Talent Corps trainees subscribe to the basic cultural values of the United States and strive for the same goals as other Americans.[115]

Cronin explicitly rejected the cultural and behavioral understandings of poverty that dominated national policy debates in 1967. It was in this same year that Congress passed amendments to the Social Security Act requiring women receiving Aid to Families with Dependent Children (AFDC) to sign up for employment or training programs. These laws forced poor women into low-wage jobs in the private labor market and were intellectually grounded in the notion that welfare created dependency.[116] After watching hundreds of women on welfare work tirelessly to train for new careers and serve their communities as paraprofessional educators, Cronin penned a stinging rebuke to this faulty framework. She drew on her own life experience to do so; as a former administrator for the New Deal's Federal Artists Project, Cronin understood that jobs, and not behavioral adjustments, were what people needed. Responding to a question about the challenges of working with paras in a 1976 interview, she chuckled that it was no harder than corralling artists and writers in Depression-era New York.[117]

Community organizers understood that community-based paraprofessional educators would be marginalized within the educational bureaucracy by behavioral theories of poverty and assumptions about care work and those who did it. They, too, sought to challenge these dominant perspectives. The United Bronx Parents (UBP) published several documents expressly for and about paraprofessional educators between 1967 and 1970 that asserted the knowledge and competence of local women. One of their first circulars informed paraprofessionals and community members in 1967 that paras were hired to "help interpret school to community and vice-versa." The flyer included a long list of resources for paraprofessionals drawn from Board of Education, Women's Talent Corps, and Bank Street College publications.[118] Another flyer, printed on the same day, listed three priorities for Title I programs, to be addressed by community members working in and with schools: "emphasis on reading improvement (not guidance or culture), emphasis on parent and community teacher assistants who would help with tutoring homework, reading drill, etc., and emphasis on teacher training under the supervision of community groups indigenous to our neighborhood."[119] Like Cronin, the Puerto Rican and African American mothers of the UBP rejected the notion that "culture" was their problem. They sought an active role for newly hired community educators in reforming local public schools.[120]

As community-based educators worked together with activists, scholars, educators, and bureaucrats in these formative years, women's shared experiences of life and labor emerged as one of the most important and enduring sources of unity. While the women who did this work did not necessarily identify as feminists or work directly in the women's movement, they all lived with the gendered division of labor, which placed the responsibility for social reproduction on women, including childcare and education. Women of different classes and races shared the challenges of balancing home and work. They recognized one another's struggles. At the Women's Talent Corps, mutual respect between program staff and the women who became paraprofessionals was not merely a product of exceeded expectations, but also a budding feminist solidarity that was cultivated by small-group conversations in many contexts. During an early meeting of staff and trainees in 1967, one paraprofessional educator told the staffers, "You seemed to understand me as a woman, and I was grateful." After the meeting, the staffer remarked, "these women want for their children what middle-class people want for theirs."[121] As Anne Cronin remembered years later, "we all had problems as women that cut across lines . . . differences are there, but common themes are even more significant."[122]

Women's needs and challenges proved a prominent source of shared discussion among gatherings of the parents, staff, and paraprofessional educators affiliated with the United Bronx Parents, as well. Lorraine Montenegro, the daughter of UBP founder Evelina Lopez Antonetty and a committed activist and leader in her own right, recalled conversations in which parents shared experiences and resources with one another, often late into the evening after meetings.[123] These collective conversations helped to generate activism, and they also connected parents with particular needs to educators who might help address them.

From the beginning, the women who trained as paraprofessionals impressed the people around them with their commitment to training and advancement. These women believed that they could, and should, do the work of education. Alida Mesrop of the Women's Talent Corps remembered the energy that trainees brought to their classes, even though "this was at night! And they're tired! And they've been working all day!" Despite this, Mesrop recalled, "They were strong, they were feisty. They were not namby-pamby. They questioned."[124] Hope Leichter, a professor at Teachers College, Columbia University, who ran the training side of the Parent-Teacher Teams program in Harlem and the Upper West Side, was similarly impressed. The parents she trained demanded a broad, humanistic education beyond the narrow parameters the district had initially suggested, and they "took advantage" of the opportunities to take classes at Teachers College. They also used the facilities regularly, bringing their children to the library to read or to the pool to swim. Community educators' embrace of these facilities also created more opportunities for interaction, discussion, and sharing between these working-class women and the professors and students who worked with them at Teachers College. The results improved the whole program, and as Leichter recalled, "I think it was welcoming and democratic beyond what we, in some ways, would have consciously been able to plan."[125]

For their part, paras regularly cited the opportunity to train for careers in education as one of the most enticing reasons to become a paraprofessional. One para surveyed by the UFT in 1968 called it the "opportunity of a lifetime."[126] Oneida Davis, who became a teacher herself after starting as a para, recalled that "a lot of people who were on welfare who'd never had a job . . . their lives had totally changed and they were able to live in the community in a different way. Not forgetting where they came from, but to help somebody else along the way."[127] Paras did not win extensive and regular opportunities to train as teachers until they unionized. However, their commitment to training with antipoverty organizations, parent groups, teachers, and administrators in the late 1960s demonstrated their commitment to their work and created additional opportunities to build solidarity with all these allies.

The dense web of connections that linked these various institutions and organizations, and the movement of people and ideas among them, reveals the remarkable degree of collaboration that sustained educational activism in these years. Paraprofessional programs were a product of these collaborations, and community-based educators, working at the nexus of these institutions, quickly became experts in building alliances. Antipoverty programs served as a laboratory in which paraprofessional educators developed organizing strategies that served them well as they moved into formal school settings and won the support of teachers and parents. These strategies—activist mothering, working women's solidarity, and collective advancement—would serve them well in future struggles over unionization, teacher training, and funding.

A Foundation for Future Organizing

If one thing unites the incredibly diverse range of paraprofessional programs in New York City schools in these years, it is favorable evaluation. In the comments of principals and teachers, the letters sent to the Board of Education and the Women's Talent Corps, and in the reminiscences of paraprofessionals themselves, it is clear that something new and remarkable took place in public schools as paraprofessional educators went to work. Evaluations from around the nation reinforced the notion that paraprofessional educators were reshaping public schooling. In a speech to the National Conference on the Paraprofessional in 1969, Frank Riessman cited studies from Indiana, Minnesota, Michigan, Colorado, and New York showing significant gains in reading with paraprofessional educators present, and significant instructor and principal support of, and belief in, the impact of paraprofessional educators.[128]

The comprehensive survey conducted by the Institute for Educational Development of New York City schools in 1970 confirmed the sentiments of educators and activists on the ground. Ninety-five percent of elementary school students reported enjoying school more and learning more with a para in the classroom, while four-fifths of junior high school students reported the same. Three-quarters of teachers observed improved student performance since the beginning of the paraprofessional program, and the same fraction of parents agreed. Ninety-five percent of teachers felt that community relations had improved, and nearly all principals agreed. Seventy percent of paras felt their work was improving their neighborhoods, and 95 percent felt their jobs were very important. On this last point, the Institute for Educational Development agreed heartily, describing the success of paras as "overwhelming."[129]

Paraprofessional educators began making changes in New York City schools in the three short years between 1967 and 1970. Drawing on community traditions of activist mothering and their own wealth of experience as school volunteers and community organizers, they built alliances with diverse actors and institutions and, in some cases, created new educational practices. They brought demands from freedom struggles into everyday public-school pedagogy and curricula. Slowly but surely, paras began convincing wary teachers, their deeply protective union, and a notoriously intransigent

Board of Education that their work could serve all parties involved. They did so by showing that their labor could, under the right circumstances, address education's growing crisis of care at many points and in many ways.

The programs paras worked for created thousands of jobs in impoverished communities, and thousands of new conduits and resources for the students and parents served by public schools in those neighborhoods. While these programs are difficult to characterize in a general fashion, the overall picture that emerges from quantitative data and qualitative studies in this period is one of energized collaboration and productive educational ferment. These programs' success was predicated on the ability of mothers receiving welfare to reimagine and reshape education, despite having been afforded little formal training of their own. These women exceeded every expectation. Their work was a staggering rebuke to the "culture of poverty" thesis and a major effort to address the structural poverty and racism their communities faced.

And yet, paraprofessional educators' successful classroom and community labor was not enough, in and of itself, to guarantee these programs' continued existence or living wages for the people who made them possible. Like "essential" public-sector workers across US history, particularly those providing forms of care, paras' labor was simultaneously exploited and denigrated.[130] When teachers and principals asked them to extend their days and go beyond their job descriptions to help students and parents, how could they refuse? And yet, despite their clear commitments and impact, their lack of credentials was used to justify their low pay. People above paras in the educational hierarchy were glad to have the crisis of care addressed, but they hoped to outsource the costs of this care work to the women who did it.

Despite the clear evidence of paras' aptitude for classroom labor, opportunities to train as teachers were not forthcoming. This fact particularly frustrated paraprofessional educators, many of whom found their work invigorating and hoped to continue in educational careers. As Martha McNear told one interviewer, "I have always wanted to be a teacher. I love children and like working with them. I thought life had passed me by after all these years. Now I know that I still have a chance to fulfill my lifelong dream."[131] Many paraprofessionals used the language of a "second chance" in describing the opportunities their new positions offered. They did not plan to wait for a third chance to come around.

The promise of teacher training was realized in a few pilot programs in these years; Jerome A. Greene's efforts in the Bronx were one such example. Despite the desires of paraprofessional educators, however, only a tiny fraction of them were able to receive any kind of training. Some cynics in the Board of Education argued that to keep paraprofessional educators from leaving the communities they came from, and to keep them in contact with the poor and working-class residents thereof, salaries and educational opportunities needed to be kept to a minimum. As the *New York Times* reported in 1967, "One of the professionals who trained these women speculated whether it might be natural for some of them 'to turn their backs on their environment as soon as they leave it.'" However, the reporter continued, "most of the trainees continue to express a desire to remain in and to improve their communities. 'They can accept change creatively, something the middle-class community finds hard,' another coordinator noted."[132] These sentiments reveal the ways community-based educators defined both their labor and the local geography of their neighborhoods. They did not hope to escape these places, but to improve them through collective action.

In their desire to rise with, and not from, their New York City neighborhoods, paraprofessional educators articulated a vision of collective advancement for an emerging, post-industrial working class. Doing so, however, required challenging bosses who hoped to keep the labor of these "aides" cheap and flexible. In the very same years that they strove to deliver on the promise of paraprofessional programs in classrooms and communities, paras also had to fight to make officials hold up their end of the bargain, and to provide better wages, job security, and teacher training. And they had to do so amid one of the most explosive and divisive confrontations between teacher unionists and parent activists in US history.

Within the photograph, text on posters reads:

I have a dream

Darryl

Rev. Dr. Martin Luther King Jr.
He wanted civil rights
He led the March on Washington
He believed in him
A bad man shot him

Paraprofessional and United Federation of Teachers organizing committee member Doris Hunter at work at PS 25 in Brooklyn, March 10, 1970. United Federation of Teachers Hans Weissenstein Negatives; PHOTOS.019.001, Box 11: Item 12429, Tamiment Library & Robert F. Wagner Labor Archives, New York University.

CHAPTER 3

"The Triumph of the Paraprofessionals"

Paraprofessional Educators Unionize in New York City, 1967–1970

"This Is the Civil Rights Movement"

Velma Murphy Hill was not a typical paraprofessional educator. Born in Chicago, Hill became a civil rights activist in high school with the South Side NAACP Youth Council. As the group's president, she helped organize marches and pickets at the Republican National Convention (RNC) in 1960 as part of the "march on conventions" movement spearheaded by A. Philip Randolph. At the end of that summer, Hill led an audacious "wade-in" to challenge segregation on Chicago's Rainbow Beach, defying the gradualist approach of the Chicago NAACP. A mob attacked the protestors, and Hill appeared on the cover of the *Chicago Defender* the following day with a wound that required seventeen stitches in her scalp. She was twenty years old.[1]

Hill (then Velma Murphy) was carried from the beach that day by Norman Hill, one of Randolph's lead organizers for the RNC protests. He rallied Chicago's civil rights establishment to the waders' cause, bringing a much larger crowd out to the beach the following weekend. Murphy and Hill returned to Rainbow Beach nearly every weekend in the summer in 1961, forcing the Chicago Police Department to protect Black beachgoers. They also fell in love. The Hills joined the Congress of Racial Equality (CORE) in Chicago and moved to New York City in 1963 to work CORE's campaigns to desegregate employment. They led protests for open hiring on public projects, including those at the SUNY Downstate Hospital Complex in Brooklyn and the 1964 World's Fair.[2] However, in 1966, the Hills left CORE as the organization embraced Black Power, following their mentors Randolph and Bayard Rustin into the labor movement.

While Norman went to work at the AFL-CIO's A. Philip Randolph Institute, Velma earned a master's in education from Harvard. When she returned to New York City, United Federation of Teachers organizer Sandra Feldman suggested she become a teacher, so Hill toured a school near her home in Chelsea. As she waited to meet the principal, Hill noticed something.

> I saw all these black women, and I said, "Oh my god! Oh my god! There are black teachers around," you know, "This is fantastic!" Then I was told, "They're not teachers. They are educational aides." . . . And I said—you know me—I went and started talking to some of them, and they start telling me what they did. They did small group instruction, they helped the teacher with a little tutoring. They cleaned up. So I said, "How much do you make?" and they said, "Fifty dollars a week." And I said, "What kind of benefits do you have?" None. That was enough for me. I decided, well, I want to organize these women.[3]

To Hill, these aides "seemed indistinguishable from elementary-school teachers until you asked about them, as I did." After talking to them, Hill recognized what she later called a "trap." As she wrote, "without union representation, this relatively new group of school workers could become little more than a cheap source of labor ready made for exploitation."[4]

As Hill recalled in 2011, these women also reminded her of her own mother, who had come to Chicago during the Great Migration and worked in a factory to support her seven children after her husband died. Indeed, many paras had migrated from the South during the "Second Great Migration" in the 1940s and 1950s, or from Puerto Rico. As Hill explained,

> You know, they [were] really wonderful. They've got kids. They want to be near their kids. One of the reasons they were aides was they could work and they could be near the kids, you know? And I said, "I want to do something." I had been involved in the Civil Rights Movement for years. I said, "You know, this is the Civil Rights Movement, as far as I'm concerned." I mean this is really helping people.[5]

Hill had met UFT President Albert Shanker in 1964, when she, Bayard Rustin, and several other organizers had met with Shanker to seek his support for the 1964 Freedom Day Boycott. She went to Shanker and told him that she wanted to organize paras; he told her that she needed to work as a para first, and quietly helped her secure a job through a friendly principal. So, without mentioning her degree from Harvard, Hill went to work as a para in the fall of 1968.

The UFT's support had been instrumental in convincing the New York City Board of Education to hire paraprofessional educators, and the union had begun holding organizing meetings in the first full year of paraprofessional programs. However, these efforts had stalled as the union clashed with parent activists in Ocean Hill–Brownsville in the spring of 1968. By the fall, the UFT was on strike, and Black and Latinx parents across the city were furious. Among the city's civil rights leaders, only a small group led by Bayard Rustin and A. Philip Randolph backed the union, a stance that drew tremendous criticism.[6] In the aftermath, the possibility of paraprofessional educators joining the union, or of the union welcoming them, seemed remote. Fully half of paras had found their positions through local antipoverty organizations, most of which had opposed the union and supported community control.[7] Paras were deeply rooted in long-running community struggles for school equity, and many, including Oneida Davis, crossed picket lines to teach and care for children, including their own, when the UFT struck in 1968. Many teachers, assailed by angry parents while picketing, decided that paras were scabs and spies for their enemies in the community control fight. This was the terrain on which Albert Shanker hired Velma Murphy Hill to organize paraprofessional educators.

Just six months later, however, at the end of June in 1969, thousands of paras voted to join the UFT. The Board of Education refused to negotiate with paras, but after an intensive two-front campaign in the spring of 1970, thousands of teachers voted to back a paraprofessional strike, while activists who had battled the union in 1968 publicly expressed support for the paraprofessionals' demands. The combination of community and teacher support brought the board to the table that summer. The result was a contract that transformed the city's school system, expanded job and career opportunities for working-class women amid a deepening urban crisis, and became a national model for teacher unionism in the decade that followed.

Paras won a 140 percent wage increase, grievance procedures, health care, and the creation of a paid teacher-training program.[8] Community-based paraprofessional educators had entered New York City public schools for the first time just three years earlier in "experimental" programs. This landmark contract solidified their place, and their rights, as educators.

This chapter explores the organizing drives and unlikely alliances that led to this contract. It traces the paths of paraprofessional educators, teachers, and organizers as they built solidarity across divides of race, class, and metropolitan geography. It shows how they mobilized white, middle-class teachers and working-class Black and Latinx activists to support their campaign.

This story—of community-based educators joining the anti-community-control UFT to preserve and expand a War on Poverty program that directly created jobs for Black and Latina women—seems improbable, if not impossible, in the context of our current historiography. Historians of the 1968 strikes argue that they splintered New York's liberal coalition and destroyed both the practice and the legitimacy of participatory governance.[9] Studying paraprofessional organizing reframes these narratives, revealing the power of working-class women's organizing to build coalitions in support of direct employment and community involvement in schools.[10] Paraprofessional unionization was fraught and imperfect, necessitating compromises and creating new challenges that are explored in later chapters. At a minimum, however, union organizing secured the place of thousands of working-class Black and Latinx workers in schools and the labor movement long after the end of the 1968 strikes.

This campaign has received scant attention from historians, in part because paraprofessional voices have gone unheeded. Sympathetic histories of the UFT cite paras' unionization as evidence of leadership's top-down benevolence, in contrast to the Ocean Hill–Brownsville fight.[11] Critical studies of teacher professionalism and grassroots activism, in contrast, have argued that unionization was an exercise in co-optation that used negligible gains to split paras from community activists.[12] Both interpretations render paras as passive objects: thankful beneficiaries or unwitting dupes. However, as Chapter 2 demonstrates, New York's paraprofessionals were savvy educators and organizers. Well-versed in organizing and coalition building, and well aware of their own precarity amid the upheavals of the late 1960s, paras sought membership in the UFT to secure their jobs, to improve their wages and working conditions, and to realize their aspirations to become teachers.

As a practical and strategic matter, paras worked with unionized teachers daily. Many had developed mutual respect, often through shared experiences as working women and mothers. Classroom teachers recruited paras and encouraged the UFT to organize them. Their alliance proved crucial as paras pursued their first contract. Paras also wanted the benefits of midcentury unionization: better wages and benefits, job security, and respect from bosses.

In the long term, many paras aspired to become teachers. Such opportunities had been promised by the legislation that funded their work and the administrators who hired them, but before unionization, teacher-training pathways were extremely limited. Velma Hill and her team made the case, and paras believed, that the surest path to teaching ran through the teachers' union. In joining the union, many paras also invoked local traditions of dissident and civil rights unionism.[13] They sought membership in the UFT not because they agreed with the union's every move, but because they hoped to transform it. In all these ways, para organizing was an iteration of struggles for economic independence—jobs, living wages, and workplace dignity—taking place in New York City and across the nation in these years.[14]

Studying paraprofessional organizing also reframes our understanding of the process by which teacher unions came to be some of the largest in the nation. The UFT's leadership, including its president, Albert Shanker, organized paraprofessionals in the service of their own goals, but their efforts were shaped by many forces. These included the directives of the UFT's parent union, the American Federation of Teachers (AFT), in Washington, the union's loss of standing in the city after the 1968 strikes, and both the radical and reactionary rank-and-file movements developing within the UFT in the late 1960s. Most of all, the union's commitment to paraprofessional unionization was a response to, and was informed by, paraprofessional organizers and their teacher allies. Both the union and its critics have portrayed the paraprofessional campaign and contract as masterminded by Shanker, but the reality was far more complex and contingent. In the years that followed, this organizing changed the course of the public-sector labor movement, bringing 100,000 paras into the AFT by 1988 (as discussed at greater length in Chapter 5).[15] Paraprofessional unionization is not a footnote to the expansion of teacher unions in this period, but a constitutive part of the process.

Building coalitions required compromise. Organizing on the heels of the Ocean Hill–Brownsville crisis generated limits as well as possibilities. While many activists came to support paraprofessional unionization, some never forgave paras for joining the union. The UFT and AFT framed paraprofessionals as future teachers throughout their campaign, casting them as a legitimate alternative to community control activists. These rhetorical moves had utility in the moment, but they could foreclose possibilities for building community alliances in the long term.

Finally, paraprofessionals and teachers returned to work in a scarred and uncertain school environment. While the community control experiment was over, the state began decentralizing New York City's school system in 1969. The signing of the paraprofessional contract coincided with the breakup of the nation's largest school district into thirty-one "community school districts," each of which hired paras separately. All these factors, along with the city's fiscal crisis, would render the "triumph" of paraprofessionals uncertain and incomplete in the years to come. The 1970 contract was not simply a victory in ongoing struggles for jobs and education. It laid the groundwork for a new phase of cooperation and conflict in schools and unions.

"We Need Someone Strong Behind Us": The Beginnings of Paraprofessional Organizing

The organizing that led to the 1970 contract began even before the Board of Education hired its first paras. As discussed in the preceding two chapters, the women hired in the first generation of paras often had led local campaigns for community involvement in schools, including demands for local hiring. Oneida Davis, Maggie Martin, and Shelvy Young-Abrams had all been parent-teacher association presidents before becoming paraprofessionals.

City-designated, federally funded community action agencies worked with local schools to hire for these positions, and paras remained in close contact with the local organizations that nominated them. The United Bronx Parents produced training materials for paras, and the Morrisania Education Council, which hired Davis, held regular "Paraprofessional Conferences."[16] Scholars and policymakers who worked with paras in antipoverty agencies and training institutes also sought to organize them. Frank Riessman, the author of *New Careers for the Poor* (which pushed the idea of paraprofessionalism into the policy mainstream), partnered with Women's Talent Corps founder Audrey C. Cohen to create a "New York New Careerist Association" to gather paras from disparate school and hospital sites across the city.[17]

However, paras and their allies realized that community organizations and newly created associations wielded scant power in the workplace. In 1966, the WTC sought the UFT's help in convincing the Board of Education to hire their trainees. The Corps' Board of Directors—comprised of activists, policymakers, and education scholars—worried that union involvement and unionization might prove a double-edged sword. As their minutes recorded, some board members believed the UFT could provide "recognition that they [paras] are part of the professional staff" and "the benefits of a strong negotiating body" in "working out licensing procedures." Other members worried that "job functions would harden prematurely as trainees became part of the school bureaucracy" and that the UFT might even "use the trainees as a weapon against the community."[18] These calculations would be repeated internally and in public many times during the contract campaign and in the years that followed, and the concerns the board members expressed would be borne out, in some cases, by experience. Nonetheless, the WTC decided they needed the UFT's support. The union lent it, and the city hired paras.

The UFT began reaching out to paraprofessionals in January of 1968, midway through the first full year of para programs in New York City schools. Local pressure from activists and scholars encouraged this, as did shifts in local and national union politics. In 1966, the AFT, the UFT's parent union, had begun moving toward an embrace of paraprofessional organizing, pushed in part by reports that its rival, the National Education Association (NEA), was planning a similar push.[19] The AFT's pursuit of paras grew stronger in 1968 as David Selden, a former UFT organizer, took the reins of the international union and prioritized organizing across the country.

Local rivalries played a role as well; the American Federation of State, County, and Municipal Employees District Council 37, the union to which Shanker directed school aides in 1964, had established itself as the largest and most powerful public union in the city by mobilizing hospital workers in 1965. The victory gave DC 37 the sole power to negotiate pensions, wage scales, and other citywide policies for civil service employees.[20] While the UFT had let DC 37 unionize school aides in 1966 without a challenge, AFSCME's interest in paraprofessionals, and the idea of a different union's members in the classroom, concerned the UFT. Though they worried teachers who had opposed the employment of local residents would push back, UFT leaders hoped their members would accept paras into their union.[21]

Once paraprofessionals were hired, it was at the school and classroom level where they made themselves essential, and where teachers and paras built working women's solidarity. A group of women within the UFT led the initial drive to organize paras, working along the same axis of female solidarity that shaped classroom alliances. Gladys Roth, a former teacher and field organizer for the UFT, led the initial meeting of 152 paraprofessionals on January 19, 1968, at UFT headquarters, which she described as "standing-room only" in the pages of the *United Teacher*, the UFT's newsletter. The meeting generated the appointment of a "paraprofessional steering committee," which was to meet regularly to formulate strategies and demands.[22] Among those who joined the committee was Velma Murphy Hill.

Much as working in classrooms and neighborhoods generated solidarity among paras, parents, and teachers, Hill remembers the importance of these early meetings in formulating a sense of solidarity among paraprofessionals as workers, beyond their particular schools and communities. The goal was to "get them talking about what their problems were in the schools, and then connecting those problems to each other."[23] This was a process that involved building interracial alliances; Hill recalls telling paras, "You're in this meeting, and you are not Black, and you are not white, and you are not Hispanic. You are a paraprofessional."[24] Meeting invitations read, "Since your assignment involves working beside the teacher and directly with children, it is professional in nature. The UFT is eager to represent you and to protect your rights."[25] Signed by Shanker, the letter urged paras to "take an active role in establishing policy and making decisions.[26]

The community antipoverty organizations that had recommended paras for their positions watched this early courtship with some alarm. Parents and activists had clashed with the UFT over the 1967 contract's "disruptive child" provision, and others felt betrayed when the union withdrew its support for the community control experiment in Ocean Hill–Brownsville, in Harlem, and on the Lower East Side.[27] In the Bronx, the Morrisania Education Council (MEC) circulated a memo "to all paraprofessionals of Morrisania schools" in March of 1968. It read: "[The council], which screened and recommended you to your present positions, is vehemently opposed to you joining the United Federation of Teachers . . . the UFT has alienated the community in its stand on the McBundy report [*sic*]." The council argued that teachers had opposed the employment of paras and now sought to control them, and "a teacher's union cannot possibly speak for you, inasmuch as your problems are different than those of teachers." Asking, "Should *teachers* be aware of your plans?" the memo concluded, "when there is such a thing as a permanent paraprofessional group, *we* will decide which union *we* embrace [all emphasis original]."[28] As paraprofessional positions took shape in the 1960s, community organizers and teacher unionists had advanced different visions for what paras would do in classrooms, and to whom they would ultimately be accountable. The possibility of unionization raised the stakes of these debates and created the potential for serious conflict.

While some community activists expressed dismay that paraprofessionals would consider joining the union, many paras believed strongly in the value of workplace organizing in addition to their community commitments. Some had family members in unions and considered unions a regular and essential part of the workplace, like Maggie Martin, whose husband was a unionized postal worker.[29] Others, like Shelvy Young-Abrams, had endured the long hours and poor conditions of non-unionized workplaces. When Young-Abrams left her mother's farm for New York City as a young woman, her mother's advice had been succinct: "join a union."[30] When the opportunity presented itself in her new paraprofessional job, she took it.

As the UFT courted paraprofessionals, Gladys Roth and Sandra Feldman, who supervised the early stages of the campaign, also had to address teachers' concerns about the addition of paras to their "professional" union. Paras had built unity with teachers in classrooms, but these alliances were confined to particular schools where paras worked. Because of the targeting of antipoverty funding, paras labored primarily in poor and working-class neighborhoods. Letters from teachers to the UFT expressed the widespread fear that paras would be spies. Other teachers wrote to suggest that employing local parents was not an educational goal but a jobs program, even as paras fought to define their labor as educational.[31]

Roth penned articles in the *United Teacher*, the UFT's newsletter, to emphasize the union's role in creating the paraprofessionals' positions and to urge rank-and-file teachers to support this new program. She maintained that teacher concerns about "poverty area" schools, including teacher shortages and strained relationships with parents, would be addressed by a robust paraprofessional program and career ladder.[32] A flyer circulated by UFT Field Representative Kinard Lang, who himself was Black, read, "Why should the UFT encourage the hiring and union membership of the Paraprofessionals?" Lang suggested a number of benefits for teachers, including "increased political influence," "teacher-parent empathy," "assistance for teachers," and "local community allies on future picket lines."[33] "Teachers legitimately resent being blamed for all educational failures," wrote Lang, and "with local parents involved in the educational process they will learn to appreciate the administrative and bureaucratic problems that hamper competent and dedicated teachers in the performance of their duties." Lang added, "Paraprofessionals who belong to the UFT . . . are far less likely to serve as scabs after their union improves their working conditions."[34] As Velma Murphy Hill explained, para organizers spoke in terms of teachers' "self-interest," which meant emphasizing that "if they went out on strike, and the paras went out on strike, then that would be a very, very formidable force."[35]

Rank-and-file teachers, even those that did not work with paraprofessionals, began to embrace the potential benefits of paraprofessional unionism as well. A UFT chapter from the Italian American neighborhood of Bensonhurst in Brooklyn submitted "Proposed Guidelines for the Use of Paraprofessionals" to UFT headquarters. Their recommendations mirrored those of field organizers and, for that matter, Black and Latinx community groups. These included "paraprofessionals should be interviewed by the Community Progress Corporation and the principal," "the paraprofessional is best viewed as an intern whose ultimate goal would be to attain full professional status," and "full articulation between the school and the Community Progress Corporation." The program, these teachers concluded, "is a bridge between the teachers and the community and the professional staff would be more than remiss if it did not utilize to the fullest the tremendous energies and talents of the community in achieving the common goal of educating the children."[36] By May, Roth could report a bright future for paraprofessionalism in New York City, noting extensive teacher support for paras and their work.[37]

It was Roth who undertook the extensive study of the first year of paraprofessional programs in New York City discussed in Chapter 2. In her report to UFT leaders on May 20, 1968, Roth detailed nascent solidarity among teachers and paras. In her introduction, Roth wrote that the report was inspired, in part, by "requests from classroom teachers to provide service for their assistants who were not paid promptly or who were closed out of community college courses."[38] These requests confirmed that some teachers had begun to advocate for, and with, the paras in their classrooms.

The paraprofessional educators Roth surveyed were equally enthusiastic about the program, and their replies revealed three trends in their experience. First, they believed their work was "very good for community relations" and that by giving "the people in the community a chance to take part in the education of their children," para programs were "particularly good in bettering relations between black and white in ghetto areas."[39] Second, most paras surveyed had "always wanted to go back to school" and one noted that "income while learning" was "marvelous for low-income families." Finally, paras emphasized their need for prompt pay, job security, and improved access to training, all of which informed their desire to unionize. One explained, "We are all going to join the union because we need someone strong behind us."[40] A strong current of aspiration ran through Roth's report;

paraprofessionals were united not just through classroom experiences but also by their desires to build careers there. One year in, paraprofessionals felt empowered by their work, even as it made them increasingly aware of the complex set of forces they contended with as low-wage workers within the New York City schools bureaucracy.

In the conclusion of her report, Roth proposed that the UFT could bring teachers and paraprofessionals together to further the goals of para programs: improving public schooling, forging links between schools and communities, and creating career opportunities for poor and working-class women. However, no one was paying attention. Eleven days earlier, Rhody McCoy, the unit administrator of the Ocean Hill–Brownsville Demonstration District in Brooklyn, had announced the transfer of eighteen white educators out of the schools under his jurisdiction. The decree, and UFT's response, ignited a conflict between the union and Black and Puerto Rican parent activists that had been gathering fuel for over a decade and would consume the city for months. Paraprofessional programs came of age just as New York City's public school system came apart.

"Caught in the Middle": Paraprofessionals Navigate the 1968 Teachers' Strikes

The firestorm that followed McCoy's announcement is one of the most studied and debated moments in the history of public schooling, teacher unionism, and Black and Puerto Rican education activism.[41] The UFT protested the transfers vehemently, arguing that they violated the due process guaranteed by the union's contract. McCoy replied that parents had the right to choose educators capable of teaching their children without racism or class bias. By the fall of 1968, fifty thousand white, middle-class teachers were on picket lines across New York, where parents and activists battled with them to open neighborhood schools for their children. Mayor John Lindsay failed to broker a compromise while vitriol between parents and teachers escalated, and three consecutive strikes closed schools for six weeks. By the time the state ended the experiment in community control in December of 1968, hostility and mistrust consumed the relations between schools and communities in New York City to such a degree that historian Jerald Podair wrote in 2002, "Ocean Hill–Brownsville sparked a cultural war between blacks and whites that would last for the rest of the twentieth century and on into the twenty-first."[42]

The battle over Ocean Hill–Brownsville took place amid a year of global upheaval. In the spring, Columbia University students shut down their campus to protest the university's disregard for Harlem, while residents of the Marcy Houses, a public housing development in Brooklyn, protested after an unarmed teenager was shot and killed by police.[43] The UFT was not the

first city union to strike; sanitation workers had walked off the job in February, filling the streets with garbage, and by the fall, firefighters and police
officers were threatening to follow their example.[44] New York's newspapers
ran headlines of a global student revolt, mass protests against the Vietnam
War, the assassinations of Dr. Martin Luther King Jr. and Robert F. Kennedy,
urban uprisings, and pitched battles between police and protestors at the
Democratic National Convention in Chicago. For many New Yorkers, the
Ocean Hill–Brownsville struggle confirmed their mayor's assertion, in the
introduction to a national report on "civil disturbances," that the city and
the nation were in chaos, beset by political and social upheaval and "moving
toward two societies, one black, one white—separate and unequal."[45]

Accounts of the Ocean Hill–Brownsville conflict differ in their emphases,
but most treat the 1968 UFT as a breaking point, after which teacher unionism, community-based schooling, and public education in New York City
were never the same. While paraprofessional experiences of the strike were
certainly traumatic, they endured them within the context of several ongoing struggles in their schools and communities. These included long-running
campaigns for educational equity, economic opportunity, and community
participation in the governance of schools and the broader social welfare state.

To some community organizers, the question of jobs was central to the
community control struggle. The United Bronx Parents (UBP), in a flyer
released during the strikes, argued that the UFT had the support of the "other
unions in this city who also do not want to see Black and Puerto Rican communities controlling money or power." In arguing this, the UBP contextualized the fight in broader terms than the question of whether parents would
govern their children's schools, connecting the UFT fight to union-based
defenses of white privilege broadly:

> After all, over 100 million dollars is spent each year by the Board of Edu-
> cation in repair and maintenance work alone! If communities are able to
> control this money, it may mean that Black and Puerto Rican plumbers,
> carpenters, and engineers may get jobs and contracts—and the unions won't
> take that lying down!

The UBP concluded with an appeal for unity from those without a stake in
schooling, writing: "Remember: The future of Ocean Hill-Brownsville is the
future of each of us."[46]

Leftist and community-connected teachers who worked with paras had
to decide whether to obey the strike vote. While most unionized teachers
stayed out of school during the UFT's strikes, some teachers, including many
who worked with paras in the city's poorest districts, supported community
control, such as Irving Adler, a former member of the communist-led Teachers Union (TU). As Adler recalled in 1985,

I felt sympathetic to the black parents because I thought that the children were entitled to have black teachers who would present a positive role model for them, teachers who would understand their problems and work co-operatively with the parent the way Alice Zitron and Lucille Spence and Norman London used to do in Harlem.[47]

The strike spawned or grew numerous opposition caucuses within the UFT that supported community control, including the African-American Teachers' Association—whose founders, Albert Vann and Leslie Campbell (later Jitu Weusi) worked in the Ocean Hill–Brownsville district—and the New-Left affiliated Teachers for Community Control.[48] High-profile allies also broke with the union, including Richard Parrish, the former AFT vice president who had worked with HARYOU in the early 1960s to launch some of the first parent-hiring programs in New York City.[49]

At the same time, the vast majority of UFT teachers supported the strike and believed it was necessary to protect their contractual rights and the professional status they represented. Ray Frankel, a former member of the TU's socialist rival, the Teacher's Guild (from which the UFT emerged in 1960), contributed to the same oral history project in 1985. She asserted, "to argue that the parents in Harlem have the same rights, or should be able to control their schools in the manner in which the [suburban] Bronxville parents control their schools is a very specious argument and works to the detriment of the city schools."[50] White, middle-class teachers might enjoy local democracy as parents in the suburban school districts where they lived, but many did not believe the Black and Puerto Rican parents of students they taught deserved the same rights or power.

Teacher opposition to community control and the strike itself generated explosive clashes between some paras and teachers, testing the newfound solidarity that was emerging in classrooms. Alice Marsh, a teacher, remembered standoffs with paras on picket lines.

> The paraprofessionals had just come into the system, and during the Ocean Hill- Brownsville thing those teachers, those paras, in many of the schools were standing outside screaming at us for not going to school. You know, the whole city went on strike, not just Brownsville. We all went on strike. . . . Paras were the parents of the children, by and large, and they were very angry with the teachers because they had no quarrel with us. What are you doing to me? . . . And the teachers were angry because many of the paras were taking over their jobs.[51]

Marsh's recollection captures a pervasive fear among teachers that paras would cross picket lines and act as scabs, one compounded by the earlier fears that paras were hired by community associations to act as "spies" in classrooms. During the strike, however, as paras navigated allegiances to teachers and parents, they found themselves working on both sides of picket lines.

Some paraprofessionals took up teaching roles in schools as the UFT went on strike. Preston Wilcox, one of the leading figures in the city's community control movement and the chairman of the board of the Women's Talent Corps, believed the strikes were an opportunity for paraprofessional educators to reveal the bankruptcy of teacher professionalism by demonstrating the power of their own teaching. Wilcox had been calling for "foster teachers"—parents hired by local school boards or principals—to work alongside credentialed teachers at IS 201 in Harlem for years.[52] He had worked with the WTC to place trainees from the community in these roles (where they were classified as "paraprofessionals") at both IS 201 and JHS 271, the junior high school at the center of the Ocean Hill–Brownsville demonstration district.[53]

Brownsville, in fact, had proved one of the corps' favorite summer placement sites in the year preceding the strike. As placement director Laura Pires-Hester (née Pires) noted, "Especially in the Brownsville schools, the summer experience was more creative, flexible, and substantial in training quality," offering "more creative materials, much fewer restrictions on curriculum, and the presence of teachers who 'wanted to teach.'" In her final report, Pires-Hester lamented, "Why can't this be the 'standard' rather than the 'special' fare for schools and children in low-income urban schools?"[54] Community-controlled schools, as educators' memoirs from the era have documented, generated an exciting educational environment, offering paras the chance to develop as educators and contribute to public schooling in new ways.[55]

When the crisis began in May of 1968, Wilcox made a passionate appeal to his students at a corps-wide meeting. After a report on the situation in Brownsville from Rhody McCoy—the teachers there were already on strike, though the UFT's citywide strikes would not begin until the fall—Wilcox asked how many of his audience would be willing to volunteer to teach in Brownsville. When only a few hands went up, Wilcox asked why. He received the reply that many corpswomen, as the WTC called them, did not feel they were ready. Wilcox replied that this illustrated a basic problem in public schooling: "For too long, black people have been taught to feel that they aren't ready," he argued, whether as students or teachers. "When I come back a year from now," Wilcox concluded, "I hope more of you will raise your hands."[56] Wilcox did not have to wait a year; after the meeting, some forty corpswomen, nearly half of the Women's Talent Corps trainees, decided to "drop their regular activities and spend a week teaching in Ocean Hill as a gesture of support."[57] They joined "volunteers from all over the city" in assisting parents and dissident teachers, teaching their own classes, and working in the schools' administrative offices. Their presence and labor were welcomed; in June, McCoy wrote to the corps to praise their efforts.[58]

Working in this way required the support of the Women's Talent Corps, which encouraged its corpswomen's choice and later lauded it as "an ideal opportunity for learning through action." The experience of paras in schools during the crisis, however, presented challenges as well as opportunities. In the final WTC report of 1968, Laura Pires-Hester noted that while McCoy and his staff "confirmed our impression that the students performed capably and confidently," the paras themselves "had many mixed reactions to the experience." As Pires reported from conversations with WTC trainees:

> [M]ost of them were appalled at the physical condition of the schools; many of those who had been sympathetic to the parents and children of the community began to blame them for conditions. Others continued to blame the system, and many were just confused and distressed at what they saw and heard.

For the WTC itself, Pires-Hester concluded, "much was learned from this mission," even though it "was not an unqualified success." Community control had offered opportunities "to experiment with an action approach to learning" and to "encourage a sense of social commitment among students," but it also "brought home the need for careful advance planning."[59] Many paraprofessional educators believed in community control and sought to support the demonstration districts, but their experiences in community-controlled schools demonstrated the impermanence and precarity of these efforts. These experiences would inform their decisions with respect to their own positions in schools and the union in the months and years to come.

The crisis and the strikes affected teachers, parents, and paraprofessionals across New York City, not just in the three demonstration districts. In the Bronx, organizers and paras with the United Bronx Parents kept their local schools open.[60] Like Preston Wilcox, the UBP sought to use the crisis of the strikes to demonstrate the capacity of parents to govern, teach, and improve education. As Evelina Lopez Antonetty, their founder, was fond of saying, "the parent is the professional when it comes to the education of their children."[61] Rallies in support of the community control experiment drew thousands of participants from across the city.[62]

As the strikes dragged into October, the UBP released a series of statements to rally "all parents, paraprofessionals, teachers, community people and everyone who has been working so hard to keep our schools open."[63] One flyer urged parents and teachers "not [to] permit yourself to be forced into conventional staffing and pupil-teacher ratios. This is an emergency and therefore innovative and creative utilization of all available adult resources is to be encouraged." The flyer expressly referenced paraprofessionals, noting, "contrary to rumor, it is permissible under state law for the Board of Education to employ teacher assistants and teacher aides to assist those certified teachers who have come in."[64]

To the north, the Morrisania Education Council worked with parents and paraprofessionals to keep schools open while teachers struck. Aurelia Greene of the MEC remembers sleeping in schools to keep them open and working with paras and teachers who crossed picket lines. This caused "schisms between friends," she recalled, but some teachers "wanted to teach," and most of the paras hired through the Morrisania Community Progress Corporation "crossed the picket lines" because "they were not in the union then, and they knew we were working hard to be sure they could remain in the schools."[65] Oneida Davis remembers staffing cafeterias packed with children to ensure that their parents could go to work during the strikes.[66] While Davis did not have the opportunity to do much pedagogical work under these circumstances, she considered it her duty to maintain a safe place for children while others traveled to work. Paras, she recalled, were "caught in the middle of it" but were "doing the best we could to maintain the children."[67] Working with these organizations and many others, paraprofessionals took on new roles as teachers and community-based educators across New York City during the strike.

Many other paraprofessionals, however, chose to honor the UFT's picket lines. They did so for various reasons. Some, as discussed earlier, came from families or communities with strong traditions of unionization and would not cross any picket line. The refrain from these paraprofessional educators, many years later, was succinct. Maggie Martin said she was "really proud to be a union person," while Chinese American para Marian Thom said simply, "I'm a union organizer."[68] Others stayed out at the request of their classroom teachers, or out of respect for a union they hoped to join themselves. Shelvy Young-Abrams, not yet unionized, recalled that she endured accusations of being an "uncle Tom" from other parents, but she believed staying out was the surest route to guaranteeing membership in the UFT, and its benefits, in years to come.[69] Still others, including those who spoke up in Women's Talent Corps meetings, simply did not feel qualified to run classrooms on their own.

Staying out, however, did not mean being idle. On the Lower East Side, where the Two Bridges Demonstration District was one of three community control experiments under fire, both Thom and Young-Abrams worked to provide care for children outside of school settings in local community centers and other buildings.[70] In Queens, Maggie Martin "stayed out" but "some of those children, parents brought them to churches or other areas where they didn't cross the picket lines," where Martin—along with fellow paras and teachers—taught and took care of them.[71] While they did not cross teacher picket lines, they continued to do the work of education, and they would cite their work as evidence that they could be both unionists and community-minded educators in the campaign for unionization that followed in 1969.

Gladys Roth wrote to Shanker during the strikes to advocate for paras who did not cross picket lines. In addition to risking pariah status in their communities, she argued, many of these paras were "penalized more harshly than teachers for honoring the strike" by administrators who had near-total control over their pay and hours.[72] As she explained, noting a racial divide,

> While the majority did cross our picket lines, the minority, mostly Puerto Rican, did not do so. Some have lost their jobs, others have lost their pay. On make up time, they are not asked to serve the additional hours or days and will therefore lose the additional remuneration provided for the teachers on an overtime basis as well as their salary for the entire period of the strike.[73]

Roth added that she was "receiving very angry calls and would like to be able to provide justice for this very valuable and brave group of UFT members."[74] Roth did not mention that paraprofessionals were not, as of that moment, organized members of any union.

Roth's memos reveal that UFT organizers continued to work with paraprofessionals even as they became enemies in the eyes of many striking teachers. These memos also demonstrate the diversity of paraprofessional and community responses to the shaping and framing of community control, even as Black, Puerto Rican, Chinese, and Dominican parents and activists worked together in the demonstration districts.[75] Jesse Hoffnung-Garskof argues in his study of Washington Heights that some Dominican and Puerto Rican parents questioned whether "there was room in the community control movement for Latinos to participate on their own terms, rather than simply as supporters of a 'community' politics that had already been defined by black activists."[76] Sonia Song-Ha Lee's *Building a Latino Civil Rights Movement* suggests another possibility. Lee traces the origins of Latino activism in New York City to progressive unions, including 1199, the "soul power" union, and District 65 of the United Retail and Wholesale Employees of America, and also to fights for inclusion within the labor movement, particularly in the textile industry.[77] Puerto Rican New Yorkers, including Evelina Lopez Antonetty, fought hard for inclusion in textile unions, and they won membership to an extent that African Americans did not in their campaigns to integrate the building trades unions. As a consequence, Latinx New Yorkers may have been less inclined to cross picket lines.[78]

Whether paraprofessionals went in or stayed out, they and their families suffered at the middle of this maelstrom. The immediate impacts were financial; as Roth's letter indicates, paras who stayed out suffered all the consequences of striking without any of the protection of the UFT's strike planning or strike fund, as they were not yet part of the union. Maggie Martin was-punished under New York State's draconian Taylor Law, which fined striking public employees two days' pay for every one that they struck, while others, as Roth reported, were frozen out of hours and even their jobs.[79] Paras who crossed picket lines may not have been fined, but as the United Bronx

Parents reported, "educational assistants and school aides who have worked throughout the strike have NOT been paid."[80] Paras faced hardship no matter what they did.

Beyond the challenges of doing without their salaries or labor protections, paraprofessionals experienced profound destabilization of their workplaces and neighborhoods during and after the teachers' strikes of 1968. Working in community-run schools suggested the possibility of new pedagogies and ways of governing and organizing education, but it also demonstrated how chaotic and frustrating school environments could be when teachers and the city abandoned them. As the crisis came to a close, these experiences and hardships would inform paraprofessional decisions about their place in communities, schools, and the union.

Paraprofessional Educators Join the Union of Professionals

Audrey Cohen, the president of the Women's Talent Corps, wrote to AFT President David Selden in March of 1969. "We have been the strongest and most articulate supporters of the role of the UFT in helping us open up the paraprofessional position in New York from the very beginning," she wrote. "I think it's important to point out that we had students and graduates who went in and taught during the strike, but at least an equal number refused to enter the schools."[81] Cohen copied UFT President Albert Shanker on the missive.

This letter reveals at least three things happening at once. First, by writing to Selden, Shanker's international union president, Cohen demonstrated her own knowledge that the "paraprofessional movement" had become a matter of national concern for the AFT. Second, Cohen was making a case for the alliance of paraprofessionals and the UFT based on a shared history and origin moment—one she played a major role in—and she was doing so just a few months after the bitter end of the Ocean Hill–Brownsville crisis. Third, she was defending her corps' student body of paraprofessionals as a heterogeneous group that had made their own decisions during the strike. While her count—"at least an equal number"—was vague and unexplained, Cohen argued that paras and the UFT remained compatible, even after the strike.

Perhaps the most remarkable thing about Cohen and the Women's Talent Corps's relationship with the UFT was that it continued at all. Shanker adopted a scorched-earth policy toward anyone who crossed UFT picket lines during the strike, publicly excoriating the United Parents Association and the Public Education Association, middle-class and elite civic groups that had opposed the strikes and sent volunteers in to teach and supervise children. He unleashed his towering anger on community control activists who opposed him and would continue to do so for decades to come. And yet, despite clear evidence that paraprofessionals from the WTC had crossed picket lines at the urging of Preston Wilcox, one of his most vociferous critics, Shanker held his fire. Why?

Though the strikes forced the dismantling of three demonstration districts, they proved a Pyrrhic victory, dividing the union's rank and file and damaging its standing in the city. AFT Vice President Richard Parrish had grown so infuriated with Shanker's hostility to community control that "by the final strike, Parrish was urging teachers to cross the picket lines and teach African American children."[82] In May of 1969, Parrish published a searing critique of the UFT titled "The New York City Teachers Strikes: Blow to Education, Boon to Racism" in which he demanded that the UFT leadership be deposed in favor of a "genuine partnership between the UFT and the black and poor communities to provide quality education." Parrish, who had helped HARYOU hire and train "parent aides" years earlier, singled out para programs and teacher training as key parts of such an effort. As he wrote, "unless Black and Puerto Rican people have a chance to get on the staff, to have job training and to develop as their white counterparts, they will never be able to hold their heads up and work with full efficiency" in either schools or the union.[83] Other rank-and-file opposition that emerged during 1968, including Teachers for Community Control, whose members later helped to found the leftist Teacher Action Caucus, likewise supported empowering paraprofessionals.[84]

Shanker and the UFT leadership also worried about losing paraprofessionals to a rival union, AFSCME District Council 37. After the strike, DC 37 began moving to represent paras in their new positions. Unlike the UFT, AFSCME had a local and national reputation as a progressive union with strong ties to the civil rights movement. Lillian Roberts, a Black woman who began her career as a nurse's aide in 1959 (a role similar to that of paraprofessional educators), led DC 37's successful hospital campaign of 1965. Dr. Martin Luther King Jr. had been assassinated while supporting AFSCME sanitation workers on strike in Memphis. For these reasons, DC 37 argued, it was the logical home for paras, not the UFT.

In addition to these local concerns, Shanker was under pressure from his international union's leaders. His old friend David Selden took the reins of the AFT at a paradoxical moment in 1968. The union had grown tremendously over the preceding decade and was poised to become a major player in the labor movement, but at the same time, the AFT and its locals were increasingly subject to intense criticism for their role in generating and preserving inequalities in urban school districts. In this context, Selden began promoting paraprofessional organizing, encouraged by New York's number-one advocate of "New Careers," Frank Riessman.

In June of 1968, Selden wrote to Frank Riessman of NYU's New Careers Development Center to express support for paraprofessionals. "I strongly favor the use of the teacher assistants in elementary and secondary schools," wrote Selden, as well as "the development of career lines which would permit such personnel to advance . . . until teacher status has been achieved." Selden was also "very fearful of setting up the usual civil service structure, with advancement being based on examinations. The red tape and meaningless job specifications of these systems is one of the chief sources of racial imbalance in big city school systems."[85] Shanker was copied.

The timing of this communication was remarkable, as it came just after the opening salvos of the Ocean Hill–Brownsville crisis, of which Selden was well aware. Selden's "red tape and meaningless job specifications" were, in many teachers' minds, the bulwarks of their threatened professionalism. Nonetheless, Selden persisted in his commitment to paraprofessional organizing throughout 1968, seeking and winning funds from the AFL-CIO to do so. However, because the AFL-CIO discouraged intra-federation competition, these monies went not to Shanker in New York, where the UFT and AFSCME had already begun organizing, but to Philadelphia.[86] While Shanker never spoke publicly on the matter, his vision of himself, and his union, as the leading edge of teacher organizing was no doubt challenged by aid to a rival local.

Riessman worked closely with Selden and Shanker during and after the strike to encourage their continued support of paraprofessionalism. His engagement as a broker helped the UFT and AFT's leaders articulate a vision for paraprofessionals that did not threaten the basic contours of teacher professionalism. This hinged on the idea that paraprofessionals were not alternative educators, but teachers in training. As Selden—himself of a midwestern, craft-unionism background—wrote to Riessman, the "new careers" concept offered:

> a very cogent point, one which I had not thought of so far as teachers are concerned. Reducing the number of teachers in the educational enterprise would have the effect of reducing career opportunities for aides and assistants. Therefore, teachers should not view such personnel as being in competition with them. Attrition of the teaching force will create enough promotional opportunities, I should think.[87]

Riessman and Selden corresponded regularly throughout the 1969 campaigns, with Riessman offering support for AFT organizing in New York, Philadelphia, and elsewhere. Selden increasingly embraced the language of "New Careers" and the idea of "career ladders" for paraprofessionals, a connection that ensured the AFT would fight for these kinds of opportunities across the country (with Riessman's assistance) throughout the 1970s.[88]

However, Selden envisioned apprenticeship, not a radical restructuring of the teaching profession. Writing again to Riessman in December of 1969, he was both optimistic and honest, noting, "I really think that so far as education is concerned, the AFT will be able to do a great deal to help the new paraprofessionals," but also that "there will be a certain amount of subversion of your original concept. Most teachers are not interested in revolutionizing the nature of this service."[89] The vision that Selden, Shanker, and the AFT developed for paraprofessional organizing was an assimilationist one, in which paras served as apprentices and could be fully incorporated into the union if, and when, they became teachers.

Selden's statement would certainly have confirmed the fears of community organizers and the Women's Talent Corps. It also implied a hierarchy, in which paraprofessional labor was defined as training, rather than necessary educational work in its own right. When budget cuts and political shifts undermined training for paras in the 1970s, this craft-union model, in which paraprofessionals assimilated into the ranks of teachers, became untenable. Without their status as teachers in training, paras would find themselves marginalized in schoolrooms and union halls.

Paras themselves demonstrated their desire to unionize after the strike, as well. As Audrey Cohen's letter noted, many of her corpswomen had honored the UFT's picket lines in spite of multitudinous pressures to cross them. When Cohen's Women's Talent Corps heard reports from the field in early 1969, they learned from paraprofessionals on the Lower East Side that "a minority of members joined the UFT chapter in their schools on an individual basis."[90] While paraprofessionals could not have been represented by the union, their participation in these chapters showed that their interest in the union remained strong, to Gladys Roth and Velma Murphy Hill as well as to Audrey Cohen. In 1969, they would get the chance to express this interest, as an election was set for June of 1969 between the UFT and AFSCME.

Velma Hill left her position as a para and became a full-time organizer early in 1969.[91] Hill and her team worked hard to define the UFT as an educator's union with "the experience and strength to obtain professional pay and status" for paras.[92] The UFT's leaders had to make a case that they—and not community leaders or AFSCME DC 37—could best provide the job security, increased wages, and path to advancement that paraprofessionals desired. At the same time, they had to ensure the support of their membership. The task proved a precarious balancing act. In making their case, the UFT used several strategies to differentiate the benefits it could offer from those that paraprofessionals might enjoy in DC 37.

Hill sought to build paraprofessional unity through mass meetings and the development of a steering committee. She constantly made the case to paras that "a boss is a boss is a boss," even when the "boss" in question was a community leader living next door.[93] The steering committee advertised their demands—including annual salaries, better benefits, and an improved career ladder—in flyers, highlighting para participation in the process.

Hill and her fellow organizers traveled widely across the five boroughs to reach paras and bring them together. Maggie Martin was recruited by former paraprofessional and UFT field organizer James Howard, who gathered paras in a bar on Sutphin Boulevard in Queens. Martin recalled that Howard was the "nicest man," and his message was simple: "you're going to work in the classroom with the teachers, you need to be in the same organization."[94] Howard coupled his message with a sympathetic ear for paraprofessional grievances, voiced over drinks. As Martin remembers, Howard believed fervently in paraprofessional programs: "he wanted to really get people involved in their children's lives and doing something better for the community." For Howard, the best way to address para needs and desires was in the union. As he told Martin and her fellow Queens paras, "If you're going to complain, why don't you become a part of the system, so you can see, so you can help out, so you can make changes, not as a spy."[95]

The UFT also pushed its status as an educators' union to appeal to paras' sense of themselves as part of an educational team. They created flyers and memos with messages like "Join the Only School Union," "Join the Union that Knows the Schools," and "If You Work With Children, You Belong in the UFT." One flyer touted the UFT's fight for smaller class sizes, a better curriculum "with African-American history," and "introduction of school aides and paraprofessionals." The material side of professional status was celebrated as well, with one flyer touting UFT discounts on everything from cars and stereos to access to credit cards and insurance policies.[96] These offers coincided and overlapped with the work of the welfare rights movement to win credit for poor and working-class women in New York City and elsewhere.[97] In addition to suggesting a path to stability and status through UFT membership, these flyers deliberately contrasted the professional unionism of the UFT with the civil service unionism of DC 37. In doing so, they reflected the original intent of the Women's Talent Corps, which had insisted on professional, and not "entry-level," status for paras.[98]

AFSCME DC 37 had built a sterling reputation in Black and Latinx communities through its organization of low-income workers in the city's hospitals and had represented many paras as school aides in prior jobs. Seeking to capitalize on the alienating effect of the 1968 strikes, DC 37 shaped its campaign messages in the language of community control. One brochure argued:

> Many more paraprofessionals have come to the realization that Al Shanker fears and opposes a real Career Ladder Program for Para-professionals. It is Shanker who demands continuation of the Board of Examiners and their

old, outmoded system of employing teachers. Local 372 wants to change this system, so that people from the community can rise through the ranks to become teachers. Shanker opposes such changes; he fears a real Career Ladder program because he fears the community.[99]

Though the UFT tried to position itself as a liberal union on questions of civil rights, the union drew on the legacy of 1968 in a very different way once DC 37 drew attention to it. As June approached, flyers urged paras to "Vote for the Union that has the Strength to Win." One from May featured a photograph of an unsmiling Albert Shanker staring out of the frame, as if at an unlucky adversary at the bargaining table. It bore the message, "When you vote for the UFT and Al Shanker you're not guessing! You KNOW we can do the job because we are DOING it. Vote UFT! UFT can do the job for YOU—It's STRONG [emphasis original]." The flyer stood in stark contrast to DC 37's brochure, which bore the smiling image of Lillian Roberts with the caption "Mrs. Roberts, Associate Director of DC 37, is nationally known as originator of Career Ladder Programs which have already raised 500 Nurse's Aides to Licensed Nurses."[100]

Official UFT campaign materials emphasized the mutual affinity of teachers and paraprofessionals and the desire of paraprofessionals to be taken seriously as educators. Talking to the *Baltimore Afro-American*, para Carolyn Frazier of Harlem told a different story, noting that she supported the UFT because she was "going to the highest bidder." In the same article, Robert Jackson, a faculty member at the Women's Talent Corps, argued, "the paraprofessionals ideologically prefer DC 37, but from a practical standpoint, they feel that the UFT has more muscle."[101] Critics of the unionization effort argued that the campaign was simply co-optation by the UFT leadership, but if this was the case, paraprofessionals were remarkably clear-eyed about it. "We're aware that the UFT is only using us to gain more power and get on the good side of the parents in our schools," another Harlem para told the *Amsterdam News*. However, these paras felt they could use the UFT for their own benefit, just as the union sought to use them.

In the campaign's final days, the UFT sought to leverage person-to-person contact to influence paras. A letter from Shanker to teachers on June 18, 1969, read:

> We are counting on you to convince her that UFT is the best choice and to see that she votes UFT in the coming election. . . . When the paraprofessional in your class votes next week, she should know that *you* want her in the UFT—that you need her support in teachers' struggles and that you will support her in winning benefits.[102]

Shanker's plea demonstrates his understanding of the essential locus of the UFT's appeal: the classroom, where paras and teachers shared in educational labor and had built solidarity. The paraprofessional campaign took place in the very same years that paraprofessionals proved their value in classrooms. Though it involved the highest-ranking officers in the union, the campaign was not primarily a top-down affair. Rather, it relied on chapter-by-chapter organizing and school and neighborhood-level alliances of rank-and-file working women.

Just before the election, photos of steering committee members with their schools and titles listed ran in a special election edition of the *United Teacher,* re-titled the *United Para-Professional* for the occasion. The photos were captioned with quotes from these paras declaring their support for the UFT. One Brooklyn para explained, "I like the idea of the UFT because the teachers are in it and we work with them in the classroom."[103] Putting para faces and ideas up front, the UFT hoped to refute notions of Shanker's dictatorial style and emphasize the democratic potential of membership in the UFT.

The election was chaotic, with both the UFT and AFSCME accusing each other of voter intimidation and ballot tampering. After several months of arbitration, during which time both unions circulated flyers and press releases accusing the other of stalling, some contested ballots were removed and the votes were counted. At the Board of Education's insistence, the election had been held only among paraprofessionals who worked in grades K–2, as the board claimed that they could not guarantee the continuation of the program beyond those grades because of the nature of federal funding. This group, between 3,500 and 4,000 paraprofessionals (out of about 10,000 total employed in New York City), had been further divided into two bargaining units: paras who worked in classrooms and paras who did not. In the final count of unchallenged ballots, the UFT won the classroom workers with 1,248 votes to DC 37's 1,195 (29 paras voted for no union, and 9 ballots were blank) while DC 37 won the family and parent workers with 252 votes to the UFT's 202 (5 voted no, 10 were blank).[104] In total, somewhere between 75 percent and 85 percent of eligible paras voted, the vast majority for some form of union membership.

While the UFT did not win a resounding victory, it was clear that paraprofessionals sought union representation and the material and status benefits that came with it. The teacher union was deeply unpopular in most communities where the election was contested, and it was challenging a broadly popular union that had already represented a significant minority of paraprofessionals (those who had previously served as school aides). Given these challenges, it is fair to ask how the UFT was able to win any votes at all.

The paras that chose the UFT did so for both practical and aspirational reasons. Joining the UFT affirmed paras' status as educational workers. Doing so offered immediate gains, as the UFT had demonstrated its ability to outduel the Board of Education. This fact, paras hoped, promised a more effective career ladder program, and the ultimate opportunity to become teachers. As Brooklyn para Julia Rodgers explained in *The United Para-Professional* just before the election, "The UFT is also offering us good things—a raise and the chance to go to college one day since we want to become teachers."[105] Maggie Martin voted for the UFT, as did many of her friends. As she reasoned, "why would you work in a classroom with a teacher and not be a part of the same union?"[106] Alida Mesrop, then a staff member at the Women's Talent Corps, remembered that many WTC paraprofessionals chose the UFT, with the corps's support, for a simple, pragmatic reason: "they had clout!"[107] The choice was not always easy; one para, Mrs. Gilbert, told a meeting of the Board of Education just before the election that "the UFT had promised to fight for her job in a school which was threatened by budget cuts." Gilbert was "tempted to join the UFT" but "[held] back because her sympathy is with the community and she is not convinced the two are compatible."[108]

By confirming the status of paraprofessionals as workers, by offering a vision for career advancement, and—somewhat ironically—by showing that they could fight the city and win, the UFT eked out a fifty-three-vote victory, one the union continues to celebrate to this day.[109] However, a two-percent margin victory hardly signals a resounding show of support, and though the election marked a drastic shift in their relationship, negotiations between the UFT and paraprofessionals were far from complete. In some locales, the UFT had won a major victory, especially in Ocean Hill–Brownsville, where 175 out of 200 paraprofessionals reportedly signed UFT union cards.[110] In other areas, ties to DC 37, or mistrust of the UFT, had carried the day.

Most important, before any substantive gains could come of paraprofessional unionism, the paras and the UFT had to bargain a novel contract with the Board of Education. They had to achieve this while being challenged on one flank by Black and Puerto Rican community organizers and on the other by a rank-and-file reaction among white teachers.

A Two-Front Campaign: Building a Coalition to Win a Paraprofessional Contract

Contract negotiations between the UFT and the Board of Education began in December 1969, but the final paraprofessional contract was not signed until August of the following year. The Board of Education dared the union to strike, hoping to undermine what they felt was an over-powerful but over-extended union. By provoking the threat of yet another teacher strike, the board hoped to break the UFT, either by unleashing a massive parent backlash against an unpopular tactic, or by revealing the UFT leadership's inability to make its mostly white rank and file walk out to support paraprofessionals. While opposition to paraprofessional unionism began to build in some neighborhoods and among some teachers immediately after the election results were ratified, it was the possibility of a paraprofessional strike that posed the most serious challenge to the UFT's efforts, both from within and from without.

The leaders of community action agencies had worried from the beginning that unionization might undermine their relationship with paraprofessionals, whom they regarded as their own appointees. Their own efforts at control sometimes antagonized paras. One rare complaint in Roth's 1968 survey referenced a meeting held by a community group demanding the fealty of paras, and the UFT received complaints from the Two Bridges demonstration district when paraprofessionals were ordered to join a sit-in at the office of the Manhattan borough president.[111] Community-based antipoverty organizations sometimes faced internal challenges from those they employed, as evidenced by an attempt at unionization on the part of some 300 employees of the Bedford-Stuyvesant Restoration Corporation in 1968.[112]

When the UFT announced the beginning of paraprofessional contract negotiations in late 1969, community-based organizations were still furious with the UFT for fighting the demonstration districts and for keeping their children out of school for nearly two months. They saw the UFT's unionization drive as yet another attempt to stifle community participation in education. These groups worried that a UFT contract would spell the end of their influence over paraprofessional appointments, even as the newly signed New York State decentralization law created community school boards with the power to hire paras. These organizations sought to remind paras that they were "placed in the school" by community associations and thus owed their jobs, and their loyalty, to these groups.[113] As one organization put it, "It is required that para-professionals remain in constant cooperation with the Crown Heights Education Committee." The UFT, they wrote, "does not reflect our local community culture in any positive manner." Moreover, they asserted, "a union contract concerning Title I personnel is invalid because it is in conflict with and in fact contrary to public law." Urging paras to "toss aside the concept that we need people outside of our community culture to bargain anything for us," they sought to reassert their relationships to, and authority over, these workers.[114]

Many flyers circulated by community groups, including the one cited above, quoted from an article from the *New York Amsterdam News* that described the firing of Maggie Martin's friend James Howard because of his independence from Albert Shanker and his use of the language of "Black pride." Reporting that paraprofessionals organized by Howard had turned in their union cards in protest, the article asked, "If the UFT can do away with Howard, a so-called top representative, imagine what they are going to do for you?"[115] Very few records of Howard's employment or his termination exist, but Martin's testimony confirms that he was popular, and the *Amsterdam News* report of paras turning in their cards suggests that paras expected to control their new union chapter.[116]

Local activists grew increasingly outspoken in their appeals to paras when the threat of a paraprofessional strike was broached in the spring of 1970. A "Letter to Paraprofessionals of Ocean Hill-Brownsville" from Rev. Herbert C. Oliver and Rhody McCoy used the word "para" interchangeably with "parent" to elide the two. It pleaded, "Don't let Shanker use our children and us to help him win back friends in our communities. He doesn't care about our children. He proved that with his illegal strikes of 1967 and 1968."[117] In Bedford-Stuyvesant, whose local school district employed the largest number of paraprofessionals, Bed-Stuy Youth in Action informed paras that, "if a strike is called, [we] will urge the para-professionals not to go out. They will be hurting the children from the community they are trying to serve."[118]

These attempts to sway paras, however, were tempered by the need to address the extremely low pay paras were receiving for work that community associations agreed was vitally important. UFT newspaper ads promoting the paraprofessionals' negotiations read, "Everybody knows the way out of poverty is a job. Well, we're working and we're still poor. We are paraprofessionals. We live in the neighborhoods of the schools we work in."[119] Seeking to preempt the need for a union-brokered contract, several community groups insisted that they had approved a 25 percent increase in paraprofessional wages, to be paid out of the federal funds allocated to the Board of Education, which the board had failed to honor.[120] Bed-Stuy Youth in Action's leaders noted in their monthly newsletter that they had formed their own paraprofessional organization, which had affirmed its commitment to the community and promised not to strike.[121] If they were to retain paras' allegiance, these organizations realized that they had to address paras' needs and desires directly.

Many local organizations called meetings to discuss the situation with paraprofessionals, who, they believed, would not employ the same tactic that had destroyed community control. "Some of the paraprofessionals in our immediate area have felt the need for an opportunity to meet together and discuss the possible para-professional strike," read the notice sent out by the East Harlem Community Corporation. Helen Testamark, the chair of the organization's educational committee, called an emergency meeting to address rumors "that efforts are being made by the United Federation of Teachers to remove these workers from community control."[122]

Velma Murphy Hill joined many of these meetings, some of which became heated. Paras who attended these meetings, Hill remembers, frequently met with "very hostile" crowds, including one woman brandishing a baseball bat, but she noted that "paras got to tell their side of the story."[123] Marian

Thom remembers similar meetings on the Lower East Side, in which tempers flared to such an extent that "you wondered if you were going to walk out alive."[124] Paraprofessionals understood the suffering that these communities had experienced during the teacher strikes, but they believed they could fight for their rights as workers and still remain true to their students. These meetings gave paras an opportunity to explain their desire to unionize while asserting their commitment to communities.

The UFT paraprofessional chapter's representatives voted to authorize a strike on April 22, 1970.[125] Shortly thereafter, the chapter began a series of pickets at the Board of Education headquarters. Images taken for the UFT's newspaper capture hundreds of paras walking the sidewalk along Livingston Street in Brooklyn, carrying signs printed by their union that read "Dignity for Paraprofessionals," "Annual Salaries Instead of Poverty Wages," and "Paraprofessionals Want a Decent Contract Now." Paras also brought their own hand-lettered signs, which included ones reading, "Must we all be on welfare?" and "Slave Labor No! Annual Salary, Fringe Benefits, Yes! Yes!" They were joined on the picket lines by teachers carrying "Teachers Support You" signs, as well as family and community members, including children.[126]

In addition to picketing, paras told their stories in the press in the days and weeks that followed their strike vote. The *New York Times* ran an article titled "A Portrait of the School Paraprofessional" on May 1, 1970, featuring profiles and photos of Julia Fuentes and Cruz Birkman, two Puerto Rican paras at P.S. 34 on the Lower East Side. Fuentes and Cruz both lived one block from the school, and "frequently meet their pupils' parents while shopping and have many informal chats," according to the article. Their principal lauded their work, citing "better communication between the school and parents" on account of paras' presence at school and specifically the translation services they provided. The article also noted their effective small-group work with students—particularly those learning English—their take-home pay of $47 a week, and Fuentes' desire to become a bilingual teacher, all key talking points in the UFT's struggle for a para contract.[127] The *New York Post* ran its long, glowing profile of paraprofessional Letty Concepcion and the "fantastic" relationships she had built with her students and teachers in Brooklyn (discussed in Chapter 2) on May 16, 1970.[128]

Paras also shared their perspectives with outlets that spoke directly to their communities. The *New York Amsterdam News* ran an interview with paraprofessional Margaret Boyd of PS 108 in East Harlem titled "She's for the Strike" three days after the para chapter's strike vote. As Boyd explained for the *Amsterdam News's* readership:

The paraprofessionals are doing jobs that are extremely essential to the educational process. I have been a paraprofessional for the past three years,

UFT paraprofessionals picket at the New York City Board of Education, Spring 1970. United Federation of Teachers Photographs; PHOTOS 019; Box 3, Folder 43; Tamiment Library/Robert F. Wagner Labor Archives, New York University.

and have not received any raises or benefits. I sincerely hope that the teachers will support our effort because most education aides are of Black and Puerto Rican descent.[129]

Her fellow paraprofessional Bessy Canty echoed Boyd's sentiments in an article titled "Paras Seek Parent Support," saying "she hope[d] that parents will understand their plight and support the education aides by keeping their children out of school" in the event of a paraprofessional strike.[130] East Harlem's *El Diario* and *El Tiempo* also covered the contract struggle, running interviews with paraprofessionals, whom it lauded for their work in bilingual education.[131] *El Tiempo*, the city's largest Spanish-language daily newspaper, noted, "If anyone in any Latin American country were to say that a public servant in the US earns between $2,500 and $3,000 annually, very few would believe it."[132] This coverage emphasized paras' impact in schools and broadcast their struggle to a wide audience. For *El Diario*, *El Tiempo*, and the *Amsterdam News*, embracing paraprofessional organizing meant revising their opposition to teacher strikes and, in this particular instance, endorsing UFT paras.

The *Amsterdam News* also interviewed Congressman James Scheuer, who had sponsored a 1966 amendment to the Economic Opportunity Act that provided funding for career training, and who sat on the board of the Women's Talent Corps. Scheuer was unequivocal in his support of the paras, arguing, "We intended this program to provide a ladder from unemployment to paraprofessionalism and on up to professional employment status. As the program is currently run, the paraprofessionals are being employed on an hourly basis with no job security, no sick leave, no vacation and effectively no chance for upgrading."[133] Scheuer's concerns were echoed in a report by the National Committee on the Employment of Youth released at the end of February in 1970. Paraprofessionals, the *New York Times* reported, are "found in the study to be 'extremely stable' and 'more than capable' in performing a wide variety of tasks in such institutions as schools, hospitals and welfare agencies," but the combination of continued credential requirements and a lack of available training meant "the growing national experiment with 'new careers'" was "in danger of remaining stalled at the level of dead-end jobs."[134]

It is difficult to know how community organizations and parents would have reacted had a paraprofessional strike taken place in 1970, but even some who had vociferously opposed the UFT in 1968 came around to the idea of paraprofessional unionism by 1970. Aurelia Greene, whose husband Jerome A. Greene led the Morrisania Education Council, remembered that they celebrated when paraprofessionals won their first contract, despite having tried to block the para-UFT alliance two years prior. "We thought of it as a good opportunity," Greene remembered, "because they [paras] were there on a temporary basis. We wanted the program to become institutionalized," and thus, the MEC leaders "were not unhappy that the union started unionizing them."[135] Lorraine Montenegro, the daughter of UBP founder Evelina Lopez Antonetty and a longtime South Bronx activist, was among those who slept in schools to keep them open in 1968, but by 1970, she recalled, "we supported them [the UFT] in most of their demands."[136] Montenegro recalled that her mother started out as an organizer with District 65, a left-leaning New York

City union. She believed in both the power of labor organizing and the need for progressive voices in the labor movement.[137]

As paraprofessionals contended with concerned and occasionally hostile community organizations, the UFT was scrambling to sell paraprofessional unionization to skeptical teachers. Early on in the campaign, a handwritten letter from Beatrice E. Jacob, the chapter chair of PS 106 in the Bronx, informed Shanker that her chapter was "unilaterally opposed to the continuation of the para-professionals," because, as she put it, "they will become a noose around our neck and at present offer no assistance but rather are a disturbing factor and a hindrance."[138] Similar missives, some signed by whole chapters, raised concerns about paraprofessionals acting as scabs, diluting teacher professionalism, and receiving unfair assistance in becoming teachers. When the threat of a paraprofessional strike was raised, many asserted, as did teacher Paul Engelson of Queens, "I have no intention of going on strike for this group."[139]

This last threat posed a grave problem for the UFT. A paraprofessional strike without teacher support would have little practical impact and would hinder any attempts to negotiate a contract. Images of white teachers crossing picket lines would confirm everything community organizations had said about the UFT and irrevocably damage the union's legitimacy with paras.

In response, Sandra Feldman and Velma Murphy Hill conducted what an internal UFT report later called "one of the most intensive internal education campaigns in our history."[140] Feldman answered hundreds of letters from teachers, driving home the message that "paraprofessionals are *members of our own union*" [emphasis original]. In replying to Engelson, Feldman added, "If we do not support them [paras] in their struggle for a contract . . . if our efforts to win a living wage and working conditions are defeated, that defeat will be a severe blow to the UFT and its future negotiating strength."[141]

After the UFT para chapter authorized a strike, the *New York Times* reported that Albert Shanker "admitted that the union leadership had a job to do to mobilize teacher support" but vowed to secure it.[142] The fifty-one-member UFT Executive Board voted unanimously to support the paras' strike and honor para picket lines on April 27, 1970, followed by a 432–139 vote of the union's delegate assembly in support of paras on April 29.[143] Nonetheless, the question of rank-and-file teacher support remained, and Shanker decided to call a mass vote of teachers to settle it.

The decision to hold a membership-wide vote on the question of whether to back a paraprofessional strike outraged some paras and left-leaning teachers, who felt it revealed paras' second-class status in the union. Nonetheless, the plan went forward, and Shanker once again leaned on his chapter chairs to educate the rank and file, urging them to emphasize the support of "civil rights, liberal and labor groups" for "our paraprofessional campaign" and the need for a "strong vote of support by all UFT members."[144] Many rose to the occasion with impressive materials of their own, including a one-act play composed by Brooklyn Chapter Chair Lucy Shifrin to address questions about the role and future of paraprofessionals in the union.[145] As Hill wrote in her memoir, "Our work with the paras was featured in the union publication, along with pictures and articles depicting paras and teachers happily working together in the classroom."[146]

The UFT's own retellings of this history emphasize the role of Shanker's leadership, including a letter to teachers in support of paras that he penned while serving jail time under the Taylor Law for the 1968 strikes.[147] However, Sandra Feldman relied far more heavily and regularly on the voices of ordinary teachers and chapter chairs who worked with paraprofessionals and were largely supportive of their demands. As Eloise Davis, a Harlem teacher, told the Amsterdam News, "paraprofessionals need and deserve better salaries and benefits."[148] Armed with letters and testimonials, the teachers of Harlem, the Lower East Side, the South Bronx, and Central Brooklyn hit the road to convince their brethren in the outer boroughs to support paraprofessionals. Their person-to-person campaigning drove home the value of the connections they had built with paras in classrooms over the previous two years.

Members of progressive and radical caucuses were particularly active, often in ways that worried Shanker. One flyer in support of the paras read "the paraprofessionals are a potentially progressive force in fighting for the real change in the schools . . . [they] have demonstrated their willingness to actively oppose the policies of the BOE and the present mis-leadership of the UFT."[149] Teachers did not have to be radical to believe that in the aftermath of the 1968 battles, teacher unionism had lost some of its joy in New York City. UFT staff member Dan Sanders, who joined paras at the bargaining table in the summer, remembered, "Given the recent climate of all the confrontationism and everything else, it was a wonderful thing to be able to participate in."[150] Larry Robbins, a teacher at the time, had stayed out during the strikes and felt the way teachers were treated by community members "wasn't fair," but when it came to paraprofessional organizing, he believed in it and was shocked that others opposed it. "It's quite another thing," he noted, "not to support getting more and more black and Hispanic into education and into the teaching profession by setting up a system by which they can elevate themselves."[151] For these teacher unionists, the paraprofessional campaign was a return to the core values of their union after an ugly detour into community control battles. Velma Murphy Hill emphasized that the paraprofessional campaign "succeeded in elevating minority, mostly women—mostly black and Hispanic women—without quotas . . . which tended to separate blacks and whites." Hill's integrationist strategy focused paras and teachers alike on solidarity.

A Triumph and a Beginning

On June 3, 1970, over ten thousand teachers gathered at Madison Square Garden and voted to support a paraprofessional strike by a three-to-one margin. The combination of widespread public support and the teachers' vote forced the Board of Education to the bargaining table. By August of 1970, New York City paras signed their landmark contract.

Official histories of the UFT have often deployed this victory as rehabilitation for Albert Shanker and the union leadership in the wake of the community control battle. This chapter argues, however, that paraprofessional educators and the teachers with whom they worked were as essential to this campaign as those at the top.[152] Real gains and power were won in the contract of 1970, contributing to long-running struggles to redefine the work of education and bring new workers into classrooms. The contract was a victory for and by the UFT, but it was also a product of civil rights campaigns for jobs and freedom and community struggles for power in public schools. For the women who worked at the nexus of these struggles—paras themselves—the distinction was less important than the result. The contract preserved and expanded programs that improved education in New York and created thousands of jobs for working-class women in neighborhoods bearing the brunt of a rising urban crisis.

The "triumph" of the paras was the result of strategic alliances between women working as educators. Historical studies of public-sector employment for poor women of color have rightly noted that racism, classism, and sexism all contributed to their receiving lower wages, insecure tenure, and few avenues for advancement in government positions, dividing them physically and rhetorically from "professional" workers like teachers.[153] In spite of this official discrimination, paraprofessionals and teachers found common ground. Working together built solidarity, and so did sharing the challenges of balancing home and work. This solidarity helped to bridge divides of class, race, and metropolitan space in the classroom, and, later, in the union.

The coalition of educators, activists, parents, unionists, and policymakers that supported paraprofessionals shifted, frayed, and fought fiercely during these three chaotic years in New York City. By 1970, many of these actors could agree about nothing at all save for the value of paraprofessionals in public schools. Still, their coalition held, for the time being, and the contract it produced proved generative for many strains of paraprofessional organizing going forward.

Questions remained, of course. In many neighborhoods, community organizers wondered whether the "institutionalization" of paras, as Aurelia Greene described it, could truly coexist with responsive community involvement. Not all teachers were convinced that paras would become allies in schools and the union. In a candid moment two decades later, Shanker recalled that at Madison Square Garden, many teachers "came down they voted and they were angry. They kind of looked at me and said, 'Well, we are voting the way you want us to, but we don't believe in it.'"[154] The contract was a victory, but in many ways, the work had just begun.

Teachers and their unions had embraced a particular definition of paraprofessional work, one that preserved elements of both paternalism and hierarchy. Leaders and teachers alike would continue to contrast the community control struggles with the paraprofessional campaigns that followed, demonizing parents and activists who fought them in 1968 while praising the hardworking women who joined them in 1969. It mattered little that many paras were members of both groups; a rhetorical line had been drawn between community control and paras. Such language sometimes created an impediment to connecting schools and communities through paraprofessional labor in the 1970s, one that radical union caucuses and community groups worked to overcome. Moreover, the ways Selden's apprenticeship model of paraprofessionalism tied the value of paraprofessional work to teacher training blinded many teachers and unionists to the multifaceted nature of paraprofessional labor, and it proved an insufficient link for sustaining teacher commitments to paras during budget crises in the 1970s.

How might we understand the legacy of Ocean Hill–Brownsville and community control struggles in light of the paraprofessional organizing drive? Community control was not a one-off experiment but a long-running demand in New York City. Struggles for community participation in public education were not simply fights about schooling but were connected to demands for economic opportunities—for parents as well as children—and democratic participation in the provision of social welfare. These took many forms in the 1960s, of which paraprofessional programs were one, and the three "decentralized districts" that launched the 1968 "crisis" another. "Community control" of schools as a city-sanctioned experiment may have ended in December of 1968, but the struggle continued, and some paras believed their contract was a contribution to this goal.

This is not to ignore that the 1968 teacher strikes were a significant turning point, but rather to reevaluate what turned, and how. Parents and activists tried to sustain a holistic vision of community schooling in the demonstration districts, and while that was destroyed, pieces of it lived on, in part because these parents had provoked a crisis. Resolving that crisis required concessions from the Board of Education and the United Federation of Teachers. Ideological shifts are often attributed to the legacy of the 1968 teacher strikes—a moment when some scholars contend that liberalism was eclipsed and maximum feasible participation squandered—but the paraprofessionals rarely spoke in such terms. Rather, paras strategized pragmatically with a combination of direct pressure, coalition building, and constant organizing. This was how they made themselves essential in their schools—building alliances in the process—and it is how they won a contract that reshaped New York City's educational bureaucracy and enshrined community roles in schooling for the following decade.

At the intersection of racial, class, and gender hierarchies, paraprofessionals worked as complete human beings with multiple, overlapping selves: parents, community organizers, educators, workers, and unionists. They did so through "everyday rituals of democratic practice": meetings, conversations, shared work, shared drinks, and the instruments of mass mobilization—pickets, printed materials and the popular press.[155] They articulated their own vision of themselves as legitimate educators and deserving workers, and while they did not have the power to define their roles completely, they organized in coalition with their allies to produce the best possible result that they could. The years to come would reveal where and how this victory produced para power, and what new and ongoing challenges demanded more organizing.

Albert Shanker (left) and Bayard Rustin march over the Brooklyn Bridge to demand the preservation of paraprofessional jobs, October 6, 1970. American Federation of Teachers Audiovisual Collection, Walter P. Reuther Library, Archives of Labor and Urban Affairs, Wayne State University.

CHAPTER 4

"You Can Never Believe
Your Good Luck"

Paraprofessional Educators and
Their Allies in New York City
in the 1970s

"Save Paraprofessional Jobs!"

Four thousand paraprofessional educators approved their first contract with the New York City Board of Education in August of 1970. In September, the board fired 1,500 of them.[1] City administrators argued that the expense of the contract itself made this necessary.[2] Paras who did go back to school had to navigate a chaotic transition to "decentralization," a new system of semi-autonomous district-level governance that restructured many programs in which paras worked. In some districts, this reshuffling would lead to even more layoffs. Those paras who had hoped to take up the contract's promise of career training were disappointed, as well. The Board of Education had opposed this provision at the bargaining table and insisted on a year's worth of planning. Paras had won a landmark contract, but their struggles continued.

Paras and their allies organized to respond to these new challenges. Their union, the United Federation of Teachers, formed an "Emergency Citywide Committee for the Public Schools." Led by Bayard Rustin, the committee brought together a broad coalition of New Yorkers, including civil rights organizations that had spent the preceding three years battling the union for community control of schools. Marching across the Brooklyn Bridge to a mass rally at City Hall on October 6, 1970, unionized teachers and veterans of the struggle for community control of schools demanded that the city "save paraprofessional jobs."[3]

Local news anchor John Murray laid out the stakes of paras' fight in an on-air editorial. "Our city's key educational problem during the last few years,"

Murray intoned, "has been the relationship of the schools to the community." Paras, he argued, were a key part of the solution:

> Paraprofessionals are community people, many of them poor, who work in the schools and serve as a bridge between the community and the school. They come with their own specialized knowledge of the community and children. They take some of the burden from over-worked teachers by helping them with supervision. And they serve as interpreters between teachers and pupils . . . the paraprofessional program provides jobs for poor people while enabling them to make important contributions to society. It would indeed be tragic if such large numbers of people who are serving an important function in education were now to be forced back onto the welfare rolls.[4]

Murray also looked to the future, arguing, "Paraprofessionalism is one of the new and more efficient approaches to education that is essential if decentralization is to succeed."[5]

Murray's editorial described paras' labor in the same terms they used, and it demonstrated the degree to which activist visions for this work had gone mainstream. His talking points reflected those Bayard Rustin penned in the *New York Amsterdam News* days earlier.[6] A telegram from the leaders of AFSCME DC 37 to the Board of Education read similarly: "Prior to the innovation of paraprofessional programs, education was a proven failure. With the involvement of community residents in school programs came a revitalization of the educational process and a more positive outlook of students toward schools."[7] Writing from Ocean Hill–Brownsville, three parent activists concurred. They demanded "that all paraprofessionals that worked in the schools of District 23 be rehired" and that "all 5.5 million dollars of our Title I money be used for paraprofessional salaries."[8] Fresh off the organizing drive for their first contract, paras had the allies to fight and win. The Board of Education rehired the laid-off paras.

This chapter shows how paraprofessional educators used the power, security, and legitimacy demonstrated by their contract to sustain and expand their labor in New York City's public schools and neighborhoods in the first half of the 1970s. Paras and their allies fought to make New York City's systems of public education, public-sector labor organizing, and municipal governance more equitable and democratic in these years. The institutionalization of para jobs and networks of support for them positioned these community-based educators to play a crucial role in the ongoing and intersecting struggles of Black and Latinx New Yorkers, poor and working-class women, and public-sector workers well beyond their 1960s heydays.[9]

In classrooms and schools, paras continued to work with teachers and administrators to create and support innovative pedagogies, curricula, and school-community partnerships to address the crisis of care in public education. Paras took part in political campaigns and social movements around the city, leading voter registration drives, health fairs, and workshops for social justice in their schools and neighborhoods. In the UFT—now their union—some paras joined the leadership and helped shape the trajectory of paraprofessional work from this vantage. Others joined opposition caucuses to advance alternative visions. Finally, paras went back to school, taking part in career training and expanded college opportunities by the thousands.

As paras organized, they contended with mounting devastation wrought by political neglect and disinvestment in the neighborhoods where they lived and worked. This deepening "urban crisis" presented new challenges to paras and the coalition they had built. Budget cuts were a constant problem, as the city neared bankruptcy and the federal government turned away from urban funding. Many of the social welfare and community action programs supported by the federal War on Poverty were scaled back or eliminated as Richard Nixon declared the "war" over in 1973. The decentralization of the city's school system created a new set of administrators and community leaders, generating new political formulations and new struggles over paraprofessional labor. At the broadest level, the collapse of the postwar political economy that supported working-class New Yorkers in these years put intense pressure on public-sector unions, civil rights organizations, and antipoverty programs: dividing their attention, pitting them against one another, and weakening their support for paras. While the first half of this book charted the rise of paraprofessional programs, this chapter traces their development amid increasingly difficult circumstances in the lead-up to New York's fiscal crisis in 1975.

While tensions in the coalition that supported paraprofessional educators proved productive in the late 1960s, the changes of the 1970s exacerbated these tensions, and this coalition began to pull apart. From the beginning, contests had arisen between educators, administrators, unionists, and community leaders over the shape of paraprofessional programs. In an environment of increasing scarcity, new struggles emerged over who would control access to these jobs and who would define paraprofessional roles, allegiances, and educational strategies. These struggles were compounded by external factors. Municipal budget shortfalls and the resulting threats to teacher jobs occupied the UFT's attention, while contests over local school boards divided and discouraged local organizers in many neighborhoods. The antipoverty programs that had served as midwives to the paraprofessional movement found their federal budgets slashed nearly to the bone, with the city in no position to help them continue their work.

These new challenges undermined the broad, transformative vision for community-based educational work that paraprofessionals and their allies had built in the 1960s. Without the support and attention of community organizers, and without the resources channeled through antipoverty agencies, simply hiring local residents did not transform public schools. Without continued "internal education" to promote solidarity—the process by which teacher allies had convinced their fellows to support the paraprofessional contract—the mere presence of paras in the teachers' union did not necessarily produce a more progressive or egalitarian union. In the face of scarcity and austerity, paraprofessional educators worked as hard as ever, but they found the space in which they operated shrinking and their capacity for coalition building diminished.

Changing Terrain: Deindustrialization and Decentralization in New York City

Historians have documented the damage wrought by the collapse of manufacturing-based economies in the cities of the northeastern and midwestern United States in great detail, charting the decisions and processes that led to the "urban crisis" of the 1970s and the rise of care- and service-based economies.[10] Following World War II, New York City lost hundreds of thousands of unionized manufacturing jobs to the suburbs and Sun Belt and saw millions of tax dollars move with white, middle-class residents, who used federal subsidies in highway construction and suburban home financing to follow these jobs out of the five boroughs. Discriminatory practices in lending, employment, and the districting and provision of municipal services distributed the costs and benefits of postwar urbanism unequally, in both the five boroughs and the wider metropolitan region. By the 1970s, the combination of lost tax revenue and increasing expenditures on social welfare programs strained New York City's municipal budget. Successive mayoral administrations began to implement a series of cuts to municipal services that shifted the costs of these political-economic upheavals onto residents and workers in the city's poorest neighborhoods.[11]

Paraprofessional educators witnessed the devastating impact of these urban crises in their schools and communities. Educational funding and maintenance of school buildings declined, social services for students and their families vanished, and the quality of the housing where they lived declined precipitously. Unemployment soared, particularly in New York's Black and Puerto Rican communities in Upper Manhattan, the South Bronx, and Central Brooklyn, where the highest concentrations of paraprofessionals worked.[12]

These changes made paraprofessional work in schools both more difficult and more vital for students, as other social welfare services were disappearing. They also made paraprofessional jobs themselves increasingly valuable assets for working-class Black and Latina women, providing stability in an era of scarcity. This stability allowed paras to raise their families, seek their own educational advancement, and organize in their communities. The city's expanding public sector had provided something of a cushion to deindustrialization; New York added nearly as many public-sector positions as it lost industrial jobs in the 1960s.[13] However, it took civil rights organizing to open these jobs to Black and Latinx residents of New York, who faced double the unemployment rates of white New Yorkers, and it took unionization to guarantee living wages and job security in these positions.[14] Paraprofessional organizing had combined these imperatives. As a result, paras were better positioned than many of their neighbors to respond to the "urban crisis" as educators, unionists, and community organizers.

As the city slipped deeper into economic turmoil at the dawn of the 1970s, it also radically reshaped its school system. After the struggles for community control in the late 1960s, the state legislature "decentralized" New York City's schools in 1970. The new law broke the largest school district in the nation into thirty-one (later thirty-two) separate sub-districts, with limited powers at the elementary and junior high school level.[15] As planned, each district would elect a nine-member community school board to appoint a superintendent, who would in turn appoint principals, recruit teachers, hire paraprofessionals and other support staff, and set the district's educational agenda. However, union contracts and citywide examination lists for teacher hiring remained in effect at the city level, so neither local boards nor their appointed superintendents truly controlled school staffing. The central Board of Education also retained control over budget allocations, curricular decisions, and other major decisions.

The law, as passed, infuriated community control activists. They had fought for local school boards to have control of staffing decisions, believing that the greatest threat to their children's educations came from the presence of racist and incompetent faculty in schools. The United Bronx Parents called the law a "disaster and a distinct step backwards."[16] Aurelia Greene explained, "Under community control, we would have a say on every level, which would include the budget, which would include the curriculum. Under decentralization, we had a say in everything except the budget and except the curriculum."[17] When the first elections for the new community school boards were held in 1970, many community control activists boycotted them altogether, rather than take part in what they believed to be a sham created to mollify, co-opt, and manage poor and working-class neighborhoods without offering them real power. In Ocean Hill–Brownsville, where elections for the "experimental" community control project in 1968 had brought 25 percent of the community to the polls, turnout was less than 5 percent of eligible voters in 1970.[18]

Community school districts (CSDs) inherited a limited, but highly visible, responsibility for public schooling at a moment when many New Yorkers agreed that education was in crisis. This new responsibility was, in many respects, a "hollow prize."[19] As the poor turnout for the initial CSD elections demonstrated, many New Yorkers had little faith in these district boards.

At the same time, pressure to succeed was high. Harlem's Isaiah Robinson, an advocate of community control and member of the IS 201 Governing Committee in 1968, was appointed to the Board of Education as New York City transitioned to its decentralized school system in 1969. In this capacity, he issued a scathing assessment of New York City's educational programs for children living in poverty at a forum called by Manhattan Borough President Percy Sutton. Robinson called the Board of Education's Title I programs a "colossal failure" that had enriched professionals while neglecting eligible students and federally required parent participation. He blasted teachers and administrators for claiming rights to funding through tenure, and scolded paraprofessionals for having "forgotten the purpose of Title I" and "clamoring for a larger share of the funds."[20] Robinson offered several recommendations: chiefly, that the newly created community school districts should be given "complete autonomy" in managing Title I funds, which funded most paraprofessional salaries.[21] Community school districts never received anything approaching "complete autonomy" in their operations, but after a three-year process to phase out the board's existing "centralized programs," districts did gain control of most "targeted funding" from Title I and state sources. Even then, however, proposals had to be approved through a laborious process involving the city, state, and federal government.

The shift to decentralization proved a rocky one for paraprofessionals. The phasing out of centralized programs meant many jobs disappeared, except when local administrators opted to keep them. This, however, was a difficult call for newly elected community school boards to make, as retaining existing programs left little money for school boards and superintendents to spend on their own ideas. Community education centers, in particular, funded by Title III of the ESEA, became the subject of major struggles. Central Harlem's District Five phased out much of its existing programming in the interest of controlling funding. *Kweli,* the newspaper of Robinson's former experimental district at IS 201, wrote in 1971 that diverting funding from Community Education Centers citywide meant that 800 people stood to lose their jobs, "of whom about 600 are 'non-professional' people, mostly mothers, who work as remedial teachers, community liaison representatives, counselors, and teacher aides."[22] These centers played many essential roles in providing social services, beyond what their names suggested. Women's Talent Corps trainee Mercedes Figueroa "organized an anti-narcotics campaign with her neighbors" while working at the IS 201 Community Education Center before it closed in 1972.[23]

The experiences of Community School District Four, in Puerto Rican East Harlem, and District Five, in Central Harlem, are instructive. Differential outlays of funding directly affected paraprofessional educators in these districts. In District Five, political infighting over limited funds encouraged patronage appointments. Constant turnover among superintendents and board members meant programs lacked continuity. District Four, in contrast, maintained many popular and effective programs, particularly in bilingual education, throughout the decade.[24] While federal funding shrank or held steady for many educational innovations, the implementation of national and state-level court mandates for bilingual education, coupled with the passage of explicit legislation at the federal level, spurred the expansion of bilingual programs in the 1970s. For paraprofessionals who spoke another language, this skill became a significant asset in hiring as the decade wore on, as well as a reason to seek continued educational opportunities at CUNY. Bilingual teaching positions would remain open even as hiring freezes kept many paras out of the teaching corps after the 1975 fiscal crisis. As a consequence, multilingual paraprofessionals were over twice as likely as their monolingual fellows to become teachers, according to a 1985 study.[25] These laws, court cases, and the trajectory they created for paraprofessionals and the programs they worked in all serve to explain some of the divergence between local school districts in New York City in the 1970s.

While the disappearance of centralized board programming presented one challenge, the creation of CSDs also undermined smaller units of organization within the school system. Community organizers had pushed for much smaller districts, along the lines of the IS 201 complex or the Parent-Teacher Teams clusters, but a coalition of conservative state legislators, the UFT, and the supervisor's union had pushed through a plan that offered only limited control of thirty-one sizable districts, whose boundaries were largely based on existing administrative units. Community school boards and superintendents sought to manage programs that employed paras at the district level, and this resulted in many programs that had previously been overseen by individual principals or small clusters of schools becoming more centralized. The complex but productive system for hiring paraprofessionals, which had included recommendations from community action programs, local principals, and AFSCME DC 37, was replaced by principal's discretion, often at the recommendation of the community school board or district superintendent. Programs that had once drawn exclusively from parents at a particular school, for instance, might now draw paras from the entire district. As a consequence, patronage increasingly became a problem;

in 1975, District Five Superintendent Luther Seabrook blasted the district's Title I office as a "patronage office" for community school board members.[26] Two years earlier, paras had picketed the district's headquarters to protest their layoffs after the phasing out of centralized programs, with one para carrying a handwritten sign that read "District 5, Give a Damn! Rehire Paras and Teachers Back in the ESEA Programs Now!"[27]

The creation of CSDs also generated new tensions between local activists hoping to implement new programming and UFT leadership seeking to protect existing jobs. While community activists and the union stood together to protect paraprofessional jobs in the fall of 1970, by August of 1971, union president Albert Shanker was writing to Calvin Alston, the chairman of Community School Board Five, regarding a proposal to create new programming in the district with new paraprofessional job titles. Shanker argued, "such a proposal is a blatant violation of the Collective Bargaining Agreement between the UFT and BOE covering paraprofessionals. Further, it is an unconscionable attempt to deprive hundreds of outstanding and dedicated paraprofessionals in your district of their employment."[28] These struggles over jobs were also struggles over paraprofessional allegiances and commitments.

Despite all the challenges of decentralization, paraprofessional educators remained an essential part of educational processes and planning in the 1970s. Under Chancellor Harvey Scribner's tenure (1970–1973), the city produced and disseminated a recruitment booklet for teachers. The booklet contained each district's statistical portrait, with demographic data for students and information about faculty, administration, and staff, including paras. It also contained pitches written by each district to recruit teachers to work with them.

While paraprofessional educators were new to schools all around the nation, and in many respects still considered "experimental," one-third of New York's community school districts cited community-based paraprofessional educators as assets for their school teams. District Sixteen in Bedford-Stuyvesant noted, "The district utilizes the community as a source of its classroom activities. The historic traditions of the community, its people, and its resources are interwoven into the regular classroom program." Several other Brooklyn districts, including District Twenty-Three, into which Ocean Hill–Brownsville was incorporated, claimed paras as well. District Three, on the Upper West Side and in southern Harlem, noted, "paraprofessionals assist many of the teachers in the early grades," while District Four, across Central Park, advertised that "over five hundred and fifty community workers are employed as paraprofessionals in our schools," working in programs that included bilingual interventions, small group instruction, and community education. The Bronx's District Nine, where Jerome A. Greene chaired the school board, claimed "approximately 600 paraprofessionals" among the reasons for its "reputation of being the most progressive and forward looking district in the city." In District Twelve, just north of District Nine, Greene's mentor Richard Parrish ran the school-neighborhood parapro-fessional program, over a decade after he organized the hiring of "parent aides" for after-school programs in Harlem. The district wrote to prospec-tive educators: "We offer the supportive services of a large number of well trained paraprofessionals who are, by nature, very close to the children and, by inclination, very close to their teachers." Across New York City's districts, the presence of paraprofessional educators in public education—feared and challenged by teachers and their union just a few years earlier as they entered public schools—was now sold to prospective teachers as a reason to apply.[29] This fact captured the fundamental tension surrounding paraprofessional educators: their labor was widely acknowledged as essential, but administra-tors still treated them as expendable and exploitable.

"Involved in Everything": Paraprofessional Educators at Work in Schools in the 1970s

Paraprofessional educators had already demonstrated the many ways they could transform the work of education when they won their contract. Despite the upheavals wrought by decentralization, their work continued. Those who worked in classrooms proved particularly versatile. A 1976 evaluation of Winifred Tates, a Women's Talent Corps trainee working in East Harlem, described her as "involved in everything . . . school, home visits, trips, etc." Tates, the reviewer wrote, "has her own reading group . . . the lowest achiev-ers in the class when they started with her. That group is now performing at the same level as the teacher's group. BOE representatives visiting the school constantly mistake her for the classroom teacher."[30]

Decentralization presented many problems for paraprofessionals, but in certain cases it allowed for creative new programming to develop. In North-ern Crown Heights and Bedford-Stuyvesant, Community School District Sixteen hired four local artists as paras to work with several other Caribbean paraprofessionals in the district to teach steel drums. Their grant applica-tion explained that the program was designed "for children to develop new musical skills and an appreciation of West Indian folk music."[31] The pro-gram reached 3,000 students as the Caribbean population of Crown Heights boomed in the 1970s, and its performing ensemble toured the city and ser-enaded Office of Education program leaders in Washington, D.C.

While the overall trend in the 1970s was toward defunding and shut-tering federal programs, some new institutional frameworks did provide opportunities. One example was an after-school tutoring program called

"Youth Tutoring Youth," developed by the Career Opportunities Program (COP), a national paraprofessional-training program inspired by New York City's Frank Riessman and run in cooperation with Model Cities programs.[32] Launched in 1970, Youth Tutoring Youth trained middle and high school students as reading tutors for younger children, seeking the "double thrust of enriching the young 'teacher' as well as the student who has tuned out the message of the structured classroom but may be more receptive to the efforts of a classmate, a neighbor, or a kid who could 'make it' and still communicate with the youngster who needs help."[33] Paraprofessionals and teachers shared in managing this program, which espoused the goal of involving "parents, indigenous teachers and paraprofessional personnel who have a stake in the community and an emotional investment in the progress of their children, hence improving communication and interaction between the schools and the members of Harlem—East Harlem Model Cities community."[34] Reviewing the program in 1972, the on-site director, Edward Grant, noted paras' critical role. Not only did they help select and pair tutors and students, but because paras were "able to empathize" with these students, they also were able "to make the tutor aware of the things in his experience which can be used to teach others."[35] The proposals for Youth Tutoring Youth diagnosed the crisis of care in education and prescribed community-based empathy and emotional investment. Paraprofessional labor was glue that held it all together.

As budget cuts froze teacher hiring, the work of paraprofessional educators made learning possible in overcrowded classrooms. However, their work became increasingly difficult as principals sought to fill gaps in staffing with para labor. Marian Thom, working on the Lower East Side, found herself in frequent conflict with administrators who asked her to take on secretarial tasks or work off the clock. In doing the latter, administrators frequently exploited the community commitments of paras, often in sexist fashion. In one instance, Thom's principal expected her to act as a crossing guard, arguing that she walked students home anyway as a favor to their mothers, her friends. Knowing paras cared, administrators gladly exploited that care.

Thom, who became an organizer of paras for the UFT, told her coworkers to fight back, to protect both their own jobs and those of other school workers. As she explained, "they're not going to hire another secretary because you're doing the work . . . they always try to get you to do something that you're not supposed to do. But you got to hold the line."[36] Membership in the UFT made Thom's stand possible. The contract allowed paraprofessionals across the city to assert contractual rights to work as more than catch-all maids and assistants for principals.

Clarence Taylor, who started his career in education as a paraprofessional in the mid-1970s before becoming a special education teacher and, later, a renowned historian of education in New York City, recalled serving as an all-purpose stopgap educator in Brooklyn in a 2015 interview. "My duties were to assist the teacher," Taylor noted, "but in many cases, paraprofessionals were running the classroom . . . teachers obviously relied heavily on paraprofessionals."[37] His work included everything from leading Black History month celebrations to administering discipline: tasks that combined pedagogical and curricular work with classroom management far beyond what official titles like "aide" and "auxiliary" suggested.

The Problem of Punishment Revisited: Paras as Police, Paras Instead of Police

A toxic combination of genuinely chaotic, overcrowded classrooms and sensationalized fears of Black and Hispanic students produced the United Federation of Teachers' infamous "disruptive child" contract provision in 1967. As the 1970s dawned, real chaos and sensational stories of youth violence continued their infectious spread. Nationally, the American Federation of Teachers declared an epidemic of school violence and asserted that teachers feared for their safety on the job.[38] Locally, New York City public schools implemented new policies that brought uniformed officers into public schools, slicking the pipeline from school to prison.[39]

At ground level, problems of order, discipline, and authority in schools came in many forms. Parents and community activists had protested the UFT's "disruptive child" proposal and criticized teachers for punishing their children instead of teaching them. At the same time, some parents also criticized young, often white, teachers deploying alternative pedagogies without structure or discipline.[40] These simultaneous critiques—too much discipline and not enough classroom control—seemed contradictory at first glance, but they demonstrated the degree to which the standards of classroom behavior and the disciplinary process were divorced from, and inscrutable to, students and their parents.

Paraprofessionals used their connections to parents and community to render discipline more specific to local social conditions and more legitimate for students and parents. Clarence Taylor remembers that paras in his Brooklyn school would "turn to the teachers and say, 'look, you have to do something about this,'" when teachers tried to ignore serious disciplinary problems.[41] At the same time, and particularly in special education settings, paras resisted teachers' efforts to suspend or otherwise banish students from their classrooms, often saying, "Look, maybe I can take the student out of the room, I can handle the student in another way." Particularly in junior high schools and high schools, such interventions made the difference between minor and major punishments, which held significant sway over student futures. Clara Blackman, a coordinator for the Women's Talent Corps and later the assistant director of guidance for New York City schools, noted in an interview in the late 1980s that paras "could see the problems that were encountered with certain children in the school that they could off-set to some extent in the community. . . . They would be in a position to transmit to parents in the community some of the problems that they perceived in the school."[42]

These immediate interventions surely made a difference for innumerable students at their most upset and vulnerable moments in school. As a matter of policy, however, they represented a form of humane triage in a system that was growing ever more inhumane and punitive. Where teachers had once sought unilateral authority to remove students from their classrooms, they now often abdicated such authority entirely, handing it over instead to school safety officers.[43] The presence of these officers, at the intersection of schooling and policing, ensured disruptions now led to criminal records and consequences.[44]

Some teachers and paras actively resisted administrators' and teachers' embrace of punitive policies. The Teacher Action Caucus (TAC), a leftist UFT caucus in which Taylor was active, argued for community-based discipline in response to rising calls for police and security forces in schools on the union's right wing. One of the TAC's first newsletters in 1970 offered a "position on violence" that demanded the "elimination of all police from the schools and the replacement of police by parent aides."[45] The demand echoed that of high school student organizers at Franklin K. Lane one year earlier (discussed in Chapter 2), who coupled their call to hire more Black teachers and aides in the spring of 1969 with a demand for the "immediate removal of any/all personnel who are not employed by the New York City Board of Education" (by which, Noah Remnick explains, the student organizers meant police and security personnel).[46] This alternative vision for care instead of punishment did not come to pass, but the TAC continued its resistance to punitive educational policies throughout the 1970s, advocating instead for community-based, restorative forms of discipline and conflict resolution.

Paraprofessional Educators in
UFT Chapters and Caucuses

The TAC's organizing was part of a broader debate about the place of paras in the United Federation of Teachers—and in the union's school-by-school chapters and political caucuses—that emerged after unionization. Unionization delivered significant material opportunities for paraprofessional educators, but it also revealed the limits of the paraprofessionals' supporting coalition and challenges to transforming the work of education the way activists envisioned. Nonetheless, paraprofessional educators worked to reshape official

UFT programs, local chapters, and left caucuses in the 1970s, and their work was part of a larger, national shift in the demography, policy focus, and leadership of public-sector unions.[47] Union membership offered training and resources to paraprofessionals organizing in their own communities and also created new spaces for debates about the meaning and future of their work.

Within the United Federation of Teachers, the Paraprofessional Committee, which had led the 1970 bargaining battle, became the official vehicle for paraprofessionals' continued advancement. The primary role of this committee, which was chartered as a formal chapter of the union in 1973, was coordinating collective bargaining, which included canvassing paraprofessionals at regular monthly meetings and in their schools. While shrinking city budgets made paraprofessional bargaining a constant challenge in the 1970s, the committee succeeded in expanding the bargaining unit and winning additional bread-and-butter gains for paras throughout the decade, starting with the second paraprofessional contract campaign in the fall of 1972. The Paraprofessional Committee's mobilization generated messages of support from City Councilor Carter Burden, State Assemblyman Edward H. Lehner, and Congressman Edward I. Koch, who telegrammed the Board of Education to urge "a reasonable and fair agreement for thousands of paraprofessionals in our educational system" in December of 1972.[48] When the paras' contract expired at the end of the year, the Teacher Action Caucus called for a mass demonstration "of all staff members, parents and students" at Board of Education Headquarters on January 2, 1973, asserting, "Paraprofessionals are our fraternal brothers and sisters and the traditional slogan that unity makes us all strong is just as true today as it ever was!"[49]

This groundswell of support pushed the Board of Education to add all paraprofessionals in grades K–12 to the bargaining unit, bringing the number of unionized paraprofessionals in New York City up to 10,000 (comprising roughly one-sixth of the UFT). The contract paras won in the spring of 1973 included raises above cost of living that brought para salaries closer to those of teachers, and the full inclusion of paraprofessionals in the UFT Welfare Fund, including better health and dental care, disability insurance, and college scholarships for paras' children.[50]

The UFT's Paraprofessional Committee also did the day-to-day work of addressing paraprofessional grievances and fighting to preserve paraprofessional jobs on a school-by-school, district-by-district basis. This sometimes brought the union into conflict with community school boards. Marian Thom attended budgeting meetings at her school in the 1970s because "they always try to get rid of the paras, you know, they'll spend it on other stuff."[51] Thom's principal came to expect her presence, and to budget for paras as a result.

In addition to leading continued collective bargaining efforts and coordinating the day-to-day fights, the committee held regular meetings and hosted leadership training for paraprofessional building and chapter representatives. Under Velma Murphy Hill's leadership, paras traveled to weekend conferences in Westchester and Long Island, where they heard from Bayard Rustin and A. Philip Randolph on such topics as "civil rights," "collective bargaining," and "the history of the labor movement."[52] UFT paras took their success story on the road, too, sending representatives to conferences, including one hosted by Frank Riessman in December of 1970 that brought unions and low-income workers from across the country together to discuss organizing strategies for paraprofessionals in many professions.[53]

The formation of the Paraprofessional Chapter within the UFT in 1973 broadened these efforts. The chapter's constitution bears the unmistakable stamp of its parent organization but also asserts aims particular to paras. Among the chapter's stated objectives were: "To cooperate to the fullest extent with the labor movement and to work for a progressive labor philosophy to awaken in all paraprofessionals a labor consciousness and a sense of solidarity with labor," "To promote education as a social agency for developing the capacities of the young; for enlightening adults, and for working toward a society motivated by the ideal of service and democratic participation," and "To make paraprofessionals aware of their political responsibilities."[54] The chapter published a regular newsletter, *Para Scope*, and hosted an annual "Salute to Paraprofessionals," at which graduates of the career ladder program were honored. They also organized voter registration drives and disseminated information about union and local school board elections in their communities.[55] Hill trained paras to present at community school board meetings and church services through a public-speaking training program the chapter created dubbed "Labor in the Pulpit." As Hill recalled, "when they went to church, they could talk about the program, why the program was important to the community and to the individual."[56]

The "Salute to Paraprofessionals" and other graduation ceremonies served to celebrate and legitimate paras' efforts in schools, and also to recruit community and political allies. Mayor Lindsay attended the first luncheon in 1973, and local politicians continue to make appearances yearly. It also highlighted paraprofessional achievements at the schools where they worked. As Shelvy Young-Abrams recalled, "Then the beautiful part is some paras, when they're nominated, their whole school comes out, their principals come out, just to spend the day with them."[57]

Gathering together, whether in chapter meetings or at weekend conferences and events, also gave paraprofessionals opportunities to develop solidarity across the wide range of roles they performed in schools, and to articulate their own visions for their work. Marian Thom remembers the challenge of attending monthly organizing meetings that ran late into the evening, but she felt that "in a way it helped, because it was like a camaraderie."[58]

Shelvy Young-Abrams remembered, similarly, that regular meetings helped "to make sure we continue that fight and not turn around" in the 1970s, as preserving para jobs required constant organizing.[59]

In these meetings, paras shared their experiences of balancing home and work, dealing with recalcitrant teachers and administrators, and trying to further their own education. The strength they built in these meetings carried outward to challenges both within the union and in the wider governance of their schools. Pearl Daniels, who worked as a coordinator at the College for Human Services (originally the Women's Talent Corps), noted that such conversations were often raw with emotion. As she put it,

> No matter where they go, no matter what income they get to, they stay with that low income minority mentality . . . it's probably because you kind of feel if you can move, you can't move out of the minority statistics . . . and if you start thinking and acting different then you feel like you've betrayed the people that are still there.

Daniels's assessment bore the mark of dominant thinking about poverty as culture, but she did not articulate this position to demean WTC trainees. Rather, Daniels included herself in this group, adding, "you see, with us you never can believe your good luck."[60] Negotiating the multiple levels at which they worked—family, community, school, union, and city—was a constant challenge. Gathering together helped paras move through these worlds in solidarity.

The UFT officially recognized paraprofessionals as full and equal voting members of their school chapters and the union at large, but in practice, paras had to fight for equality within their chapters and union. At her school in Queens, a teacher told Maggie Martin, "oh, you can't run for chapter leader because you're a paraprofessional." Martin showed the teacher her contract and told her, "In the UFT everyone votes: paras and teachers, guidance counselors, anyone who's a UFT member has a right to vote."[61] Martin won the election and went on to lead her school's chapter, but at other schools, paras had a harder time breaking into union officialdom. In the early 1980s, Clarence Taylor quit the local chapter at his school after they refused to create a position of "paraprofessional representative" in the building.[62]

The chartering of the Paraprofessional Chapter in 1973 helped to formalize paraprofessionals' place within the larger union and created positions for paras in the UFT's delegate assembly, a body composed of several hundred UFT members. In elections held in 1974, paras touted their commitment to their communities as well as their service in classrooms and unions, projecting their own visions of community-based education within the official space of union democracy. One para noted her work as an "active, participating parent" in the local PTA, while another cited "100 years of service," among

which she counted twenty years as a Brooklyn resident, eighteen as a member
of her church, ten as a PTA member, and seven as a paraprofessional.[63] In
defining their lives and work in this way, paraprofessional educators connected their work and organizing to the survival of their communities.

Not all paraprofessionals embraced the UFT's leadership. Some joined
with the Teacher Action Caucus and other rank-and-file opposition groups to
demand a more substantive commitment to community empowerment from
their union. The TAC called for paraprofessional salaries to be annualized
beginning in 1972, issuing statements that "paraprofessionals are regular
members and an integral part of the school staff . . . the services they perform
are essential to the operation of schools."[64] Local groups of TAC teachers
supported parent and paraprofessional campaigns in CSDs around the city.
TAC organizers backed a boycott by parents in District Four that demanded
"more paraprofessionals" and led after-school training for paras and teachers
in small-group reading in District Three.[65]

The Teacher Action Caucus, to Clarence Taylor, often felt like "the only
caucus in the union that was offering to represent paraprofessionals in any
serious way."[66] In this capacity, they frequently challenged the UFT's leadership head on, which included picketing at UFT headquarters on occasion. In
December of 1972, TAC members circulated a flyer in advance of the expira-
tion of the paras' first contract emblazoned with the words "URGENT" and
"Paraprofessionals and Teachers United" that argued "Unity of paraprofessionals and teachers is essential in order to win better contracts for both. Will
UFT President Shanker continue to treat paraprofessionals as second-class
union members?"[67] When the flyer reached Shanker's office, someone wrote
a note on it in pencil that read, "This is what I was afraid of. Next they will
ask for a teacher's license. They already believe they are qualified teachers."[68]
While only a small percentage of New York City teachers and paraprofessionals joined the TAC, their vocal presence in the UFT demonstrated that
paras were not simply managed from the top down, and that para programs
remained sites for envisioning community-based education in new ways.

A citywide movement to transform the UFT did not, ultimately, emerge
from paraprofessional organizing. Even before the 1968 teacher strikes,
Albert Shanker had moved to consolidate his power in the UFT by creating
and helming a "disciplined caucus" that did not countenance open debate
among caucus members, who dominated the ranks of the UFT's staff, executive council, and delegate assembly. Lois Weiner notes that this degree of
control was "highly unusual" when compared to other labor unions and gave
Shanker enormous power to marginalize and punish his political opponents
within the UFT.[69] This approach, Stephen Brier writes, was also informed
by Shanker's close relationship with socialist thinker and organizer Max
Shachtman, whose "kind of 'kill-or-be-killed' mentality toward his political

opponents" and staunch anti-Communism (at a time when many on the New Left were looking to Communist and Communist-affiliated anticolonial movements abroad for inspiration) shaped Shanker and the UFT leadership's hostility toward the TAC and other left caucuses.[70]

Still, at the local level, TAC paras and teachers worked together throughout this era to improve school-community relations and promote new kinds of pedagogy and curricula for their students. They also pushed key priorities like annualization into mainstream union politics, helping to improve para job security. And unlike Shanker, they encouraged paraprofessionals to embrace their community connections and to maintain their commitment to social movements, a process that played out in the challenging world of decentralized districts.

Paraprofessionals or "Community-Based Educators"? Freedom Struggles and Alliances

Community organizations fighting for civil rights and social justice had proved instrumental in creating paraprofessional programs. Organizations including the United Bronx Parents (UBP), the Harlem Parents Committee, the IS 201 Governing Board, the Morrisania Education Council, and many others had led the fight to bring local residents into public schools as part of a holistic vision of community-centered education. They aimed to generate high-quality, culturally responsive pedagogy and curriculum for students and to redistribute the vast resources of public schooling to students, parents, and community members. While the bitterness of the 1968 UFT strikes made the leaders of these organizations wary, many cautiously supported the paraprofessional unionization drive, largely at the request of the paras themselves. Still, well into the 1970s, leaders of these organizations continued to see both the paraprofessional movement and the larger fight for educational self-determination as unfinished revolutions. They frequently sought paraprofessional support for ongoing struggles and worked to redefine paraprofessional labor itself.

In making their case for paraprofessionals as community-based educators, community groups deployed language very different from that of the Board of Education or UFT in describing the work of education and the women who did it as paraprofessionals. The UFT held fast to the term "paraprofessional"—highlighting the incomplete status of these teachers in training—and the board continued to employ a range of job titles, including "educational assistant," "educational auxiliary," and "family assistant." Community organizations, in contrast, preferred to highlight paras' status either as community members or parents. In a 52-page handbook titled "A Parent Guide for Community-Based Educational Workers in Schools," the Central

A Parent Guide for Community-Based Educational Workers in Schools (cover). Published by the New York New Careerist Association and the Central Brooklyn Neighborhood College, Education Action Program, May 2, 1970. Annie Stein Papers, Box 21, Folder 5, University Archives, Rare Book & Manuscript Library, Columbia University in the City of New York.

Brooklyn Neighborhood College and the New York New Careerist Association announced, in 1970, "This book is dedicated to all 'para-professionals' and anticipates the day that they are recognized as COMMUNITY-BASED EDUCATIONAL WORKERS [emphasis original]."[71] The booklet argued that the term "paraprofessional" was not chosen by those doing this work, and that the term "limits [paras] in your own eyes, and in the eyes of the community." The authors argued that the term community-based education worker "describes *who you are* and leaves lots of room for *what you can do*—and we think that is important." The booklet offered a history of the paraprofessional movement that highlighted community contributions, emphasized the presence of provisions for community hiring and involvement in the federal funding that supported these positions, and listed resources about schools, the UFT, and community organizations for paras.

The United Bronx Parents, in a similar rhetorical move, referred to paras as "parent-professionals" in their flyers and supporting materials for these workers. The UBP produced guides for parents and "parent professionals" throughout the 1970s. Among their missives was a script for a "Decentralization Roleplay" that included lines for a "Parent-Para-Professional":

> You have just been elected to the new local school board and you are pleased and excited. Many other teacher assistants have contacted you since your election. They have asked you to push the new local board to set up annual and adequate salaries for all paraprofessionals. Also, you have heard of a program somewhere out west where paraprofessionals can go to work 3 days a week and go to college 2 days a week, but are paid full time. You think this is an excellent program for solving the teacher shortage in your schools and you intended to press for these two improvements at your first meeting today.[72]

The UBP's characterization of paras was nuanced and sensitive to many facets of their work. It points to the issue of teacher recruitment, which continued to be a major struggle in parent-led campaigns for educational equality. In this respect, questions of school roles and training overlapped significantly, as the UBP and many other organizations pushed the board and UFT to accelerate training programs and waive credentialing requirements to integrate the New York City teaching corps and to better staff schools in poor and working-class neighborhoods.

The New York Association of Black Educators reached out to paraprofessionals to seek their input on exactly this issue 1972, with a system-wide letter reading:

> All persons who are vitally interested and involved in the education of BLACK children are EDUCATORS. We believe EDUCATORS to be parents,

paraprofessionals, teachers, lunchroom staff, custodial staff, school board
members, community leaders, civic organization presidents, chairmen of
educational committees, supervisors and administrators, guidance counselors, school psychologists and all BLACK people who are responsible for
the education of BLACK children.[73]

The UFT's central office took note of the missive, which seemed to challenge
the union's own gradualist approach (one that kept the basic structure of
teacher credentialing in place).

Paraprofessional educators, even those who embraced the opportunities
the UFT provided, continued to work with and for community organizations, often as allies inside schools. Many served on PTAs, community boards,
and in other roles that their work schedules and job security allowed, and
most continued to have a strong sense of commitment to the struggles from
which they had worked their way into schools. At the College for Human
Services (CHS), formerly the Women's Talent Corps, a 1973 report of the
board proudly asserted that CHS students "are on the frontline and actually
trying to do something about very deep-rooted American problems, racism
and control by the professionals of service delivery."[74] For paraprofessional
educators, this meant a balancing act, continuing to work as employees of
the Board of Education, union members in the UFT, and community-based
activists while negotiating the tensions and conflicts among them.

Considering paras' role as liaisons between the educational bureaucracy
and local neighborhoods, Clara Blackman recalled an episode in her role as
assistant director of guidance "where paras were absolutely indispensable."
The City University of New York (CUNY) adopted an open admissions policy
in 1970, welcoming any high school graduate in the five boroughs, but it made
the announcement after schools had let their students go for the summer.
Guidance counselors were already on vacation far from the inner-city schools
where they worked, but Blackman's team "got in touch with the supervisors
of guidance in each district to corral the paraprofessionals they had on staff in
the district, to visit the homes of the high school graduates, to apprise them
and their parents of what was in the offing for them if they so choose." The
enormous uptick in college-going in New York City in the 1970s as a result of
open admissions, particularly for Black and Latinx students, is well known.[75]
Paraprofesssional educators took the time to promote this opportunity while
fighting for their own contract in the summer of 1970.

Building a Career Ladder for Paraprofessional Educators

One year later, paras were going back to school themselves. New York City
had created the most comprehensive and innovative training and "career

ladder" program for paraprofessionals in the nation, the Paraprofessional-Teacher Education Program (PTEP) at CUNY.[76] The Board of Education and CUNY jointly created PTEP in the fall of 1970 after the UFT won a provision for paid training in the paraprofessional contract in August. The program built on studies and examples developed in New York City by scholars, anti-poverty programs, and activists in the late 1960s, but unlike these pilot and demonstration projects, it was available to every paraprofessional in the city and fully integrated into union-negotiated systems of advancement within the schools bureaucracy. Thousands of women registered for classes when the program began in January of 1971, and until 1976, when the city's fiscal crises caused its closure, thousands of paras each year earned credits and degrees from PTEP. By the late 1970s, the UFT counted over 1,500 public school teachers who had started their careers as paras, and 2,000 by the early 1980s. Tens of thousands of other paras were earning higher salaries because of the training and degrees they had accumulated, whether in their original positions in schools or in the wider labor market. Paras used these newfound educational resources not just to improve their own lives, but also to advocate and organize for the collective advancement of their families, their schools, and their wider neighborhoods as the urban crisis deepened.

Arthur Pearl and Frank Riessman popularized the idea of a "career ladder" in *New Careers for the Poor*, in which they laid out a general model for human services training that began with hiring "indigenous nonprofessionals" to conduct relatively simple and rote tasks. These "new careerists," as Riessman was calling them by the 1970s, would then train as they worked, acquiring formal credentials and new workplace responsibilities over several "rungs" en route to becoming fully licensed teachers, social workers, or nurses.[77] Riessman's belief in on-the-job training was informed by his work with antipoverty agencies.

Many paraprofessionals sought work in schools because they hoped to become teachers, spurred on by promises from the Board of Education that such training would be offered. The board created a small Auxiliary Careers Education Unit in 1968, and some antipoverty groups—most notably the Morrisania Education Council, under the leadership of Jerome A. Greene—won federal grants to provide training. But for most paraprofessionals, access to teacher training was an empty promise. In Gladys Roth's 1968 study of paraprofessionals for the UFT, hundreds of paraprofessionals expressed their desire for more and better training, both to improve their effectiveness in the workplace and to allow them to advance as educators toward becoming teachers. The UFT won the allegiance of paraprofessionals in the 1969 election over AFSCME DC 37 in large part because they promised that their status as an educators' union would help them provide the access to teacher training paras sought.

United Federation of Teachers paraprofessionals take a high school equivalency exam, June 27, 1970. United Federation of Teachers Hans Weissenstein Negatives; PHOTOS.019.001, Box 14: Item 12709, Tamiment Library & Robert F. Wagner Labor Archives, New York University.

When the Board of Education and the UFT sat down to hammer out the paraprofessional contract in July and August of 1970, the paras present made it clear that they wanted a guarantee of teacher training opportunities for all paraprofessionals. Velma Murphy Hill, who chaired the para bargaining committee, recalled that the board's representatives were incredulous, saying, "You know, they don't want to go to school. These are women with families." The board also feared the cost of developing a training program at such a scale, which had never been done before.[78] Teachers were concerned, as well, with the potential cost of such a program. As teacher and union activist Leonora Farber recalled, "there was a kind of concern that the union would use too much of its resources in their para program, and that would take away from the resources being used to further the benefits of teachers."[79] Nonetheless, paraprofessionals and their union persisted in the demand for a comprehensive career-training program, and when the contract was signed, it included such a provision, enforced by language that promised millions of dollars to the UFT to train paras themselves if the board did not start the program by February 1971.

Thus, in the fall of 1970, the Board of Education began to create what became PTEP, racing against a clock that pushed the board into action. Central Board Member Seymour P. Lachman rallied a team of four Board of Education administrators, three CUNY administrators, and five union representatives from both the UFT and DC 37 (whose paras had signed a contract identical to the UFT's weeks later). The team debated questions of curriculum, program structure, and funding in the final months of 1970.[80] Three contextual factors influenced the path this committee chose for PTEP: successful training programs that served as models; cautionary tales of programs, some with promise, that failed or were discontinued; and most broadly, the scores of Black and Latinx uprisings on college campuses in the late 1960s and early 1970s.

While PTEP was to become the largest "career ladder" program in New York City's history, it was far from the first; as discussed in previous chapters, scholars and activists had created "model" and "demonstration" programs with federal grants around New York, including those run by HARYOU and Mobilization for Youth. At New York City's Bank Street College, Garda Bowman and Gordon Klopf had gathered many of the best practices for paraprofessional employment and training from around the country, including the work of Frank Riessman, in their influential 1968 report *New Careers and Roles in the American School*. Bowman and Klopf made a strong case for the added value of paraprofessional training opportunities in improving these programs.[81]

Indeed, even as the Board of Education argued that a comprehensive training program was costly and unnecessary at the bargaining table in the summer of 1970, it approved a trio of training programs designed "to promote the entrance into the teaching profession of low-income persons, particularly from minority groups, and to develop and implement a program which will allow for differentiated levels of staff utilization."[82] These included an NYU-sponsored program in Chinatown, Fordham University's "Trainers of Teacher Trainers" (TTT) program, and Riessman's federally sponsored "Career Opportunities Program."[83] All these models were discussed and dissected as the board moved forward.

The importance of building a sustainable program also influenced the board's ultimate decision to integrate paraprofessional education with the existing structure of CUNY as much as possible. Programs funded solely by federal grants, or run outside of existing institutional programming, ran the risk of being cut as funds ran out or priorities at institutions changed. One example was the Parent-Teacher Teams program discussed in Chapter 2. Despite tremendous support for the program, it was discontinued by 1970, after Columbia University's administration refused to accept paraprofessional trainees as college students in its General Studies track. Ford Foundation support for the program dried up soon afterward, and Parent-Teacher Teams disappeared as the community school districts were rearranged. Hope Leichter, who directed the training program, in which many women did earn high school diplomas, described the abrupt rejection as "traumatic." As Leichter explained, "the unions played into the creation of not just an idea of jobs, but jobs that were central to the institutional structure at the time," guaranteeing access to training in a way that her philanthropically funded program could not.[84]

The Fordham TTT program, which was repeatedly cited as a successful example by the team that built PTEP, met a similar end in 1971, despite the pleas of the paraprofessionals enrolled in it. One wrote, "We are putting forth every human effort to reach the standards that our society requires by the attainment of our Baccalaureate Degree. . . . We have made the utmost sacrifices in order to devote time and mind to this program and had expected to see the program through to its completion," but the board's reply simply noted that the state program that funded the project had been cut by 90 percent and added, resignedly, "although we believe your proposed program . . . evidences great potential for providing teachers with worthwhile educational experiences, we are unable to offer any financial support."[85] These programs' fragility and impermanence served as a reminder of the power of collective bargaining to guarantee what goodwill, hard work, and outside funding did not.

Along with their consideration of these immediate models and pitfalls, and the unionized paraprofessionals' demands, the team that built PTEP was also influenced by the revolutions on college campuses in the 1960s and 1970s. While chaotic scenes at prestigious universities are the most popularly remembered—Columbia, Cornell, Harvard—recent scholarship has emphasized that Black and Latinx students led student uprisings across the nation, in public urban universities as well as in elite enclaves. These scholars have shown that student organizing was intimately connected to the wider movements from which it sprang. In addition to well-known demands for Black and Hispanic Studies programs, the recruitment of more faculty and students of color, and the recognition of institutional racism, these campus movements pushed for universities to engage in service to the communities they served, and to create opportunities for people in the communities that surrounded them, including through new adult education programs.[86] Protests at City College of New York and Brooklyn College in 1969 and 1970 highlighted young New Yorkers' demands for CUNY to open enrollment not just to all eligible high school students, but also to all those who needed access to college education to survive in the city's increasingly post-industrial economy.

Joseph Monserrat, the Board of Education's Puerto Rican chairman, connected these movements to the task of creating PTEP in a December memo to the team. While noting the haste with which the program had to be built, Monserrat urged big ideas on the committee, warning against falling into the "familiar trap of rushing to apply band-aids where major surgery is needed." The "issue of career training for paraprofessionals," he argued, "draws attention to the entire question of teacher 'professional' training within the New York City school system." While criticism of New York City's schools by Black and Puerto Rican activists was familiar to those at the board, he noted, "there have been equally strident voices calling for reform and renewal of university programs which provide the teachers for these schools." Monserrat argued that the board should listen to them and see their task as crucial to the schools' survival.

> Major changes constantly taking place in our society and our city, including changing values, new legal requirements, changing technological needs as well as demographic and ethnic population shifts create a constant need for evaluating ongoing programs and for the development of new ones . . . educational realities of our public education system in the United States have always required this type of continuing education programs [sic] for our educators, but never has this need been greater than it is now. Never have the stakes been as high: the continued existence of public education.[87]

According to Monserrat, the building of this new career ladder program was an essential step, not just for paras but also in the remaking of teaching and learning for the modern city. After constant scrambling, and with about $1.5 million in funding cobbled together out of the Board of Education's budget, the UFT's Welfare Fund, and CUNY's budget, paraprofessionals were invited to sign up for their first semester of college training in the spring of 1971.

Velma Murphy Hill still gets overwhelmed when she remembers the way paraprofessional educators responded to these new opportunities, especially in light of the board's dismissal of their academic interest and aptitude at the bargaining table. Thousands of paras packed UFT offices in all five boroughs, jammed phone lines, and lined up around the block to sign up on the very first day they could. Hill spent the day driving across New York City to help overworked administrators with tears in her eyes.[88] "It was so beautiful to see them, you know, registering for school," she recalled years later.[89]

From the start, the Paraprofessional Teacher Education Program was part of an expansive new vision for CUNY. At the newly created LaGuardia Community College, "community outreach and continuing education, programs that would grow to become vital to both the school and the neighborhood, received a great deal of attention from the founders."[90] The college was officially slated to begin classes in the fall of 1971, but it opened its doors a semester early for over 100 paras who had enrolled in the college's new "Education Associates" degree program (one of many degrees available through PTEP)

Paraprofessionals line up to register for college classes at the United Federation of Teachers Manhattan Office, February 2, 1971. United Federation of Teachers Hans Weissenstein Negatives; PHOTOS.019.001, Box 17: Item 13047, Tamiment Library & Robert F. Wagner Labor Archives, New York University.

that spring. These paras thus became the first-ever students at LaGuardia Community College, enrolled in "the first of what would become scores of special programs based on community needs" at LaGuardia and other new CUNY colleges.[91]

Fern Khan, who went on to a long career in higher and continuing education at LaGuardia Community College and Bank Street College, directed the Education Associates program. Beginning in the spring of 1971, she welcomed older Black and Puerto Rican women to a college that was youthful and majority-white at its founding. Interviewed for the college's twenty-fifth anniversary, Khan recalled some trepidation on the part of these women. "They were all extremely motivated," she recalled, "but they underestimated their talents and skills."[92] Khan worked hard to make the program and course offerings relevant and accessible to these new students. English professor John Hyland, a former priest and community organizer who went on to become a leader in the Professional Staff Caucus (an AFT local) at CUNY, recalled teaching a course on "Community Control" in which he brought in flyers and mimeographed materials from Ocean Hill–Brownsville, as well as guest speakers from his time in Brooklyn.[93]

Middle-school teacher and UFT member Leonora Farber worked nights teaching English education at LaGuardia Community College for two very different groups of students.[94] One group consisted of paras in the Education Associates program; the other was young, male graduates of elite universities who were granted a draft deferral for joining the Teacher Corps and teaching for two years in a high-poverty district of New York City (Farber's charges worked in the South Bronx). While Farber noted that the Ivy Leaguers were far more academically prepared than the paras she taught, they found work in the South Bronx "unsatisfactory" and most left after their two years were up (much, she noted, like Teach for America graduates in the 2000s).[95] The paras she taught, by contrast, needed more academic support to get started, "but they were very enthusiastic and they were very ambitious," and they expressed a desire to continue working in the communities where they lived upon completing their coursework.[96]

Interviewed in 2015 about her time at LaGuardia Community College, Fern Khan closed by saying, "I cannot end this without saying the first graduates of LaGuardia were four paraprofessionals."[97] In December of 1972, Diane Faison, Joyce Heron, Lottie Spriggs, and Margaret Madden—who had added extra courses "to finish their degree requirements in about eighteen months"— earned their associate's degrees.[98] Fern Khan hosted a ceremony for them attended by LaGuardia Community College President Joseph Shenker.[99]

The celebrations at LaGuardia were just the beginning. Despite concerns that working mothers would not sign up for college classes, over 3,500 paraprofessionals were taking classes at CUNY by 1974, about one-fourth of those employed in New York City (the UFT, in an internal report, put the number closer to 6,000, which may have reflected yearly rather than semesterly numbers).[100] That same year, about 400 paras were earning high school diplomas each summer, over 3,000 had earned some form of advanced degree, and 400 were working as teachers in New York City.[101] By 1978, over 1,500 former paraprofessionals had become teachers.[102]

The Paraprofessional-Teacher Education Program was open to any paraprofessional educator with a high school education. Those who had begun working without one could earn a GED through union-led classes, held across the five boroughs. During the school year, paras received paid release time for two and a half hours each week to attend college or work on their own assignments, and otherwise went to class after school from 3:30 to 7:30 p.m. During the summers, paraprofessionals received a small stipend to attend classes, some of which were specially organized by the union to provide more options for paras to advance in the summer. These stipends were particularly valuable, as paraprofessionals worked on 10-month contracts until 1983 and typically registered for unemployment in the summers, even after unionization. Tuition was free, as it was at all CUNY colleges, and paras could attend classes at nearly every school in the system, including the many newly built community colleges, like LaGuardia, that absorbed thousands of new students into the CUNY system after open enrollment began in the 1970s. While working all the way up to a master's degree in teaching took roughly six years, paras earned associate's and bachelor's degrees along the way, and in between these formal degrees, they earned salary bumps and increased responsibility in schools when they met union-negotiated benchmarks for credits.[103]

The Legacy of the Paraprofessional-Teacher Education Program

Paraprofessional reviews of the Paraprofessional-Teacher Education Program were overwhelmingly positive, and many still recall it as the biggest victory of their unionization drive. Those paras who went through the program saw the opportunity as bigger than themselves and their own desire for personal advancement; to them, it was a program of community uplift. Oneida Davis, a para who became a teacher (though she did not train at CUNY herself), described the process in an interview in 2014:

> Becoming part of the UFT, we received time to go and pursue our credits . . . that's how most people continued with their higher education. And eventually became teachers, eventually became principals, assistant principals, and eventually became superintendents wherever they were. So it was a good thing that came to the community.[104]

Shelvy Young-Abrams recalled the program similarly, noting that even community control advocates who had opposed unionization were impressed by the opportunities PTEP offered:

> One of the things that struck everybody was the fact that we were given the opportunity to go to school. We were given an opportunity to make our life better. We were given an opportunity to help. Matter of fact, because we had paras who not only worked during the day, but they also worked

in a lot of community agencies after work, so they had enough time, had enough knowledge and enough respect to do that. . . . You'd be surprised how many of us became teachers.[105]

Reports on PTEP, as well those on related programs, frequently noted that despite balancing work, family, and school, paras maintained higher-than-average completion rates in their courses and programs of study.[106] These reports also cited the impact of educational opportunities on paras' families. The College for Human Services argued that sending mothers back to school legitimated education for their own children and those they taught, claiming "children were proud of their mothers, more willing to help with the housework, stopped being truant, and took a new interest in school work." They quoted one para who reported, "My husband enrolled in college when I did."[107] Velma Hill recalled "going into homes and seeing little kids sort of with brooms, not really sweeping up but trying, and saying, 'You know, my mommy's going to be a teacher, and I have to help.'"[108] The union reinforced paraprofessionals' scholastic accomplishments both through their annual "Salute to Paraprofessionals" and through holding regular graduation ceremonies at schools and community centers across the city.

The Paraprofessional-Teacher Education Program—sought by paraprofessional organizers and guaranteed through unionization—provided unique educational opportunities to working-class women of color in New York City's poorest neighborhoods. Unlike most employment training programs created through the Office of Economic Opportunity (OEO) in the 1960s and the Comprehensive Employment and Training Act (CETA) in the 1970s, PTEP was built into the contractual and institutional structure of paras' existing employment; as they learned more, they earned more—immediately. The program was not a "demonstration" or "pilot" program, but open to all paraprofessionals. Paraprofessionals—even those that did not become teachers—often remember huge percentages of their fellows moving through PTEP and related programs, and some suggest as many as "80 or 90%" became teachers.[109] As Velma Murphy Hill wrote in the *American Teacher* in 1971, the career ladder, more than any other part of the UFT's contract, defined paraprofessional work as "a profession with promise." The contract as a whole, Hill continued, was "more than a story of growth or of some improvement in New York City's public schools. It's also a story of economic justice."[110]

In spite of this enthusiasm, a complete evaluation of the program requires considering multiple scales and levels of its impact. In truth, only a small percentage—less than 10 percent—of paras became teachers. The process took six years, leading one para to worry aloud that she didn't "want to go to my teaching assignment in a wheelchair."[111] And with the baby boom receding, so too was the demand for new teachers. Of 300 paras who earned teaching

United Federation of Teachers celebration for paraprofessional educators who became teachers, 369th Regiment Armory, Harlem, New York City, February 18, 1972. United Federation of Teachers Hans Weissenstein Negatives; PHOTOS.019.001, Box 27: Item 13854, Tamiment Library & Robert F. Wagner Labor Archives, New York University.

degrees in New York City in 1974, the UFT and Board of Education were able to place only 100 in New York City public schools that same year.[112]

These numbers have led some historians to assert that the UFT courted paras with empty promises. Certainly, the number of teachers PTEP produced was not sufficient to support the UFT and Board of Education's expansive assertions that the program would equalize access to teacher training and fully integrate the teaching corps.[113] At the same time, thousands of paras earned degrees, providing higher wages from BOE schedules and expanded opportunities in the wider job market. Many paras moved laterally between governmental and nonprofit agencies in the 1970s and 1980s, taking on related roles as their family situations and workplace opportunities changed. In such a fluid employment environment, holding degrees and college credits greatly expanded opportunities.[114] Paras were also able to take their degrees into the private market. In the year PTEP began, fewer than 10 percent of women in Harlem, the South Bronx, and Central Brooklyn held college degrees. In the city's increasingly post-industrial economy, credentials were ever more valuable for employment opportunities.[115]

As PTEP developed, three notable challenges to the program appeared. First were gendered expectations and the challenge of the "double day," which many paras found overwhelming. Second were questions of training, professionalism, and power, part of ongoing struggles between the board, union, and community groups as to who could lay claim to paras' labor and loyalty. Last but not least were questions about how paras, teachers, and their unions conceptualized their work in light of their training, and whether their labor as paras was primarily for the purpose of teacher training, or of unique value on its own.

Velma Murphy Hill, who received thousands of letters as the first president of the UFT's paraprofessional chapter asking for help enrolling at college, also noted that paras attending school was not always easily negotiated within families. A common request she received was "please talk to my husband, he doesn't want me to go to school."[116] Mercedes Figueroa told her supervisors that her paraprofessional work "raised real problems at home, for her husband was not prepared for his wife to take this sort of career woman, activist role."[117] Amid rapid deindustrialization and skyrocketing male unemployment in New York City, opportunities for female advancement could threaten as well as encourage the men in the family. Marian Thom noted that she never completed her teacher training because her husband worked nights, and she worried, "if I was busy going to college, that I would lose the kids, they would lose something in the process."[118] Though the design of paraprofessional programs had directly confronted, and to some degree alleviated, the problem of the double day and balancing family life with waged labor for working-class women, such issues were never fully resolved, and PTEP took a great deal of time and energy to complete. Those paras who were able to become teachers, including Oneida Davis and Maggie Martin, cited family support in caring for children, making dinner, and doing housework to free up time for their education.

Making PTEP work required personal and family-level negotiations and the rearrangement of household labor. At a larger scale, it provoked neighborhood and citywide debates among paras, activists, and the UFT about the nature and scale of credentialing, and how this new form of "incorporation" into the system would affect paras. While community organizers including Preston Wilcox (as chair of the Women's Talent Corps), the Morrisania

Education Council, and the United Bronx Parents had worked hard to promote training opportunities for paras, they had done so in hopes of transforming systems of credentialing, not merely tracking new people into existing
hierarchies and systems.[119] Joseph Monserrat of the Board of Education
seemed to understand this, as did Audrey Cohen of the College for Human
Services (formerly the Women's Talent Corps), who told an interviewer in
1975 that at CHS, "we're really trying to redefine professional education."[120]

At the UFT, on the other hand, Albert Shanker promoted paraprofessional
education as an assimilationist path into the middle class for paraprofessionals, in deliberate contrast to the community-control visions espoused
by his 1968 adversaries. This reinforced Shanker's belief that parents in
high-poverty communities were not fit to make educational decisions without significant training and education. In a debate with Holcolm McKelvy
of AFSCME over the hiring of pre-kindergarten teachers in 1974, Shanker
hammered this point. When McKelvy expressed concerns that training and
unionization would take positions that had previously been staffed by community members and centralize and professionalize them, Shanker replied:

> The only way to keep the adults in the program in the community is to pay
> them a low wage. This is true. As soon as someone . . . makes a lot of money,
> they do the same thing as anybody else who has a lot of money—they like
> to get a better apartment or buy a nicer home elsewhere . . . that's exactly
> what we should be doing for everybody who lives in a slum or ghetto. Now,
> we had exactly the same problem when we organized paraprofessionals
> . . . the big argument by the so-called "liberals" on the Board of Education
> was that now paraprofessionals would be making so much money that
> they would move out of the community, and they wouldn't relate to the
> children anymore, which is a great argument for permanent starvation.[121]

Shanker's view left little room for community-based empowerment once
paraprofessionals were unionized, as it seems he fully expected them to leave
their neighborhoods.

Shanker's views led some community activists to worry, as Sonia Song-Ha
Lee writes, that "as paraprofessionals began to take more time away from
teaching in order to advance their own careers, parents felt that they became
more detached from their students."[122] Lee cites Sister Gwen Cottman's concern, espoused in a 1974 article, that "If a Paraprofessional is released [from
teaching] four afternoons a week, how does that Paraprofessional get to serve
that child that it's released from?"[123] In April of 1971, *The Black Worker*, the
newspaper of the revolutionary Marxist-Leninist Black Workers' Council,
ran a letter from a para in District 13 in Brooklyn that stated, "Many of us
are dissatisfied with the 'Career Ladder Program.' We must emphasize that
our experience with children plus our on-the-job training with community

provides us with the tools to educate our children."[124] This letter articulated two core dilemmas of training: whether formalized processes would undermine the local connections community organizations valued, and who would decide what forms this training took.

Preston Wilcox had led the construction of an alternative system of training and credentialing at the Women's Talent Corps, which became the College for Human Services, or CHS, in 1970. After his experiences at IS 201, Wilcox became increasingly concerned that professional training would strip the very essence of "community education" from paraprofessional jobs. As he wrote in a memo to a CHS faculty member as board chair:

> I am prepared to state that the CHS is a white racist institution and that its major mission should be to confront itself *first* as a means to deal with that reality. This cannot be reached by enabling Blacks and Puerto Ricans to become "equal to whites." Rather it can only be achieved by enabling Blacks and Puerto Ricans to acquire the skills, desire, and knowledge to refuse to participate in their own oppression.[125]

Wilcox suggested steps for a new educational model for the CHS's paraprofessional trainees, including: "They must be educated as members of their communities of origin."

Wilcox offered a more systematic expression of his position in a 1973 contribution to a national "Black Colloquy" on the Child Development Associate Consortium, in which he argued that training programs had been designed "to develop a lot of competencies designed to transmit counter insurgency, self-rejection, and a desire to colonize others" and "to turn authentic, natural Black mothers into 'professional technicians,' unrelated to the Black community, comfortably subservient to the white community—and ill equipped to reappropriate those natural skills/desires that their mothers had passed on to them."[126] Wilcox closed by stating his unqualified opposition to "the increasing requirement that Black women be trained/educated by Europeans to raise their children—or other children from their own communities." Wilcox's views represented one end of a spectrum, with Shanker's assimilationism at the other. The distance between them highlights the degree to which the purpose of continued paraprofessional education remained undefined, and how it generated conflict between paraprofessionals' allies.[127] The critiques offered by Wilcox and Cottman also demonstrate the limits of maternalism as an organizing principle for paraprofessionals. While practicing activist or community mothering helped paras serve their communities and win support from them early on, maternalist expectations could be wielded to critique paras' efforts at advancement, as well.

One final consequence of the career ladder program, noted by Clarence Taylor, was the way that its existence reinforced a notion of paraprofessionals as teachers in training, and not educators in and of themselves. While this definition of paraprofessionalism had proved crucial to uniting paras and teachers in the 1969 campaign, it perversely justified continuing to pay paras low wages. Taylor later recalled that, when he started as a para in the mid-1970s, "many of the paraprofessionals, in reality, didn't take those classes" and that while the program was valuable, it also contributed to a larger "system of exploitation."[128] Taylor recalled a confrontation with Shanker in which the union president dismissed concerns about low pay for paras and early-career teachers, noting that it was important to focus on increasing top salaries because that was where most career educators would end up. Shanker's comment not only was blind to the realities that only a few paras actually became teachers, but it also demonstrated that, in a cruel twist, the very career ladder that paraprofessionals had fought so hard for could devalue their ongoing contributions to classrooms as paraprofessionals.

Triumph and Trials in the 1970s

Five years after Bayard Rustin declared the "Triumph of the Paraprofessionals," the College for Human Services conducted a series of student interviews that revealed the scope and impact of their graduates' work in public schools. Winifred Tates was "very community focused," "involved in everything," and "constantly mistake[n] for the teacher" in her East Harlem classroom. Georgina Carlo was guiding students at Benjamin Franklin High School through the college application process. She had started as a guidance assistant without a college degree in 1967 but earned her own degree while leading students along the same path and became one of the school's guidance counselors. Mercedes Figueroa was leading anti-narcotics campaigns in East Harlem, while Leatrice Wilkerson was fighting "glaring injustices" in her Bronx school.[129] These interviews captured the wide range of paraprofessional labor in schools and the many ways in which preserving these jobs through unionization allowed community-based education to flourish amid the urban crisis in 1970s New York City.

Nonetheless, as this chapter demonstrates, paraprofessional educators faced continuing challenges in New York City in these years. Even as she led the UFT's paraprofessional chapter, Velma Murphy Hill remembered that unionization "wasn't the final word." As she noted, "I don't remember a year where we didn't have some external conflict that created internal conflict."[130]

In February of 1975, the *New York Times* ran a feel-good story about former paraprofessional educator Marion E. Rose. It was Black History Month, and Rose was being lauded for "her efforts to unite Black and Puerto Rican parents" at PS 49 in the South Bronx, where she had worked in the late

1960s. Like so many paraprofessional educators, Rose's political work began in support of her children. Getting involved with her local parent-teacher association brought her into contact with other mothers. "We didn't realize it then," Rose told the *Times*, "but by making decisions" about school fundraisers and community outreach, she and other parents "were being geared toward the political scene."[131]

Rose, a thirty-one-year-old mother of four, had recently become the first Black Democratic district leader in the South Bronx. In her new role as district leader, she promised "to give blacks an image out there," and also to build unity with Puerto Ricans and poor whites in the Bronx to "get their fair share" of local resources, including jobs at the newly rebuilt Lincoln Hospital.[132] Rose's trajectory reflected the ways paraprofessional positions had become avenues for working-class women's advancement and empowerment in New York City. Her politics demonstrated both pride in her local Black community and savvy in building interracial coalitions to seek resources—particularly jobs—for the wider neighborhood.

In the *Times*'s telling, Rose embodied the transformative vision for community education that had been nurtured by parent and community activism in the South Bronx in the late 1960s and won wide acclaim by the early 1970s. Her experience suggested the possibility that these gains in jobs, resources, and community participation might be amplified through political action in the years to come. Her ascent to this party position—traditionally doled out by Democratic bosses to loyal underlings—was also part of a larger transition in local politics in the 1970s.

As an older generation of white politicians either retired or followed their constituents deeper into the outer boroughs or the suburbs, many Black and Puerto Rican organizers and activists ran for office and won. This process was facilitated, in part, by the creation of new local political offices. In the Bronx, Jerome and Aurelia Greene were elected to the District Nine Community School Board after years of local agitation for community involvement in education. Albert Vann, a former teacher and community control leader from Ocean Hill–Brownsville, was elected to the New York State Assembly from Brooklyn in 1975. Placing people like Rose, Vann, and the Greenes in positions of real political power, coupled with the ongoing ability of the UFT's paraprofessional chapter to deliver real gains at the bargaining table, seemed to bode well for the future of paraprofessional educators in public schooling in New York. What neither the politicians nor the *New York Times* knew, however, was that the city stood at the brink of a fiscal crisis, one that would radically remake politics and policy in New York.

Paraprofessional on strike, member of the San Francisco Federation of Teachers, 1979. SFFT paraprofessionals won their first contract in 1979. American Federation of Teachers Audiovisual Collection, Walter P. Reuther Library, Archives of Labor and Urban Affairs, Wayne State University.

CHAPTER 5

A Union of Paraprofessionals?

The American Federation of Teachers and Paraprofessional Organizing in the 1970s

New Yorkers on the National Stage

While teacher aide and paraprofessional programs did not originate in New York City, New Yorkers played significant roles in their development from the start. The Ford Foundation's sponsorship and promotion of the Bay City, Michigan, experiment popularized the hiring of aides in the 1950s. The city's two programs funded by the Kennedy administration—Mobilization for Youth and Harlem Youth Opportunities Unlimited, Incorporated—served as models for the War on Poverty's embrace of "community action" while pushing the boundaries of what aides could do in schools and neighborhoods. As federal funds from the Elementary and Secondary Education Act rolled out to school districts across the country after 1965, it was Frank Riessman and his "New Careerists" at New York University who wrote the reports and drafted the follow-up legislation encouraging districts to use these funds to hire paraprofessional educators.

If New Yorkers helped to promote and popularize the hiring of local people as paras, however, such hiring remained very much local. Gotham's influence might be recognized in the availability of foundation and federal monies for paraprofessional programs in the 1950s and 1960s, but not in the day-to-day structure of paraprofessionals' labor, organizing, or advancement opportunities. New York City's own Board of Education was only just hiring its first paras in the late 1960s, and these new educational workers had not yet sorted out their places in New York's schools, communities, and labor movement.

The high-stakes, high-profile campaign for a paraprofessional contract in New York City inaugurated a new phase of influence for New Yorkers in paraprofessional programs across the country. Even before the United Federation of Teachers had finalized its first contract in August of 1970, its international union, the American Federation of Teachers, was moving to make the campaign a model for paraprofessional organizing nationwide. The inclusion of a robust career ladder program in the UFT contract both reflected and enhanced Frank Riessman's influence, and it encouraged policymakers to adopt and fund additional New Careers programs elsewhere. Preston Wilcox opposed paras' unionization and career ladder programs; he believed both undermined community control of para jobs and schools more broadly. Nonetheless, Wilcox remained committed to hiring local people to do the work of education. In the 1970s, he used his savvy in program design and grant writing to win funding and develop alternative models for what he called "parent implementation" of new educational practices and policies.

The two chapters that follow explore the ways New Yorkers used lessons learned and models developed in the five boroughs to build, grow, and organize paraprofessional programs across the United States after 1970. Their interventions in these years proved direct, sustained, and consequential. The AFT, the New Careerists, and Wilcox worked with hundreds of school districts and thousands of paras, promoting strategies for unionization, advancement, and community involvement that they had honed in New York City. Para programs remained local by design, and tensions sometimes emerged between New Yorkers and those they worked with on matters of strategy and tactics, but even these conflicts highlight the degree to which New Yorkers had come to shape the trajectory of paraprofessional programs nationally.

This chapter examines how Velma Murphy Hill, Bayard Rustin, and Albert Shanker, among others, used their experiences in New York City to develop a national committee and plan for organizing paraprofessional educators into the AFT. As the primary international union organizing paraprofessionals in the early 1970s, the AFT took a leading role in shaping every aspect of para programs through organizing and collective bargaining in these years. Chapter 6 explores the work of Frank Riessman and Preston Wilcox, who used federal grants to expand their visions for paraprofessional work, advancement, and organizing to a wide audience. These scholar-activists lacked the extensive resources, staff, and organizing capacity of the AFT, which was rapidly growing into one of the largest US unions in this decade. Their impact was less extensive than the AFT's, and in certain respects, it proved less lasting, as both Riessman and Wilcox promoted their visions with federal education funding that Congress either eliminated or let expire in the late 1970s. Still, within these limits, Riessman and Wilcox shaped both the specific programs with which they worked and broader public policies that structured the hiring of paraprofessional educators. Elements of their ideas and efforts continue to shape the work paraprofessional educators do to this day.

Finally, while they are analyzed sequentially here, the paths AFT organizers, Riessman, and Wilcox took as they carried the models and lessons of New York beyond the five boroughs did cross, albeit less frequently than they did in the city. In some cases, this proved productive; Riessman regularly cited the importance of collective bargaining in guaranteeing access to, and funding for, the career ladder programs he and his New Careerists constructed around the country. In other instances, the legacy of conflicts in New York City persisted in new locales; AFT organizers regularly inveighed against the dangers of community control, while Wilcox continued to rail against teacher unionism. While, in these cases, applying lessons from New York City proved limiting, the overall impact of New Yorkers' organizing and advocacy in these years was generative. Across the United States, from major cities to rural areas, these New Yorkers challenged school districts to transform "aide" work into para careers that paid living wages, offered opportunities for advancement, and recognized the importance of paras' labor in building sustained relationships between schools and the communities they served.

Paraprofessionals on the Move: Organizing in the 1970s

In 1985, Velma Murphy Hill sat for an oral history about paraprofessional organizing in New York City and beyond. Hill had led the organizing drives that brought paraprofessional educators into New York's United Federation of Teachers (UFT) in 1969 and secured their first contract in 1970. She chaired the UFT's Paraprofessional Chapter in the years that followed, fighting to secure living wages, basic benefits, career opportunities, and dignity in the workplace for paras across the five boroughs. But that wasn't all. "The New York City program was a very important program," Hill explained, because "it proved something not just for New York but, I think, for the country about what can be done with union organization." As Hill understood it, the New York campaign "provided the impetus for paraprofessional organizing all over the United States."[1] Hill spoke from experience. After her success in New York, the American Federation of Teachers (AFT) asked Hill to chair the National Paraprofessional Steering Committee in 1970. In this role, Hill convened organizers from AFT locals around the country and built a national campaign to unionize paras. By 1988, over 100,000 paraprofessional educators had joined the AFT and secured the benefits of union contracts.[2]

The AFT—and its largest and most influential local, New York's United Federation of Teachers—had been crucial in the evolution of paraprofessional labor in public schools in the 1960s, even though the union's leadership was initially slow to embrace paraprofessional organizing. By the end of the decade, however, it was clear both that paraprofessional educators had become an important part of school staffing, and that these educators were primed to organize for the same power, rights, and respect at school that teachers had won through unionization and collective bargaining. Such was the energy behind paraprofessional organizing in cities across the country that, by the time the UFT finally hammered out its landmark contract, it was not even the first AFT local to do so.

That distinction belonged to the Baltimore Teachers Union, where Lorretta Johnson had led the campaign to organize paraprofessional educators. Johnson's path to working as a para mirrored many of the experiences described by these workers in New York City. A Baltimore native and the ninth child of a union longshoreman, Johnson married her high school sweetheart in 1957 and started her own family shortly thereafter. As her third and youngest child reached elementary school, she began volunteering as a tutor at the school and impressed the principal.[3]

When Baltimore teachers won their first contract in 1966, they included a provision for the hiring of 600 teacher aides. At her principal's urging, Johnson was hired into this new role. She met AFT Field Organizer Godfrey Moore in 1967 and, shortly thereafter, found herself in a typical moment of administrative exploitation. As a blizzard blew in, the district ordered schools closed for the day while teachers were gone for lunch, leaving aides to spend several hours caring for the children and making sure they got home. "That started my union career," Johnson recalled in 2020, "because of the commitment from the principal who said we would get paid, but it never happened."[4] Johnson quickly became an organizer for the union, uniting paras in a fight for grievance procedures as well as raises and pensions, which they won in January of 1970.[5] Johnson joined Velma Hill on the National Paraprofessional Steering Committee in the summer of 1970 with this victory fresh in her mind and ready to spread the word.[6]

The campaigns and victories in Baltimore and New York augured many more to come. Paraprofessionals had already joined the Philadelphia Federation of Teachers and were fighting for their first contract, supported by funding from the AFL-CIO that AFT President David Selden had won for this purpose.[7] Paras in Hartford, Connecticut, voted to join the Hartford Federation of Teachers in November of 1970.[8] The following year, paraprofessional educators all across the country, including those in Detroit, Kansas City, Missouri, and Springfield, Massachusetts, voted to join AFT locals.[9] As with the construction of paraprofessional programs, local conditions and organizers shaped the specifics of these campaigns, and each took shape differently. All of them, however, benefited from the American Federation of Teachers' full-on embrace of paraprofessional organizing at the international level after the successes of 1970.

As in New York City, the AFT's leadership advanced an assimilationist vision to court paras and to pitch their incorporation into the union to reticent teachers. To paras, AFT membership offered the backing of a union that could deliver rights and power on the job, material gains at the bargaining table, and paths to advancement. To teachers, the AFT cast paras as classroom allies on the road to becoming teachers themselves. This strategy emphasized affinities between these workers and preserved the union's professional hierarchy while minimizing paras' connections to parent activists and movements for community control.

As chair of the National Paraprofessional Steering Committee, Velma Murphy Hill drew on her work with Bayard Rustin and A. Philip Randolph to expand the AFT leadership's vision. Hill argued explicitly that integration into the AFT would further the goals of the civil rights movement by generating economic opportunity and political voices for working-class Black women. Hill partnered with like-minded organizers fresh from their own struggles, including Lorretta Johnson, who would assume leadership of the Paraprofessional Committee (today the Paraprofessional and School-Related Personnel, or PSRP, Division) upon Hill's retirement. The vision this committee advanced was certainly integrationist, but it was rooted in the belief that integration would lead to transformation, not just assimilation. Hill, Johnson, and their fellow organizers did not aim to remake paras in the image of middle-class white teachers, but to organize them to win resources, job security, and political education that they could use to speak and act for themselves, their schools, and their communities.

The committee's efforts made an enormous material difference in the lives of thousands of paras across the nation in the 1970s. At a baseline level, the AFT's overall drive to unionize workers who had often been hired temporarily was essential in preserving paras' presence in public schools, particularly once federal support for para hiring declined. The contracts AFT locals won generated wage gains and access to fringe benefits, as well as opportunities for on-the-job training and career advancement in local institutions of higher education. The efforts of these local organizers, coupled with the work of the Paraprofessional Committee, amplified the voices and perspectives of working-class women of color in the AFT.

At the same time, tensions persisted in the union's vision. The AFT leadership continued to struggle with the legacy of the UFT's battle with the community control movement in New York City. As a consequence, official pronouncements played down the degree to which paraprofessional jobs had emerged from local struggles for equality and power in education. This, in turn, limited AFT organizing drives in realizing the political potential of community-school alliances, for both paras themselves and their unions.

A Powerful Weapon in Their Arsenal: The Impact of AFT Organizing

The AFT's commitment to paraprofessional organizing yielded significant gains for paras and their new union throughout the 1970s. In a 1976 study of over 1,000 school districts employing paraprofessionals, Jorie Lester Mark found that in the 265 districts where paraprofessionals were organized, "school systems consistently provide more liberal benefits," including financial and academic support for teacher training.[10] A 1977 review of the Career Opportunities Program (COP) noted similarly, "Teacher unions were involved in urban COP matters, to the considerable satisfaction of the participants, who felt themselves protected in the bureaucratic jungle and found union backing of career lattice arrangements to be a powerful weapon in their arsenal." The report added, approvingly, "The place of paraprofessionals in these teacher-dominated organizations is becoming stronger."[11] The AFT, for its part, gained thousands of new members in the same years that public-sector workers, and particularly teacher unions, faced dwindling municipal budgets, tax revolts, and increasingly hostile attacks on the labor movement from public officials.[12] Organizing paraprofessional educators not only helped the AFT expand its dues-paying membership but also linked the union to the working-class communities from which paraprofessionals were drawn. As the power of private-sector unions in urban politics faded in these years, coalitions of public-sector employees became increasingly important to progressive political efforts of all kinds.

Fully understanding why paraprofessional educators across the nation joined AFT locals—and how they organized their campaigns to appeal to their fellow educators and community members—requires studying local conditions in each particular case. However, certain common concerns and complaints appear in the papers of many locals and in their correspondence with the AFT and its National Paraprofessional Steering Committee (later renamed the National Paraprofessional Committee). As in New York City, paras aimed to achieve three related goals by joining unions: securing living wages and life-sustaining benefits; winning job security, respect, and dignity in schools and their unions; and creating or expanding opportunities for career advancement, including paths to becoming teachers for paras who chose to pursue them.

Union organizing delivered real wage gains throughout the 1970s, even as inflation ate away at raises in successive contracts. In 1976, Jorie Lester Mark found that unionized paras made 67 percent more than their non-union counterparts.[13] And throughout the decade, poor pay and the indignities and absurdities of paras' pay scales continued to motivate paraprofessional educators to organize. Linda Cook started as a paraprofessional at $2.43 an hour in San Francisco in 1970. One year later, a principal insisted she train a newly hired para who was earning more than Cook because she had a college degree. Cook pointed out the pay discrepancy and the absurdity of paying a trainer less than the trainee, at which point the principal told her, "it's your job." Infuriated, Cook called the San Francisco Federation of Teachers (SFFT) and reached Dennis Kelly, who promptly enlisted Cook as a paraprofessional organizer for the union.[14] The SFFT would form a paraprofessional committee in 1972, and when the union went on strike in 1974, seeking their first contract, they included a 15 percent pay increase and job security for paras in their demands.[15] They did so in part because SFFT para Norma Martinez had brought a grievance against the city of San Francisco for reneging on promised raises for paras in 1972 (public sector employees could not yet bargain contracts in California).[16]

The union created flyers in English and Spanish calling on community members to defend paraprofessional jobs during the SFFT's 1974 strike, noting that "paraprofessionals are the link between the school and the community"/"los paraprofesionales son la cadena entre la escuela y la Comunidad."[17] The fight for paraprofessional job security and living wages continued throughout the 1974–1975 school year but finally, after extensive community and union protest, the San Francisco Board of Examiners changed the local laws to affirm the pay raises they had promised years earlier. Martinez and Cook would both serve on the National Paraprofessional Committee in the years that followed.

The AFT's Economic Research Department conducted a survey of paraprofessional salaries in the 1978–79 school year. Using reports from a nationwide sample of 113 districts enrolling 25,000 or more pupils, they found a mean hourly wage of $3.65 ($16.89 in 2023 dollars) and a median of $3.54 ($16.38) for paras in instructional positions.[18] Even recognizing that unionized paras typically earned more than these averages, para jobs still paid working-class wages. No para was getting rich or buying a home in the suburbs on these salaries, particularly after the inflation of the 1970s. However, at the economic margins on which paras lived, the significant raises union contracts delivered made a huge impact. Coupled with the job security and basic benefits that these contracts provided, union organizing made the difference between teetering precarity and a measure of working-class stability.

Beyond raises, organizing drives by AFT locals aimed to deliver job security and dignity for paraprofessional educators. Teachers everywhere recognized that paras made an impact. In Kansas City, teacher Richard Wholf wrote to his union to protest a principal's arbitrary transfer of paraprofessional Viola

Howard from his classroom three years before paras unionized. "Our children love and respect Mrs. Howard as they would someone in their family,"
Wholf wrote, noting that he relied on her to lead small groups in reading
and perform clerical and grading work.[19] Wholf's description was typical, as
was the administration's arbitrary transfer. As ever, the impact paraprofessional educators made did not guarantee them rights or respect. As Lorretta
Johnson explained, "what was important in our first contract in 1970 was the
grievance procedure. Paraprofessionals had no due process rights," around
transfers, termination, or anything else.[20]

Absent such rights, exploitation ran rampant. Linda Cook's first principal in San Francisco—not the same one who demanded she train a higher-
paid educator—told Cook she could not use the teachers' lounge or restroom
(teachers at the school quickly told Cook otherwise). This principal also gave
another para her personal garments to mend and hem.[21] The contract the New
Bedford Federation of Paraprofessionals won in 1973 emphasized workplace
dignity by guaranteeing equal access to workrooms, teacher lounges, and
other adult spaces in schools, as well as places for paras to store their things
and receive mail.[22] That such measures needed to be spelled out in union contracts demonstrates that some teachers, as well as some administrators, did
not initially welcome paraprofessional educators into "professional" spaces.

An AFT-produced handbook titled *Organizing Paraprofessionals* (first published in 1973) explained that bringing teachers and paras together in the
same union required developing teachers' support for paras and vice versa.
Such support was not natural; it had to be built through internal education
and organizing. In one early instance, this did not happen; the leadership
of the Detroit Federation of Teachers decided to create a separate local, the
Detroit Federation of Paraprofessionals, rather than welcome paras into their
union with teachers.[23] The AFT opposed such moves going forward, but the
question of whether teachers would welcome paras remained contentious.
In Springfield, Massachusetts, organizers for the Springfield Federation of
Teachers circulated materials from New York and Philadelphia AFT locals,
noting that paras and teachers were represented together in each. "If possible,"
the accompanying memo read, "we should do the same, if only to avoid future
strife between professionals and para-professionals."[24] The suggestion of past
strife implicit in this wording was a reminder that unity could be fragile.

In October of 1971, the Boston Teachers Union (BTU) held an open vote at
a membership meeting to decide whether to admit paras.[25] The vote was so
close that BTU President Jack Doherty could not estimate the result from a
show of hands and instead had attendees line up on either side of the hall to
be counted. The motion carried by fewer than ten votes.[26] Even after it did,
some teachers challenged the union's decision to move forward in admitting
paras at future meetings, forcing re-votes on the issue in some cases (though

none as close).[27] Nonetheless, paras elected the BTU as their bargaining agent in April of 1972. Edna Morgan formed the Greater Boston School Aides Association in the same year to support aides in their work, and she, too, joined the National Paraprofessional Steering Committee.[28]

Aides, as they were still called in Boston, found themselves locked in a drawn-out battle over their employment status with the Boston School Committee, the state, and—after a federal court ruled for desegregation in Boston in 1974—the federal government.[29] While the desegregation plan included hiring "transitional aides" to travel with students on school buses, this very fact led the School Committee to claim such workers were temporary and thus could not be included in the BTU's bargaining unit (the state rejected this argument in 1975).[30] Frustrated with the slow pace of contract negotiations, a group of aides convened by Jenna Fitzgerald began meeting and decided to run one of their own for the BTU's executive board. Fitzgerald finished second out of ten, winning a spot, and immediately began urging the union to hire a field representative for aides. The union established the position in 1979, and Fitzgerald was elected. She would go on to serve in the role for decades.[31]

In San Francisco, Cook recalls having a hard time convincing some paras to honor the SFFT's picket lines in 1974. As she explained, many simply didn't make enough money to be able to afford staying out of work, while others had no idea what the union had to do with them. Much like paras in Boston and elsewhere, San Francisco's paras also faced confusion and obfuscation about who truly counted as their employer. As an organizer and, later, chapter leader, Cook, like Fitzgerald in Boston, worked hard to bring the union to paras, including creating a hotline—584-PARA—for her chapter's members to call with questions.[32] She also pushed leaders to speak always of "teachers *and* paras," whether in public or at the negotiating table with the school district. As she put it in a 2014 interview, "never say one without the other!"[33] Her union today is known as the United Educators of San Francisco.[34]

While the AFT's leaders often asserted natural unity, solidarity between teachers and paras was not guaranteed, and the process of paras joining teachers' unions could bring conflicts to the surface. In such instances, paras joining the union was not the end of the story, but the beginning. Paras and teachers might find common cause as members of the same local, but doing so sometimes meant rebuilding trust after struggles over whether paras belonged in teachers' unions (a process that included paras asserting themselves as full and equal union members).

Finally, as in New York City, paras across the country were united in their desire for career advancement and frustrated by the limited programs and opportunities that had emerged in the 1960s. This was what made the New York City contract, in particular, such an important model; while Baltimore's

1970 contract offered reimbursement for college courses that paras took, New York's created a program that was free at the point of service and offered stipends to support paras as students. In a memo explaining the needs of her fellow paras, New Bedford educator and organizer Geraldine Alves wrote to the Massachusetts Federation of Teachers' Paul Devlin to express frustration about evasive responses from the person in charge of federal aide training programs.[35] New Bedford's 1973 para contract ensured that any in-service training opportunities would be available to all paras.

In Kansas City, KCFT President Truman Holman worked with the local Model Cities program to create opportunities for para-to-teacher training as part of the Career Opportunities Program after paras unionized in 1971. In outlining his union's rationale for "a program of teacher development that elevates paraprofessionals," Holman wrote in 1973, "these newly certified teachers are well trained, already possess several years of classroom and teaching-related work experience and are knowledgeable of KCSD procedures."[36] Advancement was a core component of paraprofessional organizing for union leaders and paras alike, in no small part because teacher training provisions held together the AFT leadership's overarching vision for paraprofessional organizing.

Assimilating New Educators: The AFT Leadership and Para Organizing in the 1970s

In the summer of 1970, as UFT paras hammered out their first contract, the AFT's leaders offered a comprehensive vision for paraprofessional programs at their annual conference for the first time. Union resolutions declared, "the need to have more paraprofessionals drawn from the local community working in the schools is obvious" and committed the union to "seek national legislation to fund such programs at the state and local level."[37] The AFT created the National Paraprofessional Steering Committee and asked Velma Murphy Hill to take the reins. The union's executive committee resolved that "all locals ask their school boards for paraprofessional programs" built on five principles: no educational restrictions for entry, pay increases based on education and experience, release time to pursue college coursework, college unit equivalencies for on-the-job training, and, finally, that "persons who are successful in such a program will be encouraged to work toward the goal of entering the teaching profession."[38]

These principles codified the approach to paraprofessional organizing that AFT President David Selden and Vice President (one of several) Albert Shanker had developed in New York City (Shanker would step into the new role of "executive vice-president" in 1972 and replace Selden as AFT president in 1974). To paraprofessionals, the union offered raises, benefits, and job security, as well as a regularized path to professional advancement. To teachers, the AFT framed para programs not as liberal re-imaginings of the classroom or radical community intrusions into it, but as apprenticeship and training programs. Drawing on Frank Riessman's framework of a career ladder, and their conversations with Riessman about it, the AFT's leaders constructed a scalable professional hierarchy that appealed to paras' aspirations without threatening teachers' elevated professional status.

And even as the union's leaders affirmed paras' place in the AFT, they took steps to preserve professional hierarchy in the union's organizational structure. In New York, UFT staff had noted the possibility of para power at the local level with some trepidation. Field organizer Gladys Roth wrote in 1970 that paras "outnumber teachers in the very schools where teacher turnover is high and morale is low," and thus, "under the present chapter structure . . . para-professionals can dominate many school chapters."[39] The UFT did not adjust its chapter structure, but when some paras ran for chapter leadership, they encountered significant resistance.[40]

The AFT resolved, "wherever possible, AFT locals [should] be urged to organize paraprofessionals and teachers into one bargaining unit to facilitate greater strength in bargaining with school districts."[41] This logic had appealed to paras in New York City and elsewhere, and it stood the test of New York City's Board of Education when teachers voted to strike, if necessary, for paras to win a contract. However, some paras and their advocates, particularly those in the community control movement, worried that consolidation undermined paras' independence, particularly if paras wanted to support parents in problems they encountered with teachers.

The AFT also warned locals organizing paras to adjust their constitutions. "If your present constitution does not presently provide full democratic representation and first-class membership for aides," their organizing handbook warned, "the local could be barred from recognition as the bargaining agent."[42] Legality, in addition to solidarity, was on the table; if they did not offer full membership to paras, AFT locals would make themselves vulnerable to challenges from AFSCME, SEIU, and other unions organizing paras.

The international union, however, used a dues-based system of representation to blunt the impact of paraprofessional unionization on its power structure. As explained in the provisions for para organizing adopted in 1970, "paraprofessionals shall be counted in determining the delegate strength of the local . . . at 1/2 the constitutional formula for apportionment of delegate strength."[43] The justification for this was that paraprofessionals paid half the dues of teachers, and sometimes less. This "representation in return for per capita taxation" was an accepted form of union democracy under federal law, and in 1982, the AFT noted that the rival National Education Association (NEA) did not offer its "auxiliary" (paraprofessional) members any voting power at all until forced to by a court decision in 1979.[44] Nonetheless, structuring representation in this way reproduced the inequalities of the public-sector salary scale in the union hall, inequalities that were built on racist and sexist exclusion and segregation in the job market. By rewarding those with higher salaries and limiting the power of the most poorly compensated educators, AFT leaders subordinated their newest members within a professional voting hierarchy.

The AFT's new approach to paraprofessional organizing was apparent in the materials the union produced for paraprofessional campaigns. The introduction to *Organizing Paraprofessionals,* the union's handbook, opened by announcing "the paraprofessional movement is a nationwide phenomenon" and closed with the declaration, "Paraprofessionals are here to stay!"[45] In the text, and the executive committee resolutions in the appendix, the handbook celebrated paras' impact in schools, particularly their impact on school-community relations. One resolution, republished from 1970, asserted that "research discloses":

a) that paraprofessionals who themselves have lived in disadvantaged environments often communicate to children in ways which are neither threatening nor strange;

b) that they also are able to interpret some aspects of children's behavior to middle class professionals, and frustrations which children in inner-cities face, often are able to motivate these children to further effort; and

c) that the presence of paraprofessionals can effectuate changes in a child's self-concept as well as changes in his attitude toward schools.[46]

"Therefore," the resolution concluded, the union resolved to "actively support the use of both men and women of minority group backgrounds in paraprofessional positions."[47] In further resolutions, the union noted that paras were already "overwhelmingly women and minority people and their working conditions are therefore affected by racism and sexism," evidenced by "poor pay and working conditions, and a lack of job security and fringe benefits" in schools.

These resolutions constituted a significant change in tone and strategy from the AFT leadership's deep suspicion of paras in the 1960s. The union acknowledged paras' direct impact on students, and implicitly noted the limited ability of "middle class professionals"—teachers—to address educational, behavioral, and emotional needs without paras. The AFT recognized that paras should be hired from "minority group backgrounds"—backgrounds they shared with students—and that workers from such backgrounds faced racism and sexism on the job.

However, the AFT's handbook made no mention of the Black freedom struggle, the promise of "maximum feasible participation" in the War on Poverty, or the movement for community control of schools. Its brief history of paraprofessionalism mentioned only federal legislation, not the grassroots organizing or demonstration programs that had expanded the "teacher aide" model of the 1950s into a role for pedagogical innovation, community involvement, and career training. The question of why teachers and students had trouble communicating across divides of class and race in urban schools went unasked and unanswered, as did the broader question of why parents and students might have negative attitudes toward their schools and teachers. As for the question of how the "racism and sexism" paras faced at work should be addressed, the union's answer was simple: collective bargaining. It also resolved that "the content of the *American Teacher* [the AFT paper] should reflect the needs and struggles of para-professionals," but what these struggles were, and how they diverged from those of teachers, was left unsaid.[48]

These omissions revealed a problem in the AFT leadership's approach to para organizing in these years: the assertion that the interests of paras and teachers were inherently aligned. *Organizing Paraprofessionals* also reproduced Executive Council resolutions that declared, "the teacher and paraprofessional share a common concern for the improvement of the educational program" and "the interests of teachers, leaders, and paraprofessionals can best be served by an alliance."[49] Experience showed that solidarity between these groups of workers was not guaranteed and had to be built, but these resolutions presumed their unity—and paras' fealty to teachers. Aides, *Organizing Paraprofessionals* read, were hired to "relieve teachers of non-teaching chores" and to "reinforce the teaching process under the direction of the teacher."[50] This was, perhaps, true of the early "teacher aide" model as implemented by administrators in the 1950s, when the union had bargained not with aides but for their labor. It was not, however, an accurate description of paraprofessional work as envisioned or practiced during the 1960s.

Building from the campaign of internal education that Sandra Feldman and Velma Hill had led in New York, the handbook included conversation templates for teachers about paras joining the union. To the assertion "they'll be spies," the handbook replied, "It doesn't take too long for the paraprofessional to identify with the problems of the classroom teachers," including "the impossible demands that 32 children make, problems of discipline, problems of violence, the problem of little preparation time and the problem of overcrowding." Paras, said the AFT, "will be your best allies back in the community concerning the real plight of the teacher."[51]

These imagined conversations with teachers diagnosed very real challenges that shaped educators' working conditions. Left unsaid was that all these problems—impossible demands, discipline, violence—could easily

become flashpoints for conflict as well as sources of solidarity if paras and
teachers disagreed about how to respond. Indeed, they had triggered conflict
between some paras and teachers in New York. The union's internal concerns about paras "dominating" local chapters and skewing AFT delegate
apportionment also belied declarations of inherent allegiance. If interests
were aligned, what threat did paras pose?

Albert Shanker and David Selden based their blueprint for para organizing on the New York campaign, and thus the UFT's conflicts with Black and
Puerto Rican activists in New York shaped their assimilationist vision. The
AFT's organizing drives made a tremendous impact on paras' wages, job
security, and working conditions in the 1970s, and their support of career
ladders opened up pathways to teaching for thousands of working-class
women. However, the leaders regarded the third key component of paraprofessionalism—connecting school and community—as a one-way street.
Paras would support teachers and carry their concerns and needs back to
the community, not act as tribunes for students and parents. They would
deploy their local knowledge to help students adjust to the classroom, but
they would not adjust schools to students. Paras' connections to local freedom
struggles, and particularly to campaigns for community control of schools,
went largely unmentioned and uncultivated. As Shanker and Selden understood it, paras' labor, and their presence in AFT locals, would not challenge
the union's political orientation or its professional hierarchies.

Shanker and Selden, however, did not lead day-to-day paraprofessional
organizing during the 1970s. That task fell to Velma Murphy Hill and the
National Paraprofessional Steering Committee. The Black women who led
this committee cultivated a strategic vision that married labor and civil rights
organizing, building on the ideas and support of Bayard Rustin and A. Philip
Randolph. Hill shared the AFT leadership's antipathy to community control,
but she and her partners did not play down the connections between paras
and the civil rights movement. Rather, Hill and the committee fought to
define union organizing as the next logical phase in a long struggle for integrated educational work and economic opportunities for working women.

Speaking for Themselves: The National
Paraprofessional Steering Committee

When the AFT created the National Paraprofessional Steering Committee
in 1970, it stipulated that the committee should be made up of "a majority
of paraprofessionals."[52] For Hill, privileging the voices of paras was paramount. As she recalled in 1985, "there were all kinds of forces in Washington
and the community who had an agenda for these women . . . there were all
these people speaking for paraprofessionals, but paraprofessionals weren't

speaking for themselves."[53] Hill believed unionization should make paras' voices heard.

The process of amplifying para voices began with the committee's formation. By April of 1972, four paras, three Black women and one Latina, had joined, after being nominated by state and local union leaders: Lorretta Johnson of Baltimore, Violet Larry of Detroit, Norma Martinez of San Francisco, and Edna Morgan of Boston.[54] They represented geographically and demographically diverse AFT locals and school districts, and all of them had either led or were in the process of developing paraprofessional organizing campaigns.[55] They were joined on the committee by Phyllis Hutchinson, president of the Oregon Federation of Teachers, and Demosthenes DuBoise, president of the St. Louis Teachers Union, whose experiences as one of St. Louis's first Black teachers were reflected in the trials paras faced in schools.[56]

Building on their own experiences in early paraprofessional organizing drives, the steering committee pursued a three-pronged strategy. They circulated materials among AFT locals, including organizing pamphlets, para contracts, job and career ladder descriptions, and scholarly studies demonstrating the impact of paras in classrooms. They traveled widely to bring their stories to far-flung districts and to lend support to organizing efforts. And as paras' numbers in the AFT grew, they hosted national and regional conferences for paraprofessional educators.

To supplement its members' knowledge and experience, the steering committee launched an information-gathering project in the fall of 1972. Their "AFT Para-Professional Survey," circulated to locals across the country, asked how many paraprofessionals worked in local districts, what their duties were (and who defined them), whether these paras were unionized (and if so, in what union), and whether they would send a paraprofessional representative to the AFT's convention or to a National Conference on Paraprofessionals in 1973. The survey asked locals to attach "any materials which are related to Para-Professionals (organizing literature, contracts, state regulations, job descriptions, etc.)."[57] They amassed a vast collection from the replies.

The steering committee gathered materials from allies in the policy world, as well. Scholars and administrators affiliated with Frank Riessman's New Careers Training Laboratory, as well as those in state and federal positions, sent the guidelines they drafted to AFT leaders, who forwarded them to the committee.[58] The "New Careerists" shared two major goals with the union. Both groups wanted to ensure that paraprofessionals were not used as all-purpose cheap labor by principals and administrators, and both sought to turn promised career ladder programs into realities, as paraprofessionals and union organizers had done in New York City.

Once these materials were collected, the National Paraprofessional Steering Committee distributed copies to AFT locals and prospective para organizers around the country. As a UFT organizer, Velma Murphy Hill had sent materials to union organizers and educational administrators in Philadelphia and San Francisco, and she knew the value of circulating materials.[59] The papers of AFT locals that organized paras in the 1970s reveal a remarkable level of intellectual and material exchange, facilitated by the steering committee. Lorretta Johnson's Baltimore Teachers Union sent a copy of their new contract to the Detroit Federation of Teachers almost immediately upon ratification.[60] Organizers from the Kansas City Federation of Teachers, which won its first paraprofessional contract in 1971, studied articles by Bayard Rustin about Black workers in the trade union movement, paraprofessional job descriptions from the Los Angeles Unified School District, a "working agreement" between the school district and the association of paraprofessionals in Tacoma, Washington, and Boston's career ladder program.[61] Organizers in Springfield, the first local to win a paraprofessional contract in the state of Massachusetts, kept complete copies of New York City's landmark contract on file and used highlights from both New York City and Philadelphia in their campaign literature.[62] Norma Martinez brought materials back to her home local, the San Francisco Federation of Teachers, including contracts and flyers from New York City, Baltimore, Detroit, Philadelphia, and Pittsburgh. The SFFT also worked with policy studies from Garda Bowman and Gordon Klopf of Bank Street College in New York City, as well as paraprofessional handbooks from New York City and Oakland.[63] Writing in the *Boston Union Teacher*, BTU aide Laurel Goodrich cited the UFT's contract, the Paraprofessional-Teacher Education Program, and Bowman and Klopf's work in a long article titled "Aide and Teacher: A New Alliance."[64]

When locals succeeded in their unionization drives, they added their own materials to the circuit. By 1974, the KCFT was forwarding its contract and flyers to the St. Louis Teachers Union and the Indiana Federation of Teachers, noting that in their local, "paras are full members with equal voting power and representation on executive board."[65] Springfield's SFT shared its contract with locals in industrial cities across Massachusetts, including Lynn and New Bedford, and San Francisco forwarded its materials to the national steering committee.

As recommended in the AFT's resolutions from 1970, the steering committee celebrated paras in the pages of the AFT's *American Teacher*. These articles not only announced successful unionization drives but also provided inspiration, information, and images for ongoing campaigns. Locals in Kansas City, Springfield, and San Francisco kept articles from the *American Teacher* in their clippings files, and the SFFT turned an article titled "NYC Paraprofessionals ok first contract" into a flyer, with the addendum "The AFT can help paraprofessionals."[66]

The National Paraprofessional Steering Committee—which was renamed the National Paraprofessional Committee in 1973—used the materials it gathered and disseminated to shape its contributions to the *Organizing Paraprofessionals* handbook.[67] The committee's focus, in this publication, was on para voices and appeals to paras themselves. First and foremost, the handbook advocated para leadership in any prospective campaign. "It has been proven," the committee wrote, "that paraprofessionals do very well in explaining to other paraprofessionals why they need your local to represent them. They also help bridge the gap between the two groups." A steering committee of "paraprofessional leaders" was recommended to establish "well-planned and frequent *personal* contacts," to draft letters to paras regarding unionization, to schedule meetings and rallies, and to formulate the constitution for the para chapter. The local could supplement these efforts with leaflets on recommended topics, including "Why you need a united team" and "What the AFT can do for you." Paraprofessional concerns such as "we will get second class status" and "they are a professional group, not a labor union" were addressed in the Q&A section, as well as in template slogans for flyers, such as "If you work with children, you belong in the AFT" and "Paraprofessional + Teacher = A Better Way."[68]

Education, the handbook emphasized, was "the heart of the campaign." By this, the authors meant educating paras about the benefits of AFT membership, including "increased pay," "seniority—protection against layoff," "paid sick leave," "health plan," "insurance," "travel discounts," "book discounts," and "career ladder—high school equivalency and college courses." These lists captured the essence of the AFT's appeal: for workers who had been recruited from poverty and whose positions were proving tenuous in the face of municipal and federal budget cutbacks, the union offered job security, benefits, career advancement, and some of the privileges of the American middle class. Along with the material it collected from AFT locals, the National Paraprofessional Committee distributed the *Organizing Paraprofessionals* handbook far and wide in the 1970s.[69]

In addition to circulating materials, National Paraprofessional Committee members and their allies traveled extensively to promote paraprofessional unionism, support active campaigns, and recognize successful drives. As Lorretta Johnson recalled, "Shanker was sending me all over to help organize paras. I put that first in my life . . . it became a symbol of what I wanted to do."[70] Velma Hill traveled up to Boston twice in 1973, first to speak with UFT Vice President Sandra Feldman at the Massachusetts Federation of Teachers Annual Conference, and then again with fellow UFT para and organizer Maria Portalatin to speak at the first annual conference of the Greater Boston School Aides Association in December of 1973.[71] Speaking to the Massachusetts state federation, Hill emphasized the need for teachers to "join with other groups . . . blacks, other minorities, labor people, liberals—any who are concerned" to build "an open, integrated society."[72] Thousands of paras in Massachusetts joined the MFT (today AFT-MA) in these years, including in Boston, Springfield, New Bedford, Peabody, and Lynn. In between her trips to Boston in 1973, Hill flew west to join the Detroit Federation of Paraprofessionals at a mass meeting for their members in October.[73]

The San Francisco Federation of Teachers invited Hill to visit during its 1975 campaign for para raises, and the Lynn Teachers Union asked her back to Massachusetts the same year.[74] Shelvy Young-Abrams, who, like Portalatin, worked with Hill in New York City, traveled to Houston and Atlanta to meet with paraprofessional educators and share New York City's story.[75] Relatively local travels were common, as well; MFT President Rose Claffey, an early supporter of para organizing, drove ninety miles west from Lynn to Springfield to be present when Springfield agreed to hold a union election for paras, while KCFT paras traveled east across Missouri for an intercity meeting of paras in St. Louis in 1974.[76]

The committee's travels took its members to many big-city locals where the AFT was seeking to expand its presence, but they also sought to break new ground for the AFT in smaller towns, as well as the right-to-work states of the American South and Southwest. In 1978, Eugene Didier, director of the AFT's Special Organizing Project in the South, wrote to Hill to thank her for visiting the Albuquerque Teachers Aides Association, an independent group. "Your willingness to spend several hours with such a relatively small group as the ATAA, which may or may not even decide to affiliate," he noted, "gives evidence of your devotion to our great movement."[77] *Organizing Paraprofessionals* had reminded prospective unionists of the value of personal contacts in organizing. The committee lived up to its words across the country.

National Paraprofessional Committee members proved excellent hosts as well as guests. In addition to bringing their experiences and expertise to paraprofessional educators across the country, the committee gathered paras together at AFT conventions and at two focused paraprofessional conferences in 1973 and 1978. These conferences, which continued on a biennial and then annual basis in the 1980s (and to the present day) brought paraprofessional educators together as a class of workers, building solidarity among them and demonstrating their increasing presence in the AFT. They promoted conversations among paras working in different classroom and school contexts, as well as different regions of the country. They allowed paras to liaise as a group with the AFT and the Department of Health, Education, and Welfare (after 1979, the Department of Education), both headquartered in Washington, and to lobby Congress directly for continued funding for their jobs.

The first National Paraprofessional Conference, held in Washington on May 18, 1973, brought over 200 paraprofessionals together from dozens of locals.[78] Planned by Velma Murphy Hill, Lorretta Johnson, and Edna Morgan, the one-day conference opened with a welcome address from AFT President David Selden and included sessions on "The Congress, the President, and the Paraprofessional" and "Minorities and Unions," featuring Don Slaiman, the director of the Civil Rights Department of the AFL-CIO, along with Hill and Albert Shanker. The conference included practical workshops on organizing techniques (led by Hill), the "career ladder," and "The Paraprofessional and the Teacher: Partners on the Job." Vernon Jordan, president of the National Urban League, and Congressman Andrew Young were invited to speak at lunch, while Bayard Rustin closed out the day with a discussion of "Building Coalitions for Educational Change."[79] The design and themes of the conference reflected Rustin's focus on improving the lives of poor and working-class Black workers through political participation and coalition-building to unite the civil rights and labor movements.

Creating a political voice for paraprofessional educators in the nation's capital was a crucial part of conference planning. In addition to hosting sessions on legislative and administrative educational policies, the National Paraprofessional Committee planned a press conference with members of Congress "from areas of major paraprofessional concentration."[80] The committee also asked paraprofessional educators to arrive in Washington a day early for a rally at the Capitol to support legislative funding for paraprofessional jobs. President Richard Nixon had threatened vetoes of childcare and educational bills in 1973, and according to David Selden, "the whole federal aid question . . . [was] up for grabs." Selden, along with Lorretta Johnson's friend and mentor, AFT Vice-President Godfrey Moore of the Baltimore Teachers Union, were "strongly supportive of the rally idea," having already hosted an "Educational Survival Day" in April.[81] The rally was not the first time the AFT had petitioned Congress to support funding for paraprofessionals; Selden had partnered with Frank Riessman to plan a New Careers "materials raid" on the Capitol in conjunction with an AFT Leadership Convention in Washington in 1969.[82] It was, however, the first time that AFT paraprofessionals spoke directly for themselves at an AFT-sponsored event in Washington.

Organizing paraprofessional conferences presented the AFT with unique challenges. When the 1973 conference was announced, paraprofessionals from forty-four locals of the AFT expressed interest in attending, but eleven of those locals indicated that they had "no funds to send a representative."[83] Asking working mothers to take time off, and spend money, to travel during the school year was onerous. By the time the next National Paraprofessional

Conference was planned, in 1978, the union was offering $100 to each local to send a representative.[84]

The 1978 conference, titled "Paraprofessionals on the Move: Past, Present, and Future," followed the form of the 1973 effort in many respects.[85] Panels included broad discussions of "Legislation and Lobbying," "Paras and the Political Process," and "The Role and Responsibility of Paraprofessionals," led by speakers from the AFT, AFL-CIO, and federal and state education departments. A far more extensive list of practical workshops was grouped into "educational" services ("reading, language arts, math, Title I, Follow Through, and Headstart"), "related" services ("social services . . . such as Counseling, School-Community Research, Recreational, Clerical, Food Services, Security, Transportation"), and "exceptional children," the last of which reflected the growing use of paraprofessional educators in special-education roles.

The 1978 conference also featured far more paraprofessional voices. In addition to Hill and Johnson, nearly all the members of the National Paraprofessional Committee—including Nina Marchand of New Orleans, Dorothea Bell of Philadelphia, Ernestine Brown of Chicago, and Linda Cook of San Francisco—led or moderated workshops and panels. The committee itself was now composed entirely of women who had worked as paraprofessional educators, with teacher members having stepped aside.

The 1978 conference was also far larger and better attended than the first one in 1973. AFT President Albert Shanker recruited local presidents, as well as paraprofessional representatives, to attend, writing, "The conference will highlight the level of paraprofessionals in the AFT and the importance of organizing paraprofessionals."[86] In addition to the AFT's $100-per-local offer, some locals chipped in. The UFT chartered a bus for its paras for the occasion.[87]

These two conferences helped paraprofessional educators make a place for themselves in the AFT and demonstrated the union's commitment to their vision for paraprofessionals. Writing to Barbara Van Blake, the director of the AFT's Human Rights and Community Relations Department, just after the 1978 conference, St. Louis Paraprofessional Chairperson Cheryl Houston thanked her for presenting at the conference and added that her staff and department "created a climate of unity that made me proud to be a working part of the AFT."[88] This was not an idle compliment, as the AFT and its locals had been locked in battles with community organizers in earlier years. Eugene Didier also wrote Van Blake from Atlanta, noting that both the National Paraprofessional Conference and the National Paraprofessional Committee's willingness to support small local organizing efforts such as the one in Albuquerque bolstered the AFT's overall goals for expansion in the South and West.[89]

National Paraprofessional Committee, May 27, 1979. From left: Chairwoman Velma Hill (New York City), Lorretta Johnson (Baltimore), Dorothea Bell (Philadelphia), Ernestine Brown (Chicago), Linda Cook (San Francisco), Nina Marchand (New Orleans). United Federation of Teachers Photographs; PHOTOS 019, Item 4185, Tamiment Library/Robert F. Wagner Labor Archives, New York University.

A Nationwide Movement to Achieve Equality: Civil Rights and Labor in the AFT

Velma Murphy Hill's mentor and friend, Bayard Rustin, provided institutional and intellectual support for the AFT's paraprofessional unionization efforts. Rustin had celebrated New York City's first paraprofessional contract in the pages of the *New York Amsterdam News* on August 22, 1970, by writing that he was witnessing the birth of a national movement. Rustin's vision for an interracial political coalition of poor and working-class people had faltered in the late 1960s, but the paras' contract made him optimistic. The victory, he wrote, was "one of the finest examples of self-determination by the poor, and it is likely to be repeated in other cities as part of a nationwide struggle by low-income workers to achieve equality."[90] Rustin chose his language carefully, favorably contrasting the paras' contract with both the waning War on Poverty and burgeoning Black Power organizing. Rustin had been a fierce critic of both, and in the 1970s, he sought to articulate an alternative vision for the future of Black freedom struggles rooted in liberal-labor coalitions, on-the-job integration, and advocacy for full employment.

Rustin's debates with Black Power leaders took place on the common ground of economic opportunity. As David Stein writes, "the Black Panther Party and civil rights activist Bayard Rustin did not agree on many things in 1967, but they both thought the government should ensure that everyone who wanted a job had one."[91] How to go about ensuring full employment through organizing, and what kind of transformation this process would generate, proved the substance of this debate. Public-sector jobs mattered increasingly in these conversations, as they grew in number while industrial work shrank in the 1960s and 1970s. Educational work mattered in particular: winning these jobs meant not only survival but also a role in shaping educational institutions and the futures they promised for Black children.

Rustin and Hill were close confidants in a circle of Black trade union- ists and socialists who had trained as organizers with A. Philip Randolph. Randolph and Rustin cofounded the A. Philip Randolph Institute (APRI), a constituency group of the AFL-CIO, in 1965, with the express goal of building durable alliances and campaigns between the labor movement and the civil rights movement. Rustin served as president, with Hill's husband, Norman Hill, as his vice-president. In the late 1960s, the APRI promoted Rustin's "Freedom Budget for All Americans" and expanded ongoing campaigns to integrate the building and construction trades, but it also clashed with Black Power activists, most explosively during the 1968 UFT strikes, which Ran- dolph and Rustin were the only prominent Black leaders to support. Rustin and the Hills, like Albert Shanker, were also active members of the Socialist Party of America (of which Max Shachtman was the leading theorist) and, after the party's 1972 split, Social Democrats USA, which Rustin chaired. As Velma Hill worked to organize paraprofessional educators into the UFT in the aftermath of those strikes, Rustin provided personal, political, and orga- nizational support. Both Hill and Rustin hoped that the New York victory, and the appeal to a civil rights–labor alliance they had built it on, would serve as a national model in the decade to follow.

From his position as president of the APRI, Rustin regularly advanced paraprofessional organizing as a route to repair the splintering coalition between civil rights and labor organizers. In a 1970 essay titled "The Blacks and the Unions," Rustin rued this split, noting that Black Americans were both the most unionized workers in the country and the fastest-growing seg- ment of the labor movement, particularly in public-sector jobs. Public-sector organizing—and here Rustin specifically mentioned paraprofessional labor, which was "shamefully underpaid"—should, to Rustin's mind, have been a central issue for both the labor movement and Black freedom struggle.[92] As

Rustin argued to the AFL-CIO in 1969, "we eradicate white fear and black rage by satisfying the real needs of all our people" and creating new jobs.[93] In that talk, later published as "Black Rage, White Fear: The Full Employment Answer," Rustin argued, "If there was full employment, blacks would not be in a rage because they do not have jobs, and whites would not be fearful that they will lose theirs."[94] The published version was one of many Rustin pieces that the National Paraprofessional Steering Committee circulated to AFT locals as they set out to organize paraprofessionals. As Lorretta Johnson remembers, "Bayard used to amaze me because he was so outspoken. Very outspoken. He didn't want no stuff and didn't take no stuff. He cussed a lot, but he was so brilliant."[95] Rustin brought his outspoken energy to AFT events throughout the 1970s, including both paraprofessional conferences.

In the trainings she led and conversations she had as an organizer, Hill regularly asked paras to put aside their racial and ethnic identities. "You are nothing but a trade unionist," she told them, "and you've got to think that way or you're going to lose."[96] For Hill, this was the promise of integrated trade unionism, and it contrasted starkly with the community-based hiring processes that brought paras into their jobs.[97] Lorretta Johnson was similarly committed to integrated unionism, which she pursued through the AFT's Civil and Human Rights Conferences in the 1970s. Recognizing that these conferences could easily become sites where "Latinos talked to the Latinos" and "Blacks talked to Blacks," Johnson believed, "we had to find ways of how we would work it up to get as many of our white counterparts to the civil and human rights meetings." Johnson made these efforts a focus of her conference organizing.[98]

Hill's and Johnson's commitments to integration and to defining paras first and foremost as "trade unionists" were reflected in the emphasis on unity in the AFT's organizing materials. This position also served the AFT's strategy of assuaging teacher concerns and playing down the more radical, community-based origins of paraprofessionalism. Rustin and Hill believed their strategies reflected principled integrationism and hard-headed realism, while critics of the AFT frequently accused them of co-opting paraprofessional educators and the movements from which many paras had emerged.[99] The National Paraprofessional Steering Committee developed strategies to reply, rejecting the arguments of community control advocates and casting unionism as the future of the civil rights movement. Lorretta Johnson joined the AFT's Black Caucus in the 1970s, which was dominated by opponents of Shanker at the time. Johnson believed in the need for such a caucus, but she had to address Shanker's past and reputation to gain a foothold. "That history around Ocean Hill-Brownsville," she recalled in 2020, "we fought that and changed it." When told that Shanker was a racist who needed to be opposed, and, if possible, replaced, Johnson said, "We wouldn't be out here working on social justice issues with the civil rights movement if Shanker was such a racist. He wouldn't care about that."[100] Johnson channeled her energies in the Black Caucus toward funding for schools serving majority-Black student bodies and communities.

In an article published in the *American Teacher* in 1971, Velma Hill told the story of her friend Patricia Jones. As part of the UFT's Paraprofessional Chapter, Jones had attended a Women's Liberation Conference in New York. Encountering accusations that her union, and Shanker in particular, were racist, Jones said the following:

> I used to be a domestic. I earned $50 a week and worked like a slave. It was a degrading job. Then I became a paraprofessional, joined the UFT and began to fight for a better life. Albert Shanker not only helped that fight, he led it. Now I earn a decent salary. I have paid vacations, sick leave, health insurance, and other benefits. I also study so that some day I can get a college degree. My whole life has changed. You call it racism. Well, if that's racism [and she raised a fist clenched gently, in mock imitation of the militant salute] then that's the kind of racism black people need.[101]

Jones's story was retold frequently by the UFT and the AFT at paraprofessional events, and it appears in several publications from the era.[102] Its repetition captures both the possibilities and the tensions that the New York model offered to paras. The AFT could, and did, provide real gains for paraprofessional educators, but it eschewed much of the radicalism of the era.

Hill was deeply committed to paraprofessional leadership and promoting the voices and needs of paraprofessionals within her union. As she explained to an interviewer in 1986, the campaign in New York City had succeeded, in part, due to "the emergence of a black paraprofessional leadership that was also credible."[103] At the same time, she was wholly opposed to community control programs put forth in New York City by Preston Wilcox and others, visions that remained powerful for many Black and Latinx communities around the nation in these years. For Hill, these organizations' behavior toward paras—particularly their demands that paras not vote to join the UFT in 1969—reflected the institutional hierarchies and legacies of church-based organizing in Black communities, which she knew intimately from her years in the NAACP and CORE. As she put it in 2011, "the church was not a democratic organization," whereas, for her, organizing a union was "a real experience in democracy."[104]

The ideological and strategic conflicts Hill and Rustin maintained with advocates of community control of schools did not prevent AFT locals from working productively with community activists in many specific cases.

However, coupled with the national leadership's limited interest in this element of paraprofessional labor, these differences ensured that ideas and programs for expanding community participation in public schooling remained outside the international union's official program for paraprofessional labor and organizing in the 1970s.

"Affirmative Action without Quotas": Paras' Permanence in the AFT

At the AFT's National Paraprofessional Conference in 1988, union President Albert Shanker reflected on the contributions paras had made to the union, calling the move to bring paras into the union "one of the best moments, not only in my career, but in the history of the organization."[105] He noted that the AFT had added 100,000 paras to its ranks in the preceding two decades, and that "paras and teachers have realized over the years how important it was for them to be together" in the AFT. "Sometimes," Shanker noted, paras had been at the vanguard of AFT organizing: "in Baltimore for a long time we had the paraprofessionals, but we had lost the teachers, and it was really the work that Lorretta and the paraprofessionals did as a base to bring the teachers back into the AFT."[106] Shanker cited similar efforts in Cincinnati and San Francisco in the 1980s, and he closed this portion of his speech by noting, in the language of *Organizing Paraprofessionals*, that "it is pretty clear now that paraprofessional programs are here to stay."

Questions nonetheless remained about paraprofessional educators' place in the AFT. In the 1980s, major cuts to federal spending on education and social welfare, coupled with austerity budgets in many cities, led to paraprofessional layoffs and the shuttering of career ladder programs. Shanker and the AFT, for their part, sought to address attacks on teacher and school quality through a renewed emphasis on teacher professionalism and licensing standards (the National Education Association prioritized similar positions in these years).[107] Paras facing lost career opportunities and stagnating wages were not the AFT's focus.

Rose Claffey, the longtime leader of the Massachusetts Federation of Teachers and the Lynn Teachers Union (LTU), had argued that the AFT should organize paras back in 1966. She put her philosophy of robust organizing into practice in Massachusetts in the 1970s, including in her hometown of Lynn, where paras unionized in 1973.[108] Two years later, as a strike driven by a budget fight loomed, the LTU's newsletter described the union as a "growing force," driven by "increasing awareness on the part of teachers and paraprofessionals that 'in unity there is strength' is not a hackneyed phrase but, rather, a demonstrable reality has resulted in an increase in membership in the past two years alone of 25%." The article argued that the union's 1,000 members could bring 5,000 votes, counting "family and friends," in the upcoming school board and mayoral elections in Lynn, such that for "the first time in the history of local politics, those who have the expertise to judge the educational needs of the community will be able to exert a positive influence in the direction of electing candidates conscious of those needs."[109]

In November of 1975, the *LTU Newsletter* declared victory following a campaign that included a two-week strike that September. LTU members signed new contracts with raises for paras and teachers in the months that followed.[110] Organizing paraprofessionals had helped build the LTU into a political force potent enough to face down a hostile mayor and school board and win better funding for the local public schools, as well as living wages for educators.

Interviewed in 1986, Claffey understood that the AFT's fight was not finished. As she argued, "we have to . . . decide whether or not unionism means something to us, and if it does, how much participation are we willing to offer to make the goals of that union . . . a success."[111] Claffey singled out paras, noting "in our work with the non-teaching personnel, we must see that any newly created roles in school departments employ people at living wages, not minimum wages."[112] In a decade when the AFT was once again focused on defending teacher professionalism, Claffey reminded her fellow educators that the union had to fight for everyone.

On the dais in 1988, Albert Shanker did reiterate his commitment to what he called "the career ladder concept," citing a Carnegie Foundation report on the limited number of minority teachers in public schools. "What sort of better effort can you make," he asked, "than if you have paraprofessionals who are already there and they are doing parts of the job and they understand that it is an avenue to advancement."[113] Shanker's positioning here was strategic; the AFT had routinely opposed affirmative action in the 1970s and 1980s, going so far as to file an amicus brief in the *Regents of the University of California v. Bakke* case on behalf of the challenger. However, Velma Murphy Hill believed the AFT could support "affirmative action without quotas," a phrase she had coined precisely to assuage the "white fear" Bayard Rustin diagnosed, and to promote advancement without upending seniority.[114] The AFT-sponsored career ladder contributed to the growth of the Black and Latinx teaching corps; Black teachers reached their highest-ever percentage of the full-time teacher workforce in the mid-1980s, thanks in part to the recruitment and training of people through paraprofessional and career ladder programs.[115]

When Shanker invoked the "career ladder concept," he was, of course, referring to the work of Frank Riessman, Arthur Pearl, Alan Gartner, and many other policy scholars and policymakers who considered themselves part of a wider New Careers movement. The AFT's organizing was the single greatest source of power for paraprofessional educators in the 1970s and played the largest role in shaping the permanence and trajectory of this work. The union incorporated many of Riessman's ideas, but even as it did, the New Careerists were working to promote their models and ideas for the future of paraprofessional labor as well.

Frank Riessman (in tie) meeting with Mary Dowery (to his left) and parent aides at Mobilization for Youth, 1963. Riessman's vision for the "New Careers" movement built on his experiences working with aides and paras in New York City in the 1960s. Collection of Mary Dowery.

CHAPTER 6

New Careers and Parent Implementation

New York Models for Federal Education Programs

Remaking Public Education:
Frank Riessman and Preston Wilcox

Frank Riessman and Preston Wilcox crossed paths regularly in 1960s New York. Both earned their graduate degrees at Columbia (Riessman in social psychology in 1955, Wilcox in social work in 1961), and both put their professional expertise to work in early experimental programs of community action, antipoverty policy, and educational improvement. By 1965, they were two of the most influential advocates for the hiring of paraprofessional educators in the city. Riessman authored the policy framework in *New Careers for the Poor* while at New York University; Wilcox chaired the board of the Women's Talent Corps, which developed the first program of training and recruitment for paras in public schools. Both men were key members of the coalition that pressured New York City to begin hiring paraprofessional educators in 1967.

Intellectually and politically, their paths diverged in the late 1960s. Riessman worked within the educational bureaucracy, drafting legislation, authoring white papers, consulting on Board of Education demonstration projects, and corresponding regularly with administrators, politicians, and union leaders. Wilcox turned his efforts toward dismantling this bureaucracy. He authored an influential article outlining his vision for community control of public schools in 1966—one in which he argued for hiring local residents in para-type roles—and joined Black and Puerto Rican parents in Harlem, Brooklyn, and beyond in demanding a radical restructuring of public schools and the relations of power that governed them. Riessman believed the crisis of care in public education could be addressed through new staffing, collaboration, and training within an expanded educational bureaucracy. Wilcox believed this bureaucracy was actively hostile to the care of Black children and hoped to replace it with systems in which students, parents, and their communities controlled, governed, and evaluated their own schools.

Despite these differences, Riessman and Wilcox pursued their goals for public education through many of the same institutional channels and organizational strategies. Both founded and led small institutions in New York City from which they traveled extensively, published voluminously, and hosted conferences that brought thousands of people together. From their bases in New York, both took on influential roles as advisors to federal Office of Education programs that funded the hiring and training of paraprofessional educators in the 1970s. In this capacity, Riessman and Wilcox both shaped visions for, and practices of, community-based educational hiring and training in schools and school systems across the United States.

Riessman founded the New Careers Training Laboratory (NCTL) at Queens College of the City University of New York in 1971, bringing his colleagues from NYU's New Careers Development Center with him. From 1971 to 1977, they served as the lead advisors to the Office of Education's Career Opportunities Program (COP), a demonstration program funded by the Education Professions Development Act (EPDA), which Riessman's collaborator Alan Gartner had drafted. The COP employed nearly 15,000 paraprofessional educators across its seven years, serving hundreds of thousands of students in 132 districts across the nation.[1]

Riessman and his team of scholars and educators from the NCTL traveled extensively to Career Opportunities Program sites to conduct training, provide support, and lead evaluations. They produced regular reports on their work, which they circulated within the program to share best practices and more widely to spotlight the impact the program was making and the success of its New Careers framework. They hosted conferences that showcased this work alongside scholars, policymakers, and organizers engaged with the New Careers project.

Paraprofessional educators in the COP enjoyed some of the very best opportunities and support available in the 1970s, for two reasons. The first was EPDA funding: COP paras earned more and had access to better training because of it. The second was Riessman and the COP's commitment to training and collaboration. The NCTL team's tireless efforts meant that teachers, paras, and principals prepared together in schools, and that institutions of higher learning made space for paras and career ladder programs. Where it was most effective, the COP shaped practices and policies that were adopted by local school districts and written into union contracts as well as training programs that colleges and universities maintained.

In 1970, Wilcox founded Afram Associates, Incorporated, a not-for-profit consultancy designed to support and catalyze struggles for Black Power and self-determination nationally. From his second-story office in Harlem around the corner from the IS 201 complex, Wilcox applied that summer to serve as a program advisor to Project Follow Through, a federally funded enrichment program designed to "follow through" on the gains children made in Head Start by bringing the Head Start model—specifically the hiring of local residents as educators—into K–3 classrooms nationwide. Wilcox had long admired Head Start, citing the Child Development Group of Mississippi's program as a model in his 1966 article on community control of schools.[2]

Afram worked with the schools it supported to promote a program called "Parent Participation in Follow Through" (renamed "Parent Implementation" in 1972) to build parent power in every aspect of the program. While all Follow Through programs followed Head Start's model and hired aides and paras from local communities, Afram's chief innovation was the creation and funding of new parent jobs as "local stimulators." As Wilcox explained, the goal was "to provide the *parents* with a staff person who would be solely responsible to them" (emphasis original), to ensure that parental involvement was not managed or sidelined by those in the education bureaucracy.[3] At its peak, Afram advised seventeen schools serving nearly 3,000 students.[4] Beyond these specific sites, Wilcox promoted Afram's vision throughout Follow Through, hosting conferences, circulating materials, and fighting to preserve overall program funding.

A wealth of recent scholarship has documented the many efforts to create alternative systems of education in Black communities in the 1970s.[5] These included independent schools and academies, experiments in community involvement in public schools, and street academies. Such efforts, in earlier scholarship, were often referred to as "separatist" and contrasted with the "integrationist" efforts of early-to-mid-1960s civil rights activism. The transition from "integration" to "community control" has likewise been depicted as a narrowing or turning inward of Black freedom struggles. However, as Wilcox's trajectory shows, opposition to officials in power and frustration with the bureaucracy did not mean disengagement with the public sector.[6] Wilcox was a vociferous critic of unions, bureaucrats, and officialdom throughout this period, but at the same time, he was a sponsor and organizer for federally funded educational programs in public schooling. Moreover, his investment in community control did not lead Wilcox to focus solely on Harlem or New York City. Rather, even before Afram began sponsoring Follow Through programs, Wilcox was writing and traveling widely to build what he called a "social movement" in support of community control for working-class people everywhere.[7]

As the numbers indicate, Riessman and Wilcox reached only a small percentage of the nearly half a million paraprofessional educators working in the United States by the mid-1970s. As advisors to federal programs, however, their impact was magnified in several ways. From the outset, federal money—initially from the Elementary and Secondary Education Act of 1965—had facilitated the hiring of paras in public schools, setting examples from which state and local educational agencies designed programs. "Demonstration programs," including the Career Opportunities Program and Follow Through, did just what the name suggested: they used federal money and program support to demonstrate the impact that locally hired educators could make for students, parents, teachers, and administrators. The programmatic visions that the New Careers Training Laboratory (NCTL) and Afram Associates promoted thus reached far beyond the individual paras and schools with which they worked.

Working with federal programs gave Riessman and Wilcox a platform from which to promote their particular visions for paraprofessional educational work more broadly. The NCTL and Afram seized these opportunities, generating mountains of printed material and hosting multiple conferences in the 1970s to advocate for their programs. Advising the COP and Follow Through also brought Riessman and Wilcox into debates about how "professionalism"—formal and informal hierarchies of skill and credentialing, built on assumptions about race, class, and gender—should be redefined in public education, and who should have the power to determine educators' preparation, employment, and evaluation.

Both men agreed that the paraprofessional assimilation advanced by the AFT's leadership was not sufficient or desirable in schooling, and both advanced programs of collaboration among educators, administrators, families, and communities instead. Riessman and Wilcox diverged sharply, however, on credentialing and advancement. Riessman's "career ladder" model affirmed the need for professional training and credentials and sought to create new forms of training to make these credentials more accessible. Wilcox believed that existing institutions of training and credentialing actively marginalized the needs and knowledge of students, parents, and community members. He argued for a radical reconstruction of training, hiring, employment, and advancement, in which parents would be empowered to control these processes.

Riessman deployed an evolving language of professionalism in his work from 1965 to 1975 that tracked his evolving vision for schooling. Like their sporadic collaborators in the AFT, the New Careerists did not want to do away with credentialled professionalism and its hierarchies of skill and reward. Rather, they worked to link the positions in these professional hierarchies through collaboration on the job and clear and direct opportunities for advancement between jobs: the career ladders for which the New Careerists were known. In the New Careers vision, every worker who took part in the educational process wielded some professional status, not as sole providers of professional services but as constituent parts of a greater human service whole. Riessman thus replaced the anthropological exoticism of the "indigenous nonprofessional" title that appeared in *New Careers for the Poor*, first with partial ("para-") professional and then with "new professional." In doing so, he collapsed the distance between the classroom teacher and the new worker by their side and asserted that paras should be understood as contributors to the professional process as well as future ("new") teachers.

With guidance from Riessman and the New Careerists, the Career Opportunities Program advanced a holistic version of training and collaboration. In participating classrooms and schools, the COP organized and funded training, meetings, and councils in which paras, teachers, administrators, and parents worked together to improve schooling. In colleges and universities, the COP funded and advised new career ladders: free and stipend-supported teacher-training programs for paras designed to fulfill the promise that para jobs would lead to new careers in education—and particularly teaching—for working-class women. At their boldest, the New Careerists believed these successes augured a new world of public education, in which professional advancement would be fluid, collaboration the norm, and schooling democratized through the regular, paid participation of adult community members, all of whom would earn living wages and many of whom would become regular teachers. The truth was more limited: with EPDA funds (which they had fought for and won), the New Careerists offered a glimpse of what their vision could look like at its well-resourced best.

Wilcox had long been skeptical of professionalism as both a philosophy of teachers' status and as it existed in practice. By the 1970s, he regularly penned scathing critiques of teacher professionalism and professional training for paras and Black professionals more broadly. Writing to New York City Schools Chancellor Harvey Scribner in 1970 in response to a query about teacher training, Wilcox argued that New York City must "broaden and deepen the definition of the words 'education' and 'training'" to recognize that "community selection procedures [are] a process of training and education for teachers." Teachers, Wilcox argued, "must, to be effective, feel responsible to the community (to the people that they teach and the parents of those people) and not to the school bureaucracy."[8] Wilcox believed the work of education had to be radically redefined through sustained engagement with working-class Black and Latinx communities.

While Wilcox worked through federal programs, he saw no value in incorporating paraprofessional educators into the mainstream of teaching, as the AFT did, or into the New Careerist vision of career ladders. He argued that university and educational bureaucracies were hostile to Black parents and children, and that educators who trained within them would become so, too. He contended that career training for paras was assimilationist, a "new form of technical interpretation designed to turn authentic, natural Black mothers into 'professional technicians,' unrelated to the Black community, comfortably subservient to the white community."[9] For Wilcox, professionalizing care work eliminated the possibility of care, while training parents would misalign their allegiances away from the communities from which they came.

Wilcox's argument echoes the critiques made by Cleo Silvers in describing her experience as a para in *Up from Under*. However, it also contains elements of the "supermother" stereotype diagnosed by Patricia Hill Collins as a form of gendered management of Black women's labor within patriarchal movement organizations.[10] To Wilcox's credit, in practice, he and Afram tended to adapt to the needs and local leadership of Black women in Follow Through programs, and they did support paras who sought traditional training and degrees.

Wilcox's harsh critiques extended to Black professionals in education. In 1967, he argued that "the Negro Professional . . . at I.S. 201 helped transfer the victory into defeat."[11] In 1970, he asserted,

A high number of public servants function within such communities as "company agents" for the broader city, as gatekeepers, bewilderers, neo-colonialists, eavesdroppers for the system and as professional pimps . . . they earn their livelihood by helping to keep such communities in their places.[12]

Professionalization, under extant structures of power and privilege, was anathema to Wilcox. In developing his Parent Implementation model for Follow Through, he sought to present an alternative, community-driven model for hiring and training community-based educators.

Neither Riessman nor Wilcox saw their visions realized in full. Federal support for the Follow Through program ended in 1976, and for the COP a year later. The end of these programs reflected larger shifts in educational policy and the national political economy in the 1970s, discussed more fully in the following chapter. At the same time, the shuttering of Follow Through and the COP revealed limits in Riessman and Wilcox's visions and programs for community-based paraprofessional educators.[13]

The New Careerists' ambitions ran up against two challenges. The first was broad scalability. Riessman and his team believed the success of their demonstration programs would encourage their widespread adoption. Union contracts proved the most durable way to maintain training programs and career opportunities after demonstration dollars dried up, but in many cases, programs disappeared when the money did. States and local districts simply did not have the resources in the mid-1970s to pick up the slack when federal dollars disappeared. The second problem was that the New Careerists lacked a political strategy and constituency. Riessman was an adept broker, bringing diverse and even hostile groups of people together and promising to realize the goals of each, at least partially. However, when funds ran dry and conflicts emerged, no stakeholder—neither school districts nor local activists nor universities nor teacher unions—considered preserving the COP their primary priority. After Congress declined to renew its funding, the COP disappeared almost overnight in 1977.

Wilcox's Parent Implementation model, by contrast, had a clear constituency and political perspective. The parents in his programs fought hard for them, and Wilcox understood that parental support and advocacy was essential to preserving Follow Through as a whole. However, having built a program premised on outsider critiques, and one particularly hostile to teacher unions, Wilcox could not enlist power brokers within the educational bureaucracy to preserve and expand the work that Afram did with its individual sites.

The end of the Career Opportunities and Follow Through programs meant an immediate loss of support for the paras, school districts, and local communities with which they worked. The disappearance of these alternative models had a larger impact, as well, as their presence had pushed both school districts and American Federation of Teachers locals to adopt some, if never all, of the collaborative and critical ideas that Riessman and Wilcox advanced. The New Careers Training Laboratory and Afram Associates were, at one level, small New York institutions working hard to promote their particular visions, but they also served as highly visible national arms of what the New Careerists dubbed the "paraprofessional movement." Their disappearance foretold an oncoming narrowing of the possibilities for these workers and their labor. Studying the COP and Afram's Follow Through programs helps us understand how paraprofessional educators established themselves in schools permanently, while recovering their visions offers examples of how collaborative and capacious para programs were—and could be.

Creating Career Opportunities:
Frank Riessman and New Careers Advocacy

Frank Riessman would have been surprised, in 1970, to hear his "New Careers" model for paraprofessional hiring described as an "alternative" vision. Announced in 1965 by Arthur Pearl and Riessman's *New Careers for the Poor*, the New Careers model had gained considerable traction in the five years that followed. By the time Riessman moved from NYU to CUNY in 1971, he could claim influence on federal legislation and international union

organizing. As Riessman argued in 1968, the New Careers movement was
an "evolutionary revolution" that would remake urban political economy
through an expanded public sector providing new jobs and new forms of
political engagement.[14]

Riessman's program and vision for what he called the New Careers movement evolved dynamically from 1965 to 1970. In expanding and revising his
ideas, Riessman responded both to national policy debates and to the performance of "indigenous nonprofessionals" in paraprofessional programs in
New York. Riessman's early work, particularly *The Culturally Deprived Child*
(1962), reflected the postwar "culture of poverty" paradigm popularized by
Oscar Lewis. However, as Robin Marie Averbeck writes, his later publications
"are marked by a willingness to reconsider, or at least cast in a different light,
some of his earlier positions."[15] It surely helped that Riessman surrounded
himself with younger and more radical scholars at the New Careers Development Center (NCDC) at NYU. Chief among these was Alan Gartner, who
joined the NCDC after research and organizing stints with the Congress of
Racial Equality in Boston, Massachusetts, and Suffolk County, New York.

The publications Gartner and Riessman collaborated on after 1965 laid out
a program to remake urban political economy through an expanded public
sector that would provide new jobs and new forms of political engagement.
They repudiated the "culture of poverty" thesis and behavioral antipoverty
policies in favor of what Gretchen Aguiar and Michael Katz call, paraphras-
ing Riessman and Gartner, "maximum feasible employment."[16] As Riessman
wrote in 1967, "the notion is jobs first, training built in; that is, the job becomes
the motivator for further development on the part of the nonprofessional."[17]
In framing their work this way, the New Careerists joined a burgeoning multiracial movement for full employment.[18]

Public-sector employment, Riessman hoped, would also generate political empowerment. As he argued in 1968, "If today's revolution is to do more
than protest, it must be based on programs designed, through group action,
to increase the power of every individual by helping him acquire the means
on which to base the central decisions concerning his life."[19] Riessman's framing—"more than protest"—echoed that of fellow full-employment advocate
Bayard Rustin, whose 1965 essay, "From Protest to Politics" in *Commentary,*
presaged Rustin's efforts to build a multiracial movement for a robust program of public-sector investment and job creation.[20] Rustin's position would
bring him into conflict with other thinkers in the Black freedom struggle;
Riessman's pursuit of politics beyond protest included debating Saul Alinsky
regarding Alinsky's strategies for organizing outside of, rather than within,
municipal bureaucracies.[21]

Up from Poverty, a collection edited by Riessman and Hermine Popper in
1968, showcased the range and reach of the New Careers vision in politics

and public policy in the late 1960s.[22] The volume was dedicated to Dr. Martin Luther King Jr., citing a letter he had written promising to attend a New Careers conference in June of 1968. Socialist Michael Harrington contributed, citing A. Philip Randolph and Bayard Rustin's proposed "Freedom Budget" and arguing that New Careers positions did double duty, offering "material value" in the form of jobs as well as "contribut[ing] to the democratization of society."[23] Robert F. Kennedy re-published his floor speech in support of the defeated 1967 Emergency Employment Act, lauding the hiring of 116,000 teacher aides through the Elementary and Secondary Education Act and noting "employment is the only true long-run solution" to poverty.[24] The mention of the ESEA, which Kennedy's erstwhile rival Lyndon Johnson had signed in 1965 while describing education, not employment, as "the only valid passport from poverty," was surely no coincidence.

Up from Poverty also summarized and explained the recent legislation influenced by the New Careerists: the Scheuer Subprofessional Careers Act and the Education Professions Development Act. The authors encouraged educational administrators and local activists to take advantage of these new resources and hire paraprofessional educators. To support their appeal, the collection gathered new scholarship on paraprofessionals showing "very positive" early reviews of programs. These included studies conducted at sites run in partnership with the NCDC in New York City, as well as two massive studies of paraprofessional programs by Garda Bowman and Gordon Klopf of Bank Street College of Education in New York.[25]

The predominance of material on education in the *Up from Poverty* volume pointed to an emerging reality for the New Careerists. Pearl and Riessman's *New Careers for the Poor* had highlighted schooling as one of several human service areas in which "indigenous nonprofessionals" could make an impact. However, by the late 1960s, it was clear that public education was the largest site of paraprofessional hiring and the bureaucracy most amenable to the creation of career ladders. Barriers to career advancement were far higher in health care, while social and community work opportunities were spread across an increasingly disparate network of community-run and nonprofit programs.[26] Thus, as paraprofessional hiring soared in New York City and nationally after 1967, the NCDC came increasingly to focus on education.

In addition to publishing scholarship and promoting legislation, the NCDC served as a trainer and lead consultant on para programs in East Harlem, and Riessman himself spent many hours with the new educators of Harlem Youth Opportunities Unlimited and Mobilization for Youth. From these experiences, Riessman and his partners developed more generalizable models for training and employing paras, which they published through the Office of Education in 1967 and 1968.[27] Alan Gartner co-edited a "New Careers Newsletter" that included updates on policies and programs from the federal

Departments of Labor and Health, Education, and Welfare. Gartner's newsletter also contained supportive quotes about community-based education
from President Richard Nixon and AFSCME, reports of successful para programs from around the country, and a New Careers bibliography.[28] The New
Careerists also cheered the unionization of paras and supported the UFT
and AFT organizing drives, as discussed in Chapter 3. As Riessman told the
House Committee on Education and Labor in 1968, "We have moved from
the demonstration program to programs that are an integral part of the labor-
management relationship."[29] This was, in truth, the work of paras and their
unions more than Riessman's doing, but the New Careerists undoubtedly
had aided the process.

Funding and political support for the antipoverty programs and research
Riessman and the NCDC conducted began to dwindle in the late 1960s. However, the federal government's continued investment in education programs
offered the New Careerists a new opportunity in 1970. As advisors to the
Career Opportunities Program, they would further develop their model and
put it into action in classrooms and communities around the country.

Training and Collaboration:
Building the Career Opportunities Program

The Career Opportunities Program was created by the Office of Education
using funding from the Education Professions Development Act of 1967,
which Alan Gartner had drafted. As the name implied, the program's focus
was on creating career opportunities for paraprofessional educators. Of the
original three goals of hiring "indigenous nonprofessionals" in the New
Careers framework—improving service provision, building connections
between providers and the communities they served, and creating new career
pathways in the human services—building career ladders had proved the most
challenging, and the least likely to be done effectively. As Claire Dunning has
shown, jobs in community agencies and their nonprofit successors regularly
promised career training but did not deliver.[30] The failure to create career ladders left Black and Latina women stuck in poorly paid entry-level jobs, from
which they could neither enter the professional workforce nor democratize
its relationship with communities. The lack of career opportunities was a
core reason paras voted to join AFT locals, as well. If paras worked in a fixed
hierarchical structure—in which the care-work elements of schooling were
handed off to poorly paid aides while teachers did the "professional" work
of education—then para programs were simply reinforcing racial, gender,
and class inequalities.

New Careerists had to create career pathways to truly transform public
services, but building new career paths required significant investment from

training institutions, as well as the renegotiation of credentialing and hiring processes shaped both by public sector law and union contracts. At a broader level, building these pathways also required buy-in from K–12 school districts, whose administrators had happily deployed additional workers but often balked at sponsoring career training (as New York City's Board of Education did in fighting the creation of CUNY's program). It was for this reason that the New Careerists put so much energy into training and creating collaborative spaces for teachers, parents, and administrators as well as paras: to ensure that all these stakeholders saw and understood the potential of these programs, and that they understood paras and their labor as an essential part of the whole educational process.

The Career Opportunities Program aimed to overcome the institutional obstacles to career advancement with money from Washington and expertise from New York. The COP's directors helped to cement this connection. Wilton Anderson, who had previously served as director of the Auxiliary Education Career Unit for the New York City Board of Education (a forerunner to the Paraprofessional-Teacher Education Program at CUNY), was the COP's first director, succeed by Gladstone Atwell. Both men had extensive experience with paraprofessional programs and had authored their own work on the topic. Both also corresponded regularly with Riessman and Gartner.[31] Their leadership of the COP ensured that the New Careerists would be an integral part of the operation, beyond a mere consultant role.

The COP formally launched on July 1, 1970, with an annual budget of $24.3 million. The program hired 9,000 initial participants as paraprofessional educators to work with nearly a quarter of a million schoolchildren.[32] Over the next five years, it grew to include nearly 15,000 paras at 132 sites across the nation. According to a midpoint evaluation, 86 percent of participants came from low-income families, while 63 percent had previously worked in governmental programs. These figures suggest that the COP attracted paras with community-program experience who were seeking better pay and career advancement opportunities, some of whom had already worked themselves out of officially recognized poverty in local jobs. In Oakland, for instance, COP paras earned between $2.60 and $3.74 an hour, above what district-employed paras had previously earned (and on par with wages in union contracts elsewhere).[33]

Nationwide, the Office of Education identified 54 percent of COP paras as Black, 14.3 percent as Hispanic, 4 percent as Asian or Pacific Islanders, 3.7 percent as Native American, and the remaining quarter as white.[34] All of them lived in the districts, and typically the school zone boundaries, where they worked. As a report from Minnesota noted in 1974, "COP has been based on the belief that the education of children from economically disadvantaged families can be improved by aides and teachers who come from economic and

ethnic backgrounds similar to those of their students."[35] Roughly 85 percent
of COP paras were female, below the national average, in part because the
program explicitly targeted veterans; in Oakland, nearly one-quarter of paras
hired by the local COP (fourteen of sixty) had served in Vietnam.[36] Nationally,
the average participant was in their early thirties, though ages ranged from
eighteen to seventy.

While COP paras were concentrated in urban areas, they worked at a
wide range of sites. George Kaplan's final report listed, among others, the
major cities of New York, Cleveland, Nashville, and Oakland; smaller cities
and towns including Yakima, Washington, and Cedar Rapids, Iowa; and rural
sites. These rural sites included Hardin, Montana, where educators hailed
from the Crow and Northern Cheyenne tribes; Martinsburg, West Virginia,
not far from the Appalachian porch Lyndon Johnson visited while promoting the War on Poverty in 1964; and Crystal City, Texas, where paras were
drawn from migrant Mexican and Mexican American farmworkers. Student
leaders in Crystal City schools had listed the hiring of parent aides among
their demands in their 1969 "blowouts."[37]

In its general structure, the COP ran much like other paraprofessional
programs. Participating community educators were selected by community
antipoverty agencies, which were associated with Model Cities programs in
urban districts. Paras worked in a wide range of capacities under the supervision of teachers and guidance counselors, determined jointly by faculty,
administrators, and local COP staff. As described in the COP's final report,
the "aide was the adult in individualized instruction settings, the point person in bilingual and bicultural activity, the main two-way communicator
on behavioral matters, and the principal subject of a school's first tentative
probes into differentiated staffing patterns."[38]

What made the COP different was its top-to-bottom commitment to training and collaboration in the classroom and at school. Paraprofessional educators regularly gathered with school faculty and staff for planning sessions and
training at schools after hours. According to the "Project Director's Handbook" issued in 1970, "the concept of a partnership between school (Local
Education Agency), college, and community is to characterize the entire
developmental process." The COP, as its final report noted, aimed to create
a "galaxy of institutional ties" in support of paraprofessional programs.[39]
This commitment to partnership stood in stark contrast to paras' experiences being locked out of staff bathrooms and teacher lounges, and left out
of planning meetings and professional development in many districts before
the COP's arrival.

Riessman, Gartner, and many others employed by the New Careers Training Laboratory hit the road in the 1970s, traveling extensively to COP sites
across the nation to help them develop training, share best practices, and

build connections with both communities and institutions of higher learning.[40] They also created and circulated tremendous quantities of promotional materials. These included a regular newsletter, the *COP Bulletin*, which celebrated individual programs from Alaska to the Bronx and included bibliographies of additional resources for paras, teachers, and administrators.

This process of training and building connections began in the classroom. In a report in the *COP Bulletin* from Minneapolis, the COP's Alan Sweet noted, "while it is important that a paraprofessional be well trained, it is equally important that the supervising teacher or other staff member be trained in the effective utilization of the paraprofessionals."[41] The COP in Minneapolis developed training for first-year teachers working with COP paras. Successful "teacher/paraprofessional teams" taught in these training sessions, and the local district even created a film—"The School Aide Story"—and handbook for working with paras that drew on COP materials.[42] The Minnesota Department of Education explained, in its own report, that hiring paras meant "a new role for the teacher." As the state report outlined, para-teacher teams were successful because teachers "have expanded their role . . . to include being a supervisor, a trainer, and an evaluator of another adult in the classroom."[43] Citing this report, Sweet argued:

> The uninitiated may think that paraprofessionals make a teacher's job easier. They do not; they should not. The duties a paraprofessional assumes release the teacher to initiate activities at a higher and broader professional level. As a result, the teacher and paraprofessional team provide a better learning environment.[44]

It is clear, from these formulations, that the COP model did not dissolve or replace classroom hierarchies. However, both the emphasis on the para-teacher "team" and the provision of training for teachers and paras demonstrated the COP's commitment to producing a new, collaborative classroom experience. Paras, in this context, were not simply aides or even apprentices, as in the AFT's formulation, but essential components of a new educational model.

Beyond the on-site training for classroom educators, the COP institutionalized training and collaboration with local parents and residents. Each COP site created and maintained a local council modeled on the War on Poverty's Community Action Program, comprising parents, paras, teachers, and COP staff. The COP explicitly linked these councils to ongoing struggles for self-determination. "The COP," George Kaplan wrote, "was lineally descended from the Black civil rights and economic struggles of the generation that preceded it, and it was synchronized with the Hispanic-American and American Indian quests for equality." New Careerists were explicit in their belief that paraprofessionals could, and should, enhance community involvement in public education. COP staff, Kaplan reported, encountered an "increasingly popular acceptance of a role for the neighborhood in the affairs of its schools ... located somewhere on a spectrum between token committee membership and full community control." The COP, he noted, "at least in the program's early days ... was a notable tilt toward the latter."[45] Those who had organized for community control in New York argued that anything less than full control would not deliver change, and to be clear, the Career Opportunities Program did not operate on such a model. They did, however, recognize that the relationship between schools and the communities they served needed to change, and that parents needed to play a role. This did not always come easy; Gartner recalled being "too much of a New Yorker" in certain midwestern and southern school districts, where "the straight human power aspect" of paraprofessional hiring "was more compelling than community relations" as a logic for these programs.[46]

By involving parents and community members in the program's oversight, and by designing training that emphasized the immediate educational impact that paras hired from their communities could make, the Career Opportunities Program stood against both the "culture of poverty" thesis and deficit models of educational intervention. As George Kaplan argued, the COP "was a program of, by, and for minority Americans ... to demonstrate that minority Americans could seriously address problems that the majority society had failed to solve."[47] In Oakland, one para responded to a district-wide evaluation of the COP in the 1971–72 school year by noting, "People from *supposedly* low income backgrounds [emphasis added] ... can understand and relate more positively to students."[48] The impact of their presence, COP program officers believed, would be magnified exponentially if paras had free, accessible, and well-organized opportunities to train to become teachers.

In its design, the COP guaranteed full and equal access to comprehensive training programs—career ladders—for all its participants. To create these, the COP used federal monies to build and fund partnerships among local colleges, universities, and school districts. These programs engaged institutions that were initially "oblivious" to the COP's vision and sometimes to paraprofessional educators more generally. The goal was to generate a "precedent-setting arrangement" that, for many institutions, was "regenerative," spilling over into normal activities.[49] This regenerative, spillover effect, which Kaplan celebrated in an issue of the *COP Bulletin* in 1975, was at the heart of the COP's vision for transforming the work of education and the training of new educators.[50]

Implementing new training programs required site-by-site coordination and planning, and the process yielded decidedly uneven outcomes. In the most successful sites, of which Minneapolis was one, the COP worked with cities and states to build networks of opportunity. Minneapolis paras had the option of taking classes at several local community and technical colleges and could ultimately matriculate to the flagship campus of the University of Minnesota. "The Minneapolis paraprofessional training staff was moved both physically and administratively to the Minneapolis Public Schools/ University of Minnesota Teacher Center on the Main University Campus," Alan Sweet wrote in 1975, a move that "enhances both teacher and para-professional training."[51] Minneapolis was nearly unique in this regard; in a *COP Bulletin* report on "The COP and Academe," Kaplan noted that only a small minority of major state universities embraced paraprofessional train-ing, preferring to leave this work to community colleges and branch state universities traditionally focused on teacher training.[52]

The story in Oakland was more typical. Through the COP, the district engaged six local colleges as training institutions for the COP trainees and ESEA Title I aides as well. By the end of the 1971–72 school year, fifteen COP trainees and four ESEA aides had earned bachelor's degrees through these career ladders, and thirteen of these graduates had been offered teach-ing contracts in Oakland, which had adjusted its credentialing processes to accelerate their hiring.[53] The program seemed to be working, but the school district balked when paras and advocates pushed to expand it to all parapro-fessionals working in Oakland schools. Finally, in 1975, the Oakland Federa-tion of Teachers joined the Model Cities Program and COP in pushing for the expansion of the career ladder, and they won training opportunities for all of Oakland's paras.[54] The mutual reinforcement of COP innovation and AFT organizing consistently proved the best way to preserve and expand career opportunities for paraprofessional educators. This victory, too, was celebrated in the *COP Bulletin* as an example for other sites to emulate.

Just like early reports and studies on paraprofessional programs in New York City, initial evaluations of the Career Opportunities Program were overwhelmingly positive. In Minnesota, the state's 1975 report—based on interviews with paras, parents, teachers, and administrators—found "pre-dominant and pervasive" evidence of "the positive impact of COP aides upon the individualization of instruction" and "the importance of COP aides as a resource to the professional staff."[55] Alan Sweet argued in the *COP Bulletin* that "the greatest impact on the actual instructional process" made by any innovation of federal policy in Minneapolis "has been achieved through the introduction of paraprofessionals in the schools."[56]

In Oakland, where Model Cities and Black Panther Party organizer Paul Cobb described schools as part of the "urban plantation," the district's report said much the same.[57] Most administrators, teachers, and paras in Oakland, reported the COP, "reacted positively to most aspects of the program" and felt it had "a positive effect on the students, the school, the teachers, and the community."[58] One principal wrote that paras in the COP "bring with them priceless backgrounds in both the cognitive and affective domains" from their communities. A COP "team leader" noted that most paras were parents, and thus could "interpret" problems between "the community, the classroom, and the school site," while one Oakland teacher described the COP trainee she worked with as "an exceptional skilled teacher" who had brought her "valuable classroom help and understanding of the children."[59]

Positive evaluations, however, did not prevent conflict from emerging. As George Kaplan noted in his report on Oakland for the *COP Bulletin*, the "galaxy" of ties that COP programs relied on could become a "millstone," as "each funding source was banking on a share of governance."[60] These questions of control focused most directly on jobs: the hiring of paras and their re-hiring as teachers if, and when, they completed their training.

In New York, Albert Shanker wrote to the Office of Education's Allan Lesser in 1970 to complain that his union "has serious reservations about the Career Opportunities Program in NYC for paraprofessionals." The program, Shanker argued, "did not provide for objective standards of entry . . . thus allowing politics, patronage, discriminatory practices and other factors to determine which paraprofessionals are chosen for this career opportunity."[61] Two years later, the UFT recorded with dismay that the Bronx Career Opportunities Program Council—staffed in large part by community activists from Jerome and Aurelia Greene's Morrisania Community Progress Corporation—was pushing for new laws to allow "preferential hiring" of paraprofessionals who had earned their teaching licenses. The idea—which did not come to fruition—was to grant community school boards the power to hire these newly credentialed paras to work at their old schools.[62] While a policy of hiring paras as teachers in their former schools made sense, it threatened the UFT's control of teacher hiring and placement through the collective bargaining process. Though the AFT was often an essential partner in creating and preserving career ladders, the union and its locals did not plan to give up contractual control over the placement of new teachers.

Parent Implementation:
Institutionalizing Radical Educational Practices

Preston Wilcox, for his part, would not have been surprised that Albert Shanker and the UFT opposed the COP's partnership with a Black-led community organization in the Bronx. While the AFT hoped to see paraprofessional educators incorporated into public education on its relatively traditional terms, and the New Careerists believed in incremental transformation from within the system, by the late 1960s, Preston Wilcox wanted to see that system torn down and rebuilt from the ground up. Wilcox had fought for community control of public education in New York City since 1966 and had regularly called for hiring parents as part of these efforts. He clashed repeatedly with the United Federation of Teachers, blasting the union for insulating teachers from parent and community needs. Wilcox did not see a future for the freedom struggle in teacher unions, and he debated Bayard Rustin in the press.[63] While he had worked closely with Riessman and other New Careerists as a social work practitioner, he was deeply skeptical of professionalization through credentialing and formal education. The balance of power in these institutions, Wilcox believed, militated against radical transformation.

Wilcox had risen to prominence as a radical intellectual in the fight for community control of IS 201 in Harlem, and he became a fixture at educational conferences, gatherings, and networks in the late 1960s. This included traveling beyond New York City, as when he joined David Spencer of IS 201 and Al Vann and Herbert Oliver of Ocean Hill–Brownsville in Detroit in 1968 to promote community control.[64] The legitimation and hiring of parents as educators remained central to Wilcox's vision of community control throughout his writings and travels. In a proposal for a book on community control in 1968, Wilcox described his vision as "heavily weighted toward para-professional indigenous 'local influentials' who share in common: firing line experience; sustained involvement and participation in a similar anti-establishment-oriented group self-interest movement—the struggle for school community control."[65] In the same year, he wrote to Gene Bivins, a Black teacher unionist in Philadelphia, to share his "general principles on decentralization," which included an express endorsement of moving parents "from mere consumers to participants; from support parents to 'teacher parents' or better yet, 'foster teachers' . . . team members in the educational process."[66]

President Lyndon Johnson introduced Project Follow Through in his 1967 State of the Union address as a companion program to Project Head Start.[67] Unlike Head Start, which was housed in community-run or leased spaces, the Follow Through program ran within existing public schools, serving students from kindergarten through third grade. The program was also designed as a "demonstration" program—much like the Career Opportunities Program—to test different models of instruction to "follow through" on the learning gains made by student participants in Head Start. Participating school districts selected their sponsors and programs from a range of twenty institutions, including colleges, universities, consultancies, and not-for-profit organizations. With Wilcox at the helm, Afram joined the list of project sponsors in 1970.

Modeled on Head Start, Follow Through sites established parent councils to advise and shape programs. They hired "parent coordinators" to facilitate communication between schools and parent councils. Like Head Start, the project was initially funded and managed through the Office of Economic

Opportunity (OEO), and Follow Through retained the War on Poverty ethos of maximum feasible participation. Its founding documents declared that community action agencies should be consulted in hiring, and that all programs "must provide for significant parent participation in all aspects of the project," including participation in the classroom and school as "paid employees, volunteers, or observers."[68]

As Afram joined the Follow Through ranks in 1970, they hired a consultant, Nancy Mamis, to review the program as a whole. She approved. "The parent-student encounter is being enhanced. Parents are legitimating learning on behalf of their children even as they learn themselves. Students are also being exposed to seeing their own parents as being significant people in the learning process."[69] Nationally, Project Follow Through expanded rapidly from thirty-nine sites serving 2,900 children at a cost of $3.7 million in 1967–68 to 160 sites serving 70,000 students at a cost of $6.9 million in 1971–72. According to data from that year, the students Follow Through served were 48 percent Black, 13 percent "Spanish-Surname," 33 percent Anglo (White), and 6 percent Indian. Nearly half (48 percent) had been through the Head Start program.[70] At its peak in 1975, Follow Through ran 173 programs serving 94,594 students in over 3,700 classrooms.[71]

Afram's program was dubbed "Parent Participation in Follow Through," a name that Wilcox changed to "Parent Implementation in Follow Through" for the 1972–1973 school year. The shift reflected Wilcox's concern that "parent involvement has been used mainly by ambitious, politically-oriented professionals to gain the sanctions to do as they choose." Wilcox believed "parental involvement in the education of their own children has recently become an educational, political, and cultural necessity."[72] Afram's "Parent Implementation Model" established parents as "full partners in the educational process" and offered a six-point plan for their involvement. These included parent involvement in the recruitment, selection, and evaluation of all staff and consultants, the development of "educational methodology," the negotiation of contracts, the allocation of resources, and the establishment of links between schools, communities, and education agencies at the local, state, and federal level.[73] In Wilcox's formulation, community-based educational work was neither apprenticeship nor a rung on a ladder. He believed parents and communities possessed the knowledge and skills to educate children, administer schools, and govern every aspect of school district business.

Afram's program sought to implement and institutionalize a Black Power, community-control approach to schooling, based on Wilcox's own work and ideas. Charles V. Hamilton, the political scientist and coauthor of *Black Power* (with Stokely Carmichael), laid out the ways the movement for Black Power aimed to reshape state institutions at a conference Wilcox attended in 1968.[74]

Citing Wilcox's own work at IS 201, Hamilton urged the participants "to talk and act not only in terms of intense involvement of black people, but to be concerned about the implementation of control by black people of institutions affecting the black community."[75] Hamilton noted that "Black Power has been accused of emphasizing decentralization," but he explained that the philosophy was more sophisticated and engaged with state power. "As the federal government becomes more involved (and it must) in the lives of people," Hamilton declared, "it is also imperative that we broaden the base of citizen participation. It will be the new forms, new agencies and structures developed by Black Power that will link the centralizing and decentralizing trends" in order to "activate people, instill faith (not alienation) and provide a habit of organization and a consciousness of an ability to act." Hamilton closed by noting, "Black Power, then, speaks not only to the substance, the end results (more jobs, houses, etc.) but also to the process (more power in decision making) by which the results are achieved."[76]

The program of self-determination that Wilcox articulated for Afram's Follow Through sites was based in Black Power and developed in part through Afram's work with Black-led experiments in community schooling in New York City, Boston, and Washington, DC. However, as Wilcox made clear, it was not a racially exclusive vision. In public statements, Wilcox argued that public schools had failed "to effectively provide educational justice to black, Spanish-speaking, Indian, and poor white children," and Afram's sites included members of all these groups.[77] In 1972, when an article on "educational prophets" in the *Phi Delta Kappan* described Wilcox as a "radical pluralist," he embraced the moniker and sent the article to Afram sites.[78] The following year, he wrote to reject "an educational philosophy of assimilation over cultural pluralism in which minorities are 'outcast' and the preference is for evacuating the ghetto, not elevating it."[79] This stood in stark contrast to Albert Shanker's assimilationist goals and, to a lesser degree, the "evolutionary revolution" proposed by the New Careerists.

At Afram's sites, Wilcox applied this radical pluralism to schooling. Afram's program debuted in 1970, working with clusters of schools in five states and the District of Columbia. These included public schools in Atlantic City, New Jersey, East St. Louis, Illinois, and Little Rock, Arkansas. They also included the East Harlem Block Schools in New York City, the Highland Park Free School and Roxbury Community School in Boston, and the Morgan Community School in Washington, DC.[80] Half of Afram's initial sites—in East Harlem, Boston, and Washington, DC—had been developed and run by community-control advocates.[81] Their presence helped shape and realize Afram's program. Afram added three additional sites in 1971: Alcona, Michigan (a rural district, mostly white with a small Native population), Flint, Michigan, and Scott County, Arkansas (a rural, largely Black district on the Oklahoma border). By the end of the school year, Afram served a total of 2,984 children at seventeen schools.[82]

While other Follow Through sponsors focused their efforts on implementing particular pedagogies and curricula and working with teachers, Afram's program was built entirely around generating and facilitating parent and community involvement in public schooling. Like all Follow Through sites, Afram sites chose a parent council, which Afram called a "Policy Advisory Committee" (PAC) to emphasize its educatory role. Afram employed "Field Coordinators" including radical black educators Al Vann (of Ocean Hill–Brownsville) and Kenneth Haskins (of Washington, D.C.'s Morgan Community School), as well as Charles Isaacs, a young white teacher who had worked at Junior High School 271 in Ocean Hill–Brownsville during the 1968 strikes.[83] These coordinators traveled to work with local councils and visit their sites for three days every month. They also, uniquely, created an interschool Advisory Committee, comprised of one representative elected from each PAC to advise Afram. This committee inspired Wilcox and Afram's central staff; as he wrote after a series of site visits in 1970, "parents are laden with teaching talents . . . and that these talents have largely gone unrecognized." Afram's PACs "care with feeling," Wilcox wrote, and when the program took off at the sites, "school becomes a place where both children and parents learn to love learning."[84] To further the exchange of information, and to better listen to its partner schools, Afram instituted annual conferences, which began with Afram sites and grew to attract Follow Through parents from across the nation.[85] However, on the question of educational practice, Afram was deliberately agnostic. As their grant continuation proposal described it in 1975, "An effective 'Afram presence' implies the development and formulation of a local parent educational model identity," not any curriculum, pedagogy, or educational practices specific to Afram.[86]

Afram's most unique and influential innovation was having each PAC choose one parent to work full-time as a "Local Stimulator," defined as "an agent of other parents."[87] Afram trained and paid local stimulators from their grant funds, but these individuals were entirely supervised by local PACs and encouraged to "draw the community into school affairs, to introduce non-PAC members to PAC and the school, and to develop leadership skills in other parents."[88] As he wrote in 1974, Wilcox believed "concern for the child has been enhanced by the variable of the selection and hiring of 'paraprofessionals,'" but "paraprofessionals hired by the school system usually become overt advocates for the system even if they are covert advocates for the children."[89] Local stimulators, by contrast, were parent-employed parents, fulfilling Wilcox's vision for paraprofessionalism in its most community-based form. This strategy's ultimate goal, Wilcox explained, was "to enable them [Afram sites] to strengthen their potential for contributing to the education of their own children and their potential for sustaining their own efforts *without* Afram's continued assistance" (emphasis original).[90] The catch, as for the demonstration programs Frank Riessman ran, was the funding: paying parent-employed paras would quickly become a challenge without Afram's grant money.

Throughout these innovations, Afram and Wilcox emphasized an idea of ownership-as-power that was both material and political. On multiple occasions, Wilcox argued that traditional approaches to parent participation rendered parents "tenants" and teachers and administrators landlords, while his program of "implementation" confirmed "parents as owners."[91] Ownership of schools, for Wilcox, was not simply about control and legitimacy but also about resources. Organizers in New York City—including Wilcox, the United Bronx Parents, and Harlem Youth Opportunities Unlimited—had sought access to educational resources in their campaigns of the mid-1960s. These included school buildings, educational and training materials, and, of course, jobs. Such demands did not simply seek parents' integration into existing structures of power. They demanded a restructuring of the access to, and distribution of, state resources.

In a planning document for Afram's Follow Through program, Wilcox noted the need for both "full employment of community residents" and "availability of adult education programs for all, including both academic and job training courses."[92] The program Wilcox designed was expressly committed to modeling such full employment. In Afram's continuation proposal for 1971–1972, Wilcox noted that through salaries for Local Stimulators, stipends for Policy Advisory Councils, and travel expenses, including per diems, for both groups of local hires, "Afram will have invested rather directly into the concerns of the parents the amount of $72,618. This represents almost one fourth of its total grant." Wilcox added that Afram did business with Harlem-based firms and that its field consultants "try to live with local families and pay 'rent' to them when they are in the field." The goal, as the proposal explained, was simple: "to get money into the hands of those who need it the most." Afram did not conduct experiments on or about its sites but aimed to "make it possible for the consumers to participate in changing their own lives." For poor and working-class people, they averred, "that usually costs money."[93]

The goal of full employment was the one major philosophic and programmatic point of overlap among the otherwise divergent ideas of Wilcox, Bayard Rustin, and Frank Riessman. Across the ideological and strategic gulf that separated them, AFT organizers, New Careerists, and community-control activists agreed that the urban political economy in the 1970s did not and could not deliver adequate sustenance to working-class people. While they disagreed on how to go about it, Rustin and Wilcox both believed that a key goal of community-based educational programs should be paying living wages to those who needed them most. The public-sector evangelists of the

New Careers movement concurred. Rustin, Wilcox, and the New Careerists coupled demands for jobs with the belief that these new workers would not simply rise from their communities but, through their work as educators, rise with them.

In developing their Parent Implementation model and hiring local stimulators, Wilcox and Afram benefited from working with established parent-engagement programs at community schools. This process of learning from local experimentation mirrored the development of ideas for para programs in wider experiments of community action and control in New York City in the mid-1960s. The power of successful local innovations to shape national policy and politics also presented itself in the Career Opportunities Program, which learned from success in New York and Minneapolis, and in the AFT, whose national strategies were modeled on particular local campaigns. In 1971, Wilcox commissioned a report on "The Interaction between Parents and Professionals" from Dorothy Stoneman, the executive director of the East Harlem Block Schools, for use in Afram's grant proposals and planning.[94] During Highland Park's and Roxbury's tenure as Afram sites, parents raised money for scholarships and met with public school parents in Boston, while "the Morgan Community School has been meeting with other Follow Through programs in the DC School District program ... to spread the concept of parent implementation."[95] Sharing these materials inspired Afram's other sites, where reports described the program's positive impact on parent organizing, and particularly on local stimulators. Afram also benefited from the life experiences of the women it recruited to work as local stimulators, a constant refrain throughout paraprofessional programs.

As in COP sites, Afram's local sites reported that the Parent Implementation model made a broad impact on student learning, parent empowerment, and school-community relations. Writing from Flint, Michigan, Local Stimulator Liz Chisum wrote that "the Follow Through Program is the best thing that could have happened in the predominantly Black Schools that were denied ... their educational needs." Among the reasons for her glowing assessments, Chisum cited "the opportunity for so many parents of young children to obtain meaningful jobs," "the children, teachers, and parents have a closer relationship," and "our young Black children have a great capacity of learning."[96] Many sites reported, as did Kate Young in Scott, Arkansas, that the program "taught parents of their rights as parents and community people."[97] PAC member Jimmy Jackson of East St. Louis felt the program empowered his PAC, pushing their schools to recognize "the parent is the first teacher, the parents must know what's going on in school, must participate in all the activities and have a voice in the decisions made in the school."[98] In a remarkable assertion of community rights, the PAC of College Station, Arkansas, opposed a one-way busing plan, arguing, "since 1954 black students, parents and communities have borne the total burden of working toward a unitary system." To rectify this, they demanded "a school in our community which is vowed to our community . . . we refuse to sacrifice our children and our community any longer to satisfy the whims of individuals who do not know or care about us and our problems."[99]

Roy Beard of Alcona, Michigan—the site Charles Isaacs visited—argued that the "radical pluralism" of Wilcox's vision was applicable everywhere, even if Wilcox's ideas were forged in the crucible of the Black Power movement. Writing to the Office of Education in support of Afram's model in 1973, Beard acknowledged that his school district in rural Michigan was "lily white," but he explained that Wilcox's strategies for parent involvement had improved his district's ability to reach marginalized Native American and poor white students and families. "To me," Beard wrote, "this is what it's all about. This is parent participation."[100]

Reports from local stimulators featured in many Afram grants and materials. "The more I learn, the more they learn," wrote Antoinette Sargeant of East St. Louis, while Loretta Farmer of Atlantic City added, "It gives you such a good feeling to be able to become a part of the school system and not just a parent."[101] Several were inspired to seek careers as educators, as Kate Young reported. In College Station, Arkansas, the PAC noted, "Some parents are natural born teachers, [but] without Follow Through they wouldn't have the initiative to further their education. It provides jobs for parents and better acquaints them with the school and their children."[102] In May of 1974, Afram circulated an announcement of an "An AFRAM Community First," the completion of a four-year college degree by Doris Jean Beasley at Arkansas Baptist College.[103] Like community-based educators across the country, the local stimulators in Afram's programs espoused a vision of collective advancement that included their own higher educations, which would be put to use in service of the community.

At a philosophical level, these local stimulators' efforts to seek traditional credentials and professional status may have frustrated or worried Wilcox, but he adapted to the needs and desires of Afram's parent educators. When notice came that Afram would lose its funding in 1976 as Follow Through began to contract, Wilcox asserted that "the advent of the phasing out of the Follow Through program has heightened the importance of local development to ensure that Follow Through as a social movement persists even without funds." In service of this goal, Afram had begun creating and distributing "certificates of achievement to regular participants" in the hope that, along with Afram's written support, they would allow local stimulators to earn "experience credits" in college courses.[104] Wilcox may have wanted to see the credentialing system that shaped the educational workforce remade wholesale, but in the meantime, he and Afram did their best to give their parents the chance to succeed within it.

For all the very real philosophical and programmatic differences between Riessman's New Careers vision and Wilcox's Parent Implementation model, the people who worked in them had much in common. In his final COP report, *From Aide to Teacher*, George Kaplan sang the praises of Roberta Ellis of Minneapolis, who started as a COP para in 1971. A single mother in her forties, Ellis ran a home daycare during the day before heading off to her evening shift at a local country club. Once she secured a job in the public school system, she was determined to make the most of it. Ellis took nearly a full load of courses at the University of Minnesota while working as a para, taking advantage of the COP's robust, well-funded training programs, and still found time to teach Sunday school. By 1977, she had earned her bachelor's degree and teaching certification and worked full time as a fifth-grade teacher in Minneapolis.[105]

Katheryn Virginia Ann "Kate" Young of Scott, Arkansas, wrote to Preston Wilcox to describe her work after being chosen by her fellow parents in the Follow Through Parent Advisory Council to work as a local stimulator. She had worked as an educator since the 1960s, first as an aide with Head Start and then in public schools as a social work aide. She was an active member of her local church, the parent-teacher association at her children's school, the Head Start Parent Club, the Follow Through Parent Advisory Council, the Legal Aid Society of Pulaski County, and the Scott Area Action Council, and she coached a youth softball team on the side. As she wrote to Wilcox, "I was involved in many community organizing activities and now [as a local stimulator] I still work as much as I can to make Scott a better community for all the people who live here." Young also noted that she had been inspired by her experience in Follow Through to further her education at the University of Arkansas–Little Rock in the year to come.[106]

Gathering the stories and experiences of these "caring citizens" who jumped at the opportunity to expand the work they were doing with the aid of federal funding confirmed for Riessman and Wilcox that their programs truly had something to demonstrate.[107] In their own ways, they each sought to amplify these gains beyond the COP and Follow Through to politicians, policy scholars, educators, and the wider public. In so doing, they articulated broad visions for the transformation of public education in ways that would better incorporate the labor and wisdom of working-class Black women like Roberta Ellis and Kate Young. They also ran headlong into rightward shifts in policy and politics in the 1970s that systematically undercut their efforts and programs, in significant part through new forms of educational evaluation.

Imagined Futures and the Fate of
New Careers in Public-Sector Employment

As the New Careerists worked to build the Career Opportunities Program around the country, they continued to promote their broad vision to transform the public sector. The most ambitious statements of this vision appeared in a 1973 collection, *Public Service Employment: An Analysis of Its History, Problems and Prospects*, edited by Riessman, Gartner, and Russell A. Nixon. Building on a national conference hosted by these New Careerists the previous year, the collection opened with a broadside from Michael Harrington, then the leader of the Democratic Socialist Organizing Committee. Harrington blasted the Nixon administration and governors, including Ronald Reagan and Nelson Rockefeller, who "want to instruct some of our most abused, and sometimes marginal, citizens in the glories of work by using legal compulsion to rub their noses in menial labor." The alternative, Harrington argued, were careers with dignity and a future, in the New Careers mold. Ultimately, he wrote, the movement was a stepping stone to "a formal federal guarantee of a right to work" with the government not as an employer of last resort, but first resort, so that "labor might be put to needed social ends."[108] Later in the volume, radical economist Bennett Harrison put the issue simply, writing, "the guarantee of a job as a right of citizenship would be a revolutionary action."[109]

Frank Riessman followed Harrington's foreword with an argument that "the emerging service state . . . is the battleground of neocapitalism," because it was increasingly the locus of both work (as automation meant fewer industrial workers, despite growing production) and rights (to education, welfare, and health). Riessman scolded those on the left who sought to "ignore" or "strain" the service sector, and he argued that fears of co-optation were unfounded.[110] In his closing essay toward the end of the volume, Riessman contended that New Careers was "an attempt to deprive the capitalist class of a large portion of its surplus value as well as its power" through "radical reform."[111] Riessman's vision for an expanded public sector was part of an upsurge of such thinking in the mid-1970s. In 1975, Coretta Scott King told a reporter, "there are not enough hospitals and there is not enough medical care provided for people. There are not enough public schools. There are not enough teacher aids [sic]—nursing aids and that kind of thing." Scott King led the National Committee for Full Employment/Full Employment Action Council in these years, which, as David Stein explains, was focused on creating a "nonviolent economy" that "served human needs" through full employment legislation.[112]

Francis Fox Piven, whom Riessman critiqued for proposing "straining the system," took up the question of expanding the public sector in the volume's final essay. Piven, who worked alongside Riessman at Mobilization for Youth in the 1960s, warned the New Careerists that their program needed a better understanding of political engagement and political power. A public service employment program "that is both large-scale and socialistic in structure," the contributors had argued, "can be forged if we work to arouse certain potential constituencies with a stake in public service employment—minorities, the poor, women, students, and consumers."[113] Piven's question was simple: how? These constituencies, she argued, "simply do not have the political resources or organization" to make such a claim, particularly as a large—and hardly equitable or socialistic—public sector already existed. Piven warned that the "powerful interests" entrenched in the public sector—and here she included professionals, public-sector unions, and politicians—would continue to shape this sector for their own benefit. Responding to the New Careerists' assertion that their movement was an iteration of the larger freedom struggles of the era, she asked: "Who is it, or what is it, that is going to shape the stirrings of discontent into clearly articulated demands for a public service employment program?"[114] It was a question for which the New Careerists never found a satisfactory answer.

Nonetheless, Riessman, Gartner, and their fellow travelers remained committed to the belief that successful demonstration programs could not only deliver excellent short-term outcomes but also win the continued support of policymakers. In the halls of Congress, however, legislative priorities were changing. By the middle of the 1970s, the expansion of federal education funding led ascendant fiscal conservatives to attack the Elementary and Secondary Education Act of 1965—which still funded many paraprofessional programs and jobs—as an example of big government run amok.[115] Lawmakers and administrators within the Office of Education attempted to adjust the law to fit the times, emphasizing analytics and individualism and shifting away on equity and community action.

Nowhere was this more visible than in the reworking of the law's Title III. This lesser-known and lesser-funded title had begun with a "community action" mission, seeding community education centers (CECs) in local school districts to innovate beyond the strictures of the K–12 classroom. Many of the most innovative programs in New York City developed from within CECs, including El Museo del Barrio in East Harlem.[116] In 1972, part of this title was reworked for "consumer education," and by 1976, Title III was completely devoted to consumer education.[117] Under this new policy regime, seed money would not empower and hire working-class women as educators to innovate collectively for students; instead, it would hire experts to teach the poor how to best spend their limited income in the free market. Programs funded by Title III in 1976 included scam-avoidance programs for seniors in Arkansas, Utah, and several other states; introductions to "consumer economics" for elementary and middle-school students, including energy consumption curricula in Colorado; and lessons on frugal shopping for the poor in cities including Ocean City, New Jersey.[118] Somewhat incredibly, Alan Gartner won funds from the repurposed Title III for a program of "Consumer Education and the Human Services" in 1976, to be run by Gartner and Riessman's New Careers Training Laboratory at CUNY. Gartner's wording suggested they would study and evaluate the delivery of health and education services to the "consumers"—i.e., the residents—of Central Harlem.[119]

The transformation of Title III reflected the larger shifts taking place in the world of "poverty knowledge," in Alice O'Connor's formulation, as "community action" fell from favor and was replaced with increasingly "analytic" models. In an early example, Richard Nixon had ordered an audit of Head Start during his first year in office. The "impact evaluation confined itself to variables it could easily measure . . . and ignored or devalued more subtle, less easily quantifiable program objectives." Consequently, O'Connor notes, Head Start was judged "according to the measures of individual gains—such as cognitive ability or raised income—rather than more elusive indicators of community-level change."[120] This approach soon came to be applied to studies of paraprofessional educators in public schools.

These shifts in policy and politics threatened paraprofessional educators and their established visions for their work. "Neutral experts" using cost-benefit evidence of paras' impact would invariably underestimate or ignore the thick, multi-layered community connections and organizing that paras brought to their jobs. Policymakers and evaluators steeped in the "culture of poverty" would see these working-class Black and Latina mothers not as repositories of "indigenous" knowledge, but as fonts of matriarchal pathology.

In addition to the transformation of Title III, the ESEA's much larger and more significant Title I came under attack in the 1970s. Passed originally in 1965, the ESEA was shaped by both the civil rights movement and the War on Poverty. Its design and implementation laid out what scholars of education describe as an "equity regime."[121] Strategically designed to appeal to a wide range of lawmakers and infused with the "maximum feasible participation" ethos, the ESEA dispersed funds widely to combat poverty in a host of settings. As a consequence, one administrator noted, there was not one single vision for Title I funding for compensatory education, but "something more like thirty thousand separate and different Title I programs."[122] This variation had made room for the wide range of experiments in community-based hiring that paras and their allies seized upon to create para programs.

However, this variation also left the ESEA vulnerable to political attacks for its incoherence. Invoking the new analytic regime in 1970, President Nixon argued that most existing Title I programs were "based on faulty assumptions and inadequate knowledge."[123] The faulty assumptions to which Nixon referred included, pointedly, community action, while the knowledge he decried as inadequate was insufficiently quantitative and individualized.

Critiques of Title I came, as well, from advocates for educational equity, including a suit from the NAACP charging that state and local districts diverted Title I dollars away from poor children. The ESEA also became the vehicle by which specific protections for language learners and students with disabilities became enshrined in law. The rights of students to be educated necessitated new programs and new standards of evaluation and shifted the administration of the ESEA away from generalist and experimental programming toward explicit (and sometimes conflicting) directives and evaluations.[124] Paraprofessional positions followed this federal money. Bilingual paras, for instance, continued to find work even amid the recessions of the 1970s and during New York City's fiscal crisis.[125]

A broader shift occurred as the federal government moved to recognize and codify the rights of students with disabilities in the 1970s, notably in the 1975 Education for All Handicapped Children Act (since reauthorized and known today as the Individuals with Disabilities Education Act, or IDEA), which guaranteed access to a "free and appropriate public education in the least restrictive environment."[126] These students needed individual attention, which required new hiring and staff patterns in schools, even as general funding for compensatory education was increasingly diverted away from paraprofessional programs. By the 1980s, more than half of New York City's paraprofessional educators worked in special education, a ratio that holds today across a workforce of nearly 25,000 people.[127]

A Social Movement for an Alternative Public School System: Promoting Follow Through and Parent Evaluation

Like the New Careerists, Wilcox worked unrelentingly to promote Afram's program and vision, and to publicize the accomplishments of sites implementing it, to make a broader impact on public education. Afram "views itself much more as a social instrument than it does as a social institution," he wrote, and its goals included the "the taking of collective action by parents—and the shaping of public policy."[128] Much as the American Federation of Teachers and the Career Opportunities Program did, Afram circulated materials constantly through its network, aiming to connect sites to one another, to share best practices and accomplishments, and to establish a sense of a national movement. Afram's regular broadsides, many dubbed "Parent Stimulators" or "Action Stimulators," included a report about a successful fight to allow paraprofessional educators to serve on Title I advisory committees in New York City; a compilation of "Parent Insights, Proverbs, and Poems" from Afram sites; a report on the "Cost of Parent Participation" (noting Afram's commitment to paying parents); and an announcement of the creation of a "Parent Library" by the local stimulator in Alcona.[129]

Afram also intended these materials to be used by PACs working with Follow Through project administrators in local school districts. Several dealt with the role of project staff (who did not fall under Afram's direction), urging project directors to "keep all members of PAC fully informed" in "dealings with other authorities," and encouraging them to become "'naturalized' citizens of the host communities" by attending weddings, funerals, birthday parties, and other local events in and around their schools.[130] Beyond their self-produced materials, Afram also circulated parent-empowerment materials produced by Black parent organizers across the nation, including Milwaukee Legal Services' "Handbook for Parents" and a collection of "Education Materials" from the Federation of Southern Cooperatives.[131]

Just as the AFT's National Paraprofessional Committee planned conferences in Washington, Afram hosted conferences of parent advisory committees. These gatherings became sites for celebrating the work of local stimulators and putting their roles—along with those of parent councils—in the spotlight. Begun among Afram's own sites, these conferences grew to encompass representatives from nearly all 173 Follow Through sites by the time of Afram's August 1972 gathering in St. Louis. Afram, Wilcox reported, "had come to feel a sense of responsibility to the entire 'Follow Through School System.'" Representatives from the US Office of Education, which took over the program from the Office of Economic Opportunity in 1971, attended as well. Among the parent-led activities in St. Louis were the election of a national parent advisory committee for Follow Through and the launch of a letter-writing campaign to preserve funding for Follow Through sites (including Afram's own in Alcona, Michigan). Afram's report declared the conference "an effort of a variety of people involved in a federally-funded educational program to participate in shaping that program into a movement to impact public education."[132] Afram's next conference, in Hampton, Virginia, in May of 1973, drew similar numbers to what Preston Wilcox deemed a "family affair."[133]

These conferences contributed to Afram and Wilcox's larger goal of building "a social movement designed to create a federally-funded alternative public school system."[134] Unlike the New Careerists, Wilcox did not believe demonstration programs would be enough to convince educational bureaucrats to make parent participation and parent hiring permanent. Follow Through, he wrote, had "established the legitimacy of a federal role in transforming—not merely reforming—the public school system." In working with the whole program, his goals were the "stimulation of a broader community interest in the concept of parent implementation" and "training and development of a local cadre of parent trainers/consultants," to fight for these programs even if Afram or Follow Through lost their funding.[135]

While Afram did not effect a radical transformation of the school system, it made an impact well beyond the sites it served, particularly in the arena of evaluation. Wilcox fought hard to promote community-based roles in the planning, collection, and interpretation of evaluative data, writing both to the Office of Education and its contracted consultants to this effect in the early 1970s.[136] Wilcox's argument was echoed on the Senate floor by Minnesota's Walter Mondale. "No one really knows more about whether a program is working or not," declared Mondale, "than those whom it is supposed to benefit." He continued, "If we do nothing else in the 1970s we must make it our goal to achieve participation in programs by those who are supposed to benefit from them."[137] In a 1971 report on national evaluation procedures, the US Office of Education concurred, writing, "data which are not valued by their audiences will be seen at best to be irrelevant and at worse to be invalid."[138]

Debates about how to evaluate Follow Through, and paraprofessional programs more broadly, raged throughout the 1970s and are the subject, in part, of the following chapter. Throughout, Wilcox's efforts ensured that parent voices would be, at least in some cases, part of this process. His critique was prescient. Even before major cuts to Follow Through began to threaten programs in the mid-1970s, Wilcox understood that parents and communities needed to exert at least some control in the production of "poverty knowledge." Otherwise, they would see their hard work and local interventions deemed unworthy by outsiders using unfamiliar criteria and methods to pass judgment on these programs.[139]

As the creator and promoter of a particular model for Follow Through, Wilcox understood that evaluations of this model would matter. His focus on evaluation as a key site for community participation, however, ran deeper, back to arguments he made during the community control struggles in New York City. Parents, Wilcox believed, needed to set the agenda for evaluating public education, especially when their own work was on the line. In addition to the constant activism he organized on behalf of Follow Through programs and parents, Wilcox also wrote regularly and strenuously to the Office of Education to insist that parents and community-based educators take part in evaluating programs. Wilcox's Afram Associates promoted this model to their own Follow Through sites, urging that parents be regularly involved in the assessment of their children's education.[140]

Wilcox took his concerns up the chain, as well, insisting that the Office of Education (OE) implement programs that included parents in evaluation at every level. The OE had contracted the Stanford Research Institute to evaluate Follow Through, and it had produced a glowing report of the program's first year in 1969 and 1970, using survey data to show increased parent involvement as well as test data to show individual student gains.[141] Nonetheless, Wilcox was concerned. In February of 1971, he wrote to Richard Snyder, OE's chief of research and evaluation for Follow Through, to argue that test-score data collected by the institute should "not be presented by itself or interpreted by anyone other than the parents and the Parent Action Councils" in conjunction with "soft data" collected by parents themselves.[142]

In July, OE committed, in a draft of evaluation procedures, to openly sharing evaluations and procedures with communities and to giving community members "the opportunity to determine, at least in part, what data should be collected."[143] Wilcox continued to emphasize the need for parent participation in evaluation throughout the life of Afram's Follow Through sites. In 1973, he expounded on Afram's "Philosophy of Evaluation" in its annual report to OE, writing, "Afram seeks to involve locally-designated persons in paid positions as collectors of data, conveners of meetings, research assistants, and the like." In this context, he added, evaluation was a "learning tool" for parents as well as a method for producing feedback and accountability.[144] Self-evaluation was a final link in the chain of community control and accountability in Wilcox's definition, allowing communities to decide themselves what worked.

Wilcox's emphasis on the need to couple "hard" test score data with "soft" surveys of parents and communities anticipated many present-day movements to improve testing, as did his demand that communities have a say in the accountability measures imposed on their schools. Like the New Careerists, his concerns were gleaned from experience, and from the realization that Afram's model of community empowerment through paraprofessionalism was not easily measured by cost-benefit analysis. As Afram site coordinator Roy Beard (of "lily white" Alcona County, Michigan) wrote in a letter to Wilcox, "This is parent participation but how do you get this to show up in an evaluation study as a statistic?"[145] For Wilcox, the answer was, in part, to have the parents who participated evaluate the program themselves.

Struggles over evaluation and knowledge production took time and energy even when administrators—like those Wilcox worked with at OE—were sympathetic in the early 1970s. However, by the late 1970s, and particularly after the fiscal crisis in New York, the "analytic" revolution in policy was coupled to a political revolution whose commitments to cutting the public sector and social spending placed paras square in its crosshairs.

The End of the Career Opportunities Program and Follow Through

As the COP wound down in 1977, its chronicler, George Kaplan, sought to position the program's success within a changing world of policy and politics.

Conceived in the 1960s, the COP ran in the 1970s, and as Kaplan put it, the "climate of that decade was far different than earlier."[146] Freedom struggles "had crested" and were "ebbing," but despite the community action ideas built into the COP, Kaplan argued, the program in fact "epitomized the changed ambiance of the 1970s." Writing for an audience of politicians and administrators in 1977, Kaplan tried to walk back the New Careerists' socialistic visions and fit his story to the times. The COP, he wrote, promoted "old fashioned work ethic . . . not only didn't it attack the prevailing political and economic system, its participants were ambitious to become part of it."[147] For ascendant conservatives and opponents of antipoverty spending, Kaplan tried to refashion the COP's definition of paraprofessional labor as by-the-bootstraps individualism. It was a far cry from Riessman's calls for full employment earlier in the decade. Kaplan also strove to redefine the idea of the "indigenous nonprofessional" within this new rubric, writing that the use of "indigenous participants" made for "internal accountability" to communities.[148]

However, Kaplan's linguistic contortions, as he noted, were likely for naught, as the COP had "nonexistent public relations" and, according to one Office of Education official, "no one in Congress has ever heard of it."[149] The COP, by its own measures and according to the sociological studies conducted on its various programs, had been a smashing success, but it was unclear that anyone in power had either noticed or cared. Kaplan characterized it as a "scarcely-known offshoot of the underpublicized Education Professions Development Act" that received only "fleeting publicity . . . within the project locality, not at a national level."[150]

In the final offing, Kaplan recognized that the COP's multifaceted impact was difficult to capture, echoing Wilcox's critical assessment of the problem of evaluation emerging in education at the time. Of the COP's overall impact, Kaplan wrote, "low-income communities reawakened to their schools. Individual lives acquired new importance," but all of this was "frustratingly immune to quantification."[151] Without adequate evaluations to take account of the thick, multilayered impact that paraprofessional educators had in classrooms, communities, and unions, these educators and their work were vulnerable to political attack.

The New Careerists were fierce advocates for their vision at all levels of government in the 1970s, but they put their faith in the power of demonstration programs to persuade politicians and the public. In his conclusion, Kaplan cited congressional staffers, Black Studies scholars, and a "high-level Federal education functionary," all of whom agreed "our national interest in education was beginning to slip, a trend the Nixon Administration was pleased to encourage."[152] Reflecting on what became of most War on Poverty programs, Alice O'Connor writes, "In reality, it was the strength and organization of a political constituency, not cost-effectiveness, that would determine the[ir] fate."[153] The New Careerists were learning this the hard way.

The COP was "just the right size for a demonstration project," Kaplan argued, but it "played a role out of all proportion to its relatively small size." Kaplan ran through a robust list of accomplishments, examples of which are evident in the Minneapolis and Oakland case studies cited earlier. However, he closed only by saying: "by any measure, this Federal program did its job, often with high distinction. Its participants and the society they served were thereby enriched." Facing imminent closure, Kaplan's milquetoast conclusion is difficult to square with the visions of "revolutionary action" foretold by New Careerists just a few years prior. Riessman and the New Careerists had believed that a consensus in support of these programs could be built from the ground up, with support from diverse and even antagonistic actors. They united unlikely groups in many instances, but they did not build a sustained membership or movement to support their vision in the halls of power. When the time came for a political fight, the COP went quietly.

Afram's Follow Through grant was discontinued at the end of the 1975–1976 school year. Wilcox wrote furiously to the Office of Education to preserve his program, noting, "Our investment . . . has helped to shape the Follow Through program into an educational reform movement, hopefully to impact the larger system of which the Follow Through School System is a part."[154] Wilcox cited the materials he had created and disseminated, the conferences he had hosted, and the organizing efforts he put in to "save" Follow Through with a congressional letter-writing campaign in the spring of 1972.[155] His missives make clear the outsize impact of Afram's Harlem-based vision for paraprofessionalism and parent involvement on Follow Through, but they were to no avail. Federal policy was shifting away from models of community engagement in all policy arenas, and programs like Afram's were casualties of ascendant conservative policy regimes. Wilcox's own presence as a gadfly and unapologetic radical may also have made him a target. As he noted in pencil on one report, Afram lost its place in Follow Through because he and his team "refused to go along to get along."[156]

One group in particular, with which Wilcox refused to collaborate, was teacher unions, and a noteworthy omission in many Afram materials and reports is teachers themselves. In a précis on the "Parent Implementation Model" in 1972, Wilcox mentions teachers in passing, once to say that "The classroom is modified into a family group in which the teacher functions as a 'family' member and as a teacher" and elsewhere to assert that, at Afram sites, "Teachers operate as members of the local community."[157] These, however, are imperatives, not programmatic initiatives. They elide the fact that, as one report on Follow Through put it in 1975, "across all models there are features of Follow Through in general that mean a change, a redefinition of roles, that is often unsettling and threatening to teachers." The report noted "extra adults in classrooms requiring teachers' skills in supervision," and cited one sponsor who said, "we're asking them to do a lot more than in a regular classroom."[158]

Wilcox's opposition to teacher unionism—one Afram flyer asserted, "Unions are for people who do not trust themselves and each other" and "Parents are the children's union"—prevented a more systemic engagement with this workforce, but the absence of a plan for engaging teachers is nonetheless striking.[159] The AFT established paraprofessional educators as future teachers and worked extensively to make teachers comfortable with paras. The Career Opportunities Program built extensive training regimes to encourage parent-teacher teams in the classroom. Afram, however, did not seek to build the kinds of solidarity or alliances among teachers, paras, and parents that had sustained and expanded paraprofessional programs in New York City, relying almost entirely on the power of parent activism to transform schooling.

The ending of the Career Opportunities and Follow Through programs in the late 1970s meant the loss of millions of dollars for the hiring, training, and empowerment of local residents in working-class public school districts across the United States. The end of these programs also diminished the ability of Riessman, Wilcox, and their teams in the New Careers Training Laboratory and Afram Associates to advance their programs and visions for paraprofessional programs more broadly. While they reached only a comparatively small number of educators directly, the alternatives the NCTL and Afram presented to school districts and the American Federation of Teachers had proved influential. Riessman and the New Careerists had helped AFT presidents David Selden and Albert Shanker embrace career ladder programs and write them into contracts, and the COP had built ladders that AFT locals preserved and replicated in other cities. Wilcox had proved a powerful voice for parent empowerment in Follow Through and the Office of Education more broadly, and the programs he coordinated on the ground helped sustain emancipatory visions of education in Black, Hispanic, and Native American communities well into the 1970s. The end of these programs both reflected and hastened the breakdown of the coalition of forces that had fought for, and with, paraprofessional educators for a decade.

The New Yorkers who ventured forth from the five boroughs in the 1970s made a clear and significant impact on education nationally. In a decade that witnessed the shuttering of the Office of Economic Opportunity and the decimation of antipoverty programs, a rash of urban fiscal crises, and a rising backlash against "community action," the AFT, the New Careers

Training Laboratory, and Afram helped make community-based paraprofessional educators a permanent feature of public schooling from shore to shore. Their visions varied widely, but they shared underlying commitment to the power and potential of paras. By 1975, nearly half a million paraprofessional educators worked in public education, many with access to living wages, opportunities for career training, and connections to community movements for parent participation in schooling.

The AFT, NCTL, and Afram were not comparable institutions in terms of their size, structure, mission, or impact. What united them was their prominence within wider national contexts—the labor movement, social policy, and radical community organizing—as advocates for paras and para programs. The AFT, NCTL, and Afram agreed on the three principles of para hiring that emerged in New York City in the 1960s: improving education in classrooms, linking schools and communities, and creating jobs and careers in education. They all sought to secure the place of these workers in schools through legislation, demonstration programs, advocacy, and direct action. They all advised paraprofessional programs around the nation, sent organizers to far-flung destinations to support these programs, circulated materials they created, and convened conferences of paras and allies that defined paras as a class of workers. They all spoke of their work, and paraprofessional educators in general, as part of larger movements.

While they collaborated on occasion, the AFT, NCTL, and Afram differed significantly on how paras should be hired and trained, who they should be responsible to, and the meaning and purpose of their work within larger educational struggles. Each institution also encountered a range of new local contexts that reshaped their own work and expectations as they promoted their New York–born ideas and strategies throughout the United States.

As the AFT, NCTL, and Afram worked with paraprofessional educators in the 1970s, the historical phenomena that created the demand for this work and shaped its evolution faded from prominence. School overcrowding eased as the baby boom generation grew up. The Black freedom struggle was slowed by political backlash and criminalization. President Richard Nixon, building on this backlash, declared the War on Poverty over in 1973, and Congress slashed funding for social welfare programs amid a rising recession. While teacher union organizing continued, it did so in an increasingly hostile political climate that slowed the growth of public-sector unions and weakened their ability to bargain by the end of the decade.

As the rapid demise of the COP and Follow Through in the late 1970s make clear, the political winds were changing. In New York City, home to the strongest career ladder and most robust paraprofessional union chapter in the country, a fiscal crisis in 1975 was followed by the election of Mayor

Edward I. Koch in 1977, who promised to slash social spending. His first target, and the subject of the following chapter, was the effort of New York's paraprofessional educators to win annual salaries. His attack on their labor, and their legitimacy as educators, prefigured a broader attack on community-based paraprofessional educational work that came to limit the power of paraprofessionals in schools and cities as the 1970s drew to a close.

I Love New York, Mayor Koch.
Why Doesn't New York Love Me?

My name is Shelly Young. I've been a school paraprofessional for the last 10 years. And before that I was on welfare. I'm the head of my household and the mother of two children, 17 and 19 years old.

At P.S. 127, Manhattan, I work with 4-year-olds in a pre-kindergarten program. My day starts early. I greet the children and their parents at the school door and have breakfast with the children. Then it's a full day of helping the classroom teacher in a program of learning and play . . . drawing the children out and teaching them to relate to each other and the school experience . . . starting them off on the right foot.

At night I go to college. Someday I'll be a teacher. I'll be a good teacher, because I'm learning as much on my job as I am at college.

I'm paid on an hourly basis and earn about $9,000 over a year. Say I'm on the job every school day for the whole school year. In the summer I'm "laid off" and have to stand in line to collect unemployment. My union, the UFT, negotiated a new contract with the Board of Ed which would pay me year-round and but meth a pension system. And the city would actually save money on it. But Mayor Koch turned it down. He says I'm only a part-timer and not entitled to an annual salary . . . or something for my old age.

Mayor Koch, I'm a full-timer, doing a hard but exciting job. I'm the city's future. I love New York. Why doesn't New York love me?

United Federation of Teachers, Local 2, AFT, AFL-CIO
260 Park Avenue South, New York, N.Y. 10010.
Albert Shanker, President.

I Love New York, Mayor Koch.
Why Doesn't New York Love Me?

My name is Shelvy Young. I've been a school paraprofessional for the last 10 years. And before that I was on welfare. I'm the head of my household and the mother of two children, 17 and 16 years old.

At P.S. 137, Manhattan, I work with 4-year-olds in a pre-kindergarten program. My day starts early. I greet the children and their parents at the school door and have breakfast with the children. Then it's a full day of helping the classroom teacher in a program of learning and play . . . drawing the children out and teaching them to relate to each other and the school experience . . . starting them off on the right foot.

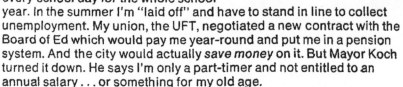

At night I go to college. Someday I'll be a teacher. I'll be a good teacher, because I'm learning as much on my job as I am at college.

I'm paid on an hourly basis and earn about $6,000 over a year. I'm on the job every school day for the whole school year. In the summer I'm "laid off" and have to stand in line to collect unemployment. My union, the UFT, negotiated a new contract with the Board of Ed which would pay me year-round and put me in a pension system. And the city would actually *save money* on it. But Mayor Koch turned it down. He says I'm only a part-timer and not entitled to an annual salary . . . or something for my old age.

Mayor Koch, I'm a full-timer, doing a hard but exciting job. I'm the city's future. I love New York. Why doesn't New York love me?

United Federation of Teachers, Local 2, AFT, AFL-CIO
260 Park Avenue South, New York, N.Y. 10010
Albert Shanker, President

CHAPTER 7

"Mayor Koch, Meet a Workaholic"

Fiscal Crisis, Political Realignment, and the End of the Paraprofessional Movement

A Decade of Gains Under Fire

Shelvy Young-Abrams still gets angry when she talks about Ed Koch. Elected in 1977 in the aftermath of New York City's fiscal crisis, Koch ran, and governed, on a platform of rage and resentment directed at those he blamed for the city's near bankruptcy: people who relied on the city's social services and the unionized public-sector workers who provided them. Embracing a bipartisan turn toward punitive solutions to social problems, Koch campaigned on a "law-and-order" platform, even calling for the death penalty (over which the mayor has no control).[1] Upon his election, he attacked Black and Latinx organizers and their neighborhoods. Koch denigrated local activists receiving federal funds as "poverty pimps" and made a point of ignoring community pleas as he closed Harlem's Sydenham Hospital in his first term in office.[2]

Paraprofessional educators, as unionized public servants drawn from the ranks of those eligible for public assistance, found themselves squarely in Koch's crosshairs. In the mayor's first year in office, the United Federation of Teachers sought annual salaries and pensions for paras in its contract negotiations. Koch signed off on all the union's contract demands but this one, vetoing it over the objections of his own appointed schools chancellor, Frank Macchiarola.[3] Koch claimed that annualizing paras' salaries would "set a dangerous precedent" for future contracts and suggested paras should collect unemployment or welfare in the summers instead.[4]

Young-Abrams, like many paras, had received public assistance before she was hired, and she found Koch's suggestion shocking and cynical. "Mayor Koch felt that we should still be on welfare. That pissed me off. I didn't think that. Why should I still be on welfare when I'm trying to better myself, so that the city would not have to take care of me?" Young-Abrams recalled in

2014. "We were ready to do a sleep-in at City Hall. No, we were. When that happened, we were ready to strap ourselves to the tables. That's how strongly we felt about it."[5] Annualizing paraprofessional salaries was no great cost. The mayor's pointed attack was part of his full-scale assault on the movements and institutions that had created and sustained paraprofessional jobs in New York City: civil rights organizing, antipoverty programs, and the public-sector labor movement. By singling out paras, Koch also laid bare the racist and sexist assumptions that undergirded the emerging political backlash to social welfare. His acquiescence to teachers' demands contrasted sharply with his diminution of paras' labor and his suggestion that they collect welfare. Koch made room for white, middle-class professionals in his coalition, but not for working-class Black and Latina educators whose work prominently involved care.

Paras fought back, defining themselves as "workaholics" who had improved public education through their love of their children and their city.[6] They rallied their union and community groups to their cause, but in Koch's New York, paras and their allies lacked the influence they had once enjoyed. The Board of Education had laid off thousands of paras during the 1975 fiscal crisis. Many were eventually rehired, but the UFT was unable to preserve the Paraprofessional-Teacher Education Program (PTEP) at the City University of New York (CUNY), depriving paras of free educational opportunities and the union of its most important symbolic link between paras and teachers. Local, state, and federal funding for antipoverty programs, including some that funded paras' salaries, receded across the 1970s. And while community organizers did rally against cuts to schools and programs, their actions could not stop the imposition of austerity measures by the state-appointed managers of the city. By 1978, paras lacked power. After a two-year struggle in arbitration, they won summer stipends to supplement their yearly salaries in 1980, but paras had to wait another three years for full access to pensions.

This final chapter charts the ways that the political and economic changes of the late 1970s brought about the end of the "paraprofessional movement" in New York City. New York had been an early, influential site of innovation in community-based hiring and paraprofessional organizing in the 1960s. By 1975, however, the city had become the leading edge of attacks on para programs and educators. These attacks began with the city's near bankruptcy in 1975, resulting in the layoffs of thousands of paras and the gutting of the PTEP program at CUNY.

Paraprofessional layoffs hit New York's poorest communities doubly hard, depriving students and schools of essential services while generating financial instability for families that relied on public-sector employment for survival in the postindustrial city. The destruction of the career ladder that PTEP offered likewise dismantled a path to stability for these families. Massive layoffs and the elimination of paid training opportunities also damaged the United Federation of Teachers' credibility with its newest members. Job cuts during the crisis disproportionately affected Black and Latinx workers and their communities, due in part to union and civil service seniority rules. All these factors pulled apart the coalition of unionists, educators, and activists who—despite long-simmering tensions—had supported community-based paraprofessional educators in New York City over the preceding decade.

Emergency federal funding and the slow recovery of the city's credit allowed many paras to return to work in the late 1970s, but they did so in a rapidly changing environment. President Nixon had shuttered the Office of Economic Opportunity, which had administered the War on Poverty's Community Action Program, in 1973. Congress restructured the Elementary and Secondary Education Act several times in the 1970s to shift the emphasis in spending away from community-based programming and toward targeted, measurable interventions in individual student performance. Congressional support for special and bilingual education continued to fund paraprofessional jobs in these areas, but monies dwindled for comprehensive programs that tried to simultaneously improve instruction, connect schools and communities, and create jobs.

New York City's fiscal crisis set the stage for a new urban politics, and Koch's election brought these politics to fruition. The famously pugnacious mayor helped shape "the Democratic Party version of neoliberalism" in the wake of the crisis: slashing social services, subsidizing private development, and abandoning traditional allies in the labor and civil rights movements.[7] Koch was a Democrat, but his politics prefigured the strategies associated with the "Reagan Revolution" at the national level. In singling out paras in the UFT's 1978 contract negotiations, Koch employed a version of Reagan's favorite racist trope, that of the "welfare queen." Paras, to Koch, were not educators, and to treat them as such in a city contract would be "dangerous."[8]

A decade removed from their 1970 "triumph," New York City's community-based educators had consolidated their positions in classrooms, but the alliances and conditions that had made their work transformative were crumbling away. They continued to make incremental advances in benefits in the 1980s, but they no longer featured at the vanguard of community-based educational struggles, teacher unions, or poverty policy. Their labor continued, and does to this day, but the capacious vision and practice of community-based education that paras and their allies had shaped was eclipsed by the rise of neoliberal education reform.

"Disproportionately on the Shoulders
of Blacks and Puerto Ricans":
Paraprofessional Educators during
New York City's Fiscal Crisis

New York City's 1975 budget shortfalls were years in the making.[9] The city
had been a leader in social welfare innovation and spending since the LaGuardia era. New programs had grown precipitously under Mayors Wagner and
Lindsay in the 1960s, aided in large part by the expansion of federal spending
in the War on Poverty. Public-sector job creation and unionization—which,
this book has argued, should be understood as part of the expansion of the
social welfare state—likewise increased city budgets. As discussed in the
introduction, approximately 250,000 New Yorkers worked for the city by
1965.[10] The growth of the public sector created many new opportunities for
Black and Latina women who had long been relegated to the city's least
desirable jobs. As Michael Woodsworth demonstrates, Black women in Bedford-Stuyvesant, Brooklyn's largest African American neighborhood, seized
these opportunities to leave domestic work for new positions in municipal
employment throughout the postwar era.[11] In Harlem, where few people,
male or female, had access to government employment in 1960, roughly 20
percent of all employed people, and thirty percent of women, worked in the
public sector by 1980.[12] As historians including Jane Berger, Michael Katz,
and Rhonda Williams have argued, the creation of public sector jobs remains
an underappreciated but enormously significant legacy of both the War on
Poverty and civil rights organizing, particularly for women.[13]

The city's growing workforce and social welfare state meant growing budgets; by 1965, New York City's annual spending totaled $3.4 billion.[14] In the
following decade, however, the flight of middle-class taxpayers to federally
subsidized suburban developments in the wake of deindustrialization—the
city lost half a million jobs between 1969 and 1976—began to severely undermine the city's economy and tax base.[15] Declining federal and state support—
New York City paid the highest proportion of its hospital, Medicaid, and
welfare bills of any municipality in the nation—exacerbated the problem,
and successive mayors and their administrations turned to short term bond
issues to manage increasingly untenable debt loads.[16] By 1974, the city's debt
stood at $11 billion, and 11 percent of annual spending went to debt service.[17]

In this moment, historian Joshua Freeman argues, "bankers, financiers,
and conservative ideologues made an audacious grab for power."[18] Observers
had speculated that the city was in trouble, but the extent of the crisis was
not clear until New York's bankers abruptly closed the bond market to the
city in March of 1975. Panic set in, and the State of New York stepped in to

manage the crisis by creating a "Municipal Assistance Corporation" (MAC). By late April, at the MAC's urging, Mayor Abe Beame had announced the elimination of nearly 4,000 employees on the city payroll and another 8,000 positions from the Board of Education's budget, which was being cut by $132 million for the year, all to take effect on July 1, 1975.[19]

These cuts, as Black and Latinx New Yorkers were quick to realize, did not fall evenly on all city workers. Responding to the announcement, Deputy Schools Chancellor Bernard Gifford told the *New York Amsterdam News* in May that the cuts would "fall disproportionately on the shoulders of Blacks and Puerto Ricans."[20] Gifford explained the double thrust of these cuts, noting the loss of both jobs and services. "The Mayor has targeted the elimination of large numbers of school aides and paraprofessionals, positions in which Black and Puerto Rican women are in the majority," Gifford noted, and their firings meant the "cutback of extracurricular activities like vacation daycare, adult education, and recreation" that were "very important" to Black and Puerto Rican New Yorkers who could not afford such services on the private market. Also, Gifford worried, minority teachers might be fired because they lacked seniority. Combined with the layoff of paras, Gifford was "very concerned about this because we need an integrated school staff."[21] The central goals of the paraprofessional movement and the wider struggle for educational equity in New York were now under attack.

Paraprofessional educators and their parent allies took to the streets when the cuts went into effect in July. The PTAs of PS 76 and PS 144 blocked traffic at 125th Street and Adam Clayton Powell Jr. Boulevard in Harlem, and PS 76's UFT chapter joined the protest after learning that their school would lose twenty-five of its forty-three paras. "This is a rip-off of Central Harlem," Ethel Hughes, president of PS 144's PTA, told reporters. "We are losing the most compared to other areas." Parent leader Annelle Munn added, "The budget cut is throwing a lot of us out of jobs."[22] Later in the month, longtime Harlem activist Isaiah Robinson, now president of the Board of Education, echoed their concerns in a news conference at the board's headquarters, in which he blasted the city for "painfully placing its priorities everywhere but in the classroom."[23] The actions of these parents and their local union allies were part of a summer of wildcat strikes and protests in response to the layoffs, which included police blocking traffic on the Brooklyn Bridge and a group of highway workers shutting down the Henry Hudson Parkway.[24]

The UFT had just celebrated its annual "Salute to Paraprofessionals" when the first round of drastic cuts to the educational budget were announced. In the materials and articles that surrounded the fete, UFT president Albert Shanker had celebrated the capacity of unionized paras to "improve the quality of education for the City's children and to provide an affirmative action program which would . . . encourage further racial and social integration both within the schools and the union itself."[25] The graduates of CUNY's Paraprofessional-Teacher Education Program (PTEP) marched across the stage at the "Salute," and Shanker celebrated their climb up the career ladder as an annual high point. As he bragged to the *New York Times*, "this is the finest self-help educational program in this country."[26]

Shanker's celebration of "self help" reflected his strategic and ideological thinking about paraprofessional educators in the 1970s. Since 1968, the UFT had defined and described this work as a kind of apprenticeship. By positioning paras as future teachers, the union had simultaneously appealed to paraprofessional hopes for advancement and assuaged rank-and-file teachers' fears that these new educators might undermine or replace them. The CUNY career ladder program, PTEP, which the UFT had won for paras at the bargaining table in 1970, was the mechanism that held Shanker's ideology and its material basis together. As Velma Hill explained in 1986, "As more and more paras become teachers, then . . . the differences fade away."[27]

The fiscal crisis, however, undermined the political and economic order in which Shanker and the UFT operated so effectively. In the process, the crisis put the union's commitment to paraprofessional educators and their advancement to the test. Shanker's initial response to the cuts was direct and unwavering: they were "totally unacceptable." However, as he noted the following week, "the major losses will not occur in the jobs of presently full-time teachers" but primarily in the "the services provided children and in the quality of education."[28] The decision to cut "auxiliary" positions first, as Gifford noted in his comments to the *Amsterdam News*, lay with the Board of Education and the mayor, not with the union. Nonetheless, Shanker's language rankled the small but influential band of organizers in the union's left-leaning Teacher Action Caucus (TAC).[29] "Aren't these remedial teachers, BCG personnel and paras full time employees and union members?" asked the TAC's newsletter in May of 1975.[30] Paraprofessional educators had officially joined the UFT as equals, but the implied hierarchy of Shanker's phrasing suggested that the union planned to prioritize teachers in the fight ahead.

While parents and paras protested over the summer, the MAC again took its knife to the city's education budget. By August, new cuts had been announced, leading to reports that as many as an additional 7,000 to 8,000 positions would be cut.[31] In addition to the positions lost in the spring, such cuts would total 15,000 people, or nearly one-fifth of the Board of Education's workforce.[32] These numbers proved inflated, but the board's detailed figures, released in mid-September, revealed that 4,542 regular teachers and supervisors would lose their jobs. The paraprofessional workforce, however, took the biggest hit: the board's memorandum noted the elimination of 5,970 positions. This accounted for nearly two-thirds of all New York City paraprofessionals, nearly all of whom were unionized with the UFT.[33]

By sheer coincidence, the UFT faced these massive cuts at the same moment its three-year contract expired. The MAC hoped to use the occasion to break the union's power in the city, while the union tried desperately to hang on to a decade of contract gains. Shanker, by his own recollection, did not intend to call a strike against a Board of Education facing a $220 million shortfall, but his agitated rank and file demanded it.[34] The walkout was a strange one, as it effectively saved the city money. Shanker later mused, "We could have stayed out for two years. They were not interested in opening the schools."[35] The weeklong strike, however, gave both the UFT leadership and the TAC, in opposition, an opportunity to articulate their vision for teacher unionism and the place of paraprofessional educators within it.

Shanker, in his regular "column" (a paid advertisement that ran every Sunday in the *New York Times*), argued that the board insisted on "stripping teachers of long-held and hard-won rights."[36] Shanker charged that the board was violating the UFT's contract, particularly the class-size provisions, which could not be met after the loss of so many staff. Any new contract, the UFT's leadership argued, "would not yield benefits and working conditions given to the teachers in previous contracts."[37] The heads of the city's public-sector unions, led by Victor Gotbaum of AFSCME DC 37, had decided together to forgo annual raises in their contracts, and the UFT told the Board of Education that it was willing to freeze any salary increase. However, givebacks on previous contract gains were out of the question. The union's flyers highlighted the issue of class size, in particular, both as a way of courting parent support and to remind their restive teachers of one of the major gains made since the UFT's first contract in 1962.[38]

After five days, Shanker wrote to his membership asking them to ratify a contract with terms much like the UFT's previous one. He celebrated the restoration of class size limits to previous contract maximums and the preservation of seniority rights, sabbaticals, and "relief from administrative duties and non-teaching chores."[39] The letter also promised that "over two-thirds of all laid-off members will be rehired beginning immediately, and all of us will be back in a short period of time." What Shanker's letter did not say was that these re-hirings were contingent on relief monies from New York State and the federal government, particularly the Comprehensive Employment and Training Act (CETA) funds, whose allocation was not formally announced until October.[40] Shanker urged his membership to "remain united and strong" and "by *mutual* sacrifice . . . go back to school [emphasis original]."[41]

By stressing rights, contract gains, and seniority as the yardsticks by which the UFT's success should be measured, Shanker deployed a vision of unionism fully in line with the mainstream AFL-CIO position in the collective bargaining era. His focus on class size, sabbaticals, and non-teaching chores demonstrates the premium Shanker placed on teacher autonomy and privileges accrued through seniority. Shanker's own trajectory as a unionist from the early 1960s, and his firm embeddedness in the AFL-CIO tradition, ensured that he defined the power of his union by the material gains secured in each successive contract, all of which contributed to the protected status of veteran teachers.

Critics at the time and since have argued that Shanker privileged the needs and desires of his white, middle-class veteran teachers over both newly hired teachers and paraprofessional educators. The Teacher Action Caucus, in opposition, advanced a different measuring stick. In their own strike flyers, they repurposed Shanker's own statement, "No one goes back till we all go back" to argue "the minimum conditions for a contract must be no layoffs—rehire all workers who were on staff in May '75."[42] Shanker's words were surrounded with a hand-drawn chain linking "teachers," "paras," "subs," and "counselors." While the TAC stressed the issue of class size as well, their fundamental argument was that the union's strength should be measured by its members, not its contracts. Although the TAC claimed that the money was available to rehire everyone, their basic argument suggested that, given the choice between preserving contract gains and preserving unionized jobs in a moment of austerity, the union should opt for the latter. The TAC was further incensed when Shanker, under pressure from the city and other union leaders, invested hundreds of millions of dollars from teacher pension funds in the city, which had just "clipped the wings" of the union, in the words of one former Board of Education president.[43]

The TAC argued that the UFT should protect jobs above all from within the union, but it was not the only group in the city to argue for taking extraordinary measures to protect city workers, particularly given the outsize impact of layoffs on Black and Puerto Rican educators. A report in the *Village Voice* quoted District 5 Community School District Superintendent Luther Seabrook in Central Harlem on the deleterious effect of preserving seniority during teacher layoffs: "Young teachers, minority teachers have been let go." As Seabrook explained, "These are teachers who believe black kids can learn, and they get that belief across. But we've lost most of them because they've been either subs or they became regular teachers after 1972."[44]

Seabrook's statement pointed to another problem for paraprofessional educators. Union and community support for paraprofessionals had proved complementary in the paras' 1970 contract campaign. However, in 1975, union seniority regulations put parents and the union at odds with one another. In January of 1976, a newly formed "Concerned Parents and Educators of District 5" in Harlem described the effect of the educational cuts as the "destruction of parent power."[45] "If we allow Black paraprofessionals, guards, aides, secretaries, teachers, principals, guidance counselors, and superintendents to be fired," the group held, "the images that we have struggled so hard and so long to get for our children will be lost."[46] According to the *Amsterdam News*, the group had "prevailed on District Five officials to cease honoring the UFT's seniority transfer plan," which, practically, meant laying off Black and Latinx teachers and replacing them with older white teachers. Alice Kornegay, a longtime Harlem activist, stated unequivocally, "White teachers failed us all these years and in the last 10 years, Blacks have been coming in and doing the job."[47] Harlem parents and educators continued to seek ways to retain Black educators in the face of cuts throughout 1976. The local chapter of the NAACP announced that it would challenge the discriminatory effect of city layoffs in court. In October, the New York State Association of Black Educators took up a collection among its cash-strapped members and managed to donate $4,000 to the cause.[48]

In April, a report by New York City's Commission on Human Rights confirmed what parents and activists had been saying: "minorities and women have borne a disproportionate share of layoffs," and if trends continued, the city would have "an all-white, predominantly male workforce."[49] Between July of 1974 and November of 1975, the city's mayoral agency workforce had shrunk 28.2 percent, from 164,894 to 118,459 workers: 46,435 people had lost their jobs, including over half of all Hispanic-identified city workers and 35 percent of Black workers, as compared to 22 percent of white workers. A staggering 85 percent of the workforce had been laid off in the "paraprofessional" category, which included workers in health, sanitation, and social work as well as education.[50] The report explained that the crisis generated a "double-barreled effect" of unemployment and cuts to essential social services:

> First, it left jobless individuals whose low skills and education severely limit their future employment options, deprived them of the training opportunities traditionally provided by paraprofessional work, and in some cases returned to welfare people who have been deliberately accorded jobs as an alternative to public assistance. . . . [Second,] para- professional jobs are usually those which provide direct community services . . . their loss deprives the population of low income and minority New Yorkers of these needed services.

While the report was careful to note that drastic budget cuts were the root of the problem, seniority rules in civil service codes and union contracts exacerbated their impact.[51] Membership in the UFT had provided enormous gains to paraprofessional educators in the five years since their first contract, but now their allies in communities—and some paras themselves—began to wonder whether their union still had the power, or desire, to protect them.

Albert Vann, the Brooklyn teacher and community control advocate who had become a state assemblyman, called a meeting of 300 paraprofessionals

in Brooklyn in October. At the meeting, Vann offered a brief historical overview of community-based education, saying, "the creation of paraprofessional
positions in the NYC school system came about from parental and community pressure to make our schools meaningful to the children." Vann added,
"The system accommodated a lot of our parental and grass-roots leadership
by providing jobs for them in the schools. To the surprise of many, you made
yourselves invaluable in the classroom." At Vann's suggestion, the gathered
paraprofessionals created a steering committee to directly challenge the UFT,
which, in Vann's estimation, "no longer wants you around."[52]

The *Amsterdam News* reported that Velma Murphy Hill, the UFT's paraprofessional chapter chair, met with the new steering committee shortly after
Vann's meeting and promised "all paras will be rehired in 2–3 weeks by using
CETA money." Vann remained skeptical, telling the *News,* "I strongly suggest
that the paras in my district remain organized and keep the pressure on the
union where they paid their dues. There is nothing in the law that says our
paras must be the last priority."[53]

Hill's meeting with these Brooklyn paras was one of dozens she attended
during the crisis, both at UFT school chapter meetings and in community
settings. Committed as she was to realizing civil rights gains through labor
organizing, Hill was torn between supporting paraprofessional educators in
every context and honoring the union's longtime commitments to seniority
and to autonomy from community activism. Layoffs, as she was well aware,
threatened not just paraprofessional jobs but the community support for
unionized paraprofessionals that she and her chapter had worked so hard
to build in 1969 and 1970.

At UFT headquarters, Hill ran a makeshift "hiring hall" to reassign and
re-employ paras, doing her best to honor their own seniority as money
slowly became available to rehire these workers. However, the layoffs, even
if they proved temporary, forced many paras to look for other jobs to support their families. Working-class women, many of them the heads of their
households, could hardly afford to wait out the uncertainty of being rehired.
Shelvy Young-Abrams, by then a union activist in her Lower East Side school,
recalled that in her district, "we lost about 300 . . . practically all of them. I
don't know where they all went." Young-Abrams herself "was shaking in my
boots. Lord, I can't afford to lose my job." While she survived without being
laid off, she realized that some of her colleagues "would never be back."[54]

Schools and students across New York City suffered throughout the academic year as paraprofessional educators were laid off. One *New York Times*
story cited cancellations of after-school programs in the South Bronx, bilingual parent outreach and health services in East Harlem, and community
programming in Bedford-Stuyvesant as a consequence. The piece quoted
one principal who said that, because of the layoffs, "there is no release, no

outlet for the kids" and "that hostility comes back to us."[55] At PS 40, in Bed-Stuy, ten of the school's twenty-two paraprofessional educators were laid off. Principal Seymour Lachman noted that those who were able to secure unemployment "come around on their own and serve as volunteers."[56]

As they had done during previous crises, including the 1968 teacher strikes, New York City's community-based paras remained committed to serving the children of their neighborhoods, going so far as to work for free in certain instances. They knew students and parents depended on the work that they did and the services they provided, both during and after school. Their sacrifices reflected the sexist paradox built into care work: the very fact that paras cared enough to work for free in emergency situations was used by administrators and politicians in the years following the fiscal crisis to define paras' labor as a natural product of their gender, rather than skilled work deserving of proper recognition and reward.[57]

The Crumbling Career Ladder

During the summer of 1975, Velma Hill and Albert Shanker negotiated to allow paras attending classes at CUNY through the Paraprofessional-Teacher Education Program to continue in their programs with all related union benefits, including their summer stipends, despite being laid off.[58] Hill fought hard to preserve these opportunities, as they allowed workers to stay active in their union and continue their education with small stipends as they waited to be rehired. However, not all paraprofessionals could make time for school while seeking other jobs. Marian Thom remembers that she "resigned" from classes after being laid off in 1975 (she was rehired later in the year).[59] Even as CETA funding arrived in New York City to allow paraprofessional educators to return to work, the aftershocks of the fiscal crisis imperiled the free, open career ladder at CUNY, which was the most innovative contract victory paraprofessionals won in 1970.

The first cut to the Paraprofessional-Teacher Education Program took place abruptly in May of 1976, when the Board of Education announced that it no longer had the money to pay stipends to paraprofessionals attending summer classes. In a twenty-page report to Bernard Gifford, the board's personnel director, Frank C. Arricale, spelled out a doomsday scenario: "In the Mayor's Executive Budget the entire amount of 2.8 million dollars for the paraprofessional career training program was eliminated."[60] To make matters worse, the Emergency Financial Control Board (EFCB), which had taken over city management from the MAC, had imposed tuition at CUNY. Arricale reported, "our staff was told that in no way would CUNY waive tuition costs for the paras; since the paras are part-time students they do not qualify for tuition assistance." CUNY was asking for $5 million for tuition (to begin in the fall of 1976), while summer stipends—$80–85 per week for six weeks—would cost about $1.5 million to replace. The Board of Education simply didn't have the money. Thinking aloud, Arricale suggested that paras could apply for unemployment or welfare to fund themselves over the summer, as many paras who did not take classes already did. When this suggestion went public, it became a flashpoint as a particularly cruel result of the fiscal crisis.

Shanker penned a strongly worded letter to the Board of Education on June 16, insisting it "reconsider this direct contract violation."[61] These words were chosen carefully; Shanker had defined his union's strength on unyielding protection of contract gains. However, the reply was the same: "the Board has no funds for this purpose."[62] Shanker replied with a public telegram on July 27 that averred, "the paraprofessional career training program has been the ladder to economic advancement for thousands of Black and Hispanic paraprofessionals and promises an infusion of minority group members into the ranks of New York City teachers. Every dictate of conscience, morality, and social decency demands the continuation of this vital program."[63]

The timing of Shanker's telegram was not a coincidence. On the same July day, a small but vocal group of paraprofessional educators rallied in front of UFT headquarters to demand the union defend their contract and win back their stipends. Led by a group calling itself "Concerned Teachers for Quality Education," the rally slammed Shanker and the union's leadership for being "insensitive" to their needs and "sell[ing] out to the Board of Education."[64] Flyers distributed by the group argued that paras "need more effective union representation."[65] Theirs was not the first action by rank-and-file paraprofessionals. The *Civil Service Leader* reported that "angry" union paras from both DC 37 and the UFT rallied at City Hall in the last week of June.[66] Shanker had promised to preserve contract gains; when he did not, UFT paraprofessionals protested.

Velma Murphy Hill tried to reassure members in the paraprofessional chapter newsletter, but in the face of such drastic cuts, her words offered little comfort. "This year closes on a very sad note," read the June 1976 issue of *Para Scope*. "The city's financial crunch has placed the career ladder program in serious jeopardy."[67] The newsletter closed with a promise and a plea: "We will continue our efforts to keep our college program and to maintain it, but in these serious times, we need the support and the solidarity of every member of the UFT."[68] Writing to UFT paraprofessional chapter representatives across the city before the demonstration at UFT headquarters, Hill took a more frustrated tone. "We are sure that this precipitous action comes from the frustration and anxiety about the state of the program," she wrote, "but we should be conscious of who the enemy is and who it is not. The UFT is committed to doing all within its power to maintain this program. To demonstrate the Union only creates the impression of disunity among the paraprofessionals."[69] The protests went on as planned.

Within the rubric of formal collective bargaining, the UFT's only option was to file a grievance and go through the laborious process of arbitration. In the meantime, summer faded into fall without a single paraprofessional educator receiving a stipend, and the school year's opening brought the announcement of more cuts and chaos.[70] Shanker tried to keep public attention focused on the paraprofessionals' continued fight for their career ladder. In his "Where We Stand" column in September, he called the destruction of PTEP "ridiculous," arguing "we are saving next to nothing, but we are denying the children the services of the paras, we are pushing far into the future the genuine integration of our schools staff, and we are once again needlessly placing people on the treadmill of poverty and welfare."[71] Finally, in late October, the union won its arbitration case.[72] The board was ordered to pay out stipends of $500 to 1,700 paras who had fulfilled the requirements for the summer, and the UFT hailed the decision as an overdue victory.[73]

However, these 1,700 paraprofessionals represented only half of those who had originally planned to take summer classes. As Marian Thom's story indicates, many could not continue their educations without the financial support their contract promised. Moreover, the larger problem remained. CUNY now charged tuition, and the board no longer had any funding to pay either tuition or stipends. Throughout the following school year, Velma Murphy Hill and the paraprofessional chapter continued to fight for stipends and tuition, but budgets did not budge, and participation in the program began to wither badly, as it was now contingent on paras' ability to pay their own way before perhaps being reimbursed.[74] PTEP was eventually shuttered in the early 1980s, though paraprofessional educators continued to seek higher education at CUNY through a series of more specific and targeted programs developed in piecemeal fashion.

While city budgets and paraprofessional jobs slowly stabilized in the late 1970s, the fiscal crisis had done lasting damage to unionized paras on two levels. Unionization had helped some paras preserve and regain their jobs during the crisis, but the UFT's seniority provisions had demonstrated their lowly place within the union's hierarchy. While driven by circumstances far beyond the union's control, the leadership's success in preserving key contract gains for veteran teachers contrasted starkly with their inability to retain paras' contractually guaranteed career ladder program. For the left-leaning unionists in the TAC, the unequal results of the "mutual sacrifice" promised by Shanker called the UFT's entire model of organizing into question. Ewart Guinier, a leading Black trade unionist and founding director of Harvard's African American Studies program, asked, "is collective bargaining passé in a time of fiscal crisis?" at a TAC event in December of 1976.[75] Paras who lost jobs and training opportunities despite their contract might well have thought so. As Joshua Freeman argues, the damage the crisis did to "the idea and reality of an expansive, democratic state sector was immediate, strong, and irreversible." Over the next five years, the city would shed 63,000 jobs through layoffs and attrition.[76]

PTEP's destruction weakened the collegial and rhetorical link between teachers and paras by eliminating the possibility of paras becoming teachers. In the 1970 contract campaign in New York City, and around the nation afterward, UFT leaders and organizers described paraprofessional educators not as parent activists but as teachers in training. As Hill recalled in 1986, the creation of PTEP had also demonstrated the union's commitment to paras, "to go out . . . and try to keep its word" by using all its power to demand a significant investment of resources from the city in paras' advancement. For many paras, Hill believed, "that career ladder become very important to them and to the credibility of the union."[77]

Clarence Taylor, who started as a special education paraprofessional just after the fiscal crisis, observed a cruel sort of irony in the persistence of the career ladder after 1976. Paras who sought better working conditions in schools were often told to become teachers, even though the process, by that point, "sort of went on forever" and required significant personal financial investment.[78] Absent real opportunities for advancement, defining paraprofessional work as apprenticeship could relegate these workers to second-class status in classrooms and union halls.

In the first half of the 1970s, it seemed that paraprofessional educators in New York had carved out a space for themselves in the city's schools, unions, and political power structure. In addition to their longtime collaborators in grassroots struggles and antipoverty programs, these educators now had allies and representatives in party politics and one of the city's largest and most powerful unions. However, just as paras gained access to these levers of power, the midcentury political and economic order in which they were embedded began to collapse.

Watching the fiscal crisis unfold, leftist activists both inside and outside of the United Federation of Teachers argued that the union should take drastic action to defend its newest members. They blasted the union for taking part in a "corporatist" resolution to the crisis, in which municipal unions bailed out the city with their pension funds in exchange for the preservation of their existing contracts. These organizers and activists were particularly incensed by the UFT's adherence to strict seniority in the face of inequitable layoffs. For better or worse, these were the principles that the UFT, and the midcentury public-sector labor movement more broadly, were built on.[79] Their strategies had driven the tremendous growth of teacher and municipal unionism. However, the world in which they had succeeded was now disappearing. As a new world of austerity took shape in the years following the fiscal crisis, the coalition of antipoverty workers, unionists, and civil rights activists that had supported the creation and growth of an expansive vision of community-based hiring and education broke down.

What did the future hold for community-based educators in this new landscape? Writing in the *Amsterdam News* in 1976, William L. Hamilton, the African American dean of LaGuardia Community College, mused on this question. In his years at community colleges in New York City, Hamilton had watched paras "struggling up the educational ladder to reach for the American dream," and he saluted their "tremendous physical, emotional and intellectual stamina." As opportunities for advancement waned, Hamilton argued, "a lesson is to be learned from the experience of the paraprofessional movement": paras and their allies "must develop into political advocates of their programs to protect their vested interests and to sustain their gains by developing the momentum into an institution, thus keeping the movement alive for others."[80]

Hamilton's call for political mobilization echoed arguments that New Yorkers including Preston Wilcox and Frances Fox Piven had been making across the nation for years. Piven, whose critique of the New Careerists had been their lack of political strategy, was teaching at CUNY's Brooklyn College in 1975. As the Teacher Action Caucus did in K–12 schools, Piven argued against job cuts based on seniority during the 1975 fiscal crisis. She proposed, instead, a more equitable distribution of fiscal hardship across the CUNY faculty to retain maximum numbers.[81] Piven understood the fundamentally political nature of public-sector job creation and antipoverty policy, and the need to organize to defend these jobs at precisely the moment that the political coalitions that had sustained the War on Poverty and Great Society were breaking down. Paras had done exactly this for a decade from 1965 to 1975, organizing in their schools, communities, and the labor movement. Maintaining this political activity, and the uneasy alliances underlying it, would prove far more difficult in the post-crisis city.

"Why Should I Still Be on Welfare?": Paraprofessional Educators under Attack

Edward I. Koch, the three-term mayor of New York City, upended the city's old progressive Democratic politics.[82] And while most "New Democrats" hailed from the Sun Belt and suburbia, Koch was in many ways the first urban neoliberal Democrat, as evidenced by everything from his embrace of gentrification as development policy to his aggressive cuts to social services. His attack on paras demonstrated the political distance Koch had traveled in just five short years; as a congressional representative for Greenwich Village in 1972, he had telegrammed the Board of Education in support of the paras' push for a second contract.[83]

In rejecting the annualization of paraprofessional salaries in his first year in office, Koch and his aides took their cue from what the city's Board of Education had done during New York's fiscal crisis and suggested paras could simply collect unemployment or welfare in the summers instead.[84] However, while the board's suggestion had been a tone-deaf exercise in bureaucratic arithmetic, Koch's was a pointed attack. The mayor simultaneously linked paras to the social spending that Koch blamed for the fiscal crisis and devalued their work in classrooms.

Paraprofessional educators and their allies protested furiously. While Young-Abrams and her fellow paras readied themselves "to do a sleep-in at City Hall," Velma Murphy Hill told the mayor, "you can't discriminate against one group" and threatened legal action for discrimination in addition to the union's move to arbitration, which began in the spring of 1979.[85] The UFT also pulled together an advertising plan in response to Koch's argument that paras were part-time employees who did not deserve the benefits that teachers and other professionals received. In one ad, Young-Abrams appeared below the headline "I Love New York, Mayor Koch. Why Doesn't New York Love Me?" The ad explained that Young-Abrams was a single mother of two working full-time and attending school. Her composed presence in the *Amsterdam News* offered a staunch rebuke to Koch's rhetoric about "poverty pimps" and pushing paraprofessionals back onto the welfare rolls.[86] Chinese American paraprofessional Marian Chin appeared in a similar ad that read "Mayor Koch, Meet a Workaholic," and para Victor Vasquez appeared alongside a description of a boy with cerebral palsy, whom Vasquez had helped to walk for the first time.[87]

The *Amsterdam News* authored an editorial in support of Harlem's paras and ran several articles on the fight. One piece ran photos from the UFT's annual Salute to Paraprofessionals and quoted Velma Hill on the virtues of unionization for paras: "Today, being a paraprofessional in a New York City public school is clearly a job with a future." The *Amsterdam News* added a note on activist mothering, writing that "most paras live in the communities in which they work and many spend their own time on an informal basis reaching out to the parents of children."[88]

Despite these efforts, by 1978, the coalition of allies that had once created and sustained paraprofessional jobs and programs no longer wielded the clout it once had. As arbitration dragged on for a year, Koch made a show of giving "grades" to New York City agencies on live television. Unsurprisingly, the schools did poorly, and Koch took the opportunity to blame the UFT for costing the city money. Al Shanker responded in his paid column by critiquing Koch's "school destruction program" and by noting that his budgets had slashed support staff—including paras—for the very children Koch purported to defend.[89]

Finally, in March of 1980, Koch's administration yielded a small summer stipend for paras in lieu of an annualized contract. An exhausted Velma Murphy Hill told *New York Teacher*, the UFT's magazine, "It just always does take a lot of time, patience, and much aggravation before working people get anything like what we deserve."[90] The stipends were something "like" the annual salaries that the TAC had demanded since 1972, and which the UFT's leadership had been seeking since 1978, but the arbitration gains of 1980 otherwise shared little with the "triumph" of the first contract a decade earlier. It was not until 1983 that paraprofessionals received full pensions, by an act of New York State government.[91]

While community-based educators managed to preserve their jobs amid the fiscal crisis, and even win small gains on the new, unfavorable terrain of urban politics, Koch's efforts in 1978 set the tone for further attacks in the 1980s. The mayor's thinly veiled racism and sexism framed paraprofessional educators as expendable: not educators but "welfare mothers," their jobs not work but patronage. New York City Schools Chancellor Joel Klein would make similar arguments as he tried to fire hundreds of paras twenty-five years later in 2003.[92]

The vision and practice of community education that paras and their allies had articulated combined public-sector employment with antipoverty organizing to address the crisis of care in public education. Their vision was equitable, transformative, and rooted in the knowledge and ability of local communities. The coalition of unionists, activists, and educators they assembled in support of this vision made these positions permanent within the schools bureaucracy and provided jobs, training, and empowerment to thousands of working-class women and their communities in the 1970s. By the end of the decade, however, changing political, fiscal, and analytic practices at every level of government not only undermined this vision but also cast paraprofessional labor as expendable, even wasteful. These political shifts also weakened the support networks paras had built for their programs by undercutting freedom struggles, attacking public-sector unions, and slashing antipoverty and social service funding. Paras and their allies could still gather in support of specific measures by the 1980s, but the transformative moment—the "paraprofessional movement"—had passed.

From the Career Ladder to the "Sticky Floor": Paraprofessionals in the 1980s

Ed Koch's attack on paras in 1978 presaged a much larger, broader attack on public education, public-sector jobs, and public-sector organizing at every level of government in the 1980s. The contours of the national story are well known. In his first two years in office, Ronald Reagan broke the Professional Air Traffic Controllers Organization (PATCO) strike and pushed Congress to cut federal spending on education by 20 percent and to replace the Comprehensive Employment and Training Act with the scaled-back Job Training Partnership Act of 1982.[93] In the face of this massive attack, the AFT chose "Year of Survival" as the theme of its 1982 Paraprofessional Conference.[94]

Cities across the nation faced bankruptcies and near-misses, and state and local governments found their capacity to spend hamstrung by "tax revolts" that took many forms, from ballot measures to voted-down school budgets. Reliant as public schools were, and are, on property taxes, these measures badly exacerbated inequality.[95] Coupled with Reagan's requested 20 percent cut to the Elementary and Secondary Education Act, these budget shortfalls led to an overall decline in paraprofessional positions nationwide during the first half of the 1980s.[96] Much as happened in the larger labor movement in the 1980s, layoffs put paraprofessional educators and their unions on the defensive, making it much harder to pursue gains at the bargaining table or new innovations in staffing, training, or pedagogy.

Beyond budget cuts and layoffs, education policy underwent a seismic shift in the 1980s as the "analytic" approach to poverty knowledge, as Alice O'Connor defined it, eclipsed community-based efforts to improve public education.[97] In addition to cutting federal education funding, Ronald Reagan had hoped to eliminate the cabinet-level Department of Education entirely, but in this, at least, he failed. In part to preserve the department, Reagan's Secretary of Education, Terrel Bell, convened the National Commission on Excellence in Education in 1981. Its report, *A Nation at Risk*, published in 1983, declared American students dangerously ill-equipped to maintain the nation's standing in the world and prescribed a new focus on test scores, job preparation, and economic competition.[98]

In New York City, paraprofessional educators did retain their jobs, but the coalition that had supported their efforts continued to lose influence in city and state politics. In the mid-1970s, paras and many others had celebrated the election of community organizers to local and state offices. When the New York State Assembly finally passed a law to grant pensions to paraprofessionals in 1983—over Mayor Koch's objections—former community control leaders Albert Vann and Aurelia Greene cast votes for it as members of the assembly. The chair of the Education Committee, which brought the bill to the floor, was Jose E. Serrano, who had been hired as a paraprofessional in the Bronx's District Nine by Greene's husband, Jerome Greene.[99] These former activists and community-based educators had moved into formal positions of power, and when the opportunity arose, they served as valued allies.[100]

Black and Latinx politicians, however, faced constant demonization by Ed Koch as corrupt.[101] These accusations, and the language in which they were couched, were always political beyond the particulars; they were designed not just to accuse individuals but also to delegitimize the social welfare state that these politicians now controlled. New York City's semi-decentralized school districts faced these accusations regularly. As Heather Lewis shows, many hardworking educators and activists achieved tremendous success in these decentralized districts. Nonetheless, every mayor from Abe Beame onward damned them as corrupt and sought mayoral control of schools.[102]

Still, instances of corruption cropped up with depressing frequency, leading to a vicious cycle in some districts that drove committed parent activists out of school board politics and left these posts to unscrupulous political operators. Corruption in District Five—Central Harlem—led to seemingly endless cycles of recrimination, while in District Nine, the entire school board was dissolved in 1988 after allegations of extortion, drug dealing, and teacher intimidation surfaced. While the Greenes were not personally implicated in these events, they found themselves on trial two years later for the alleged theft of a baby grand piano from a nearby school.[103] They were not convicted, but the accusations generated more turmoil in the district and made it harder for them and their allies to seek funding and build political coalitions.

Even for administrators and politicians without legal trouble, the increasingly limited funds available for education and social programs more broadly made it difficult to support robust programs of public-sector job creation. Community-based educators surely benefited from the security and incremental gains these allies provided. However, as a path to expanding these programs and realizing their potential, political office proved a hollow prize in the 1980s and beyond.[104]

The United Federation of Teachers continued to fight for paraprofessionals on particular issues in the 1980s. In 1980, the union challenged a state assembly law that would have required all paras, including those who had been on the job for a decade, to acquire high school diplomas and college credits.[105] However, as austerity budgets continued to plague the public school system, the UFT also developed a program called PRESS (Paraprofessionals Retrained for Employment as School Secretaries) to retrain laid-off paraprofessionals as school secretaries and as secretaries for private industry.[106] Far more limited in scope and ambition than the shuttered PTEP program at CUNY, PRESS seemed, in many ways, an admission that the vaunted "ladder" from para to teacher was no longer available to many of these educators.

The UFT did continue to celebrate this career ladder, despite its disappearance as a guaranteed, free program for all chapter members. In 1988, the union published a small pamphlet for its members titled "Yes, I Can: The Triumph of the UFT's Classroom Paraprofessionals." It opened with the assertion, "The story of New York's paraprofessionals is the story of the American Dream."[107] Such assertions served the union well as publicity and inspiration to members in all job categories, but as critics such as Clarence Taylor noted, they did not necessarily translate to paras' empowerment in either classrooms or union halls.[108]

On the question of the career ladder's impact, a study from 1985 offers a brief statistical portrait. Fourteen years after the Paraprofessional-Teacher Education Program (PTEP) was launched at CUNY, two thousand paras had become teachers, and they "generally experience[d] great success in their new career, due mainly to their experience as paraprofessionals."[109] In addition to moving into teaching, the career ladder had promoted mobility in other ways. Since 1970, author Gary Goldenback noted, six thousand paras had earned associate's degrees, five thousand had earned bachelor's degrees, and three hundred had earned "other" master's degrees (outside of teaching degrees). Goldenback cited general studies on paras' success and noted bilingual paras, in particular, "had proven invaluable in promoting student growth."[110] However, the path to teaching remained arduous, and far more so following PTEP's closing in the early 1980s. For most paras, the opportunity to become teachers was indeed a dream.

By 1990, paraprofessional educators occupied an almost contradictory position in New York City's public school system, cited regularly as "excess" workers while still looked to, by some organizers and politicians, to solve the myriad problems schools faced. In February of that year, the Board of Education announced the "first affirmative action plan" in its history, citing a need to hire "more black, Hispanic, and Asian" teachers in a system whose students were 80 percent nonwhite but whose educators remained 70 percent white.[111] The proposed plan included "expand[ing] training for paraprofessionals to become teachers."[112] Little seems to have come of the effort, though 1990 is notable as the founding year for another teacher-recruitment program: Teach for America, which recruited and fast-tracked elite college students, not paraprofessional educators, into teaching positions in urban public schools.

On March 14, 1991, the *New York Times* covered the revelations by two Brooklyn district superintendents and the Board of Education's inspector general that "the practice of hiring paraprofessionals and school aides was 'peculiarly vulnerable to corruption.'" The superintendents claimed that over half of these employees in their districts were unnecessary; the community school district board members, for their part, defended themselves by saying, "These are community people and they deserve to work."[113] On the same day in the same section of the paper, another story noted the work of paraprofessionals alongside other educators in a program designed to reach families living in shelters in Far Rockaway, Queens.[114] No mention was made of either article in its counterpart, despite the dissonance.

Looming over all this coverage was an impending fiscal crunch, first reported in July as a $62.3 million cut to the board's budget.[115] As that number swelled to a $94 million cut by November, the *Times* ran a story headlined "The Schoolteacher as Budgetary Sacrificial Lamb," with the subtitle "What about all those aides and paraprofessionals?"[116] The piece itself explained that many paras now worked in federally mandated roles in special education (though it cited a superintendent claiming they were ineffective). It quoted the chancellor's office explaining that paras didn't make enough for massive cuts to yield sufficient savings, and that "support positions—many of which are crucial for security and discipline—are hard to cut." The article's overall presentation, however, was ripped straight from Koch's playbook and reflected a growing consensus among education policy people: teachers were lambs, paras were leeches.

Crisis was averted early in 1991 when the city, Board of Education, and UFT agreed to a settlement that included all educators taking a three-day furlough to ensure no jobs were lost.[117] Once again, paras retained their jobs, but with the value of their labor publicly denigrated and opportunities for advancement still not forthcoming. The following year, sociologist Catherine White Berheide concluded a detailed study of pay equity in New York State, part of a years-long project.[118] Observing that women workers primarily occupied positions in which they earned less than $20,000 per year with little hope for advancement—including 74 percent of the paraprofessionals in education, health care, and social work—Berheide coined a phrase. While public attention often focused on the "glass ceiling" elite women faced, most women workers in the public sector were stranded on a "sticky floor," working jobs that paid little and offered little hope of advancement, including those working as paraprofessional educators.[119]

Paraprofessional Labor in the Shadow of Neoliberal Education Reform

In 2003, New York City Schools Chancellor Joel Klein announced the largest round of faculty and staff layoffs in the public school system since 1991. As in the 1975 fiscal crisis, these layoffs fell hardest on Black and Latina women. Of the 3,200 layoffs announced, nearly 1,000 targeted paraprofessional jobs. The cuts, ostensibly, were a necessary response to a budget shortfall, but in the very same month they were announced, New York City and state jointly launched a new recruitment program for "highly qualified" teachers.[120]

Klein, a former corporate litigator with no educational credentials or experience, had been chosen by New York City Mayor Michael Bloomberg to restructure the school system, which was re-centralized at Bloomberg's request in 2002.[121] Klein, like Bloomberg, spoke a colorblind, market-based language of evaluation and accountability. He regularly attacked local politicians and school boards for making "patronage hires" and assailed the UFT for supposedly defending bad educators and broken policies for political gain.[122] When the cuts were announced, Klein blamed the union, saying (through a spokesperson), "the mayor gave the unions months to come up with potential savings and they never materialized."[123] UFT president Randi Weingarten replied by pointing to the dissonance between announcing layoffs and recruiting new teachers. Noting that many paraprofessional educators had worked their way up career ladders to become teachers, Weingarten argued, "This isn't sending a message that we want those teachers and that we value their work."[124]

As the layoffs loomed in June of 2003, the UFT filed suit against Klein, arguing that the disproportionate impact of the cuts amounted to racial discrimination. In announcing the suit, Weingarten pointed to Klein's recent hiring of 132 highly paid administrators and argued, "The fact that two-thirds of our paras are black and Latino and that the executives who have just been hired are not makes this a clear violation of the state's and the city's human rights laws."[125] The UFT was joined in its protests by the New York City Chapter of the Association of Community Organizations for Reform Now (ACORN). Bertha Lewis, the director of New York ACORN, explained, "the laying off of these black and brown women who spend their money in the neighborhoods and live in the neighborhoods is tantamount to writing off low-income black and brown students in our school system."[126] In response, the Department of Education issued a categorical rejection of the charges, claiming simple economic necessity and adding, "It's unfair and really quite sad that they are injecting race and discrimination into the conversation."[127]

This 2003 conflict served to highlight the many facets of paraprofessional labor and organizing in New York City at the turn of the millennium. As a *New York Times* article on the lawsuit explained, paraprofessional positions were created "in response to pressure from minority residents who wanted more control over local schools" and who hoped "many paraprofessionals would become teachers, diversifying the overwhelmingly white teaching force." The story noted that thousands of paras had become teachers since the 1970s, but that the school district still employed a majority—62 percent— of white teachers. The article continued: "Paraprofessionals are also more likely than teachers to live near the schools where they work," and most of them "work in overcrowded classrooms, where parent and student advocates say their presence would be most acutely missed." Finally, the *Times* added, these educators were among the lowest-paid people in the school system, taking home about $23,000 per year, on average.[128]

Nearly all these characteristics would have been familiar to the first generation of community-based educators, who had gone to work over four decades earlier. New York City's paraprofessionals, in 2003, earned salaries that barely cleared the poverty line. Despite this low pay, they worked tirelessly, bringing local knowledge into schools and carrying official knowledge back to neighborhoods, where they used their experience and dollars to support their communities. Against steep odds, many strove to become teachers. And while they lacked educational significance in the eyes of the schools chancellor, they had allies in their union and local community organizations that would stand up for them and for the value of their labor.

Klein, for his part, was not particularly unique in his attack on community-based educators. He trod a path blazed by Mayor Ed Koch in the fight over para pensions with the UFT in 1978, repeated by the Dinkins administration in 1991. Klein's strategies and ideas drew from the mainstream of educational reform policy and scholarship as it had evolved from the 1980s through the early 2000s. In his own postmortem writing, Klein traced his intellectual lineage to the publication of A Nation at Risk in 1983 and the report's assertion that American public schools were being swamped by a "rising tide of mediocrity." Klein, in his telling, had hoped to "ignite a revolution" in New York City Public Schools before being waylaid by "those defending the status quo—the unions, the politicians, the bureaucrats, and the vendors."[129] He sought to fight these entrenched interests by hiring the best and the brightest of young, elite teachers and policymakers, including the aforementioned 132 administrators, whom Klein insisted were necessary to "tame the bureaucracy," even amid budget cuts and city layoffs.[130]

The evolution of the "reform" ideas that Klein made his guiding philosophy reflects, in many respects, the broader evolution of social policy.[131] The shift to "excellence" as the goal of public education—as both described and defined by A Nation at Risk—was constructed, in scholarly and political accounts, as being fundamentally in tension with the goal of educational equity from the 1950s and 1960s.[132] The approaches of many "reformers" privileged econometric cost-benefit analyses of teacher and program performance, metrics of achievement that rely on test scores to determine value. These reformers were enamored, as Klein was, with elite education and business acumen, and they were deeply suspicious of longtime educators, local political networks, and community-based knowledge. As Weingarten pointed out, it appears Klein never considered paras as potential teachers as he was laying them off.

In 2003, the combination of the union's suit and local pressure forced Klein to modify his layoffs and retain most, though not all, of these jobs. His desire to eliminate paraprofessional positions remained, spurred on by education reformers' thinking. Much mainstream policy writing about education in these years defined paraprofessional educators as "poorly educated aides" or "unqualified aides." In their assessment of the history of federal educational spending published in 2009, David Cohen and Susan Moffitt told a different story about paras than the one the *New York Times* told in 2003. In Cohen and Moffitt's telling, paras were hired as workers of last resort, because "given poor salaries and tough working conditions in high-poverty schools, it was difficult to find well-qualified teachers," and because "aides were paid less."[133] Asking why policymakers did not "keep unqualified aides from teaching," Cohen and Moffit answered that "federal involvement in local personnel practices" was blocked by the structures of American federalism and because the AFT, in particular, "organized and represented aides and was unlikely to put them out of work."[134]

Cohen and Moffit's history depicted community-based educators purely as passive bodies in schools: hired to work because they, and their school systems, had no other options, stumbling along ineptly without formal education, protected by a union that wants them for their dues, not their abilities. This history is flawed in several ways. Civil rights activists campaigned for years to push cities to launch local hiring programs. They partnered with antipoverty practitioners and progressive teacher unionists to develop experimental programs and exert more pressure on local boards of education. Together, they developed a three-part rationale for local hiring: improving instruction, connecting schools and communities, and creating jobs—all in the service of addressing the crisis of care in postwar public education.

The historical perspective on paraprofessional educators advanced by Klein, Cohen, and Moffit, however, continues to have political power in the present. It defines these educators as uneducated, rendering them definitionally incapable of contributing to educational "excellence." It renders local knowledge suspect, not salutary, and defines these jobs as "patronage hires," not the work of education. As Weingarten noted in 2003, it passes judgment not just on the value of their particular labor, but on the possibility of finding high-quality teachers in neighborhoods where opportunities for elite credentialing have not historically been made available. While paraprofessional educators in the 1960s made educative spaces out of segregated places, the rhetoric of reform returned to the deficit model, consigning these places and the people who inhabited them to poverty unless they could secure the aid of powerful outsiders.[135]

Throughout the decades since 1980, paraprofessional educators have continued doing the work of education, including providing care. Recruited to address overlapping crises that emerged within the postwar liberal order, they have found themselves undervalued, attacked, and harried in neoliberalism's new crisis of care. In many respects, their experience has proved a harbinger of things to come: attacks on the most marginalized educators have snowballed into attacks on all educators, while paras have endured their position on the bleeding edge of neoliberal reform. For this reason, they also occupy a pivotal position in the ongoing fight to preserve, rebuild, and reimagine public education.

Paraprofessional Educators
on the Front Lines, Once Again

As of May 2023, the Bureau of Labor Statistics estimates 1,337,320 teaching assistants (as it terms paras) are at work in the United States, taking home a median annual wage of $ 35,550.[1] As reported by journalists and scholars, many work one or two additional jobs, often in childcare roles as after-school or weekend tutors, caretakers, or program supervisors. Working alongside a teaching and administrative corps that, after trends toward desegregation in the 1970s and 1980s, continues to hail predominantly from white middle and upper-middle-class backgrounds and training, paras often encounter marginalization and exploitation in schools.[2]

Where does this leave a history of the "paraprofessional movement"? In many ways, paraprofessional labor has followed a downward trajectory similar to a great many service-sector jobs worked primarily by Black and Latina women in the age of austerity and neoliberalism. While highly trained, mostly white professionals are paid well for their credentials and expertise, the work of social reproduction—including care work, discipline, and community building—is left to women workers who labor "in the shadow of the welfare state."[3] The stratification of educational labor reflects the larger stratification of the American workforce.

At the same time, paraprofessional educators who earn similar salaries to those who work in home health care, sales, food service, and similarly precarious industries remain unionized. This provides some core baseline benefits and protections: access to health care, pensions, and a measure of job security that, while not equivalent to teacher tenure, provides some stability. After paras finally received pensions in 1983, paraprofessional and UFT organizer Marian Thom made the rounds of schools on the Lower East Side, urging her colleagues to sign up. Many of them, she recalled, did not fully comprehend the benefit, and decades later, she received stunned phone calls from these women. One para reported bringing the first pension statement home to her husband and son, who exclaimed, "We never knew you had that much money!" Thom was thrilled and reminded her friend of the years they had spent organizing to win these funds.[4]

These benefits, of course, are meager compared to those most "professional" public-sector employees receive. They are much reduced from the gains paras made in the 1970s, when their salaries approached, and rose with, those of teachers, and opportunities for training and advancement were not just free at the point of service but paid through their contract. However, union membership does not only confer bread-and-butter benefits. It opens the door to collective action, to the possibility not just of contract gains but also remaking public education.

Attacks on paraprofessional educators in the late 1970s proved to be the tip of the neoliberal spear. Ed Koch may have singled out paras in 1978, but teachers themselves soon found their own positions and contract gains under attack and public support for their demands dwindling.[5] In the 1980s, Albert Shanker and the American Federation of Teachers tried to respond by doubling down on professionalism, releasing their own reports on teacher excellence and envisioning ways to raise the professional profile of teachers through unionization.[6] Neoliberal reformers, however, not only continued their attacks on unionized teachers but also developed new forms of teacher recruitment and training that bypassed traditional pathways.[7] By the turn of the twenty-first century, neoliberal education reform had become a bipartisan consensus and teacher unions had become perhaps the most vilified unions in the United States.[8] Then, in 2010, a wave of Republican victories in gubernatorial and state legislature campaigns across the country seemed to herald the end of teacher unionism itself in many places, exemplified by Wisconsin governor Scott Walker's successful crusade to eviscerate public-sector collective bargaining in the state where it had begun six decades prior.[9]

In this same year, educators in Chicago elected a radical new leadership slate, the Caucus of Rank-and-File Educators (CORE), to lead the Chicago Teachers Union (CTU). Two years later, the CTU led a campaign and strike that was widely hailed in the American labor movement as a model for the future.[10] They overcame the high hurdles that billionaire governor Bruce Rauner and a right-wing state legislature had erected to teacher strikes, and faced down Chicago mayor Rahm Emmanuel, a darling of the Democratic Party who had previously served as President Barack Obama's chief of staff. The union built tremendous parent and community support for its contract demands—which included student and community needs as well as salary increases—drawing on community ire at Emmanuel's devastating program of school closures in Black and Latinx neighborhoods. This visible backing when the CTU went out on strike helped push the city to the bargaining table, where CTU won a landmark contract.

Afterward, CTU President Karen Lewis explained that paraprofessional educators were invaluable conduits between her union and local residents. "Paraprofessionals, those are the people that actually have experience with children in that neighborhood, because they by and large work in the neighborhood where they live," Lewis noted in an interview with *Dissent*. "We're working together with them because school closings affect all of us."[11] In a campaign that reimagined teacher unions as agents of social justice who could bargain for the common good, Lewis reframed paraprofessional labor as essential both for the union and for public education. Her acknowledgment of the value of paras' local knowledge was radical in 2012, but it also recalled the origins of paraprofessional jobs as they emerged from the social movements of the 1960s.

The CTU's campaign inspired a wave of educators to mobilize and organize both inside and beyond their unions to challenge the devastating effects of neoliberal education reform. AFT locals in cities from Los Angeles to Boston elected radical and progressive leaders, while affiliates of the National Education Association (NEA) did the same both at the local and state level across the nation.[12] In 2018, a wave of rank-and-file teacher walkouts now remembered as the "Red for Ed" movement began in West Virginia and spread quickly to Kentucky, North Carolina, Oklahoma, and Arizona.[13] This wave of walkouts in 2018 was followed in 2019 by a pair of major victories by the Chicago Teachers Union and United Teachers Los Angeles, the second- and third-largest AFT locals in the country. Both CTU and UTLA won huge increases in spending on public education, including essential social and health services for students.[14]

Paraprofessional educators featured in this upsurge of mobilization: helping coordinate food delivery for students in West Virginia, marching alongside teachers in Arizona, and winning contract gains themselves in Los Angeles and Chicago. The Philadelphia Federation of Teachers negotiated a new paraprofessional-to-teacher program with multiple pathways to meet the needs of working educators.[15] Paras have organized themselves with renewed vigor. The Massachusetts Teachers Association (MTA), a statewide NEA affiliate, has supported living wage campaigns for "ESPs" (education support professionals, the NEA's preferred term for paras) in cities and towns across the commonwealth since 2016. As of this writing, the MTA is one of several NEA state organizations pushing for an "ESP Bill of Rights."[16] Paras in northernmost Washington State and Lawrence, Kansas, have organized their own locals to fight for living wages and job security.[17] Running through these campaigns are reassertions of the value of paras' labor, their importance in building links between schools and communities, and the need for para-professionals to have adequate opportunities for advancement without their living wages or job security being contingent on becoming teachers.

Paraprofessional educators organizing today do not need the inspiration of history to know that they deserve living wages, job security, respect, and opportunity in the present. What this history can demonstrate is that para-professional educators once did fight for, and win, the kinds of gains that school boards, elite commentators, and some journalists often scoff at today. Raises of 30 to 40 percent, as paras sought and won in Minneapolis in 2022 and Brookline, Massachusetts, in 2023—two examples among many—deserve to be contextualized in a proud tradition of organizing that, in the late 1960s and early 1970s, regularly yielded salary increases of 100 percent (double) or more.[18]

Moreover, this history reveals the capacious visions and radical move-ments of which paraprofessional campaigns were a part. These efforts to make public education more equitable, democratic, humane, and collectively empowering for the entire school community find their echoes in today's calls for educators to "bargain for the common good."[19] While, as recent schol-arship shows, paras' position at the nexus of school and community is still underappreciated and under-rewarded, progressive unionists have begun to recognize and engage the potential of "para power" once again.[20]

The "paraprofessional movement" of the 1960s and 1970s created thou-sands of jobs for working-class women, primarily Black and Latina, but also Asian American, Native American, and white (particularly in rural areas). These have always been working-class jobs, even at the height of local and national investment in this work, but they were and remain valuable assets, both for the individuals who work them and for the schools and neighbor-hoods in which these women work. Today, they share many characteristics with other exploited working-class care workers, but paras are not nearly as precarious in their positions as many such workers.

The continued presence of paraprofessional educators in schools is not just a testament to the struggles of an earlier generation. While they are not necessarily empowered to do so, or even compensated for their extracurricu-lar labors, most of these educators, in New York and nationally, continue to live in the neighborhoods where they work, and to work as conduits between home and school in many capacities. Their efforts in schools, communities, and union halls create opportunities to reimagine community-based educa-tion in the twenty-first century.

Studying paraprofessional educators, then and now, reveals a history of social and political organizing in and about schooling that transformed public education, freedom struggles, the labor movement, and the social welfare state. This organizing continued long after the flashbulbs and funding that put these movements in the spotlight began to dissipate in the late 1960s. By charting the long trajectory of this organizing deep into the 1970s, we can see, as the late British social theorist Stuart Hall wrote, that "social forces which lose out in any particular historical period do not thereby disappear from the terrain of struggle; nor is struggle in such circumstances suspended."[21] Paraprofessional educators worked for two decades at the forefront of movements for educational transformation and equity, and they have continued to pursue those goals up to the present day, albeit under adverse circumstances. However, as the consensus that supported the educational reforms of the 2000s dissipates, and as new demands for school equity emerge alongside new movements for social and economic justice, the everyday power and the transformative potential of paraprofessional educators' work is coming back into focus.

Despite the budget cuts and policy shifts that have impoverished urban public education, over 1 million community-based paraprofessional educators work in public schools today. Community-based paraprofessional educators and their allies once imagined a more equitable, democratic future for American schools, unions, and cities. The history of their organizing in the 1960s and 1970s cannot offer simple lessons or portable models, but it can help us think anew about how we might strive for such a future today.

Notes

Abbreviations

AFP	Anne Filardo Papers
AFT-Inventory	American Federation of Teachers Inventory
AFT-OH	American Federation of Teachers Oral Histories
AFT-President	American Federation of Teachers, Office of the President Collection
AFT-Selden	American Federation of Teachers Records, Office of the President Collection, David Selden Papers
AFT-Shanker	American Federation of Teachers, Office of the President Collection, Albert Shanker Papers
BOE	Records of the Board of Education of the City of New York
BTU	Boston Teachers Union Collection
ELP	Ellen Lurie Papers
JHS Papers	Congressman James H. Scheuer Papers
KCFT	American Federation of Teachers Local 691, Kansas City Federation of Teachers Records
MCNY	Archives of the Women's Talent Corps, College for Human Services, and Audrey Cohen College, Metropolitan College of New York
MFT	AFT Massachusetts Federation of Teachers Records
MAA	Morningside Area Alliance Records
NARA	Office of Education Records, National Archives, College Park, MD
NEA	National Education Association Papers
PWP	Preston Wilcox Papers
RPP	Richard Parrish Papers
SFT	Springfield (MA) Federation of Teachers Records
USAR	Union Settlement Association Records

UBP   Records of the United Bronx Parents
UESF   United Educators of San Francisco
UFT   United Federation of Teachers Records
UFT-OH   United Federation of Teachers Oral History

Introduction. In Search of Para Power

1. Bayard Rustin, "The Triumph of the Paraprofessionals," *New York Amsterdam News*, August 22, 1970, 4.

2. Rustin, "The Triumph of the Paraprofessionals."

3. This figure comes from Henry M. Brickell et al., *An In-Depth Study of Paraprofessionals in District Decentralized ESEA Title I and New York State Urban Education Projects in the New York City Schools* (New York: Institute for Educational Development, 1971). Pilot programs expressly targeted mothers for hiring, and this figure likely was even higher, though comprehensive numbers across these pilots identifying mothers are not available.

4. Velma Murphy Hill, interview with the author, November 7, 2011 (interview transcripts available from author). Hill discusses her organizing work with paraprofessional educators in the UFT and AFT in Chapters 8 and 9 of her memoir, coauthored with her husband, Norman Hill, *Climbing the Rough Side of the Mountain: The Extraordinary Story of Love, Civil Rights, and Labor Activism* (New York: Regalo Press, 2023).

5. Hill, interview.

6. On the struggle for community control, see Daniel Perlstein, *Justice, Justice: School Politics and the Eclipse of Liberalism* (New York: Peter Lang, 2004); Jonna Perrillo, *Uncivil Rights: Teachers, Unions, and Race in the Battle for School Equity* (Chicago: University of Chicago Press, 2012); Jerald E. Podair, *The Strike That Changed New York: Blacks, Whites, and the Ocean Hill-Brownsville Crisis* (New Haven, CT: Yale University Press, 2002).

7. On the disruptive child provision, see Perrillo, *Uncivil Rights*.

8. Cleo Silvers, "Who Are the Para-Professionals?" *Up from Under*, August/September 1970. Collection of New-York Historical Society Library, New York, NY.

9. Silvers, "Who Are the Para-Professionals?"

10. Alondra Nelson, "'Genuine Struggle and Care': An Interview with Cleo Silvers," *American Journal of Public Health* 106, no. 10 (October 2016): 1744–48.

11. Nelson, "'Genuine Struggle and Care.'"

12. Nelson, "'Genuine Struggle and Care.'"

13. Silvers, "Who Are the Para-Professionals?"

14. Silvers, "Who Are the Para-Professionals?"

15. Silvers, "Who Are the Para-Professionals?"

16. Dulcie Garcia, "More about Para-Professionals?" *Up from Under*, August/September 1970.

17. Rustin, "The Triumph of the Paraprofessionals."

18. William P. Jones, *The March on Washington: Jobs, Freedom, and the Forgotten History of Civil Rights* (New York: W. W. Norton & Company, 2014).

19. Paul Le Blanc and Michael D. Yates, *A Freedom Budget for All Americans: Recapturing the Promise of the Civil Rights Movement in the Struggle for Economic Justice Today* (New York: Monthly Review Press, 2013).

20. Rustin, "The Triumph of the Paraprofessionals."

21. Bureau of Labor Statistics, Occupational Outlook Handbook, 2021, https://www.bls.gov/ooh/education-training-and-library/teacher-assistants.htm.

22. On the rise of jobs deemed care work in the US economy, see, among others: Claire Dunning, "New Careers for the Poor: Human Services and the Post-Industrial City," *Journal of Urban History* 44, no. 4 (July 2018): 669–90; Sarah Jaffe, *Work Won't Love You Back: How Devotion to Our Jobs Keeps Us Exploited, Exhausted, and Alone* (New York: Bold Type Books, 2021); Premilla Nadasen, "Rethinking Care Work: (Dis)Affection and the Politics of Caring," *Feminist Formations* 33, no. 1 (2021); Gabriel Winant, *The Next Shift: The Fall of Industry and the Rise of Health Care in Rust Belt America* (Cambridge, MA: Harvard University Press, 2021).

23. E. P. Thompson, *The Making of the English Working Class* (New York: Vintage, 1966).

24. These campaigns are discussed in more detail in the epilogue. For example, see "MTA PreK-12 ESP Bill of Rights Is a Framework for Contract Gains," *MTA Today* (Winter 2023), https://massteacher.org/news/2023/04/esp-bill-of-rights.

25. Madeline Will, "Paraprofessionals: As the 'Backbones' of the Classroom, They Get Low Pay, Little Support," *Education Week*, June 15, 2022, https://www.edweek.org/leadership/paraprofessionals-as-the-backbones-of-the-classroom-they-get-low-pay-little-support/2022/06.

26. Biraj Bisht, Zachary LeClair, Susanna Loeb, and Min Sun, "Paraeducators: Growth, Diversity and a Dearth of Professional Supports," *EdWorkingPaper* (2021) 21–490. Retrieved from Annenberg Institute at Brown University: https://doi.org/10.26300/nk1z-c164.

27. LeShawna Coleman and Gemayel Keyes, "Recruiting the Talent Within: Philadelphia's Paraprofessional-to-Teacher Pipeline," *American Educator* (Winter 2022–2023), https://www.aft.org/ae/winter2022–2023/coleman_keyes.

28. Johanna S. Quinn and Myra Marx Ferree, "Schools as Workplaces: Intersectional Regimes of Inequality," *Gender, Work & Organization* 26, no. 12 (2019).

29. Quinn and Ferree, "Schools as Workplaces."

30. Jennifer E. Gaddis, *The Labor of Lunch: Why We Need Real Food and Real Jobs in American Public Schools* (Berkeley: University of California Press, 2019).

31. Nancy Fraser, "Contradictions of Capital and Care," *New Left Review* no. 100 (August 1, 2016), https://newleftreview.org/issues/ii100/articles/nancy-fraser-contradictions-of-capital-and-care.

32. Discussed in greater detail in the epilogue. See, among others, David K. Cohen & Susan L. Moffitt, *The Ordeal of Equality: Did Federal Regulation Fix the Schools?* (Cambridge, MA: Harvard University Press, 2009).

33. National Center for Education Statistics, Digest of Education Statistics: 2016, https://nces.ed.gov/programs/digest/d16/ch_1.asp.

34. A note on terminology: wherever possible, I refer to people with specificity (e.g., as Puerto Rican). "Hispanic" was used as the most common catchall term

during the era this book covers, and when discussing sources and events from this era, I use "Hispanic" for consistency. When discussing recent historical literature and how it informs my understanding of this history, I use the term "Latinx," following the pattern of recent scholarship.

35. Diana D'Amico Pawlewicz, *Blaming Teachers: Professionalization Policies and the Failure of Reform in American History* (New Brunswick, NJ: Rutgers University Press, 2020), 108; Bethany Rogers, "'Better' People, Better Teaching: The Vision of the National Teacher Corps, 1965–1968," *History of Education Quarterly* 49, no. 3 (August 2009).

36. Podair, *The Strike That Changed New York*, 182.

37. Jack Dougherty, *More Than One Struggle: The Evolution of Black School Reform in Milwaukee* (Chapel Hill: University of North Carolina Press, 2004). On the breadth of Black struggles beyond the traditional civil rights–Black Power dichotomy, see Russell Rickford, "Integration, Black Nationalism, and Radical Democratic Transformation in African-American Philosophies of Education, 1965–74," in Manning Marable and Elizabeth Kai Hinton, eds., *The New Black History: Revisiting the Second Reconstruction* (New York: Palgrave, 2011); and Nikhil Pal Singh, *Black Is a Country: Race and the Unfinished Struggle for Democracy* (Cambridge, MA: Harvard University Press, 2005). On the wide range of activist philosophies and practices in schooling, see Dougherty, *More Than One Struggle*; Tomiko Brown-Nagin, *Courage to Dissent: Atlanta and the Long History of the Civil Rights Movement* (Oxford, UK: Oxford University Press, 2011); and Russell Rickford, *We Are an African People: Independent Education, Black Power, and the Radical Imagination* (New York: Oxford University Press, 2016).

38. Among others, see Perlstein, *Justice, Justice*; Podair, *The Strike That Changed New York*; and Diane Ravitch, *The Great Schools Wars: New York City 1805–1973* (New York: Basic Books, 1973). For recent studies of New York City that move beyond the integration-separation dichotomy, see Christopher Bonastia, *The Battle Nearer to Home: The Persistence of School Segregation in New York City* (Stanford, CA: Stanford University Press, 2022); Sonia Song-Ha Lee, *Building a Latino Civil Rights Movement: Puerto Ricans, African Americans, and the Pursuit of Racial Justice in New York City* (Chapel Hill: University of North Carolina Press, 2014); Heather Lewis, *New York City Schools from Brownsville to Bloomberg: Community Control and Its Legacy* (New York: Teachers College Press, 2013); Perrillo, *Uncivil Rights*; and Grace G. Roosevelt, *Creating a College That Works: Audrey Cohen and Metropolitan College of New York* (New York: SUNY Press, 2015).

39. Rickford, "Integration, Black Nationalism, and Radical Democratic Transformation in African-American Philosophies of Education," 308.

40. Jane Berger, *A New Working Class: The Legacies of Public-Sector Employment in the Civil Rights Movement* (Philadelphia: Penn Press, 2021).

41. Stephen Gregory, *Black Corona: Race and the Politics of Place in an Urban Community* (Princeton, NJ: Princeton University Press, 1999); Harvey Kantor and Robert Lowe, "Class, Race, and the Emergence of Federal Education Policy: From the New Deal to the Great Society," *Educational Researcher* 24, no. 3 (April 1, 1995): 4–21; Harvey Kantor, "Education, Social Reform, and the State: ESEA

and Federal Education Policy in the 1960s," *American Journal of Education* 100, no. 1 (November 1, 1991): 47–83; David F. Labaree, "The Winning Ways of a Losing Strategy: Educationalizing Social Problems in the United States," *Educational Theory* 58, no. 4 (November 1, 2008); Margaret Weir, "States, Race, and the Decline of New Deal Liberalism," *Studies in American Political Development* (June 2005).

42. Claire Dunning, "New Careers for the Poor: Human Services and the Post-Industrial City," *Journal of Urban History* 44, no. 4 (July 1, 2018): 669–90.

43. Annelise Orleck, *Storming Caesars Palace: How Black Mothers Fought Their Own War on Poverty* (Boston: Beacon Press, 2005); Annelise Orleck and Lisa Gayle Hazirjian, eds., *The War on Poverty: A New Grassroots History, 1964–1980* (Athens: University of Georgia Press, 2011); Nancy A. Naples, *Grassroots Warriors: Activist Mothering, Community Work, and the War on Poverty* (New York: Routledge, 1998); Tamar W. Carroll, *Mobilizing New York: AIDS, Antipoverty, and Feminist Activism* (Chapel Hill: University of North Carolina Press, 2015); Dunning, "New Careers for the Poor."

44. Naples, *Grassroots Warriors*, 2–10. Naples's formulation builds on the concept of "othermothering" discussed by Patricia Hill Collins in her reading of bell hooks in *Black Feminist Thought: Knowledge, Consciousness and the Politics of Empowerment* (London: Routledge, 2000). Bottom-up histories of the War on Poverty deploy this analytic framing. See Orleck and Hazirjian, *The War on Poverty*, Part II, "Poor Mothers and the War on Poverty."

45. Premilla Nadasen, *Welfare Warriors: The Welfare Rights Movement in the United States* (New York: Routledge, 2005); Rhonda Y. Williams, *The Politics of Public Housing: Black Women's Struggles against Urban Inequality* (New York: Oxford University Press, 2005); Naples, *Grassroots Warriors*.

46. Rhonda Y. Williams, *Concrete Demands: The Search for Black Power in the 20th Century* (New York: Routledge, 2014).

47. Naples, *Grassroots Warriors*, 2–10.

48. "Introduction," in Jeanne Theoharis and Komozi Woodard, eds., *Groundwork: Local Black Freedom Movements in America* (New York: New York University Press, 2005), 2–3.

49. Jessica Wilkerson, *To Live Here, You Have to Fight: How Women Led Appalachian Movements for Social Justice* (Urbana: University of Illinois Press, 2019).

50. On the rise of violence in public schools in New York City, see John Devine, *Maximum Security: The Culture of Violence in Inner City Schools* (Chicago: University of Chicago Press, 1996).

51. Elizabeth Hinton, *From the War on Poverty to the War on Crime: The Making of Mass Incarceration in America* (Cambridge, MA: Harvard University Press, 2016).

52. Stuart Hall, *Cultural Studies 1983: A Theoretical History* (Durham, NC: Duke University Press, 2016), 223.

53. Labaree, "The Winning Ways of a Losing Strategy"; Miriam Cohen, "Reconsidering Schools and the American Welfare State," *History of Education Quarterly* 45, no. 4 (Winter 2005).

54. Jane Berger, "'A Lot Closer to What It Ought To Be': Black Women and

Public Sector Employment in Baltimore, 1950–1970," in Robert Zieger, ed., *Life and Labor in the New New South* (Gainesville: University of Florida Press, 2012); Berger, *A New Working Class*; Nancy MacLean, *Freedom Is Not Enough: The Opening of the American Workplace* (Cambridge, MA: Harvard/Russell Sage, 2008). On the importance of these campaigns for the making of an African American middle class in the late twentieth century, see Michael B. Katz and Mark J. Stern, "The New African-American Inequality," *Journal of American History* (June 2005); Crystal Sanders, *A Chance for Change: Head Start and Mississippi's Black Freedom Struggle* (Chapel Hill: University of North Carolina Press, 2016).

55. Ansley T. Erickson, *Making the Unequal Metropolis: School Desegregation and Its Limits* (Chicago: University of Chicago Press, 2016); Andrew R. Highsmith, *Demolition Means Progress: Flint, Michigan, and the Fate of the American Metropolis* (Chicago: University of Chicago Press, 2015); Jack Dougherty and contributors, "On the Line | Book-in-Progress," accessed March 13, 2017, http://ontheline.trincoll.edu/book/.

56. On the "distribution of people and jobs" into homogeneous political units concerned primarily with defensive protection of resources and exclusion of outsiders, see Ira Katznelson, *Schooling for All: Class, Race, and the Decline of the Democratic Ideal* (New York: Basic Books, 1985). The argument here is that community-based educational hiring was an effort to lean against this tendency in American schooling.

57. See Carroll, *Mobilizing New York*; Roberta Gold, *When Tenants Claimed the City: The Struggle for Citizenship in New York City Housing* (Urbana: University of Illinois Press, 2014); Stephanie Gilmore, ed., *Feminist Coalitions: Historical Perspectives on Second-Wave Feminism in the United States* (Urbana: University of Illinois Press, 2008).

58. Joshua B. Freeman, *Working-Class New York: Life and Labor Since World War II* (New York: New Press, 2000), 183.

59. Michael Woodsworth, *Battle for Bed-Stuy: The Long War on Poverty in New York City* (Cambridge, MA: Harvard University Press, 2016), 135.

60. U.S. Census Bureau, Occupational Data, 1950–1980. Prepared by Social Explorer, https://www.socialexplorer.com. Accessed May 2016.

61. Figures from Joseph Slater, *Public Workers: Government Employee Unions, the Law, and the State, 1900–1962* (Ithaca, NY: Cornell University Press, 2004).

62. See MacLean, *Freedom Is Not Enough*; Paul Frymer, *Black and Blue: African Americans, the Labor Movement, and the Decline of the Democratic Party* (Princeton, NJ: Princeton University Press, 2009); Freeman, *Working-Class New York*; Michael K. Honey, *Going Down Jericho Road: The Memphis Strike, Martin Luther King's Last Campaign* (New York: W. W. Norton, 2008).

63. Berger, *A New Working Class*.

64. Perrillo, *Uncivil Rights*.

65. Pawlewicz, *Blaming Teachers*; Diana D'Amico, "Teachers' Rights Versus Students' Rights: Race and Professional Authority in the New York City Public Schools, 1960–1986," *American Educational Research Journal* 53, no. 3 (June 1, 2016): 541–72; Mark Maier, *City Unions: Managing Discontent in New York City* (New Brunswick, NJ: Rutgers University Press, 1987).

66. On the problem of professionalism in public education, see Leo Casey, *The Teacher Insurgency: A Strategic and Organizing Perspective* (Cambridge, MA: Harvard Education Press, 2020), Chapter 10, as well as Lois Weiner, *The Future of Our Schools: Teachers Unions and Social Justice* (New York: Haymarket Press, 2012).

67. Jon Shelton, "Against the Public: The Pittsburgh Teachers Strike of 1975–1976 and the Crisis of the Labor-Liberal Coalition," *Labor* 10, no. 2 (June 20, 2013): 55–75. See also Jon Shelton, *Teacher Strike! Public Education and the Making of a New American Political Order* (Urbana: University of Illinois Press, 2017).

68. On the AFT's verticality, see Diana D'Amico Pawlewicz, Nick Juravich, and Jonna Perrillo, "Defining and Defending Professionalism: A Long View of Teacher Unionism," in Diana D'Amico Pawlewicz, ed., *Walkout! Teacher Militancy, Activism, and School Reform* (Charlotte, NC: Information Age Publishing, 2022).

69. Berger, *A New Working Class.*

70. Kim Phillips-Fein, *Fear City: New York's Fiscal Crisis and the Rise of Austerity Politics* (New York: Metropolitan Books, 2017); Jonathan Soffer, *Ed Koch and the Rebuilding of New York City* (New York: Columbia University Press, 2010).

71. Hall, *Cultural Studies 1983*, 223.

72. As Michael Woodsworth explains in *Battle for Bed-Stuy*, examining the interplay between local practices and national policy reveals "just how *creative* 'creative federalism' could be" (9).

73. Aurelia Greene, interview with the author, July 24, 2014.

74. On pioneering antipoverty efforts in New York City, see Carroll, *Mobilizing New York*; Noel E. Cazenave, *Impossible Democracy: The Unlikely Success of the War on Poverty Community Action Program* (Albany, NY: State University of New York Press, 2007); and Woodsworth, *Battle for Bed-Stuy*. On teacher segregation, see Christina Collins, *"Ethnically Qualified": Race, Merit, and the Selection of Urban Teachers, 1920–1980* (New York: Teachers College Press, 2011).

75. On the education of children with disabilities and the construction of "special education" as a category, see, among others, Francine Almash, "New York City '600' Schools and the Legacy of Segregation in Special Education," *Gotham: A Blog for Scholars of New York City History*, June 21, 2022, https://www.gothamcenter.org/blog/new-york-city-600-schools-and-the-legacy-of-segregation-in-special-education; Adam Nelson, *The Elusive Ideal: Equal Educational Opportunity and the Federal Role in Boston's Public Schools, 1950–1985* (Chicago: University of Chicago Press, 2005); Christine Sleeter, "Learning Disabilities: The Social Construction of a Special Education Category," *Exceptional Children* 53, no. 1 (1986).

Chapter 1. From Aides to Paras

1. Benjamin Fine, "Aides in Midwest Classrooms Help Relieve Teacher Shortage," *New York Times*, December 1, 1956.

2. "Introduction," *Journal of Teacher Education* 7, no. 2 (June 1, 1956): 100.

3. Fine, "Aides in Midwest Classrooms Help Relieve Teacher Shortage."

4. "Editorial Comments," *Journal of Teacher Education* 7, no. 2 (June 1, 1956): 98.

5. National Center for Education Statistics, Digest of Education Statistics: 2016, https://nces.ed.gov/programs/digest/d16/ch_1.asp.

6. Michael R. Glass, "Schooling Suburbia: The Politics of School Finance in Postwar Long Island" (PhD diss, Princeton University, 2020).

7. "Editorial Comments," *Journal of Teacher Education* 7, no. 2 (June 1, 1956): 153.

8. Ford Foundation, *Decade of Experiment: The Fund for the Advancement of Education, 1951–61* (New York: The Ford Foundation, 1961).

9. Diana D'Amico Pawlewicz, *Blaming Teachers: Professionalization Policies and the Failure of Reform in American History* (New Brunswick, NJ: Rutgers University Press, 2020), 108.

10. Pawlewicz, *Blaming Teachers*, 47.

11. Charles B. Park, "The Bay City Experiment . . . As Seen by the Director," *Journal of Teacher Education* 7, no. 2 (June 1, 1956).

12. Paul W. Briggs, "The Bay City Experiment . . . As Viewed by the Staff of the City Schools," *Journal of Teacher Education* 8, no. 1 (March 1, 1957): 3–6.

13. Dorothy McCuskey and Ablett H. Flury, "The Bay City Experiment . . . As Seen by a Curriculum Specialist," *Journal of Teacher Education* 7, no. 2 (June 1, 1956): 111–18.

14. Park, "The Bay City Experiment . . . As Seen by the Director." Note here the gendered language.

15. James L. Hymes, "The Bay City Experiment . . . As Seen by a Child Psychologist," *Journal of Teacher Education* 7, no. 2 (June 1, 1956): 126–31.

16. John McLean, "US Education Watches Bay City Experiment: Eight Women at School Do Noneducational Chores So Teachers Can Do Teaching," *The Milwaukee Journal*, February 14, 1956.

17. Hymes, "The Bay City Experiment . . . As Seen by a Child Psychologist."

18. On the definition of poor and working-class mothers as problems—and the resistance of these mothers to such designations and their policy implications—see Annelise Orleck and Lisa Gayle Hazirjian, eds., *The War on Poverty: A New Grassroots History, 1964–1980* (Athens: University of Georgia Press, 2011), Section II: Poor Mothers and the War on Poverty.

19. Hymes, "The Bay City Experiment . . . As Seen by a Child Psychologist."

20. Park, "The Bay City Experiment . . . As Seen by the Director."

21. McLean, "US Education Watches Bay City Experiment"; Hymes, "The Bay City Experiment . . . As Seen by a Child Psychologist"; Dorothy McCuskey and Ablett H. Flury, "The Bay City Experiment . . . As Seen by a Curriculum Specialist," *Journal of Teacher Education* 7, no. 2 (June 1, 1956).

22. McLean, "US Education Watches Bay City Experiment."

23. McLean, "US Education Watches Bay City Experiment."

24. Lucille Carroll, "The Bay City Experiment . . . As Seen by a Classroom Teacher," *Journal of Teacher Education* 7, no. 2 (June 1, 1956): 142–47. The final report of the Bay City faculty and staff appears to contradict this assertion.

25. Wayne J. Urban, *Gender, Race and the National Education Association: Professionalism and Its Limitations* (New York: Routledge, 2000): 171.

26. Pawlewicz, *Blaming Teachers*, Chapter 5.

27. Park, "The Bay City Experiment . . . As Seen by the Director."

28. Carroll, "The Bay City Experiment . . . As Seen by a Classroom Teacher."

29. Park, "The Bay City Experiment . . . As Seen by the Director."

30. Park, "The Bay City Experiment . . . As Seen by the Director."

31. *Decade of Experiment*, 48–50.

32. Fred Hechinger, "Teachers for Tomorrow: New Answers to an Old Question," *New York Herald Tribune*, November 13, 1955; Yale-Fairfield Study of Elementary Teaching, *Teacher Assistants: An Abridged Report,* prepared by John H. Howell (New Haven: Yale University Press, 1959); "Yale Plans Study of Public Schools: Project on a Ford Foundation Grant Will Focus on Teaching in Fairfield, Conn., System," *New York Times*, October 25, 1953.

33. *Decade of Experiment*, 50.

34. Letter from Charles Cogen to William B. Nichols, December 7, 1955, UFT Box 7, Folder 38.

35. Martha Biondi, *To Stand and Fight: The Struggle for Civil Rights in Postwar New York City* (Cambridge, MA: Harvard University Press, 2003); Brian Purnell, *Fighting Jim Crow in the County of Kings: The Congress of Racial Equality in Brooklyn* (Lexington: University Press of Kentucky, 2015); Thomas J. Sugrue, *Sweet Land of Liberty: The Forgotten Struggle for Civil Rights in the North* (New York: Random House, 2009); Clarence Taylor, ed., *Civil Rights in New York City: From World War II to the Giuliani Era* (New York: Fordham University Press, 2011).

36. Christopher Bonastia, *The Battle Nearer to Home: The Persistence of School Segregation in New York City* (Stanford, CA: Stanford University Press, 2022); Ansley T. Erickson and Ernest Morrell, eds., *Educating Harlem: A Century of Schooling and Resistance in a Black Community* (New York: Columbia University Press, 2019); Purnell, *Fighting Jim Crow in the County of Kings*; Taylor, *Civil Rights in New York City*.

37. Adina Back, "Exposing the 'Whole Segregation Myth': The Harlem Nine and New York City's School Desegregation Battles," in Jeanne F. Theoharis and Komozi Woodard, eds., *Freedom North: Black Freedom Struggles Outside the South, 1940–1980* (New York: Palgrave Macmillan, 2003); Ashley D. Farmer, "'All the Progress To Be Made Will Be Made by Maladjusted Negroes': Mae Mallory, Black Women's Activism, and the Making of the Black Radical Tradition," *Journal of Social History* 53, no. 2 (November 1, 2019): 508–30.

38. Kenneth Clark, Address to the "Children Apart" Conference, April 24, 1954.

39. Clarence Taylor, "Conservative and Liberal Opposition to the New York City School-Integration Campaign," in Taylor, *Civil Rights in New York City*.

40. Barbara Ransby, "Cops, Schools, and Communism," in Taylor, *Civil Rights in New York City*.

41. Barbara Ransby, *Ella Baker and the Black Freedom Movement* (Chapel Hill: University of North Carolina Press, 2003), 153–55.

42. On the TU, see Clarence Taylor, *Reds at the Blackboard: Communism, Civil Rights, and the New York City Teachers Union* (New York: Columbia University Press, 2012), 239. Similar campaigns took place across the country, even after the *Brown v. Board of Education* decision focused attention on pupil segregation in the South. In Milwaukee, the "creative application" of *Brown* included demands for the hiring of African American teachers and increased resources for majority-Black schools. See Dougherty, *More Than One Struggle*.

43. Back, "Exposing the 'Whole Segregation Myth'"; Michael Glass, "From Sword to Shield to Myth: Facing the Facts of De Facto School Segregation," *Journal of Urban History* 44, no. 26 (2016). Mae Mallory, who became the leading voice of the protests, explained later that they were "never about wanting to sit next to white folks." Farmer, "All Progress Will Be Made by Maladjusted Negroes."

44. Purnell, *Fighting Jim Crow in the County of Kings*.

45. Collins, *Ethnically Qualified*.

46. Within the Black educational tradition, the use of laypeople and community members as educators has a long history, dating back to the practice of "each one, teach one," by which enslaved people shared literacy covertly. After emancipation, the state's abdication and active hostility to Black education made schooling a community exercise by necessity, one that generated community-focused teaching by "caring teachers" and also networks in individual towns and cities to support schools and students where the official system would not. See, among a great many others, James Anderson, *The Education of Blacks in the South, 1860–1935* (Chapel Hill: University of North Carolina Press, 1988); Vanessa Siddle Walker, *Their Highest Potential: An African American School Community in the Segregated South* (Chapel Hill: University of North Carolina Press, 1996). Charles Payne and Carol Sills Strickland, eds., *Teach Freedom Education for Liberation in the African-American Tradition* (New York: Teachers College Press, 2008). These traditions served as foundations in imagining new roles for "aides."

47. The most famous example of this framework appears in Daniel P. Moynihan's 1965 report for the Department of Labor, "The Negro Family: The Case for National Action."

48. Elizabeth Hinton, *From the War on Poverty to the War on Crime: The Making of Mass Incarceration in America* (Cambridge, MA: Harvard University Press, 2016).

49. On the burgeoning carceral state and its entanglement with public education, see the special section of the *Journal of Urban History*, "Public Education and the Carceral State," 49, no. 5 (September 2023), edited by Walter C. Stern, particularly essays by Stern, Matthew B. Kautz, and Noah Remnick. See also Mahasan Chaney, "Discipline for the 'Educationally Deprived': ESEA and the Punitive Function of Federal Education Policy 1965–1998" (PhD diss., University of California, 2019).

50. Mary Dowery, interview with the author, January 30, 2014.

51. Dowery, interview.

52. Laura Pires-Hester, interview with the author, March 9, 2015.

53. Lee, *Building a Latino Civil Rights Movement*, 108–9.

54. This phrase borrowed from Cheryl Townsend Gilkes, "Successful Rebellious Professionals: The Black Woman's Professional Identity and Community Commitment," *Psychology of Women Quarterly* 6, no. 3 (Spring 1982).

55. For a detailed discussion of the possibilities and limits of "place-based politics" in antipoverty organizing and community organizing in New York City, see Woodsworth, *Battle for Bed-Stuy*.

56. See Ira Katznelson, *City Trenches: Urban Politics and the Patterning of Class in the United States* (Chicago: University of Chicago Press, 1982); Gregory, *Black Corona*; Weir, "States, Race, and the Decline of New Deal Liberalism."

57. Richard A. Cloward and Lloyd E. Ohlin, *Delinquency and Opportunity: A Study of Delinquent Gangs* (Glencoe, IL: The Free Press, 1960).

58. Dowery, interview.

59. See Tamar Carroll, *Mobilizing New York: AIDS, Antipoverty, and Feminist Activism* (Chapel Hill: University of North Carolina Press, 2015) for an extended discussion of Mobilization for Youth and the challenges aides faced when they encountered entrenched bureaucrats and politicians.

60. Dowery, interview.

61. Quoted in Felicia Kornbluh, *The Battle for Welfare Rights: Politics and Poverty in Modern America* (Philadelphia: University of Pennsylvania Press, 2007), 98.

62. Shelvy Young-Abrams, interview with the author, September 5, 2015.

63. Young-Abrams, interview.

64. Gerald Markowitz and David Rosner, *Children, Race, and Power: Kenneth and Mamie Clark's Northside Center* (New York: Routledge, 1999).

65. "Negro Teachers Form a New Assn. To Aid Harlem Kids," *New York World-Telegram and Sun,* November 13, 1963, Richard Parrish Papers, Reel 1, Schomburg Center for Research in Black Culture, New York Public Library, New York, NY.

66. Ronnie Almonte, "Richard Parrish, the Black Caucus, and the 1968 Ocean Hill–Brownsville Strikes," *International Socialist Review* 111 (Winter 2018–19), https://isreview.org/issue/111/richard-parrish-black-caucus-and-1968-ocean -hill-brownsville-strikes/index.html.

67. "Negro Teachers Form a New Assn. To Aid Harlem Kids," *World-Telegram and Sun,* November 11, 1963, RPP, Microfilm, Reel 1.

68. "A Proposal to Establish after School Study Centers in the Central Harlem Area and to Develop New Approaches in the Area of Remediation, Academic Instruction, Guidance, and the Training of Teachers," Community Teachers Association, RPP, Microfilm, Reel 3.

69. Oneida Davis, interview with the author, September 3, 2014.

70. Davis, interview.

71. Meeting Minutes, April 5, 1963, PS 192, Manhattan, UFT Box 115, Folder 3.

72. Harlem Youth Opportunities Unlimited, Inc., *Youth in the Ghetto: A Study of the Consequences of Powerlessness and a Blueprint for Change* (New York, 1964).

73. As William Cutler writes in *Parents and Schools*, the 1940s and 1950s saw an explosion of middle-class parent voluntarism in public school classrooms, with local mothers volunteering as aides and both mothers and fathers taking active

roles in shaping new curricula for their children. See Cutler, *Parents and Schools: The 150-Year Struggle for Control in American Education* (Chicago: University of Chicago Press, 2000), 165–70.

74. Laura Pires-Hester, interview with the author, March 9, 2015.

75. "Youth in the Ghetto," in Arthur Pearl and Frank Riessman, *New Careers for the Poor: The Nonprofessional in Human Service* (New York: Free Press, 1965), vii.

76. Quoted in Pearl and Riessman, *New Careers for the Poor*, viii-ix. On maximum feasible participation, see Alice O'Connor, *Poverty Knowledge: Social Science, Social Policy, and the Poor in Twentieth-Century U.S. History* (Princeton, NJ: Princeton University Press, 2001).

77. See, among many others, Ira Katznelson, "Was the Great Society a Lost Opportunity?" in Steve Fraser and Gary Gerstle, *The Rise and Fall of the New Deal Order, 1930–1980* (Princeton, NJ: Princeton University Press, 1990).

78. Alan Gartner, *Paraprofessionals and Their Performance: A Survey of Education, Health, and Social Service Programs* (New York: Praeger Publishers, 1971).

79. For analysis of Head Start's impact on the struggle for "full freedom" by parents and working-class women in the Child Development Group of Mississippi, see Crystal Sanders, *A Chance for Change: Head Start and Mississippi's Black Freedom Struggle* (Chapel Hill: University of North Carolina Press, 2016).

80. Harvey Kantor, "Education, Social Reform, and the State: ESEA and Federal Education Policy in the 1960s," *American Journal of Education* 100, no. 1 (November 1, 1991): 58.

81. Michael Katz, ed., *The "Underclass" Debate: Views from History* (Princeton, NJ: Princeton University Press, 1993); Katznelson, "Was the Great Society a Lost Opportunity?"; O'Connor, *Poverty Knowledge*.

82. David Labaree, "The Winning Ways of a Losing Strategy: Educationalizing Social Problems in the United States," *Educational Theory* 58, no. 4 (November 1, 2008).

83. Gloria Ladson-Billings, "Getting to Sesame Street? Fifty Years of Federal Compensatory Education," *RSF: The Russell Sage Foundation Journal of the Social Sciences* 1, no. 3 (2015): 96–111.

84. William S. Bennett, *New Careers and Urban Schools: A Sociological Study of Teacher and Teacher Aide Roles* (New York: Holt, Rinehart and Winston, 1970), 18. Preston Wilcox later consulted on Follow Through programs.

85. See Kantor, "Education, Social Reform, and the State," on the contest over who would control the education centers created by Title III of the ESEA, as well as their "subversive" potential and its decline.

86. Department of Health, Education, and Welfare Press Release, June 30, 1966. American Federation of Teachers Inventory, Part I, Box 30, Folder "School Aides," Walter P. Reuther Library, Wayne State University, Detroit, MI.

87. Quoted in Johanna S. Quinn, "Unequal Work in Unequal Schools: Working in NYC Middle Schools in an Era of Accountability" (PhD diss., University of Wisconsin, 2017), 53.

88. O'Connor, *Poverty Knowledge*, 170.

89. O'Connor, *Poverty Knowledge*, 172.

90. O'Connor, *Poverty Knowledge*, 177–80. On the broader impact of Head Start, see Gretchen Aguiar, "Head Start: A History of Implementation" (PhD diss., University of Pennsylvania, 2012), and Sanders, *A Chance for Change*.

91. Aguiar, "Head Start."

92. Frank Riessman, *The Culturally Deprived Child* (New York: Harper, 1962).

93. Audrey J. Gartner, "Biography of Frank Riessman," *The Journal of Applied Behavioral Science* 29, no. 2 (June 1, 1993): 148–50.

94. Pearl and Riessman, *New Careers for the Poor*, vii.

95. Pearl and Riessman, *New Careers for the Poor*, viii-ix.

96. While federal funds supported New Careers hiring in the public health care sector as well, career ladder and community-based hiring programs faltered in this context, where aides were limited to "low level and peripheral functions . . . with no real entry onto professional ladders." Eileen Boris & Jennifer Klein, *Caring for America: Home Health Care Workers in the Shadow of the Welfare State* (New York: Oxford University Press, 2012), 108–10. On the limits to career ladders in nonprofit contexts, see Dunning, "New Careers for the Poor."

97. Kenneth Clark, *Dark Ghetto: Dilemmas of Social Power* (New York: Harper & Row, 1965), quoted in Pearl and Riessman, *New Careers for the Poor*.

98. Pearl and Riessman, *New Careers for the Poor*, Chapter 4.

99. Clipping, *New York Herald-Tribune*, January 23, 1966, in the James H. Scheuer Papers, Box 6, Folder 3, Swarthmore College, Swarthmore, PA.

100. Miriam Cohen, "Reconsidering Schools and the American Welfare State," *History of Education Quarterly* 45, no. 4 (Winter 2005).

101. Matthew F. Delmont, *Why Busing Failed: Race, Media, and the National Resistance to School Desegregation* (Oakland: University of California Press, 2016).

102. Clarence Taylor, *Knocking at Our Own Door: Milton A. Galamison and the Struggle to Integrate New York City Schools* (New York: Columbia University Press, 1997); Delmont, *Why Busing Failed*.

103. Michael W. Flamm, *In the Heat of the Summer: The New York Riots of 1964 and the War on Crime* (Philadelphia: University of Pennsylvania Press, 2016).

104. Russell Rickford, "Black Power as Educational Renaissance: The Harlem Landscape," in Erickson and Morrell, eds., *Educating Harlem*.

105. Marta Gutman, "Intermediate School 201: Race, Space, and Modern Architecture in Harlem," in Erickson and Morrell, eds., *Educating Harlem*.

106. Preston Wilcox, "The Controversy at IS 201—One View and a Proposal," *Urban Review*, July 1966, PWP Box 24, Folder 2.

107. Wilcox, "Controversy at IS 201." On the Child Development Group of Mississippi, see Sanders, *A Chance for Change*.

108. Harlem Parents Committee, "Views," April 1966 and September 1967, UFT Box 87, Folder 25.

109. McGeorge Bundy, ed., *Reconnection for Learning: A Community School System for New York City* (New York: Mayor's Advisory Panel on the Decentralization of Schools, 1967), 26.

110. Mercedes Figueroa, MCNY Student Interviews, 1976.

111. Orleck, *Storming Caesars Palace.*

112. Wendell Pritchett, *Brownsville, Brooklyn: Blacks, Jews, and the Changing Face of the Ghetto* (Chicago: University of Chicago Press, 2003). For similar analyses of campaigns for, and gains made by, African American women in public sector employment, see Rhonda Williams, *The Politics of Public Housing* (New York: Oxford University Press, 2004); Katz and Stern, "The New African-American Inequality."

113. Garda Bowman and Gordon Klopf, "New Partners in the Educational Enterprise" (Report for the Office of Economic Opportunity, 1967), Bound Material in the Bank Street College of Education Archives, Bank Street College, New York (hereafter Bank Street).

114. "Training Parents and Others in Low Income Neighborhoods to Work in the Schools," Application for Operational Grant ESEA Title III, Ellen Lurie Papers, Box 1, Folder "Publications.."

115. Garda W. Bowman and Gordon J. Klopf, "Auxiliary School Personnel: Their Roles, Training, and Institutionalization," Report for the Office of Economic Opportunity (October 1966); Garda W. Bowman and Gordon J. Klopf, *New Careers and Roles in the American School* (New York: Bank Street College of Education, 1968).

116. Bowman and Klopf, *New Careers and Roles in the American School,* Appendix III.

117. Bowman and Klopf, *New Careers and Roles in the American School,* 17.

118. Aurelia Greene, interview with the author, July 24, 2014.

119. Rep. Serrano of New York, Tribute to Reverend Jerome A. Greene, 109th Cong., 2nd sess., *Congressional Record,* Vol. 152 No. 46, E597, https://www.congress.gov/congressional-record/2006/4/25/extensions-of-remarks-section/article/e597-3?r=42.

120. Lee, *Building a Latino Civil Rights Movement;* Lorraine Montenegro, interview with the author, September 24, 2014. Montenegro is Evelina Lopez Antonetty's daughter and worked closely with her mother on these campaigns.

121. Montenegro, interview.

122. "The Use of Auxiliary Personnel (Paraprofessionals)," October 20, 1967, ELP Box 1, Folder "Paraprofessionals." Center for Puerto Rican Studies, Hunter College, New York, NY.

123. "Title I: Some Questions to Ask," October 20, 1967, ELP Box 1, Folder "Title I."

124. "Information on Title I," August, 1968, ELP Box 1, Folder "Title I."

125. For a comprehensive look at the United Bronx Parents and Black-Latinx solidarity in New York City, see Lee, *Building a Latino Civil Rights Movement.*

126. Jesse Hoffnung-Garskof, *A Tale of Two Cities: Santo Domingo and New York after 1950,* (Princeton, NJ: Princeton University Press, 2007), 194. Hoffnung-Garskof suggests that these fissures emerged because of leadership concerns, and whether "there was room in the community control movement for Latinos to participate on their own terms, rather than simply as supporters of a 'community' politics that had already been defined by black activists." Chapters 5

and 6 of Hoffnung-Garskof's book examine cooperation and contention among Dominican immigrants and African Americans in the context of education. See also Mark Brilliant, *The Color of America Has Changed: How Racial Diversity Shaped Civil Rights Reform in California, 1941–1978* (New York: Oxford University Press, 2009); and Emily Straus, "Unequal Pieces of a Shrinking Pie: The Struggle between African Americans and Latinos over Education, Employment, and Empowerment in Compton, California," *History of Education Quarterly* 49 (November 2009), for a considered look at the battles for jobs and resources embedded in schools.

127. Johanna Fernandez, "The Young Lords and the Social and Structural Roots of Late Sixties Urban Radicalism," in Taylor, *Civil Rights in New York City*.

128. Velma Murphy Hill, interview.

129. Alida Mesrop, interview with the author, January 28, 2015.

130. Grace G. Roosevelt, *Creating a College That Works: Audrey C. Cohen and Metropolitan College of New York* (Albany: State University of New York Press, 2013).

131. Women's Talent Corps Progress Report (No. 2), October 1966, UFT Box 108, Folder 5.

132. "Albert Shanker, 1973" (Transcript of Oral History with Audrey Cohen), MCNY Folder 156.

133. Freeman, *Working-Class New York*.

134. Frymer, *Black and Blue*.

135. Leonora Farber, interview with the author, January 21, 2014.

136. Collins, *Ethnically Qualified*; Pawlewicz, *Blaming Teachers*; Perrillo, *Uncivil Rights*.

137. Letter from Charles Cogen to William B. Nichols, December 7, 1955, UFT Box 7, Folder 38.

138. "To Chapter Chairmen of the Schools Which Are Receiving Teacher Aides in February 1963," from Neil Lefkowitz, November 30, 1962, UFT Box 20, Folder 60; Gladys Roth, "UFT Opens Career Doors for Educational Assistant," *The United Teacher*, January 24, 1968, UFT Box 155, Folder 1.

139. Elizabeth Todd-Breland, *A Political Education: Black Politics and Education Reform in Chicago Since the 1960s* (Chapel Hill: University of North Carolina Press, 2018).

140. Board of Education Special Circular No. 66, 1962–63, June 25, 1963, UFT Box 93, Folder 5.

141. Letter from School Aides of Bronx Science to Shanker, March 26, 1964, UFT Box 93, Folder 5.

142. Letter from Charles Cogen to Richard Parrish, December 21, 1964, AFT-Inventory, Box 41, Folder "Richard Parrish."

143. Department of Health, Education, and Welfare Press Release, June 30, 1966, AFT-Inventory, Part I, Box 30, Folder "School Aides."

144. For more on this move and its meaning for teacher unionism, see Diana D'Amico Pawlewicz, Nick Juravich, and Jonna Perrillo, "Defining and Defending Professionalism: A Long View of Teacher Unionism," in Diana D'Amico

Pawlewicz, ed., *Walkout! Teacher Militancy, Activism, and School Reform* (Charlotte, NC: Information Age Publishing, 2022).

145. Executive Council Minutes, July 9, 1966, AFT-Inventory Part I, Box 30, Folder "School Aides."

146. AFT Executive Council Minutes, July 9, 1966.

147. AFT Executive Council Minutes, July 9, 1966.

148. Pawlewicz, *Blaming Teachers*, 149.

149. Executive Council Minutes, July 9, 1966, AFT-Inventory Part I, Box 30, Folder "School Aides."

150. AFT Executive Council Report, March 31, 1969, AFT-Inventory Series II, Box 31, Folder 3.

151. Letter from Albert Shanker to Audrey C. Cohen, March 8, 1967, MCNY, Folder 4657.

152. AFT Executive Council Report, March 31, 1969, AFT-Inventory Series II, Box 31, Folder 3.

153. Women's Talent Corps Progress Report (No. 6), March-April 1967, UFT.

Chapter 2. "They Made Themselves Essential"

1. On the segregation of the teaching corps, see Collins, *Ethnically Qualified*.

2. United Federation of Teachers, Video: Paraprofessionals Chapter 50th Anniversary, https://www.uft.org/news/videos/paraprofessionals-chapter-50th-anniversary (accessed August 7, 2019).

3. Maggie Martin, interview with the author, February 2, 2015.

4. Shelvy Young-Abrams, interview with the author, September 5, 2015.

5. Women's Talent Corps, Progress Report July-December 1967, MCNY Folder 14.

6. Nancy D. Garcia to Albert Shanker, October 23, 1967, UFT Box 93, Folder 5.

7. On the "disruptive child" provision, see Francine Almash, "New York City '600' Schools and the Legacy of Segregation in Special Education," *Gotham: A Blog for Scholars of New York City History*, June 21, 2022, https://www.gothamcenter.org/blog/new-york-city-600-schools-and-the-legacy-of-segregation-in-special-education, and Jonna Perrillo, *Uncivil Rights: Teachers, Unions, and Race in the Battle for School Equity* (Chicago: University of Chicago Press, 2012).

8. Gladys Roth, "Auxiliary Educational Assistants in New York City Schools," UFT Box 80, Folder 11.

9. Roth, "Auxiliary Educational Assistants." Quotes are drawn from three different paraprofessionals at three different schools.

10. Brickell et al., *An In-Depth Study of Paraprofessionals*.

11. Aurelia Greene, interview with the author, August 27, 2014.

12. On the construction of care work and the exploitation of jobs defined as such, see, among others, Boris and Klein, *Caring for America*; Evelyn Nakano Glenn, *Forced to Care: Coercion and Caregiving in America* (Cambridge, MA: Harvard University Press, 2010); Jaffe, *Work Won't Love You Back*; Nadasen, "Rethinking Care Work"; Quinn and Ferree, "Schools as Workplaces."

13. Collins, *Black Feminist Thought*. Sociologist Nancy Naples developed the framework of "activist mothering" by applying Patricia Hill Collins's concept of "othermothering" to the narratives she collected from community-based antipoverty workers who were active in the 1960s and 1970s, including some paraprofessional educators. See Naples, *Grassroots Warriors*. Othermothering, as Collins defines it, is a form of social reproduction under conditions of subordination. "In confronting racial oppression," she writes, "maintaining community-based child care and respecting othermothers who assume child-care responsibilities serve a critical function. . . . Experiences as othermothers provide a foundation for Black women's political activism." Collins in turn invokes an earlier generation of Black feminist writers, including bell hooks, Angela Davis, and Alice Walker, who conceptualized othermothering as a Black women's survival strategy for Black communities. See Collins, *Black Feminist Thought*, especially 119–20, 132. Scholars of the welfare rights movement and the War on Poverty "from the grass roots up" have deployed Naples's framework to reveal the centrality of working-class Black and Latina women's thought and action to these movements, and to unpack and upend hierarchies of race, class, and gender that marginalized this work, both at the time and in historical memory. On the welfare rights movement, see Nadasen, *Welfare Warriors,* and Kornbluh, *The Battle for Welfare Rights*. On the War on Poverty era, see Orleck and Hazirjian, eds., *The War on Poverty*; Orleck, *Storming Caesars Palace*; and Williams, *The Politics of Public Housing*.

14. On feminist coalitions, see Gilmore, ed., *Feminist Coalitions*, and Kirsten Swinth, *Feminism's Forgotten Fight: The Unfinished Struggle for Work and Family* (Cambridge, MA: Harvard University Press, 2019). In New York, see Carroll, *Mobilizing New York,* and Gold, *When Tenants Claimed the City*.

15. Patricia Hill Collins, drawing on the work of Cheryl Townsend Gilkes, calls this practice "going up for the oppressed," a strategy deployed by Black women professionals that mirrors Eugene Debs's famous assertion that he hoped to rise "with the ranks, and not from the ranks" of the working class. See Collins, *Black Feminist Thought*; Cheryl Townsend Gilkes, "Going Up for the Oppressed: The Career Mobility of Black Women Community Workers," *Journal of Social Issues* 39, no. 3 (Fall 1983): 115–39; Eugene V. Debs, "The Canton, Ohio, Speech," June 16, 1918, https://www.marxists.org/archive/debs/works/1918/canton.htm (accessed March 17, 2017). On professional advancement as collective uplift, see also Naples, *Grassroots Warriors*; Sanders, *A Chance for Change*.

16. Working-class women of color developed and deployed sophisticated theoretical understanding of education, organizing, and political action, and should be recognized as intellectuals and education reformers. See Keisha M. Blain, "Writing Black Women's Intellectual History," *Black Perspectives,* November 21, 2016, http://www.aaihs.org/writing-black-womens-intellectual-history/ (accessed March 16, 2017). See also Mia E. Bay et al., eds., *Toward an Intellectual History of Black Women* (Chapel Hill: University of North Carolina Press, 2015), and Elizabeth Todd-Breland, *A Political Education*, Introduction.

17. Quinn and Ferree, "Schools as Workplaces," 1806–15.

18. Nancy Naples argues that politics and mothering are mutually constitutive processes for "women whose motherwork has often been ignored or pathologized," in "Activist Mothering: Cross-Generational Continuity in the Community Work of Women from Low-Income Urban Neighborhoods," *Gender and Society* 6, no. 3 (1992). The "culture of poverty" thesis—developed by Oscar Lewis and deployed by Daniel Patrick Moynihan and many others—is the archetypical example of elites' tendency to pathologize poor mothers of color in the 1960s.

19. "Resolution 31: Authorization for Funding under Title I ESEA, A Planning Grant for the Recruitment, Training, and Classification of Non-Professional Personnel in the New York City School System." March 8, 1967, *Journal of the Board of Education* (1967): 334–35, Series 116, City Hall Library, New York.

20. On the hiring of paraprofessional educators with Title VII funds in New York City, see Laura J. Kaplan, "P.S. 25, South Bronx: Bilingual Education and Community Control" (Ph.D. diss, 2018), particularly the subsection titled "Paraprofessionals at P.S. 25" in Chapter 5.

21. Board of Education Special Circular No. 30, "Creating Paraprofessional Positions," October 30, 1967, UFT Box 155, Folder 1.

22. Brickell, *An In-Depth Study of Paraprofessionals.*

23. Brickell, *An In-Depth Study of Paraprofessionals.*

24. These organizations were funded through the Community Action Program of the Office of Economic Opportunity, both creations of the Economic Opportunity Act of 1964.

25. All these organizations are discussed in the following chapters. On Youth in Action, see Woodsworth, *Battle for Bed-Stuy.*

26. *Journal of the Board of Education*, 1968–1969, Ed 8.16, Series 116, City Hall Library, New York.

27. Brickell et al., *An In-Depth Study of Paraprofessionals.*

28. All the data presented in this section are drawn from Brickell, *An In-Depth Study of Paraprofessionals.* The Women's Talent Corps, in a similar review of its graduates in the same year, found that over half of its corpswomen were involved in formal volunteering programs in their local communities.

29. Anne Cronin, quoted in "1968 Progress Report," MCNY Folder 15.

30. Progress Report 4, 1966, MCNY Folder 10.

31. Laura Pires-Hester, quoted in Progress Report 5, January-February 1967, MCNY Folder 11. On paraprofessionals in Harlem in particular, see Nick Juravich, "Harlem Sophistication: Paraprofessional Educations in Harlem and East Harlem," in Erickson and Ernest Morrell, eds., *Educating Harlem*, 234–54.

32. Greene, interview.

33. Martin, interview.

34. Oneida Davis, interview with the author, September 3, 2014.

35. Young-Abrams, interview; Marian Thom, interview with the author, September 3, 2013.

36. Young-Abrams, interview.

37. Greene, interview.

38. Martha McNear Interview, MCNY Folder 160.

39. Thom, interview.

40. Naples, *Grassroots Warriors*. In both HARYOU's "Youth in the Ghetto" (1964) and Pearl and Riessman's *New Careers for the Poor*, community-based educators are referred to as "indigenous nonprofessionals," a formulation that drew on emergent analysis of ghettoized urban neighborhoods as colonies, particularly Kenneth Clark's *Dark Ghetto* (1965). See also Rickford, *We Are an African People*.

41. Bernard Bard, "It's More Than Watering Plants," *New York Post Magazine,* May 16, 1970.

42. Bard, "It's More Than Watering Plants."

43. Bard, "It's More Than Watering Plants."

44. Garda W. Bowman and Gordon J. Klopf, *New Careers and Roles in the American School* (New York: Bank Street College of Education, 1968), 10–11, http://eric.ed.gov/?id=ED027266.

45. New York City Board of Education Special Circular No. 30, UFT Box 155, Folder 1.

46. "A College for Human Service," Episode of "New York Illustrated," on NBC New York, January 4, 1969, Collection of MCNY.

47. "A College for Human Service."

48. Christine Sleeter, "Why Is There Learning Disabilities? A Critical Analysis of the Birth of the Field in Its Social Context," *Disability Studies Quarterly* 30, no. 2 (June 1, 2010), https://doi.org/10.18061/dsq.v30i2.1261; David J. Connor and Beth A. Ferri, "Introduction to DSQ Special Issue: 'Why Is There Learning Disabilities?'—Revisiting Christine Sleeter's Socio-Political Construction of Disability Two Decades On," *Disability Studies Quarterly* 30, no. 2 (April 9, 2010), https://doi.org/10.18061/dsq.v30i2.1229.

49. These are the categories described by Sleeter in "Why Is There Learning Disabilities?"

50. Leanora Nelson to Bernard Donovan, March 27, 1967, MCNY Folder 323.

51. "Title III Teacher Training Manual," 1969 Isaiah Robinson Files, BOE Series 378, Box 28, Folder 23.

52. Kaplan, "P.S. 25, South Bronx."

53. Cited in Kaplan, "P.S. 25, South Bronx," 195–96.

54. Kaplan, "P.S. 25, South Bronx," 195.

55. Thom, interview.

56. Thom, interview; Young-Abrams, interview.

57. Davis, interview.

58. Bowman and Klopf, *New Careers and Roles in the American School.*

59. Davis, interview.

60. "Parents Go Back to School—As Teacher Assistants and TC Students," TC Week, February 7, 1969, Morningside Area Alliance Records, Series III, Box 55, Folder 16, Columbia University Archives, New York, NY.

61. Thom, interview; Virginia Eng, interview with the author, September 10, 2013.

62. Hymes, "The Bay City Experiment . . . As Seen by a Child Psychologist," discussed in Chapter 1.

63. Davis, interview.

64. Martin, interview.

65. Leatrice Wilkerson Interview, Folder 160, MCNY Student Interviews.

66. Wilkerson, MCNY Student Interviews.

67. Eng, interview.

68. On the history of teachers' organizing to respond to disruptions and physical violence in schools, see, among others, Elizabeth Faue, "Battle for or in the Classroom: Teachers' Strikes in the Context of the 'Epidemic' of School Violence and the Working Environment," in Rebecca Kolins Givan and Amy Schrager Lang, eds., *Strike for the Common Good: Fighting for the Future of Public Education* (Ann Arbor: University of Michigan Press, 2021); Judith Kafka, *The History of "Zero Tolerance" in American Public Schooling* (New York: Palgrave, 2011).

69. On racialized disciplinary policies in postwar schools, see Mahasan Chaney, "Discipline for the 'Educationally Deprived': ESEA and the Punitive Function of Federal Education Policy 1965–1998" (PhD diss., University of California, 2019); Judith Kafka, *The History of "Zero Tolerance" in American Public Schooling* (New York: Palgrave Studies in Urban Education, 2011); Matthew B. Kautz, "From Segregation to Suspension: The Solidification of the Contemporary School-Prison Nexus in Boston, 1963–1985," *Journal of Urban History* 49, no. 5 (September 2023); Rachel E. Lissy, "From Rehabilitation to Punishment: The Institutionalization of Suspension Policies in Post-World War II New York City Schools" (PhD diss., University of California, 2015); Noah Remnick, "'The Police State in Franklin K. Lane': Desegregation, Student Resistance, and the Carceral Turn at a New York City High School," *Journal of Urban History* 49, no. 5 (September 2023).

70. Hinton, *From the War on Poverty to the War on Crime.*

71. Almash, "New York City '600' Schools and the Legacy of Segregation in Special Education." Almash's study offers a concrete example of the wider phenomenon explored by Christine Sleeter, in which the categories used by educators and administrators to identify students with learning, social, and developmental disabilities have served as tools of racial segregation.

72. Clara Blackman Interview, MCNY Folder 83.

73. Clara Blackman Interview, MCNY Folder 83.

74. On suspensions, see Lissy, "From Rehabilitation to Punishment."

75. Thom, interview.

76. Remnick, "The Police State in Franklin K. Lane," 1078.

77. Silvers, "Who Are the Para-Professionals?"

78. Marietta J. Tanner, "Community Conscious," *New York Amsterdam News,* March 9, 1968.

79. Leonora Farber, interview with the author, January 18, 2014.

80. Jacqueline Watkins, interview with the author, August 29, 2014.

81. Thom, interview.

82. Alida Mesrop, interview with the author, January 28, 2015.

83. Watkins, interview.

84. Martin, interview.

85. Young-Abrams, interview.

86. "Title III Teacher Training Manual," 1969 Isaiah Robinson Files, BOE Series 378, Box 28, Folder 23.

87. Student Interviews, MCNY Folder 160.

88. Louise Burwell, interview with the author, December 3, 2013.

89. Thom, interview.

90. Young-Abrams, interview.

91. Thom, interview.

92. "Information on Title I," United Bronx Parents, August 1968, ELP Box 1, Folder "Title I."

93. Kaplan, "P.S. 25, South Bronx," 198.

94. Elementary and Secondary Education Act of 1965, Pub. L. No. 89-10, 79 Stat., HR 2362 (April 11, 1965).

95. Adult Education Act of 1966, Pub. L. No. 89-750, 80 Stat., HR 13161 (November 3, 1966).

96. Ansley T. Erickson, "HARYOU: An Apprenticeship for Young Leaders," in Erickson and Morrell, eds., *Educating Harlem*.

97. Undated Report, District 4 Community Education Centers 1970, Isaiah Robinson Files, BOE Series 378, Box 12, Folder 14: CSB 5 July 1970–Dec. 1970.

98. *Journal of the Board of Education*, 1969–1973, Series 116, Ed 8.16, City Hall Library, New York.

99. El Museo Del Barrio, "History and Timeline," https://www.elmuseo.org/about/history-mission.

100. Litwin to Donovan, March 2, 1967, MCNY 322.

101. Levey to Laura Pires, March 3, 1967, MCNY 321.

102. "Talent Corps Points Way out of Welfare Coils," *New York Daily News*, June 23, 1967.

103. Program Overview: Career Development and Utilization of Auxiliary Personnel, September 1969, UFT Box 80, Folder 14.

104. Audrey C. Cohen to Ted Bleeker, United Teacher Editor, January 12, 1968, MCNY 4657.

105. For a detailed discussion of Parent-Teacher Teams and paraprofessional educators in Harlem more broadly, see Nick Juravich, "'Harlem Sophistication': Community-Based Paraprofessional Educators in Central Harlem and East Harlem," in Erickson and Morrell, eds., *Educating Harlem*.

106. Untitled Report, MAA Box 55, Folder 16. HARYOU merged with another Harlem antipoverty organization, Associated Community Teams (ACT), when it was taken over by Congressman Adam Clayton Powell Jr. in 1965.

107. "Center C for Development, Parent Teacher Teams," Spring 1968, MAA Box 55, Folder 16.

108. Untitled Report, MAA Box 55, Folder 16.

109. "Developing Parent Teacher Teams," MAA Box 55, Folder 16.

110. My access to the data used in making these maps was made possible through digitization and collaborative work done through the Harlem Education History Project, Teachers College, Columbia University. See http://harlemeducationhistory.library.columbia.edu/.

111. "Parents Go Back to School," MAA Box 55, Folder 16.

112. Davis, interview.

113. The most (in)famous statement of the "culture of poverty" thesis is Moyni-han, "The Negro Family." On Black and Latina women activists' rejection of the report, see Adina Back, "'Parent Power,' Evelina López Antonetty, the United Bronx Parents, and the War on Poverty," in Annelise Orleck and Lisa Gayle Haz-irjian, eds., *The War on Poverty: A New Grassroots History, 1964–1980* (Athens: University of Georgia Press, 2011.)

114. Progress Report 2, October 1966, MCNY Folder 8.

115. Progress Report 6, March-April 1967, MCNY Folder 12.

116. On welfare policy, see Marisa Chappell, *The War on Welfare: Family, Pov-erty, and Politics in Modern America* (Philadelphia: University of Pennsylvania Press, 2011); Kornbluh, *The Battle for Welfare Rights*; Nadasen, *Welfare Warriors*.

117. Anne Cronin Interview, MCNY Folder 102.

118. "The Use of Auxiliary Personnel (Paraprofessionals)," United Bronx Par-ents Flyer, October 20, 1967, ELP Box 1, Folder "Paraprofessionals."

119. "Title I: Some Questions to Ask," United Bronx Parents, October 20, 1967, ELP Box 1, Folder "Title I."

120. See Back, "'Parent Power" for an extended discussion of how Antonetty and the UBP redefined local residents and mothers as bearers of knowledge and change agents in their community and the wider city.

121. Women's Talent Corps Final Report, 1966–1967, MCNY Folder 1.

122. Anne Cronin Interview, MCNY Folder 102.

123. Lorraine Montenegro, interview with the author, July 10, 2014.

124. Mesrop, interview.

125. Hope Leichter, interview with the author, October 23, 2014.

126. Gladys Roth, "Auxiliary Educational Assistants in New York City Schools," Internal Report, United Federation of Teachers, May 20, 1968, UFT Box 80, Folder 11.

127. Davis, interview.

128. Frank Riessman and Alan Gartner, "The Instructional Aide: New Devel-opments," 1969, UFT Box 210, Folder 6.

129. Brickell et al., *An In-Depth Study of Paraprofessionals.*

130. On the long history of public sector work and organizing, see Frederick W. Gooding Jr. and Eric S. Yellin, eds., *Public Workers in Service of America* (Urbana: University of Illinois Press, 2022).

131. Martha McNear Interview, MCNY Student Interviews, Folder 160.

132. "Self-Help in the Ghetto," *New York Times,* July 2, 1967.

Chapter 3. "The Triumph of the Paraprofessionals"

1. For a full accounting of Velma Murphy Hill's life in her own words, see Hill and Hill, *Climbing the Rough Side of the Mountain*. On the wade-ins, see Nicholas Juravich, "Wade in the Water: The NAACP Youth Council, the Sit-In Movement, and the Rainbow Beach Wade-Ins in Chicago, 1960–1961," *Chicago Studies* 1, no. 1 (November 2008).

2. Liz Robbins, "Around the Unisphere at the World's Fair, Lives Changed" *New York Times*, April 18, 2014, https://www.nytimes.com/2014/04/20/nyregion/around-the-unisphere-at-the-worlds-fair-lives-changed.html.

3. Velma Murphy Hill, interview with the author, November 7, 2011.

4. Hill and Hill, *Climbing the Rough Side of the Mountain*, Chapter 8 (quote from advance proofs)

5. Hill, interview.

6. Marietta J. Tanner, "Community Conscious," *New York Amsterdam News*, December 20, 1969.

7. The hiring structure for paraprofessional educators in New York City before 1970 required principals to hire 50 percent at the recommendation of city-recognized "Community Action Agencies," 25 percent from existing school staff at their discretion, and 25 percent at the recommendation of AFSCME DC 37, which represented school aides. See Brickell, *An In-Depth Study of Paraprofessionals*.

8. Bayard Rustin, "The Triumph of the Paraprofessionals," *New York Amsterdam News*, August 22, 1970, 4. An extended analysis of this op-ed appears in the introduction.

9. See, among many others, Freeman, *Working-Class New York*; Kahlenberg, *Tough Liberal*; Lee, *Building a Latino Civil Rights Movement*; Perlstein, *Justice, Justice*; Perrillo, *Uncivil Rights*; Podair, *The Strike That Changed New York*; Pritchett, *Brownsville, Brooklyn*; Ravitch, *The Great Schools Wars*.

10. The process of developing working women's solidarity is discussed at greater length in Chapter 2. Para organizing serves as an example of the intergenerational, cross-class aspects of women's activism, within and beyond what is typically considered the "feminist movement" in these years. See Carroll, *Mobilizing New York*; Gold, *When Tenants Claimed the City*; Gilmore, ed., *Feminist Coalitions*.

11. For a sophisticated statement of the union's position, see Kahlenberg, *Tough Liberal*.

12. On professionalism, see Collins, *Ethnically Qualified*; Pawlewicz, *Blaming Teachers*.

13. Fink and Greenberg, *Upheaval in the Quiet Zone*; Freeman, *Working-Class New York*; Lee, *Building a Latino Civil Rights Movement*; Taylor, *Reds at the Blackboard*.

14. Berger, *A New Working Class*; Dorothy Sue Cobble, *The Other Women's Movement: Workplace Justice and Social Rights in Modern America* (Princeton, NJ: Princeton University Press, 2005); MacLean, *Freedom Is Not Enough;* Katz and Stern, "The New African-American Inequality."

15. AFT PSRP Conference Speech, American Federation of Teachers, Office of the President Collection, Albert Shanker Papers, Box 65, Folder 61, Walter P. Reuther Library, Wayne State University.

16. "Title I: Some Questions to Ask" and "The Use of Auxiliary Personnel (Paraprofessionals)," October 20, 1967, ELP Box 1, Folder "Paraprofessionals"; Memo: To All Paraprofessionals in Morrisania Schools, March 20, 1968, UFT Box 133, Folder 7.

17. "Second Annual Report and Evaluation of the Talent Corps/College for

Human Services 1967–68" (prepared April 1969) MCNY Folder 2. As part of their advocacy for paraprofessionals, these organizations promoted unionization. At a "National Council for New Careers Organizing Conference" in Detroit June 20–23, 1968, Cohen was the only speaker not affiliated with a labor union. "Jobs and Career Development," Progress Reports 1968, MCNY Folder 15.

18. Minutes of the Board, March 30, 1967, MCNY Folder 655.

19. Report, August 1967, UFT Box 155, Folder 1.

20. See Freeman, *Working-Class New York*; Maier, *City Unions*. The city under Mayor Robert F. Wagner had insisted that a majority of workers across city agencies had to be represented by a single union before the city would bargain on citywide policies. Teachers, as professional staff in a specific role, were not classified as such.

21. Women's Talent Corps Progress Report (No. 2), October 1966, UFT Box 108, Folder 5.

22. Gladys Roth, "Educational Assistants 'On Move with UFT' to Professional Status, Career Opportunities," *United Teacher,* February 7, 1968, UFT Box 93, Folder 5.

23. Hill, interview.

24. Hill, interview.

25. Memo: To All: Educational Assistants, Teacher Assistants, Family Workers, Family Assistants, Educational Aides, from Joan Fisher and Gladys Roth, February 13, 1968; Memo: A Special Meeting of District 19 Para-Professionals Will Be Held at IS 292, March 20, 1968, UFT Box 133, Folder 7.

26. Shanker to Members, February 28, 1968, UFT Box 133, Folder 7.

27. The "disruptive child" provision is discussed in greater detail in Chapter 2. See also Perrillo, *Uncivil Rights*.

28. Memo: To All Paraprofessionals in Morrisania Schools, March 20, 1968, UFT Box 133, Folder 7. McGeorge Bundy of the Ford Foundation had authored the report, known throughout the city as the "Bundy" report.

29. Maggie Martin, interview with the author, February 3, 2015.

30. Shelvy Young-Abrams, interview with the author, September 5, 2014.

31. Nancy D. Garcia to Albert Shanker, UFT Box 93, Folder 5. Debates about the relative merits of local employment in education are discussed in greater detail in Chapters 1 and 6.

32. Gladys Roth, "UFT Opens Career Doors for Educational Assistant," *United Teacher,* January 24, 1968, UFT Box 155, Folder 1.

33. Kinard Lang, "Why Should the UFT Encourage the Hiring and Union Membership of the Paraprofessionals?" UFT Box 133, Folder 27.

34. Lang, "Why Should the UFT Encourage the Hiring and Union Membership of the Paraprofessionals?"

35. Hill, interview.

36. "Proposed Guidelines for the Use of Paraprofessionals," Letter from the Arturo Toscanini Chapter to UFT Headquarters, UFT Box 133, Folder 27.

37. Gladys Roth, "Auxiliary Educational Assistants in New York City Schools," May 20, 1968, UFT Box 80, Folder 11.

38. Roth, "Auxiliary Educational Assistants in New York City Schools."

39. Roth, "Auxiliary Educational Assistants in New York City Schools." Quotes are drawn from three different paraprofessionals at three different schools.

40. Roth, "Auxiliary Educational Assistants in New York City Schools."

41. Freeman, *Working-Class New York;* Kahlenberg, *Tough Liberal;* Lee, *Building a Latino Civil Rights Movement;* Perlstein, *Justice, Justice;* Perrillo, *Uncivil Rights;* Podair, *The Strike That Changed New York;* Pritchett, *Brownsville, Brooklyn;* Ravitch, *The Great Schools Wars.*

42. Podair, *The Strike That Changed New York,* 182.

43. Stefan Bradley, "'Gym Crow Must Go!': Black Student Activism at Columbia University, 1967–1968," *Journal of African American History* 88, no. 2 (Spring 2003): 163–81; Fritz Umbach, *The Last Neighborhood Cops: The Rise and Fall of Community Policing in New York Public Housing* (New Brunswick, NJ: Rutgers University Press, 2011).

44. Freeman, *Working-Class New York.*

45. *Report of the National Advisory Commission on Civil Disorders* (New York: Bantam Books, 1968). Mayor Lindsay served as vice chairman of the commission and is widely credited with writing the lines cited.

46. United Bronx Parents, "To All Parents, Paraprofessionals, Teachers, Community People and Everyone Who Has Been Working So Hard To Keep Our Schools Open," October 28, 1968, ELP Box 1, Folder "Strike Material."

47. Irving Adler Interview, 1985, UFT-OH Box 1, Folder Irving Adler. On Lucille Spence and the Teachers Union, see Lauri Johnson, "A Generation of Women Activists: African American Female Educators in Harlem, 1930–1950," *The Journal of African American History* 89, no. 3 (Summer 2004), 223–40; Taylor, *Reds at the Blackboard.*

48. Perlstein, *Justice, Justice.*

49. See Chapter 1.

50. Ray Frankel Interview, 1985, UFT-OH Box 1, Folder Ray Frankel.

51. Alice Marsh Interview, 1985 UFT-OH Box 1, Folder Alice Marsh.

52. "The Community Centered School," 1968, PWP Box 11, Folder 12. See also "A Letter: General Principles on Decentralization," addressed to Brother Gene Bivins, Philadelphia Federation of Teachers, July 26, 1968, PWP Box 12, Folder 7. On professionalization, see Collins, *Ethnically Qualified;* D'Amico, "Claiming Profession."

53. Progress Report 6, March-April 1967, Placements, MCNY Folder 12.

54. Progress Report July-December 1967, MCNY Folder 14.

55. On the creative pedagogies employed in community-controlled schools, see Bonastia, *The Battle Nearer to Home,* and Charles S. Issacs, *Inside Ocean Hill-Brownsville: A Teachers' Education, 1969–69* (New York: State University of New York Press, 2014).

56. Minutes of Open Board Meeting, May 23, 1968, MCNY Folder 656.

57. Final Report 1968, MCNY Folder 2.

58. Progress Reports, 1968, MCNY Folder 15.

59. Final Report 1968, MCNY Folder 2.

60. Lorraine Montenegro, interview with the author, September 24, 2014.

61. "Organizational History," Records of the United Bronx Parents, Box 2, Folder 14, Center for Puerto Rican Studies, Hunter College, New York, NY. On the UBP's commitment to the community control experiments, see also Lee, *Building a Latino Civil Rights Movement*.

62. Bonastia, *The Battle Nearer to Home*, 158–59.

63. United Bronx Parents Flyer, October 28, 1968, ELP Box 1, Folder "Strike Material."

64. United Bronx Parents Flyer, October 28, 1968.

65. Aurelia Greene, interview with the author, August 27, 2014.

66. Oneida Davis, interview with the author, September 3, 2014.

67. Davis, interview.

68. Maggie Martin, interview with the author, February 3, 2015; Marian Thom, interview with the author, September 3, 2013.

69. Shelvy Young-Abrams, interview with the author, September 5, 2014.

70. Thom, interview; Young-Abrams, interview. On debates between parents and paraprofessionals, see Siok Ee Yeo, "Two Bridges Demonstration District: Defying the Patterns of Community Control" (master's thesis, Columbia University, 2015).

71. Martin, interview.

72. Memo from Gladys Roth to Albert Shanker and Vito DeLeonardis, October 17, 1968, UFT Box 80, Folder 14.

73. Memo from Gladys Roth to Albert Shanker and Vito DeLeonardis, October 17, 1968.

74. Memo from Gladys Roth to Vito and Al, November 19, 1968, UFT Box 80, Folder 14.

75. For discussions of "black-brown" solidarity in the community control struggle, see Lee, *Building a Latino Civil Rights Movement*; Johanna Fernandez, "The Young Lords and the Postwar City: Notes on the Geographical and Structural Reconfigurations of Contemporary Urban Life," in *African American Urban History Since World War II* (Chicago: University of Chicago Press, 2009), 60–82.

76. Hoffnung-Garskof, *A Tale of Two Cities*, 194. Chapters 5 and 6 of Hoffnung-Garskof's book examine cooperation and contention among Dominican migrants and African Americans in the context of education, including student interactions, the decentralization crisis, and school board elections.

77. Lee, *Building a Latino Civil Rights Movement*, 80.

78. Fink and Greenberg, *Upheaval in the Quiet Zone*; Purnell, *Fighting Jim Crow in the County of Kings*.

79. Martin, interview.

80. "Shanker Wants a Whole Hog and a Pint of Blood," October 28, 1968, ELP Box 1, Folder "Strike Material."

81. Audrey C. Cohen to David Selden, March 10, 1969, UFT Box 80, Folder 14.

82. Marjorie Murphy, "Militancy in Many Forms: Teachers Strikes and Urban Insurrection, 1967–1974," in Aaron Brenner, Robert Brenner, and Cal Winslow,

eds., *Rebel Rank and File: Labor Militancy and Revolt from Below During the Long 1970s* (New York: Verso, 2011).

83. Richard Parrish, "The New York City Teachers Strikes: Blow to Education, Boon to Racism," *Labor Today*, May 1969, RPP, Microfilm, Reel 1. See also Almonte, "Richard Parrish, the Black Caucus, and the 1968 Ocean Hill–Brownsville Strikes."

84. "What Does Control Mean?" Teachers for Community Control Newsletter, December 1968. Anne Filardo Papers on Rank and File Activism in the American Federation of Teachers and in the United Federation of Teachers (TAM 141) Box 1, Folder 1B, Tamiment Library/Robert F. Wagner Labor Archives, New York University, New York, NY.

85. Selden to Riessman, June 3, 1968, UFT Box 155, Folder 2.

86. Selden to Riessman, June 3, 1968.

87. Selden to Riessman, February 24, 1969, American Federation of Teachers Records, Office of the President Collection; David Selden Papers, Part II, Box 5, Folder 1: New Careers, Paraprofessionals 1967–1971, Walter P. Reuther Library, Wayne State University, Detroit, MI.

88. George R. Kaplan, "From Aide to Teacher: The Story of the Career Opportunities Program" (Washington, DC: U.S. Government Printing Office, 1977). On Frank Riessman's commitment to employment as an antipoverty strategy, see also Aguiar, "Head Start: A History of Implementation," and the "Career Opportunities Bulletin," which Riessman edited from Queens College's New Careers Training Laboratory throughout the 1970s. A complete run of the "COP Bulletin" is contained in the Records of the Office of Education, 1870–1980, Records Relating to Teachers' Qualifications, Educational Opportunity, and Educational Services, 2/1968–1980, RG 0012, Container 51, National Archives at College Park, MD.

89. Selden to Riessman, December 12, 1969, AFT-Selden Box 5, Folder 1.

90. Second Annual Report and Evaluation of the Talent Corps/College for Human Services 1967–68, MCNY.

91. Sandra Feldman continued to supervise paraprofessional organizing efforts for Shanker, while Gladys Roth's involvement with the campaign seems to have ended. She moved to a position with the union's grievance office.

92. Flyer, June 1969. UFT Box 155, Folder 3.

93. Hill, interview.

94. Martin, interview.

95. Martin, interview.

96. UFT Flyers, UFT Box 155, Folders 2–4.

97. Nadasen, *Welfare Warriors*; Kornbluh, *The Battle for Welfare Rights*.

98. Progress Report 3, November 1966, MCNY-WTC Folder 9.

99. DC 37 Flyers, UFT Box 155, Folders 2–4. The Board of Examiners had been a particular target of community leaders' ire, and it was seen as representing the over-rigid bureaucracy with which the UFT was associated. See Collins, *Ethnically Qualified*.

100. UFT Flyers, UFT Box 155, Folders 2–4.

101. "Unions Fight to Enlist NY's Teacher Aides," *Baltimore Afro-American,* December 27, 1969.

102. Letters from Shanker to Teachers and Chapter Chairs, June 18, 1969, UFT Box 155, Folder 6. This note followed a flurry of urgent correspondence with chapter chairs, with much the same message.

103. *The United Para-Professional,* June 1969, UFT Box 155, Folder 3.

104. Election Report, *New York Times,* November 8, 1969, UFT Box 255, Folder 2.

105. *The United Para-Professional,* June 1969, UFT Box 155, Folder 3.

106. Martin, interview.

107. Alida Mesrop, interview with the author, January 28, 2015.

108. Minutes of Board Meeting, June 11, 1969, MCNY Folder 657.

109. Kahlenberg, *Tough Liberal;* "Not for Teachers Only," *The United Teacher,* February 2010.

110. "UFT Scoring Gains in Ghetto," *New York Post,* January 12, 1970.

111. Gladys Roth, *The United Para-Professional,* June 1969, UFT Box 155, Folder 3.

112. Michael Woodsworth, "The Forgotten Fight: Waging War on Poverty in New York City, 1945–1980" (PhD diss., Columbia University, 2013).

113. Memo No. 1, Crown Heights Education Committee, December 29, 1969, UFT Box 80, Folder 11.

114. Memo No. 1, Crown Heights Education Committee.

115. Tanner, "Community Conscious. Copies of this article appear throughout the UFT Collection, as reproduced in all five boroughs.

116. The UFT archive contains a one-line letter firing Howard, but no other information as to why he was terminated (Hill does not remember the cause of his termination). Howard later worked for the Board of Education and with Lillian Roberts at DC 37. Howard and another UFT paraprofessional organizer, Marvin Rogers, later filed an NLRB complaint against Shanker, alleging that he paid them at a lower rate than other organizers and fired them to avoid giving them tenure. See Albert Shanker and Herbert Hill, "Black Protest, Union Democracy, and the UFT," in Burton Hall, ed., *Autocracy and Insurgency in Organized Labor* (New Brunswick, NJ: Transaction Books, 1972).

117. A Letter to Para-Professionals of Ocean Hill-Brownsville School District, April 22, 1970, UFT Box 80, Folder 15. McCoy cites both the 1967 "disruptive child" strike and the better-known 1968 strikes.

118. Memo: Para-Professional Crisis, Bedford-Stuyvesant Youth in Action, May 1, 1970, UFT Box 80, Folder 15.

119. "Work or Welfare," March 23, 1970, UFT Box 155, Folder 3.

120. Materials from Ocean Hill–Brownsville, Crown Heights, and Bedford-Stuyvesant all contain this identical claim. The structure of paraprofessional programs (discussed in greater detail in Chapter 2) gave community development corporations (also known as community action agencies) a voice in hiring paraprofessionals, but the board never extended control over funds to these groups, including wages paid to paraprofessionals. See "New York City Council

against Poverty Approval for Board of Education ESEA Proposals," March 14, 1967, conditioned "on the expressed commitment of the BOE that teacher aides are to be hired from within the community and wherever possible through the local community action agency." BOE Series 282, Box 11 (Elementary and Secondary Education Act), Folder 171.

121. "Community News Service," May 1970, UFT Box 155, Folder 5.

122. Perrillo, *Uncivil Rights*; "Emergency School Meet," *New York Amsterdam News*, November 29, 1969.

123. Hill, interview. Hill and Hill, *Climbing the Rough Side of the Mountain*, Chapter 9 (citation from advance proofs).

124. Marian Thom, interview with the author, September 3, 2013.

125. "School Workers Vote to Strike," *New York Times*, April 23, 1970.

126. Undated Contact Sheet, United Federation of Teachers Photographs; PHOTOS 019; Box 3, Folder 43; Tamiment Library/Robert F. Wagner Labor Archives, New York University.

127. Andrew H. Malcolm, "A Portrait of the School Paraprofessional," *New York Times*, May 1, 1970.

128. Bernard Bard, "It's More Than Watering Plants," *New York Post Magazine*, May 16, 1970.

129. "She's For the Strike," *New York Amsterdam News*, April 25, 1970.

130. "She's For the Strike."

131. Clipping from *El Diario*, June 15, 1970, UFT Box 255, Folder 2.

132. "Las Demandas de Los Paraprofessionales," *El Tiempo*, May 1970, UFT Box 155, Folder 6. Translation by the author.

133. "Paraprofessionals Seek Parent Support," *New York Amsterdam News*, May 2, 1970. Scheuer, who also sat on the board of the Women's Talent Corps, is discussed in greater detail in Chapter 1.

134. Frances X. Clines, "Dead End Found in 'New Careers,'" *New York Times*, March 1, 1970. On the challenges of securing training and advancement for paras, particularly outside of schools, see Dunning, "New Careers for the Poor."

135. Greene, interview.

136. Montenegro, interview.

137. Montenegro, interview. See also Lee, *Building a Latino Civil Rights Movement*.

138. Beatrice E. Jacob to Albert Shanker, January 12, 1969, UFT Box 80, Folder 14.

139. Paul Engelson to Albert Shanker, April 4, 1970, UFT Box 155, Folder 3.

140. Internal Report, 1974, UFT Box 80, Folder 13. Hill and Hill echo this description in *Climbing the Rough Side of the Mountain*, Chapter 9 (quotation from advance proofs).

141. Feldman to Paul Engelson, April 24, 1970, UFT Box 155, Folder 3.

142. "School Workers Vote to Strike."

143. "UFT Leaders Vote Backing for Strike," *New York Times*, April 28, 1970; "UFT Vote Backs School Workers" *New York Times*, April 30, 1970.

144. Shanker to Chapter Chairs, May 26, 1970, UFT Box 133, Folder 27.

145. Newsletter from UFT Chapter Chairman Lucy Shifrin at PS 189K, April 1970, UFT Box 155, Folder 6.

146. Hill and Hill, *Climbing the Rough Side of the Mountain*, Chapter 9 (quotation from advance proofs).

147. Kahlenberg, *Tough Liberal*.

148. "Paraprofessionals Seek Parent Support,"

149. "A Call to Unity" Teachers Workshop, UFT Box 80, Folder 15.

150. Dan Sanders Interview, 1985, UFT-OH Box 2, Folder Dan Sanders.

151. Larry Robbins Interview, 1985, UFT-OH Box 2, Folder Larry Robbins.

152. For a sophisticated statement of the union's story, see Kahlenberg, *Tough Liberal*.

153. Among others, see Berger, *A New Working Class*; Collins, *Ethnically Qualified;* Gooding Jr. and Yellin, eds., *Public Workers in Service to America*, particularly chapters by William P. Jones and Jon Shelton.

154. Speech at AFT PSRP Conference, 1985, AFT-Shanker Box 65, Folder 61.

155. The concept of "everyday rituals of democratic practice," which I first encountered in the work of Heather Lewis on New York City schools, comes from Charles M. Payne and Adam Green, eds., *Time Longer than Rope: A Century of African American Activism, 1850–1950* (New York: New York University Press, 2003).

Chapter 4. "You Can Never Believe Your Good Luck"

1. At the time, about 10,000 people worked in paraprofessional positions in New York City, of which 4,000 had been included in the UFT's bargaining unit for the 1970 contract. Before the contract (and for nearly a decade afterward, until 1978), paraprofessionals worked on ten-month contracts and were forced to collect unemployment in the summers. Thus, the city tried to claim that the decision to re-hire fewer paraprofessionals in the fall of 1970 did not constitute layoffs, even though most of those laid off had been promised work when schools reopened.

2. Memo: To: All Para-Professionals in District 29 From: Max G. Rubinstein, Community Superintendent, September 30, 1970, UFT Box 80, Folder 15. As Rubinstein wrote, "the increased salaries of paraprofessionals does mean that the same money cannot buy the same services."

3. Letter from Albert Shanker, UFT President, to membership, September 25, 1970 (flyer for "Mass Demonstration at City Hall" attached), UFT Box 80, Folder 15.

4. New York 9 Editorial, "Paraprofessionals," John Murray Reading, October 28–29, 1970, UFT Box 80, Folder 15.

5. New York 9 Editorial, "Paraprofessionals."

6. Bayard Rustin, "Paraprofessionals and Schools," *New York Amsterdam News*, October 3, 1970.

7. Telegram from Victor Gotbaum, Lillian Roberts, and Charles Hughes to Isaiah Robinson, September 28, 1970, Isaiah Robinson Papers, BOE Series 378, Box 1, Folder 2.

8. Telegram from Bernice Cox (Chairman of the Board of the Brownsville Parents Association), et al., to Isaiah Robinson, September 24, 1970, Isaiah Robinson Papers, BOE Series 378, Box 2, Folder 31.

9. This research contributes to a burgeoning literature on the continuities between activism in New York City's well-studied midcentury era and continued efforts for social justice amid the austerity of the 1970s and the rising neoliberalism of city governance in the 1980s. See, among others, Lee, *Building a Latino Civil Rights Movement*; Gold, *When Tenants Claimed the City*; Carroll, *Mobilizing New York*.

10. On the urban crisis, see Robert O. Self, *American Babylon: Race and the Struggle for Postwar Oakland* (Princeton, NJ: Princeton University Press, 2005); and Thomas J. Sugrue, *The Origins of the Urban Crisis: Race and Inequality in Postwar Detroit* (Princeton, NJ: Princeton University Press, 1995), among any others. On the fall of industry and the rise of care-work-based economies, see Davarian Baldwin, *In the Shadow of the Ivory Tower: How Universities Are Plundering Our Cities* (New York: Bold Type Books, 2021); and Winant, *The Next Shift*.

11. Phillips-Fein, *Fear City*, Part I, "Origins."

12. Freeman, *Working-Class New York*, 256.

13. Freeman, *Working-Class New York*, 201.

14. Freeman, *Working-Class New York*, Chapters 11–13.

15. High schools remained under centralized control. On decentralization, see Lewis, *New York City Public Schools from Brownsville to Bloomberg*.

16. "Summary and Analysis of School Decentralization Bill," April 30, 1969, Ellen Lurie Papers, Box 1, Folder "Decentralization Materials," Center for Puerto Rican Studies, Hunter College, New York, NY.

17. Aurelia Greene, interview with the author, August 27, 2014.

18. Podair, *The Strike That Changed New York*; Perlstein, *Justice, Justice*; Lee, *Building a Latino Civil Rights Movement*.

19. H. Paul Friesema, "Black Control of Central Cities: The Hollow Prize," *Journal of the American Institute of Planners* 35, no. 2 (March 1, 1969): 75–79; Neil Kraus and Todd Swanstrom, "Minority Mayors and the Hollow-Prize Problem," *PS: Political Science and Politics* 34, no. 1 (March 1, 2001): 99–105.

20. "The Effect of Title I ESEA Funds on Student Achievement," October 27, 1970, Isaiah Robinson Files, BOE Series 378, Box 26, Folder 6.

21. "The Effect of Title I ESEA Funds on Student Achievement." Recognizing the legitimacy of the paraprofessional contract, Robinson recommended that paraprofessional salaries be paid by tax levy funds and that separate legislation be passed to fund paraprofessional college training.

22. *Kweli: The IS 201 Newspaper*, March 1971, Annie Stein Papers, Box 3, Folder 5.

23. Mercedes Figueroa Interview, MCNY Folder 161.

24. On divergent trajectories of community school districts, see Lewis, *New York City Public Schools from Brownsville to Bloomberg*.

25. Gary D. Goldenback, "Teaching Career Aspirations of Monolingual and Bilingual Paraprofessionals in the New York City School System" (PhD diss., Hofstra University, 1985).

26. Audit of the District 5 ESEA Programs from 1975–77, released in 1979, Amelia H. Ashe Files, BOE Series 312, Box 61, Folder 13, ESEA Program Audit 1979.

27. Photo, September 1973. United Federation of Teachers Photographs, PHO-TOS 019, Box 7, Folder 88, Tamiment Library/Robert F. Wagner Labor Archives, New York University.

28. Letter from Shanker to Calvin Alston, August 13, 1971, UFTR Box 80, Folder 12.

29. "The Decentralized School Districts of the City of New York," Annie Stein Papers, Box 5, Folder 3.

30. Winifred Tates, MCNY Student Interview, Folder 160.

31. Acceptance of EPDA Title V Grant for Community School District 16 for program "Project Steel Drums," October 4, 1972, *Journal of the Board of Education* 1974, City Hall Library, New York, NY, 1652.

32. The COP, which drew heavily on Riessman's practical experience working with parent activists and early parent-aide and paraprofessional programs in New York City, became the most progressive federal program of local hiring and perhaps the most fully realized arm of the "paraprofessional movement." It is discussed at greater length in Chapter 6. See also Kaplan, *From Aide to Teacher*.

33. "Youth Tutoring Youth Harlem-East Harlem," May 27, 1970, Office of the Chancellor, Harvey Scribner Files, BOE Series 1101, Box 14, Folder 7.

34. "Youth Tutoring Youth," June 7, 1970, Office of the Chancellor, Harvey Scribner Files, BOE Series 1101, Box 15, Folder 25.

35. Edward Grant, "Proposal Draft for YTY," May 18, 1972, Office of the Chancellor, Harvey Scribner Files, BOE Series 1101, Box 15, Folder 25.

36. Marian Thom, interview with the author, September 3, 2013.

37. Clarence Taylor, interview with the author, February 11, 2015.

38. Faue, "Battle for or in the Classroom."

39. Remnick, "The Police State in Franklin K. Lane."

40. Most famously, a junior high math teacher who let students disassemble his classroom and taught nothing under the guise of an "open classroom" in Ocean Hill–Brownsville was among those unilaterally transferred from the district, and parents cited his methods as evidence that teachers made no effort on behalf of their students. See Perrillo, *Uncivil Rights*.

41. Taylor, interview.

42. Clara Blackman Interview, MCNY Folder 83.

43. John Devine, *Maximum Security: The Culture of Violence in Inner-City Schools* (Chicago: University of Chicago Press, 1996). See also Kafka, *The History of "Zero Tolerance" Policies in American Public Schooling*; Kautz, "From Segregation to Suspension"; Remnick, "The Police State at Franklin K. Lane."

44. Megan French-Marcelin and Sarah Hinger, *Bullies in Blue: The Origins and Consequences of School Policing* (New York: American Civil Liberties Union, 2017).

45. "TAC Position on Violence," TAC Newsletter, January 1970, Anne Filardo Papers, Box 1, Folder 4.

46. Remnick, "The Police State at Franklin K. Lane," 1078.

47. For context on this transition, see Berger, *A New Working Class*; MacLean, *Freedom Is Not Enough*; Honey, *Going Down Jericho Road*.

48. Telegram from Carter Burden to Board of Education, December 19, 1972; Letter from Edward H. Lehner to Board of Education, December 22, 1972; Telegram from Edward I. Koch to Board of Education, December 27, 1972; all found in UFT Box 80, Folder 12.

49. "Support the Paraprofessionals!" Teacher Action Caucus Flyer, UFT Box 80, Folder 12.

50. "Summary of New Contract Provisions," UFT Box 80, Folder 12.

51. Thom, interview.

52. Program, Paraprofessional Retreat in Tarrytown, January 1971, UFT Box 175, Folder 6; Paraprofessional Week-End, Harrison House, Glen Cove, Long Island, February 10, 1973, UFT Box 149, Folder 30.

53. Correspondence between Riessman and UFT, September-November 1970, UFT Box 155, Folder 6.

54. "Constitution of the Para-Professional Chapter of the UFT, Article II: Objectives," UFT Box 149, Folder 30.

55. Thom, interview. Thom remembers that she and several other paras would rise early on election days to vote, read through the "confusing" ballots, and then stand by to explain them to parents and other school staff.

56. Velma Murphy Hill, interview with the author, November 7, 2011.

57. Shelvy Young-Abrams, interview with the author, September 5, 2014.

58. Thom, interview.

59. Young-Abrams, interview.

60. Pearl Daniels Interview, MCNY Folder 92.

61. Martin, interview.

62. Taylor, interview.

63. "Para Scope" vol. 1, no. 2, October 1974, UFT Box 149, Folder 30.

64. "Support the Paraprofessionals," December 19, 1972, AFP Box 1, Folder 6.

65. "Viva El Boicot!" TAC Newsletter, December 4, 1972, AFP Box 1, Folder 6; "Let's Help Our Children Read Better," District 3 TAC, February 1, 1973, AFP Box 1, Folder 6.

66. Taylor, interview.

67. "Paraprofessionals and Teachers United," UFT Box 210, Folder 6.

68. "Paraprofessionals and Teachers United," UFT Box 210, Folder 6.

69. Weiner, *The Future of Our Schools*, 87–88.

70. Stephen Brier, "The Ideological and Organizational Origins of the United Federation of Teachers' Opposition to the Community Control Movement in the New York City Public Schools, 1960–1968," *Labor / Le Travail*, 73 (Spring 2014), 179–93.

71. "A Parent Guide for Community-Based Educational Workers in Schools," May 2, 1970, Annie Stein Papers Box 21, Folder 5.

72. ELP Box 1, Folder Decentralization.

73. Meeting of NY Association of Black Educators, April 16, 1972, with UFT

note that "This was enclosed in Para Professional payrolls as distributed by District [illegible] in Brooklyn," UFT Box 80, Folder 12.

74. Fifth Annual Report of the College for Human Services 1971 Program, MCNY Folder 5.

75. Biondi, *The Black Revolution on Campus*.

76. For a detailed discussion of the origins and significance of the Paraprofessional-Teacher Education Program, see Nick Juravich, "Reclaiming the Promise: Union Advocacy for Paraprofessional-to-Teacher Pathways," *American Educator* (Winter 2022–2023), https://www.aft.org/ae/winter2022–2023/juravich.

77. Pearl and Riessman, *New Careers for the Poor*. Riessman's vision for New Careers and its connection to on-the-ground antipoverty activism in New York City is discussed in far greater detail in Chapters 1, 3, and 6.

78. Hill, interview.

79. Leonora Farber, interview with the author, January 18, 2014.

80. Memos dated October 27, November 17, and December 4, 1970, Isaiah Robinson Files, BOE Series 378 Box 18, Folder 38.

81. Bowman and Klopf, *New Careers and Roles in the American School*.

82. Resolution 55, July 30, *Journal of the Board of Education*, 1970.

83. Resolution 55; Resolution 61, June 22, 1970, Education Professions Development Act, p. 1358–9, Working with Fordham to implement TTT Program in District 3, *Journal of the Board of Education*, 1970.

84. Leichter, interview.

85. Memo from Joseph Monserrat to Board of Education Re: Education Program for Paras (Lachman Memo), December 16, 1970, Isaiah Robinson Papers, BOE Series 378, Box 18, Folder 38; "Appeal by the Fordham University Urban Teacher Corps," Office of the Secretary, Harold Siegel Subject Files, 1971, BOE Series 1028, Box 22, Folder 383.

86. Biondi, *The Black Revolution on Campus*; Ibram H. Rogers, *The Black Campus Movement: Black Students and the Racial Reconstitution of Higher Education, 1965–1972* (Albany: SUNY Press, 2012).

87. Lachman Memo, December 16, 1970.

88. Velma Murphy Hill, Address to Second Annual Paraprofessional Conference, SUNY-ESC Harry Van Arsdale Center, April 2014. See also Hill and Hill, *Climbing the Rough Side of the Mountain*, Chapter 9.

89. Hill, interview.

90. Terry Golway, "LaGuardia Works: LaGuardia Community College, the First 25 Years," *CUNY Digital History Archive*, accessed April 9, 2024, https://cdha.cuny.edu/items/show/1201.

91. Golway, "LaGuardia Works." See also Unknown, "Joe Shenker, Founding President of LaGuardia with the First Group of Students Who Were Paraprofessionals," *CUNY Digital History Archive*, accessed April 9, 2024, https://cdha.cuny.edu/items/show/1771, and Khan, Fern, "Celebration for the First Group of LaGuardia Community College Paraprofessional Students, May 1971," *CUNY Digital History Archive*, accessed April 9, 2024, https://cdha.cuny.edu/items/show/1761.

92. Golway, "LaGuardia Works."

93. Friedheim, Bill, and Vásquez, Andrea Ades, "John Hyland Oral History Interview," CUNY Digital History Archive, accessed April 9, 2024, https://cdha .cuny.edu/items/show/51.

94. Farber, interview.

95. Farber, interview. For a detailed assessment of the Teacher Corps and its legacy, see Rogers, "'Better' People, Better Teaching."

96. Farber, interview.

97. CDHA, "Oral History Interview with Joan Greenbaum, Fern Khan, and Sandy Watson of LaGuardia Community College," *CUNY Digital History Archive*, accessed April 9, 2024, https://cdha.cuny.edu/items/show/2331.

98. Golway, "LaGuardia Works."

99. Golway, "LaGuardia Works."

100. Raymond Murphy, "The New Students at the City University of New York: How Are They Faring?" in Alan Gartner, Frank Riessman, and Vivian Carter Jackson, eds., *Paraprofessionals Today: Volume I: Education* (New York: Human Sciences Press, 1977); Internal report, undated, UFT Box 80, Folder 11.

101. Draft of full-page advertisement for *New York Times*, March 1974, UFT Box 149, Folder 30.

102. "Career Ladder Demonstrates Mobility: Union Moving for EFCB Approval of Para Contract," *The United Teacher*, UFT Box 159, Folder 31.

103. "The Paraprofessional-Teacher Education Program of the City University of New York" (Pamphlet), UFT Box 255, Folder 3; Murphy, "The New Students at the City University of New York."

104. Oneida Davis, interview with the author, September 3, 2014.

105. Young-Abrams, interview.

106. Kaplan, *From Aide to Teacher*; "Appeal by the Fordham University Urban Teacher Corps," April 1971, Isaiah Robinson Papers, BOE Series 378, Box 38, Folder 18.

107. "Final Report and Evaluation of the Women's Talent Corps New Careers Program 1966–67," MCNY.

108. Hill, interview.

109. Davis, interview; Young-Abrams, interview; Martin, interview.

110. Velma Murphy Hill, "A Profession with Promise," *American Teacher*, October 1971, UFT Box 255, Folder 2.

111. Collins, *Ethnically Qualified*, 64.

112. Murphy, "The New Students at the City University of New York."

113. Collins, *Ethnically Qualified*; Perlstein, *Justice, Justice*.

114. Naples, *Grassroots Warriors*.

115. U.S. Census Bureau, Educational Data, 1970. Prepared by Social Explorer. Accessed May 2016.

116. Velma Murphy Hill Interview, 1985, UFT-OH Box 2, Folder Velma Murphy Hill.

117. Mercedes Figueroa, MCNY Student Interview, Folder 161.

118. Thom, interview.

119. Collins, *Ethnically Qualified* offers a detailed assessment of these systems and these efforts.

120. Audrey Cohen Interview, MCNY Folder 93.

121. Transcript of the October 22nd Meeting of the Day Care Alliance, National Council of Organizations for Children and Youth, 1974, AFT-Shanker Box 65, Folder 73.

122. Lee, *Building a Latino Civil Rights Movement*, 227–28

123. Lee, *Building a Latino Civil Rights Movement*, 227–28.

124. "Paraprofessionals," clipping from *The Black Worker*, April 1971, UFT Box 80, Folder 11.

125. Preston Wilcox: December 22, 1970, Letter from PW to Kalu Kalu, Faculty Representative, MCNY Folder 171.

126. "Competencies, Credentialing and the Child Development Associate Program or Maids, Miss Ann and Authentic Mothers: 'My Momma Done Told Me,'" PWP Box 11, Folder 17.

127. "Competencies, Credentialing and the Child Development Associate Program."

128. Taylor, interview.

129. Figueroa, MCNY Student Interviews, Folders 160–61.

130. Hill, interview.

131. Charlayne Hunter, "School to Cite Black Parent for Unity Efforts," *New York Times,* February 13, 1975.

132. "School to Cite Black Parent for Unity Efforts."

Chapter 5. A Union of Paraprofessionals?

1. Velma Murphy Hill Interview, 1985, UFT-OH Box 2, Folder Velma Murphy Hill.

2. AFT PSRP Conference Speech (no date, appears to be 1988 based on references to that year's presidential election), AFT-Shanker Box 65, Folder 61.

3. Oral History of Lorretta Johnson, Interviewed by Leo Casey, Burnie Bond, and Vicki Thomas of the Albert Shanker Institute, December 8, 2020, https://www.shankerinstitute.org/resource/oral-history-lorretta-johnson.

4. Oral History of Lorretta Johnson.

5. Baltimore Teachers Union Paraprofessional Contract, January 5, 1970, Detroit Federation of Teachers Collection, Box 21, Folder 19, Walter P. Reuther Library, Wayne State University, Detroit, MI.

6. Oral History of Lorretta Johnson.

7. Letter from Selden to Riessman, June 3, 1968, UFT Box 155, Folder 2.

8. "Teacher Aides Vote for Union," *The Hartford Courant*, November 14, 1970, 17.

9. Election Flyers, 1971, DFT Box 22, Folder 16. The Springfield and Kansas City campaigns are discussed in greater detail further on in this chapter.

10. Jorie Lester Mark, *Paraprofessionals in Education: A Study of the Training and Utilization of Paraprofessionals in U.S. Public School Systems Enrolling 5,000 or More Pupils* (New York: Bank Street College of Education, 1976), 40.

11. Kaplan, *From Aide to Teacher.*

12. See Perrillo, *Uncivil Rights,* Chapter 7, on "Teacher Power" and challenges to it. On hostility to teacher unions, see Berger, *A New Working Class;* and Shelton, "Against the Public."

13. Mark, *Paraprofessionals in Education.*

14. Linda Cook, Interviewed by Dan Golodner for the AFT Bay Area Oral History Project: Teachers Gain a Collective Voice, March 24, 2014.

15. Dennis Kelly, "State's Oldest AFT Local Shares 100th Birthday with CFT: United Educators of San Francisco, 1919–2019," California Federation of Teachers, https://www.cft.org/article/states-oldest-aft-local-shares-100th-birthday-cft#; "The Case for Equity for Paraprofessionals," Flyer, March 3, 1974, UESF Part II: Box 31, Folder 1.

16. Letter from SFUSD to SFFT, March 22, 1972, UESF Part II: Box 27, Folder 5; Letter from SFFT to SFUSD, February 16, 1972, UESF Part II: Box 27, Folder 6.

17. "Emergency Planning Session of AFT Paraprofessionals," July 17, 1974; "Ayude, Nos Roban Puestos," August 5, 1974, UESF Part II: Box 31, Folder 1.

18. "Survey of Paraprofessional Salaries, 1978–79," A Report of the Economic Research Department of the American Federation of Teachers, September 1979, UESF Part II: Box 56, Folder 24. Wage comparison via Bureau of Labor Statistics CPI Inflation Calculator, https://data.bls.gov/cgi-bin/cpicalc.pl.

19. Richard Wholf to Robert Wheeler, November 9, 1968, KCFT Box 10, Folder 21.

20. Oral History of Lorretta Johnson.

21. Cook, Interviewed by Dan Golodner.

22. Agreement between the New Bedford School Committee and the New Bedford Federation of Paraprofessionals, MFT Box 7, Folder 3. Teachers in New Bedford were already organized with the National Education Association.

23. Election Flyers, 1971 and 1972, DFT Box 22, Folder 16.

24. Agreement between SFT and City of Springfield School Committee, MFT Box 1, Folder 15.

25. Charles E. McGowan, "Election of Bargaining Agent for Aides Set for April 6," *The Boston Union Teacher,* March 1972, https://openarchives.umb.edu/digital/collection/p15774coll27/id/113/rec/10.

26. Tom Gosnell, Interviewed by Nick Juravich and Betsy Drinan, January 29, 2020, Boston Teachers Union Oral History Project, UMass Boston.

27. Joan Devlin, Interviewed by Nick Juravich and Betsy Drinan, January 15, 2020, Boston Teachers Union Oral History Project, UMass Boston.

28. *Massachusetts Union Teacher,* January-February 1974, MFT Box 12, Folder 5.

29. On the hiring of transitional aides, see Adam R. Nelson, *The Elusive Ideal: Equal Educational Opportunity and the Federal Role in Boston's Public Schools, 1950–1985* (Chicago: University of Chicago Press, 2005).

30. Joan Buckley, "S.L.R.B. Rules for B.T.U." *The Boston Union Teacher,* March 1975, https://openarchives.umb.edu/digital/collection/p15774coll27/id/222/rec/36.

31. "Jenna Fitzgerald at the Boston Teachers Union Digitizing Day: Video Interview," November 11, 2018, https://openarchives.umb.edu/digital/collection/p15774coll37/id/443/rec/111.

32. Cook, Interviewed by Dan Golodner; Flyer "584-PARA: Announcing a New Service for Paraprofessionals," March 14, 1979, UESF Part II: Box 50, Folder 11.

33. Cook, Interviewed by Dan Golodner.

34. Cook, Interviewed by Dan Golodner.

35. Geraldine Alves to Paul Devlin, 1973, MFT Box 7, Folder 3.

36. Holman to Miriam Simon, Specialist III, EPDA Project KCSD, November 11, 1971, KCFT Box 10, Folder 21.

37. "Paraprofessionals" 1970: AFT-Selden Part I: Box 10, Folder 41: Paraprofessional National Committee.

38. "Paraprofessionals" 1970: AFT-Selden.

39. Gladys Roth to Albert Shanker, January 20, 1970, UFT Box 80, Folder 6.

40. See Chapter 4, particularly quotations from author interviews with Maggie Martin and Clarence Taylor.

41. *Organizing Paraprofessionals: A Manual Prepared by the Committee on Paraprofessionals* (Washington, DC: American Federation of Teachers, 1973), 14.

42. *Organizing Paraprofessionals.*

43. *Organizing Paraprofessionals.*

44. AFT report on the NEA, 1982, AFT-Shanker Box 55, Folder 40.

45. *Organizing Paraprofessionals.*

46. *Organizing Paraprofessionals*, 13.

47. *Organizing Paraprofessionals*, 13.

48. *Organizing Paraprofessionals.*

49. *Organizing Paraprofessionals.*

50. *Organizing Paraprofessionals.*

51. *Organizing Paraprofessionals.*

52. "Paraprofessionals," 1970: AFT-Selden.

53. Velma Murphy Hill, UFT Oral History Collection, 1985.

54. Executive Council, Abridged Proceedings, April 21–22, 1972, AFT-Inventory Box 32, Folder 3; Letter from David Selden to Lorretta Johnson, April 26, 1972, AFT-Selden Box 10, Folder 41: Paraprofessional National Committee.

55. Executive Council, Abridged Proceedings, April 21–22, 1972; Letter from David Selden to Lorretta Johnson, April 26, 1972.

56. Executive Council, Abridged Proceedings, April 21–22, 1972; Letter from David Selden to Lorretta Johnson, April 26, 1972; Chris King, "Black and Blue: An Anthology of African-American Writing on St. Louis Paints a Bleak Portrait of the City," *Riverfront Times*, December 23, 1998, https://www.riverfronttimes.com/stlouis/black-and-blue/Content?oid=2476590 ("Demosthenes DuBoise writes about being among the first black teachers to teach in a white school; he and another black teacher taught only the black students bused into the school and had to use the black janitors' toilet!") Access to teachers' bathrooms and other adult/professional spaces was a recurring demand in paraprofessional organizing.

57. AFT Paraprofessional Survey, Received Completed by William Penn Federation of Teachers (PA), January 10, 1973, AFT-Selden Box 10, Folder 41.

58. Memo: November 9, 1972, From Selden to Velma Murphy Hill and Members of Para Committee, Sharing Teacher Aide Guidelines as Adopted by the Michigan State Board of Education from November 7, 1972, AFT-Selden Box 10, Folder 41.

59. Letter from Philadelphia Board of Education to Albert Shanker, February 10, 1971, UFT Box 80, Folder 12; Letter from Tom Koren, Local 61, San Francisco, to Jules Kolodny at UFT, December 23, 1975, UFT Box 80, Folder 13.

60. Baltimore Teachers Union Paraprofessional Contract, January 5, 1970, DFT Box 21, Folder 19.

61. "The Blacks and the Unions," by Bayard Rustin from the May 1971 issue of *Harpers. The New Leader* by Rustin, "Mobilizing a Progressive Majority," KCFT Box 5, Folder 9; Boston training program and Los Angeles United School District materials, Fall 1970, copy of "working agreement" between Tacoma School District No. 10 and the Tacoma Association of Paraprofessionals, KCFT Box 10, Folder 21.

62. "To All Building Representatives": Recruitment! April 15, 1970, Copy of UFT contract, AFT Massachusetts Federation of Teachers Records, Box 1, Folder 15: Springfield Federation of Teachers, Walter P. Reuther Library, Wayne State University, Detroit, MI.

63. Baltimore Teachers Union Paraprofessional Contract, Flyer/handout made from copy of *American Teacher* article, "NYC paraprofessionals ok first contract," with handwritten note (copied) that reads "AFT can help para-professionals," Partial copy (lightly annotated) of Garda Bowman and Gordon Klopf's *New Careers and Roles in the American School* (1968), United Educators of San Francisco Local 61 Records, Part II: Box 27, Folder 5: Paras 1972. Walter P. Reuther Library Wayne State University, Detroit, MI. "A Statement of Support for Paraprofessionals (The Board of Education's Forgotten Minority)," Philadelphia Federation of Teachers Paraprofessional Contract, Pittsburgh Federation of Teachers Contract, Partial copy of "Handbook for Instructional Assistants" from Oakland, August 1974, UESF Part II: Box 34, Folder 16. Detroit Federation of Paraprofessionals Contract, UFT pamphlet "Teacher and Para-Professional: On-the-Job Partners . . . Working Together for Better Schools," UESF Part II: Box 34, Folder 17.

64. Laurel Goodrich, "Aides and Teachers: A New Alliance." *The Boston Union Teacher*, March 1975, https://openarchives.umb.edu/digital/collection/p15774coll27/id/222/rec/36.

65. Letter from Norman Hudson to Indiana Federation of Teachers, noting paras are full members with equal voting power and representation on executive board, January 14, 1974, KCFT Box 13, Folder 43; Paraprofessional Meeting, 1974 inter-city strategy session with St. Louis, Local 420, KCFT Box 13, Folder 44.

66. Flyer/handout, copy of *American Teacher* article, "NYC paraprofessionals ok first contract" with handwritten note (copied) that reads "AFT can help para-professionals," UESF Part II: Box 27, Folder 5: Paras 1972.

67. *Organizing Paraprofessionals.*

68. *Organizing Paraprofessionals.*

69. *Organizing Paraprofessionals.*

70. Oral History of Lorretta Johnson.

71. *Massachusetts Union Teacher* January-February 1974, MFT Box 12, Folder 5.

72. *Massachusetts Union Teacher,* Spring 1973, MFT Box 12, Folder 5

73. "Mass Meeting: All School Service Assistants, October 16, 1973," Michigan Federation of Teachers Part III: Box 6, Folder 15. Walter Reuther Library, Wayne State University.

74. SFFT Letter to Velma Murphy Hill, trying to bring her out to San Francisco, 1975–76, UESF Box 39, Folder 18.

75. Shelvy Young-Abrams, interview with the author, September 5, 2014.

76. Election Agreement between Springfield Federation of Teachers and Springfield School Committee, May 13, 1970, MFT Box 1, Folder 15; Paraprofessional Meeting, 1974, KCFT Box 13, Folder 44.

77. Eugene J. Didier, Director of the "Special Organizing Project" in Atlanta to Velma Murphy Hill, May 9, 1978, AFT-Shanker Box 1, Folder 10.

78. Letter from David Selden to Hubert H. Humphrey, April 23, 1973, AFT-Selden Box 10, Folder 41.

79. Letter from Selden to Hill, Schedule of National Paraprofessional Conference, April 19, 1973; Letter from Lorretta Johnson to Selden, with minutes from AFT National Paraprofessional Committee meeting, which was held on Monday, March 19, 1973, sent March 22, 1973, Preliminary schedule for conference attached, AFT-Selden Box 10, Folder 41.

80. Letter from Selden to Hill, March 26, 1973, AFT-Selden Box 10, Folder 41.

81. Letter from Selden to Hill, March 26, 1973.

82. Leadership Conference: August 11–14, 1969, Letter from David Selden to Frank Riessman, July 28, 1969, AFT-Selden Box 10, Folder 37.

83. Letter from Lorretta Johnson to Selden, March 22, 1973, AFT-Selden Box 10, Folder 41.

84. Letter from Albert Shanker to Nat LaCour, President of United Teachers of New Orleans, February 7, 1978, AFT-Shanker Box 12, Folder 14.

85. Program: "Paraprofessionals on the Move: Past, Present, and Future," April 27–28, 1978, AFT-Shanker Box 12, Folder 14.

86. Letter from Shanker to LaCour, February 7, 1978.

87. Memo from Velma Murphy Hill, "Paraprofessional Conference," UFT Box 149, Folder 30.

88. Cheryl M. Houston, Paraprofessional Chairperson for St. Louis Teachers Union, to Barbara Van Blake, Director of UFT's Human Rights and Community Relations Department, May 5, 1978, AFT-Shanker Box 12, Folder 14.

89. Eugene J. Didier, Director of the "Special Organizing Project" in Atlanta, to Barbara Van Blake, May 9, 1978, AFT-Shanker Box 1, Folder 10.

90. Rustin, "The Triumph of the Paraprofessionals."

91. David Stein, "Making Freedom a Fact," *Jacobin*, March 23, 2016, https://

www.jacobinmag.com/2016/03/coates-reparations-welfare-randolph-du-bois/. Stein's title paraphrases W. E. B. Du Bois from *Black Reconstruction* (1935).

92. Bayard Rustin, "The Blacks and the Unions," in *Down the Line; the Collected Writings of Bayard Rustin. Introd. by C. Vann Woodward* (Chicago: Quadrangle Books, 1971).

93. Daniel Levine, *Bayard Rustin and the Civil Rights Movement* (New Brunswick, NJ: Rutgers University Press, 2000), 217.

94. A. Philip Randolph Institute, 1970–1971, "Black Rage, White Fear," KCFT Box 5, Folder 9.

95. Oral History of Lorretta Johnson.

96. Velma Murphy Hill Interview, 1985, UFT-OH.

97. On community-based organizations behaving as bosses, see Chapters 3 and 4.

98. Oral History of Lorretta Johnson.

99. Critics and historians have debated the degree to which Rustin, in particular, accommodated the racism of labor leaders in the service of promoting unity as head of the APRI. On Rustin's humanism, see Jerald Podair, *Bayard Rustin: American Dreamer* (Blue Ridge Summit, PA: Rowman & Littlefield Publishers, Inc., 2008). On Rustin's accommodationism, see Daniel Perlstein, "The Dead End of Despair," in Clarence Taylor, ed., *Civil Rights in New York City* (New York: Columbia University Press, 2011). On broader critiques of para organizing as co-optation, see the discussion in Chapter 4, as well as Preston Wilcox's position on unionization, discussed in Chapter 6.

100. Oral History of Lorretta Johnson.

101. Velma Murphy Hill, "A Profession with Promise," *The American Teacher,* 1971, UFT Box 255, Folder 2.

102. Hill, interview with the author; Interview with Patricia Jones in Appendix A of Hill and Hill, *Climbing the Rough Side of the Mountain.*

103. Velma Murphy Hill, Interviewed by Renee Epstein for the UFT Oral History Project, June 19 and November 29, 1986.

104. Hill, interview with the author. The UFT, it should be noted, itself was often criticized for its lack of internal union democracy. See Stephen Brier, "The UFT's Opposition to the Community Control Movement," *Jacobin,* September 12, 2018; David Selden, *The Teacher Rebellion* (Washington, DC: Howard University Press, 1985); Weiner, *The Future of Our Schools.*

105. AFT PSRP Conference Speech (appears to be 1988), AFT-Shanker Box 65, Folder 61.

106. AFT PSRP Conference Speech.

107. On Shanker's professionalism-based response to attacks on educators in the 1980s, see Perrillo, *Uncivil Rights,* 163–72; on the NEA, see Urban, *Gender, Race and the National Education Association.*

108. Letter from Richard J. Williams, LTU President, to Paras, February 26, 1973, MFT Box 2, Folder 28.

109. LTU Newsletter, May 1975, MFT Box 2, Folder 27.

110. LTU Newsletter, November 1975; Contract Proposals for Paraprofessionals, MFT Box 2, Folder 27.

111. Rose Claffey Interview, 1986, Box 23, Folder Rose Claffey, AFT Oral Histories, Walter P. Reuther Library, Wayne State University, Detroit, MI.

112. Rose Claffey Interview, 1986, Box 23, Folder Rose Claffey, AFT Oral Histories, Walter P. Reuther Library, Wayne State University, Detroit, MI.

113. AFT PSRP Conference Speech (appears to be 1988), AFT-Shanker Box 65, Folder 61.

114. Hill, interview with the author.

115. Katherine Schaeffer, "America's Public School Teachers Are Far Less Racially and Ethnically Diverse than Their Students," *Pew Research Center*, December 10, 2021, https://www.pewresearch.org/short-reads/2021/12/10/americas-public-school-teachers-are-far-less-racially-and-ethnically-diverse-than-their-students; Leana Cabral, Mary Eddins, David Lapp, and Saxon Nelson, *The Need for More Teachers of Color* (Philadelphia: Research For Action, 2022), https://www.researchforaction.org/research-resources/k-12/the-need-for-more-teachers-of-color.

Chapter 6. New Careers and Parent Implementation

1. Kaplan, *From Aide to Teacher*, 43.

2. Wilcox, "I.S. 201." On the Child Development Group of Mississippi and the empowerment of working-class Black women as educators, see Sanders, *A Chance for Change*.

3. Memo from Wilcox to Policy Advisory Committee Chairmen, Project Directors, Parent Coordinators and Local Stimulators, Subject: The Role of the Local Stimulator, October 26, 1970, PWP Box 30, Folder 1.

4. Fact Sheet for 9 Afram-Affiliated Sites 1971–2, November 23, 1971, PWP Box 30, Folder 4.

5. Richard D. Benson II, *Fighting for Our Place in the Sun: Malcolm X and the Radicalization of the Black Student Movement, 1965–1974* (New York: Peter Lang, 2015); Rickford, *We Are an African People*; Woodsworth, *Battle for Bed-Stuy*, Chapter 7.

6. This new interpretation of Black Power is argued most cogently by Rhonda Williams in *Concrete Demands*.

7. Preston Wilcox, "The Community Centered School" (1968), PWP Box 11, Folder 12.

8. Wilcox to Scribner, January 5, 1970, PWP Box 5, Folder 5.

9. "Competencies, Credentialing and the Child Development Associate Program or Maids, Miss Ann and Authentic Mothers," PWP Box 7, Folder 17.

10. Collins, *Black Feminist Thought*. The analytics of "activist mothering" run this risk as well, particularly when deployed as a category to describe people ("activist mothers") instead of a practice ("activist mothering"). Much as the language of "mother hens" that administrators used to describe paras (see Chapter 2) assumes inborn maternal instinct and renders emotional labor invisibly

"natural," assuming that certain women are inherently "authentic" or "activist" mothers flattens the complex set of ideas, choices, and roles these women navigated in schools and neighborhoods.

11. "The Educated and the Unlettered," 1967, PWP Box 12, Folder 1.

12. May 1970: "How to Develop 'Operational Unity' Among Blacks," PWP Box 24, Folder 2.

13. On the "labor-liberal" coalition, see Shelton, *Teacher Strike!*

14. Frank Riessman and Hermine Popper, eds., *Up from Poverty: New Career Ladders for Nonprofessionals* (New York: Harper & Row, 1968), 1.

15. Robin Marie Averbeck, "The Other Riessman," *U.S. Intellectual History Blog*, February 26, 2015, https://s-usih.org/2015/02/the-other-riessman/. Averbeck argues in this piece that Riessman's "flexibility never stretched to the point of questioning capitalism or seriously tackling institutionalized racism" and that he thus represented "the ultimate failure of liberals to grapple with the structural underpinnings of social and racial injustice." Aguiar and Katz (cited below), however, demonstrate that Riessman's commitment to state-sponsored employment constituted a structural, if not radical, approach to poverty and postindustrial urban economies.

16. Aguiar, "Head Start"; Michael B. Katz, *The Undeserving Poor: America's Enduring Confrontation with Poverty* (New York: Oxford University Press, 2013).

17. Aguiar, "Head Start." (Chapter 2: "I want to underscore the fact that the New Careers believed unemployment to be a root cause of poverty. Rejecting the prevalent notion that training programs were the answer for the supposedly "hardcore" unemployed, the movement's mantra became "jobs first, training built in."); Frank Riessman, *Training the Nonprofessional* (Union, NJ: Scientific Resources Inc., 1967), http://files.eric.ed.gov/fulltext/ED014642.pdf.

18. David P. Stein, "Fearing Inflation, Inflating Fears: The End of Full Employment and the Rise of the Carceral State" (PhD diss., University of Southern California, 2014).

19. Riessman and Popper, eds., *Up from Poverty*.

20. Bayard Rustin, "From Protest to Politics: The Future of the Civil Rights Movement," *Commentary Magazine*, February 1, 1965, https://www.commentary magazine.com/articles/from-protest-to-politics-the-future-of-the-civil-rights -movement. Rustin's program for this shift to politics was laid out in the "Freedom Budget for All Americans," which he coauthored and published out of the A. Philip Randolph Institute in 1966.

21. Frank Riessman, "More on Poverty: The Myth of Saul Alinsky," *Dissent* 14, no. 4 (July 1967).

22. Riessman and Popper, eds., *Up from Poverty*. The collection's echo of the title of Booker T. Washington's autobiography, *Up from Slavery*, was surely intentional, and it points to a focus on economic development as a primary producer of future equality.

23. Riessman and Popper, eds., *Up from Poverty*, 17

24. Riessman and Popper, eds., *Up from Poverty*, 21.

25. Garda W. Bowman and Gordon John Klopf, *New Partners in the Educational*

Enterprise: Report of Phase One of a Study of Auxiliary Personnel in Education (New York: Bank Street College of Education, 1967); Garda W. Bowman and Gordon J. Klopf, *New Careers and Roles in the American School*, 1968, http://eric.ed .gov/?id=ED027266.

26. On the limits of paraprofessional jobs in nonprofit settings, see Dunning, "New Careers for the Poor," 669–90. In health care, see Eileen Boris and Jennifer Klein, *Caring for America: Home Health Workers in the Shadow of the Welfare State* (New York: Oxford University Press, 2012) and, on struggles for community control of medical care and facilities, see Merlin Chowkwanyun, *All Health Politics Is Local: Community Battles for Medical Care and Environmental Health* (Chapel Hill: University of North Carolina Press, 2022).

27. "A Design for Large-Scale Training of Paraprofessionals," New Careers Development Center, NYU, Training Laboratory (May 1967); Frank Riessman et al., "A New Careers Guide for Trainers of Education Auxiliaries," New Careers Training Laboratory, for the Office of Economic Opportunity (December 1968).

28. Alan Gartner and Jane Schroeder, eds., "New Careers Newsletter" 2, no. 5 (Fall 1968).

29. Riessman, *Up from Poverty;* "New Careers and the Employed Poor" (testimony before House Committee on Education and Labor), 188.

30. Dunning, "New Careers for the Poor."

31. "Manual for Utilization of Auxiliary Personnel" (New York: Board of Education, 1969). The document, edited by Atwell, cites Riessman's publications and the work of the NCDC extensively.

32. Kaplan, *From Aide to Teacher*, 43.

33. Career Opportunities Program, Evaluation Report 1971–1972, Oakland Unified School District, Research Department, DHEW Office of Education, RG 0012, Container 98, NARA.

34. Kaplan, *From Aide to Teacher*, 54.

35. Nancy Falk, "A Study of the Utilization of Paraprofessionals Trained under the Career Opportunities Program" (St. Paul, Minnesota: Department of Education, 1975).

36. Kaplan, "The City as COP Turf."

37. Kaplan, *From Aide to Teacher*. On the Crystal City student walkout of 1969, see Nick Palazzolo, "Chicano Students Strike for Equality of Education in Crystal City, Texas, 1969–1970," Global Nonviolent Action Database, Swarthmore College, May 16, 2013, https://nvdatabase.swarthmore.edu/content/chicano-students -strike-equality-education-crystal-city-texas-1969–1970. Of seventeen student demands, number fourteen was "Involvement of parents as teacher aides."

38. Kaplan, *From Aide to Teacher*, 69.

39. Kaplan, *From Aide to Teacher*, 62, 47.

40. Alan Gartner, interview with the author, March 21, 2013.

41. Sweet, "A Decade of Paraprofessional Programs in Minneapolis Public Schools."

42. Sweet, "A Decade of Paraprofessional Programs in Minneapolis Public Schools."

43. Falk, "A Study of the Utilization of Paraprofessionals Trained under the Career Opportunities Program."

44. Sweet, "A Decade of Paraprofessional Programs in Minneapolis Public Schools."

45. Kaplan, *From Aide to Teacher*, 13.

46. Gartner, interview.

47. Kaplan, *From Aide to Teacher*, 14.

48. Career Opportunities Program, Evaluation Report 1971–1972, Oakland Unified School District.

49. Kaplan, *From Aide to Teacher*, 69.

50. George Kaplan, "The Unlikely Alliance: COP and Academe," *COP Bulletin* 2, no. 8 (1975), http://eric.ed.gov/?q=COP+bulletin&id=ED118545.

51. Sweet, "A Decade of Paraprofessional Programs in Minneapolis Public Schools."

52. Kaplan, "The Unlikely Alliance."

53. Kaplan, "The Unlikely Alliance."

54. Kaplan, "The City as COP Turf."

55. Falk, "A Study of 'the Utilization of Paraprofessionals Trained Under the Career Opportunities Program."

56. Sweet, "A Decade of Paraprofessional Programs in Minneapolis Public Schools."

57. Self, *American Babylon*, 217.

58. Kaplan, "The City as COP Turf."

59. Kaplan, "The City as COP Turf."

60. Kaplan, "The City as COP Turf."

61. Albert Shanker to Lesser, October 17, 2011, UFT Box 155, Folder 6.

62. "Bronx Group Backs Teachers," *New York Amsterdam News,* March 25, 1972, UFTR Box 255, Folder 2.

63. "The Black Ghetto and the UFT: A Response to Bayard Rustin," Letter to the *New York Amsterdam News* in reply to Rustin's article "Why I Support the UFT." PWP Box 10, Folder 15.

64. Flyer: November 7, 1968, Detroit Citizens for Community Control, AFT-Selden Box 10, Folder 16.

65. October 23, 1968, Letter from Wilcox regarding "Change in Action" book proposal, PWP Box 5, Folder 2.

66. "A Letter: General Principles on Decentralization," addressed to Brother Gene Bivins, Philadelphia Federation of Teachers, July 26, 1968, PWP Box 12, Folder 7. In 1966, Wilcox had called for the employment of parents as "foster teachers" to work in classrooms, make home visits, and build links between schools and community-based institutions at IS 201 in what many historians regard as the founding statement of the community-control philosophy. See Preston Wilcox, "The Controversy over I.S. 201: One View and a Proposal," *Urban Review* (July 1966).

67. On the importance of Project Head Start as a source of jobs and political independence for working-class Black women, see Aguiar, "Head Start"; Sanders,

A Chance for Change. Wilcox cited Project Head Start, and particularly the Child Development Group of Mississippi studied by Sanders, in his proposals for "foster teachers." See Wilcox, "The Controversy over I.S. 201."

68. September 1970, Parent Participation and Community Involvement, PWP Box 30, Folder 6.

69. November 10, 1970, Strategies for Parent Participation, report for PPFT/Afram, Nancy Mamis, PWP Box 30, Folder 1. Mamis's observation about seeing parents "as significant people in the learning process" echoes community-based educator Maggie Martin's observation, quoted in Chapter 4, that seeing parents in schools inspired and encouraged pupils.

70. "What Happened in St. Louis? A Report of the National Conference of Follow Through Parent Advisory Committees," September 18, 1972, PWP Box 30, Folder 2.

71. Afram Continuation Proposal 1974–1975, PWP Box 31, Folder 1.

72. Preston Wilcox, "Parental Decision-Making: An Educational Necessity," *Theory into Practice* 11, no. 3 (1972): 178–82.

73. Wilcox, "Parental Decision-Making."

74. Stokely Carmichael and Charles V. Hamilton, *Black Power: The Politics of Liberation* (New York: Random House, 1967).

75. Program: "Black Power—A Positive Force" A Conference Sponsored by the New York Region National Conference of Christians and Jews, Thursday, March 28, 1968. Keynote Address: Charles V. Hamilton, PWP Box 7, Folder 4.

76. Hamilton, Keynote Address. Hamilton's framing mirrors the historical argument Rhonda Williams made in *Concrete Demands*.

77. Wilcox, "Parental Decision-Making."

78. Thought Stimulator #376: Educational Leadership, October 4, 1973. Quotes Robert J. Havinghurst on "Educational Leadership for the Seventies," published in the *Phi Delta Kappan* (March 1972, p. 404). The article lists four categories of educational prophets: "conservative anarchists" (followers of Rousseau, including Paul Goodman), "revolutionary anarchists" (Everett Reimer), "conservative oligarchists" (Max Rafferty), and "radical pluralists" (Preston Wilcox). PWP Box 30, Folder 4.

79. "Changing Conceptions of Community," 1974, PWP Box 31, Folder 1. On assimilation as a racist idea, see Ibram X. Kendi, *Stamped from the Beginning: The Definitive History of Racist Ideas in America* (New York: Nation Books, 2016).

80. Memo from PW to PAC Chairmen and Project Directors, Subject: One Time Around, August 28, 1970, PWP Box 30, Folder 1.

81. On the East Harlem Block Schools, see Tom Roderick, *A School of Our Own: Parents, Power, and Community at the East Harlem Block Schools* (New York: Teachers College Press, 2001).

82. Fact Sheet for 9 Afram-Affiliated Sites 1971-2, November 23, 1971, PWP Box 30, Folder 4.

83. Isaacs, *Inside Ocean Hill-Brownsville*, 271.

84. Memo from PW to PAC Chairmen and Project Directors, Subject: One Time Around.

85. Report of the Meeting between Afram Advisors and Washington, DC, Follow Through Staff, April 27, 1971, PWP Box 30, Folder 1.

86. Wilcox Letter to Follow Through Staff, attached document September 8, 1975, PWP Box 31, Folder 1.

87. Wilcox, "Parental Decision-Making."

88. Wilcox, "Parental Decision-Making."

89. "Changing Conceptions of Community," 1974.

90. Role of the Local Stimulator, June 1970, PWP Box 31, Folder 9.

91. Wilcox, "Parental Decision-Making"; Continuation Proposal 1974–1975, PWP Box 31, Folder 1.

92. Action Stimulator #32: A Twenty Point Program for Real Community School Control, April 1970, PWP Box 31, Folder 8.

93. "Parent Participation in Follow Through, 1971–72," June 9, 1971, PWP Box 30, Folder 2.

94. "The Interaction between Parents and Professionals," August 27, 1971, PWP Box 30, Folder 1.

95. Continuation Proposal 1975–1976, PWP Box 31, Folder 2.

96. Continuation Proposal 1973, PWP Box 30, Folder 8; For more on Flint's educational struggles, see Highsmith, *Demolition Means Progress*.

97. Letter from Katheryn (Kate) Virginia Ann Young, Social Work Aide for FT, PWP Box 31, Folder 5; Atlantic City Follow Through Highlights, August 1972, PWP Box 31, Folder 7: "the involvement of the parents in the program has led to their being more aware of the functioning of the program, and their rights."

98. "What Happened in St. Louis?"

99. *Afram as Mirror to Follow Through Parents* (compiled by Nancy Mamis, edited by Joan Eastmond, May 30, 1973): Thought Stimulator 100, PWP Box 31, Folder 4. On the unequal burdens school desegregation placed on Black families and communities, see Erickson, *Making the Unequal Metropolis*, among many others.

100. *Afram as Mirror to Follow Through Parents*.

101. *Afram as Mirror to Follow Through Parents*.

102. From College Station, Arkansas, on "Parent Participation," December 29, 1971, PWP Box 30, Folder 4.

103. Announcement of "An AFRAM Community First," May 1974, PWP Box 31, Folder 2.

104. Continuation Proposal: Parents as Community Developers 1975–76 School Year, PWP Box 31, Folder 2.

105. Kaplan, *From Aide to Teacher*, 56.

106. Letter from Katheryn (Kate) Virginia Ann Young, Social Work Aide for FT, PWP Box 31, Folder 5.

107. The idea of "caring citizenship" is articulated in Wilkerson, *To Live Here, You Have to Fight*.

108. Michael Harrington, "Introduction," in Alan Gartner, Russell Nixon, and Frank Riessman, eds., *Public Service Employment: An Analysis of Its History, Problems, and Prospects* (New York: Praeger, 1973), xiii–xxi.

109. Bennett Harrison, "Comment of a Radical Economist," in *Public Service Employment*, 120.

110. Frank Riessman, "Can Services Be Humane in this Society?" in *Public Service Employment*. Riessman here addressed himself to Frances Fox Piven and Richard Cloward, who had argued in the 1960s for "stressing" the inadequate social welfare system to pressure the government to build a better one. Piven and Cloward returned to these questions of strategy in *Poor People's Movements: Why They Succeed, How They Fail* (New York: Vintage, 1978).

111. Frank Riessman, "Can Services Be Humane in This Society?"

112. Stein, "This Nation Has Never Honestly Dealt with the Question of a Peacetime Economy."

113. Frances Fox Piven, "Public Service Employment: Vision or Reality," in *Public Service Employment*, 220.

114. Piven, "Public Service Employment," 220–21.

115. Patrick J. McGuinn, *No Child Left Behind and the Transformation of Federal Education Policy, 1965–2005* (Lawrence: University Press of Kansas, 2006), 41–42.

116. CSB 3 v. BOE, 1970, Isaiah Robinson Files, BOE Series 378, Box 12, Folder 12; El Museo Del Barrio, "History and Timeline," https://www.elmuseo.org/about/history-mission/

117. "A Look at 66 Funded Projects, 1976." RG 441 General Records of the Department of Education, Office of Elementary and Secondary Education, Elementary and Secondary Education Act Program Records, Box 14, Title III, ESEA, Part E, Folder 2, Grant Projects, NARA.

118. "A Look at 66 Funded Projects, 1976."

119. "A Look at 66 Funded Projects, 1976."

120. O'Connor, *Poverty Knowledge*, 188.

121. McGuinn, *No Child Left Behind*, 34; Nelson, *The Elusive Ideal*.

122. McGuinn, *No Child Left Behind*, 35.

123. McGuinn, *No Child Left Behind*, 40.

124. Nelson, *The Elusive Ideal*.

125. Goldenback, "Teaching Career Aspirations of Monolingual and Bilingual Paraprofessionals."

126. "History of the IDEA," Individuals with Disabilities Education Act Website, US Department of Education, https://sites.ed.gov/idea/about-idea/#IDEA-History.

127. Shelvy Young-Abrams, interview with the author.

128. "Guide to the Selection of Afram's Services for Follow Through Projects," May 1, 1971, PWP Box 30, Folder 1; "Parent Implementation in Follow Through, July 1, 1972–June 30, 1973," PWP Box 30, Folder 4.

129. Action Stimulator #50: Title I Parents Participation in Evaluation, March 1971, PWP Box 30, Folder 3 (Wilcox argued, "Para-professionals, who are both 'poverty parents' and paid workers in schools are in a unique position to evaluate and monitor programs. Their experience and judgment could be valuable to other parent members."); *Afram as Mirror to Follow Through Parents*; Action Stimulator #52: The Cost of Parent Participation, March 2, 1971, PWP Box 30,

Folder 3; "Idea Stimulator No. 8: A Parent Library," January 12, 1972, PWP Box 30, Folder 4.

130. PPFT, "Action Stimulator 46: Trust Building Procedures," December 22, 1970, PWP Box 30, Folder 1; "Thought Stimulator #95: The Role of the Follow Through Project Directors," October 9, 1970, PWP Box 30, Folder 3.

131. "A Handbook for Parents: Make the Public Schools Work for You," from Freedom Through Equality, Inc., and Milwaukee Legal Services, Inc., September 1973, PWP Box 4, Folder 2; "Education Materials" from The Federation of Southern Cooperatives, PWP Box 30, Folder 1. For more on the Milwaukee struggle that produced this handbook, see Dougherty, *More Than One Struggle*.

132. "What Happened In St. Louis?"

133. The Hampton Experience: Afram Community Conference, Parent Implementation in Follow Through, Hampton Institute, Hampton, VA, May 9–11, 1973, PWP Box 30, Folder 5.

134. Continuation Proposal 1974–1975, PWP Box 31, Folder 1.

135. Continuation Proposal 1974–1975; Continuation Proposal 1973, PWP Box 30, Folder 7.

136. Letter from Preston Wilcox to Richard Snyder, Chief of Research and Evaluation for Follow Through for the Stanford Research Institute, February 24, 1971, PWP Box 30, Folder 1.

137. Funding Proposal, 1971, Sen. Walter Mondale, Chair of the Select Committee for Equal Educational Opportunity, PWP Box 30, Folder 3.

138. US Office of Education draft of the "National Evaluation of Follow Through for Local Communities," July 27, 1971, PWP Box 30, Folder 1.

139. On the ways in which changing regimes of study and evaluation shaped the War on Poverty and its aftermath, see O'Connor, *Poverty Knowledge*.

140. "Strategies for Parent Participation," November 10, 1970, PWP Box 30, Folder 1.

141. Stanford Research Institute Report, PWP Box 30, Folder 1.

142. Letter from Preston Wilcox to Richard Snyder, February 24, 1971.

143. "National Evaluation of Follow Through for Local Communities," July 27, 1971, PWP Box 30, Folder 1.

144. Parents as Community Educators: Continuation Proposal 1974–75, PWP Box 31, Folder 1.

145. *Afram as Mirror to Follow Through Parents*.

146. Kaplan, *From Aide to Teacher*, 117

147. Kaplan, *From Aide to Teacher*, 118.

148. Kaplan, *From Aide to Teacher*, 125.

149. Kaplan, *From Aide to Teacher*, 43.

150. Kaplan, *From Aide to Teacher*, 10–11.

151. Kaplan, *From Aide to Teacher*, 3.

152. Kaplan, *From Aide to Teacher*, 10–11.

153. O'Connor, *Poverty Knowledge*, 188.

154. Continuation Proposal: Parents as Community Developers, 1975–76 School Year, PWP Box 31, Folder 2.

155. Continuation Proposal: Parents as Community Developers.

156. Handwritten sheet accompanying report of 1975, PWP Box 31, Folder 7.

157. Wilcox, "Parental Decision-Making."

158. Nero and Associates Report on Follow Through, 1975, PWP Box 30, Folder 6.

159. Humanizer 191: Teaching Ourselves to Teach, March 18, 1974, PWP Box 31, Folder 7.

Chapter 7. "Mayor Koch, Meet a Workaholic"

1. Soffer, *Ed Koch and the Rebuilding of New York City.*

2. Soffer, *Ed Koch and the Rebuilding of New York City.*

3. Marcia Chambers, "Koch's Budget Unit Urges Closing of 15 Schools, Higher Lunch Fees," *New York Times,* January 4, 1979.

4. Letter from Ed Koch to Frank Macchiarola, January 4, 1979, Stephen R. Aiello Files, BOE Series 311, Box 15, Folder 157; Albert Shanker,"Where We Stand: Some Cuts Are More Stupid Than Others," paid advertisement, *New York Times,* September 19, 1976.

5. Shelvy Young-Abrams, interview with the author, September 5, 2014.

6. "Mayor Koch, Meet a Workaholic," United Federation of Teachers Photographs (PHOTOS.019), Tamiment Library/Robert F. Wagner Labor Archives, New York University, New York, NY.

7. Soffer, *Ed Koch and the Rebuilding of New York City.*

8. On the rise of individualized econometric analyses of poverty policy, see O'Connor, *Poverty Knowledge.* On the racialized attack on welfare, see, among many others, Katz, *The Undeserving Poor*; Kornbluh, *The Battle for Welfare Rights*; Nadasen, *Welfare Warriors.* On attacks on public-sector workers, see Berger, *A New Working Class.*

9. Phillips-Fein, *Fear City.*

10. Freeman, *Working-Class New York,* 183.

11. Woodsworth, *Battle for Bed-Stuy,* 135.

12. U.S. Census Bureau, Occupational Data, 1950–1980. Prepared by Social Explorer. Accessed May 2016.

13. Berger, *A New Working Class*; Katz and Stern, "The New African-American Inequality"; Williams, *The Politics of Public Housing.*

14. Woodsworth, *Battle for Bed-Stuy,* 135.

15. Seymour P. Lachman and Robert Polner, *The Man Who Saved New York: Hugh Carey and the Great Fiscal Crisis of 1975* (Albany: State University of New York Press, 2010), 94.

16. Lachman and Polner, *The Man Who Saved New York,* 96.

17. Freeman, *Working-Class New York,* 256.

18. Freeman, *Working-Class New York.*

19. "Thousands of Blacks Facing Loss of Jobs," *New York Amsterdam News,* May 7, 1975.

20. "Thousands of Blacks Facing Loss of Jobs."

21. "Thousands of Blacks Facing Loss of Jobs."

22. "Harlem Takes to the Streets in the Battle of the Budget," *New York Amsterdam News,* July 2, 1975.

23. "Head of Schools Fears Peril in Classroom," *Village Voice,* July 16, 1975.

24. Freeman, *Working-Class New York,* 262.

25. Draft Report, 1974–1975 School Year, UFT Box 80, Folder 13.

26. "800 Paraprofessionals Honored by UFT for Earning Degrees," *New York Times,* April 19, 1975.

27. Velma Hill, Interviewed by Renee Epstein.

28. Shanker in *New York* Teacher, reprinted in TAC Newsletter, May 1975, AFP Box 1, Folder 8.

29. The Teacher Action Caucus, while never big enough to challenge the UFT's leadership in citywide elections, controlled or influenced clusters of schools around the city at the chapter level, including several on the Upper West Side in District Three that are discussed in Chapter 4. For additional information on the TAC, see Perlstein, *Justice, Justice.*

30. TAC Newsletter, May 1975, AFP Box 1, Folder 8.

31. Albert Shanker, "Where We Stand: Will the Schools be Open on Tuesday?" *New York Times,* September 7, 1975.

32. Shanker, "Where We Stand: Will the Schools Open on Tuesday?"

33. "4500 Teachers to be Laid Off in Month," *New York Times,* September 13, 1975.

34. On rank-and-file demands that Shanker fight austerity more aggressively, see Lois Weiner, *The Future of Our Schools: Teachers Unions and Social Justice* (Chicago: Haymarket Books, 2012), Chapter 7.

35. Freeman, *Working-Class New York,* 265; Lachman and Polner, *The Man Who Saved New York,* 138.

36. Shanker, "Where We Stand: Will the Schools be Open on Tuesday?"

37. "Board and UFT Near Agreement in School Strike," *New York Times,* September 11, 1975.

38. "Why We Strike," UFT Flyer, AFP Box 1, Folder 9. On the class size issue in the 1962 contract, see Murphy, *Blackboard Unions*; Leonora Farber, interview with the author, January 18, 2014.

39. Albert Shanker to UFT Membership, September 15, 1975, AFP Box 1, Folder 9.

40. "U.S Agrees to Give City Enough Funds to Re-Employ 2,000," *New York Times,* October 11, 1975.

41. Albert Shanker to UFT Membership, September 15, 1975.

42. "No One Goes Back Till We All Go Back," TAC Flyer, September 1975, AFP Box 1, Folder 9.

43. Lachman and Polner, *The Man Who Saved New York,* 144.

44. Village Voice Clipping, September 29, 1975, AFP Box 1, Folder 9.

45. "Harlem Parents and Educators Unite for Better Education," *New York Amsterdam News,* January 10, 1976.

46. "Harlem Parents and Educators Unite for Better Education." By invoking the "image" of parent educators in schools and its impact on children, this new

committee re-asserted the goal of desegregating school staff and establishing relatable role models through local hiring.

47. "Harlem Parents and Educators Unite for Better Education."

48. "NYABE Gives NAACP $4,000," *New York Amsterdam News,* October 23, 1976.

49. "Rights Panel Finds Layoffs by City Hurt Minorities," *New York Times,* April 15, 1976.

50. New York City Commission on Human Rights, "City Layoffs: The Effect on Minorities and Women," April 1976, https://www.ojp.gov/ncjrs/virtual-library/abstracts/city-layoffs-effect-minorities-and-women.

51. New York City Commission on Human Rights, "City Layoffs."

52. "Paraprofessionals Form Committee to Confront UFT," *New York Amsterdam News,* October 22, 1975.

53. "Paraprofessionals Form Committee to Confront UFT."

54. Shelvy Young-Abrams, interview with the author, September 5, 2014.

55. "Trimming Frills from School Budget Is Seen by Some as Cutting Fiber of Life," *New York Times,* June 23, 1976.

56. "Trimming Frills from School Budget."

57. Borrowing from economist Nancy Folbre, Jennifer Gaddis describes school food workers as trapped in a "prison of love" by the ways their genuine care is exploited on the job. Gaddis, *The Labor of Lunch,* Chapter 4.

58. Letter from Shanker to CUNY-PTEP, October 6, 1975, UFT Box 80, Folder 13.

59. Marian Thom, interview with the author, September 3, 2013.

60. Memo to Deputy Chancellor Bernard Gifford and BOE from Frank C. Arricale, II, May 28, 1976. Amelia Ashe Files, BOE Series 312, Box 45, Folder 559: Paraprofessionals—Rules and Regulations.

61. Shanker to Board, June 16, 1976, Amelia Ashe Files, BOE Series 312, Box 45, Folder 559.

62. John P. Finneran to Amelia Ashe (re: Shanker Letter), July 6, 1976, Amelia Ashe Files, BOE Box 45, Folder 559.

63. Telegram from Albert Shanker to Board, July 27, 1976, Amelia Ashe Files, BOE Box 45, Folder 559.

64. Telegram from Roxy Lott and Gloria Reddick of CTQE to Shanker, July 28, 1976, UFT Box 80, Folder 13; "Paraprofessionals Picket UFT," *New York Amsterdam News,* July 31, 1976.

65. Handwritten Flyer, "Support Concerned Paras for Quality Education," UFT Box 80, Folder 13.

66. "Union Paras Angry," *Civil Service Leader,* July 2, 1976, Clippings File, UFT Box 255, Folder 2.

67. *Para Scope* 2, No. 5 (June 1976), UFT Box 80, Folder 13.

68. *Para Scope* 2, No. 5.

69. Velma Murphy Hill to Paraprofessional Representatives, July 23, 1976, UFT Box 80, Folder 13.

70. "School Year Begins in New York with Numerous Signs of Cutbacks," *New York Times,* September 14, 1976.

71. Albert Shanker, "Where We Stand: Some Cuts are More Stupid Than Others," *New York Times,* September 19, 1976 (Shanker's "Where We Stand" column ran as a paid advertisement on Sundays).

72. Decision in Grievance, October 26, 1976, UFT Box 80, Folder 13.

73. "School Board Loses Arbitration on Pact: It Is Told to Pay Paraprofessionals for Training Despite Program's Removal from City's Budget," *New York Times,* October 29, 1976.

74. *Para Scope,* January 1977, UFT Box 149, Folder 30.

75. TAC Flyer: Ewart Guinier, December 10, 1976, AFP Box 2, Folder 1. For more on Guinier's fascinating trajectory from radical labor leader with the United Public Workers of America to Black Studies pioneer at Harvard, see Biondi, *The Black Revolution on Campus.*

76. Freeman, *Working-Class New York,* 270–72.

77. Velma Hill, Interviewed by Renee Epstein.

78. Clarence Taylor, interview with the author, February 11, 2015.

79. On "corporatism" in the municipal sector, see Freeman, *Working-Class New York,* 269–70; and Michael Spear, "In the Shadows of the 1970s Fiscal Crisis: New York City's Municipal Unions in the Twenty-First Century," *WorkingUSA: The Journal of Labor and Society* 13 (September 2010), 353–56.

80. William L. Hamilton "On Higher Education," *New York Amsterdam News,* July 24, 1976.

81. Frances Fox Piven, interview with the author, September 10, 2014.

82. Soffer, *Ed Koch and the Rebuilding of New York City.*

83. Telegram from Edward I. Koch to Board of Education, December 27, 1972, UFT Box 80, Folder 12.

84. Shanker, "Where We Stand: Some Cuts are More Stupid Than Others."

85. Young-Abrams, interview.

86. "I Love New York, Mayor Koch," *New York Amsterdam News,* March 10, 1979.

87. Marian Chin and Victor Vasquez, UFT Photographs.

88. "UFT Fights for Salaries," *New York Amsterdam News,* September 1, 1979.

89. Albert Shanker, "Where We Stand," *New York Times,* January 20, 1980.

90. New York Teacher photo, March 5, 1980, UFT Photos.

91. "Cuomo Signs Pension Bills Opposed by Koch as Costly," *New York Times,* August 13, 1983.

92. Abby Goodnough, "Teachers' Unions Sues Klein, Claiming Bias in Layoffs of Aides," *New York Times,* May 6, 2003, http://www.nytimes.com/2003/05/06/nyregion/teachers-union-sues-klein-claiming-bias-in-layoffs-of-aides.html.

93. McGuinn, *No Child Left Behind,* 41–42; Tamar W. Carroll, *Mobilizing New York: AIDS, Antipoverty, and Feminist Activism* (Chapel Hill: University of North Carolina Press, 2015).

94. "A Year of Survival," AFT National Conference of Paraprofessionals, UFT Box 210, Folder 8. On the air traffic controllers' strike and its chilling effect on the labor movement, and particularly the public-sector labor movement, see Joseph A. McCartin, *Collision Course: Ronald Reagan, the Air Traffic Controllers, and the Strike That Changed America,* Reprint edition (Oxford University Press, 2013).

95. Michael Glass, "Schooling Suburbia: The Politics of School Finance in Postwar Long Island" (PhD diss., Princeton University, 2020); Kelly Goodman, "Tax the Rich: Teachers' Long Campaign to Fund Public Schools" (PhD diss., Yale University, 2021).

96. Quinn, "Unequal Work in Unequal Schools," 35. Detailed data available through the Bureau of Labor Statistics and the National Center for Education Statistics.

97. O'Connor, *Poverty Knowledge*, 177–80.

98. Nelson, *The Elusive Ideal*; Cohen Moffitt, *The Ordeal of Equality*.

99. UFT Bulletin/New York Teacher, "Jose E. Serrano: From UFT Para to Top Assembly Post," May 1, 1983, UFT Box 255, Folder 2.

100. "School to Cite Black Parent for Unity Efforts," *New York Times*, February 13, 1975.

101. Soffer, *Ed Koch and the Rebuilding of New York City*; Joel Klein, "The Failure of American Schools," *The Atlantic*, June 2011, https://www.theatlantic.com/magazine/archive/2011/06/the-failure-of-american-schools/308497/.

102. Lewis, *New York City Public Schools from Brownsville to Bloomberg*, 2013.

103. Robert D. McFadden, "Jury Acquits 3 in the Removal of School Piano," *New York Times*, March 16, 1990, http://www.nytimes.com/1990/03/16/nyregion/jury-acquits-3-in-the-removal-of-school-piano.html.

104. H. Paul Friesema, "Black Control of Central Cities: The Hollow Prize," *Journal of the American Institute of Planners* 35, no. 2 (March 1, 1969): 75–79, https://doi.org/10.1080/01944366908977576; Neil Kraus and Todd Swanstrom, "Minority Mayors and the Hollow-Prize Problem," *PS: Political Science and Politics* 34, no. 1 (March 1, 2001): 99–105; Twyla Blackmond Larnell and Michael Thom, "How Hollow Is the Prize? Minority Mayors and State Government Intervention in Municipal Finance," SSRN Scholarly Paper (Rochester, NY: Social Science Research Network, November 6, 2013), http://papers.ssrn.com/abstract=2350878.

105. Letter from Sandra Feldman to Paraprofessional Chapter, May 16, 1980, UFT Box 172, Folder 50.

106. Paraprofessionals: Project PRESS, 1981, UFT Box 80, Folder 16.

107. UFT bulletin, "Yes, I Can: The Triumph of the UFT's Classroom Paraprofessionals," March 14, 1988, UFT Box 255, Folder 2.

108. Taylor, interview.

109. Goldenback, "Teaching Career Aspirations."

110. Goldenback, "Teaching Career Aspirations."

111. Joseph Berger, "Plan for Schools on Minority Hiring," *New York Times*, February 16, 1990.

112. Berger, "Plan for Schools on Minority Hiring."

113. Joseph Berger, "School Boards Said to Pad Their Payrolls," *New York Times*, March 14, 1990.

114. Fred M. Hechinger, "About Education: Educators Try to Make Homeless Children Comfortable in School," *New York Times*, March 14, 1990.

115. Joseph Berger, "New York City Schools Face $62.3 Million Budget Cut," *New York Times*, July 28, 1990.

116. Joseph Berger, "The Schoolteacher as Budgetary Sacrificial Lamb," *New York Times*, November 18, 1990.

117. Joseph Berger, "Teachers to Defer Wages in New York," *New York Times*, January 26, 1991.

118. Catherine White Berheide et al., "A Pay Equity Analysis of Female-Dominated and Disproportionately Minority New York State Job Titles," *Humanity & Society* 11, no. 4 (November 1, 1987): 465–85; Catherine White Berheide, "Women Still 'Stuck' in Low-Level Jobs," *Women in Public Service* 3 (Fall 1992).

119. "At Work," *New York Times*, November 22, 1992; Catherine Berheide, "Sticky Floor," in Vicki Smith, *Sociology of Work: An Encyclopedia* (Thousand Oaks, CA: SAGE Publications, Inc., 2013).

120. Jennifer Medina, "Budget Ax Threatens 3,200 School Workers," *New York Times*, April 9, 2003, http://www.nytimes.com/2003/04/09/nyregion/budget-ax-threatens-3200-school-workers.html.

121. Lewis, *New York City Public Schools from Brownsville to Bloomberg*.

122. Klein, "The Failure of American Schools."

123. Medina, "Budget Ax Threatens 3,200 School Workers."

124. Medina, "Budget Ax Threatens 3,200 School Workers."

125. Goodnough, "Teachers' Union Sues Klein."

126. Goodnough, "Teachers' Union Sues Klein."

127. Goodnough, "Teachers' Union Sues Klein."

128. Goodnough, "Teachers' Union Sues Klein."

129. Klein, "The Failure of American Schools."

130. Goodnough, "Teachers' Union Sues Klein."

131. O'Connor, *Poverty Knowledge*.

132. Nelson, *The Elusive Ideal*; Cohen and Moffitt, *The Ordeal of Equality*.

133. Cohen and Moffitt, *The Ordeal of Equality*.

134. Cohen and Moffitt, *The Ordeal of Equality*.

135. In describing the transformation of segregated places to spaces of empowerment, I borrow from Zaheer Ali's reading of Michel de Certeau in "Malcolm X in Brooklyn," *Black Perspectives*, February 20, 2017, http://www.aaihs.org/malcolm-x-in-brooklyn.

Epilogue. Paraprofessional Educators on the Front Lines, Once Again

1. Bureau of Labor Statistics, Occupational Employment and Wage Statistics, May 2023: 25–9045 Teaching Assistants, Except Postsecondary, https://www.bls.gov/oes/current/oes259045.htm.

2. Bisht, LeClair, Loeb, and Sun, "Paraeducators"; Quinn and Ferree, "Schools as Workplaces"; Madeline Will, "Paraprofessionals: As the 'Backbones' of the Classroom, They Get Low Pay, Little Support," *Education Week*, June 15, 2022, https://www.edweek.org/leadership/paraprofessionals-as-the-backbones-of-the-classroom-they-get-low-pay-little-support/2022/06.

3. Boris and Klein, *Caring for America*; Dunning, "New Careers for the Poor"; Fraser, "Contradictions of Capital and Care"; Winant, *The Next Shift*.

4. Marian Thom, interview with the author, September 3, 2013.

5. Pawlewicz, *Blaming Teachers*; Shelton, *Teacher Strike!*

6. See Casey, *The Teacher Insurgency*, Chapter 10; Perrillo, *Uncivil Rights*, Chapter 7.

7. James W. Fraser and Lauren Lefty, *Teaching Teachers: Changing Paths and Enduring Debates* (Baltimore: Johns Hopkins University Press, 2018).

8. McGuinn, *No Child Left Behind*.

9. Harold Meyerson, "If Labor Dies, What Next?" *The American Prospect*, September 13, 2012.

10. Tom Alter, "'It Felt Like Community'"; Micah Uetricht, *Strike for America: Chicago Teachers against Austerity* (New York: Verso, 2012).

11. "Defending Public Education: An Interview with Karen Lewis of the Chicago Teachers Union," *Dissent* 60, no. 3 (Summer 2013).

12. Cecily Myart-Cruz and Alex Caputo-Pearl, "The LA Strike: Learning Together to Build the National Movement We Need," in Givan and Lang, eds., *Strike for the Common Good*; BTU for All Platform (accessed January 18, 2022), https://btuforall.com/new-blog-1.

13. Casey, *The Teacher Insurgency*; Eric Blanc, *Red State Revolt: The Teachers' Strike Wave and Working-Class Politics* (New York: Verso, 2019); Givan and Lang, eds., *Strike for the Common Good*, Section II: Red States Rising.

14. Myart-Cruz and Caputo-Pearl, "The LA Strike"; Alexia Fernández Campbell, "The 11-Day Teachers Strike in Chicago Paid Off," *Vox*, November 1, 2019, https://www.vox.com/identities/2019/11/1/20943464/chicago-teachers-strike-deal.

15. Coleman and Keyes, "Recruiting the Talent Within."

16. James Paterson, "Education Support Professionals Campaign for a 'Bill of Rights,'" *NEA Today*, November 10, 2022, https://www.nea.org/nea-today/all-news-articles/education-support-professionals-campaign-bill-rights, See also Maryland State Education Association, ESP Bill of Rights, https://marylandeducators.org/education-support-professional-bill-of-rights/; Massachusetts Teacher Association, ESP Bill of Rights, https://massteacher.org/about-the-mta/who-we-are/esp/esp-bill-of-rights; Education Minnesota, Education Support Professionals Bill of Rights, https://educationminnesota.org/wp-content/uploads/2021/07/ESP-Bill-of-Rights-Handout.pdf.

17. Dan DiMaggio, "In the Pacific Northwest, the First Paraeducator-Led Strike of the Teacher Uprising," *Labor Notes*, November 16, 2018, https://labornotes.org/2018/11/pacific-northwest-first-paraeducator-led-strike-teacher-uprising; Tricia Masenthin, "Lawrence School Board Approves PAL-CWA Contract," *Lawrence Times*, October 24, 2021.

18. Elizabeth Shockman and Andrew Krueger, "Deal Reached To End Minneapolis Teachers Strike," *MPR News*, March 25, 2022, https://www.mprnews.org/story/2022/03/25/tentative-agreement-reached-to-end-minneapolis-educators-strike; Jeremy Margolis, "Teachers Union, Schools Agree on New Contract for Paraprofessionals," *Brookline.News*, July 1, 2023, https://brookline.news/teachers-union-schools-agree-on-new-contract-for-paraprofessionals/.

19. On Bargaining for the Common Good, see https://www.bargainingforthecommongood.org.

20. Quinn and Ferree, "Schools as Workplaces."

21. Stuart Hall, "Gramsci's Relevance for the Study of Race and Ethnicity," *Journal of Communication Inquiry* 10 (1986). As I have argued elsewhere, Hall's essay is essential reading for all those who seek what Hall, following from his reading of Antonio Gramsci, calls a "dynamic historical analytic framework" for activism in historical periods when retrenchment and backlash are ascendant (including the post-1968 urban United States). On this point, see also Michael Denning, *The Cultural Front: The Laboring of American Culture in the Twentieth Century* (New York: Verso, 1997), 37.

Bibliography

Archival Collections

American Federation of Teachers Local 691, Kansas City Federation of Teachers Records, Walter P. Reuther Library, Wayne State University, Detroit, MI.

American Federation of Teachers, Office of the President Collection, Walter P. Reuther Library, Wayne State University, Detroit, MI.

American Federation of Teachers, Office of the President Collection, Albert Shanker Papers, Walter P. Reuther Library, Wayne State University, Detroit, MI.

American Federation of Teachers Inventory, Walter P. Reuther Library, Wayne State University, Detroit, MI.

American Federation of Teachers Oral Histories, Walter P. Reuther Library, Wayne State University, Detroit, MI.

American Federation of Teachers Records, Office of the President Collection, David Selden Papers, Walter P. Reuther Library, Wayne State University, Detroit, MI.

Anne Filardo Papers on Rank and File Activism in the American Federation of Teachers and in the United Federation of Teachers (TAM 141), Tamiment Library/Robert F. Wagner Labor Archives, New York University, New York, NY.

Annie Stein Papers, Columbia University Rare Book and Manuscript Library, New York, NY.

Archives of the Women's Talent Corps, College for Human Services, and Audrey Cohen College, Metropolitan College of New York, New York, NY. *This collection is organized solely in folders; there are no boxes.*

Bank Street College of Education Archives, New York, NY.

Boston Teachers Union Collection, University Archives and Special Collections, Healey Library, University of Massachusetts Boston.

Congressman James H. Scheuer Papers, Swarthmore College, Swarthmore, PA.

Ellen Lurie Papers, Center for Puerto Rican Studies, Hunter College, New York, NY.

Massachusetts Federation of Teachers Records, Walter P. Reuther Library, Wayne State University, Detroit, MI.

Morningside Area Alliance Records, Columbia University Archives, New York, NY.

National Education Association Papers, George Washington University, Washington, DC.

Office of Education Records, National Archives, College Park, MD.

Preston Wilcox Papers, Schomburg Center for Research in Black Culture, New York Public Library, New York, NY.

Records of the Board of Education of the City of New York, Municipal Archives of New York City, New York, NY.

Records of the United Bronx Parents, Center for Puerto Rican Studies, Hunter College, New York, NY.

Richard Parrish Papers, Schomburg Center for Research in Black Culture, New York Public Library, New York, NY.

Springfield (MA) Federation of Teachers Records, Walter P. Reuther Library, Wayne State University, Detroit, MI.

Union Settlement Association Records, Columbia University Rare Book and Manuscript Library, New York, NY.

United Educators of San Francisco Local 61 Records, Walter P. Reuther Library, Wayne State University, Detroit, MI.

United Federation of Teachers Records (WAG 022), Tamiment Library/Robert F. Wagner Labor Archives, New York University, New York, NY.

United Federation of Teachers Oral History Collection (OH 009), Tamiment Library/Robert F. Wagner Labor Archives, New York University, New York, NY.

Periodical Sources

American Teacher
Baltimore Afro-American
Boston Union Teacher
Career Opportunities Bulletin
El Diario
El Tiempo
Milwaukee Journal
New York Amsterdam News
New York Teacher
New York Times

Oral Histories Conducted by the Author
(transcripts, notes, and/or audio available upon request)

Louise Burwell, October 22, 2013
Oneida Davis, September 3, 2014
Mary Dowery, January 30, 2014
Virginia Eng, September 10, 2013
Leonora Farber, January 18, 2014
Alan Gartner, March 21, 2013
Aurelia Greene, July 24 and August 27, 2014
Velma Murphy Hill, November 7, 2011
Hope Leichter, October 23, 2014
Maggie Martin, February 2, 2015
Alida Mesrop, January 28, 2015
Lorraine Montenegro, September 24, 2014
Laura Pires-Hester (today Laura Pires-Houston), March 9, 2015
Clarence Taylor, February 11, 2015
Marian Thom, September 3, 2013
Jacqueline Watkins, August 29, 2014
Shelvy Young-Abrams, September 5, 2014

Published Works

Aguiar, Gretchen. "Head Start: A History of Implementation." PhD diss., University of Pennsylvania, 2012.

Ali, Zaheer. "Malcolm X in Brooklyn," *Black Perspectives,* February 20, 2017. http://www.aaihs.org/malcolm-x-in-brooklyn/.

Almash, Francine. "New York City '600' Schools and the Legacy of Segregation in Special Education," *Gotham: A Blog for Scholars of New York City History,* June 21, 2022. https://www.gothamcenter.org/blog/new-york-city-600-schools -and-the-legacy-of-segregation-in-special-education.

Almonte, Ronnie. "Richard Parrish, the Black Caucus, and the 1968 Ocean Hill–Brownsville strikes." *International Socialist Review* 111 (Winter 2018–19). https://isreview.org/issue/111/richard-parrish-black-caucus-and-1968-ocean -hill-brownsville-strikes/index.html.

Alter, Tom. "'It Felt Like Community': Social Movement Unionism and the Chicago Teachers Union Strike of 2012." *Labor* 10, no. 3 (September 21, 2013): 11–25.

Anderson, James D. *The Education of Blacks in the South, 1860–1935.* Chapel Hill: University of North Carolina Press, 1988.

Averbeck, Robin Marie. "The Other Riessman." *U.S. Intellectual History Blog,* February 26, 2015. https://s-usih.org/2015/02/the-other-riessman.

Baldwin, Davarian. *In The Shadow of the Ivory Tower: How Universities Are Plundering Our Cities.* New York: Bold Type Books, 2021.

Bay, Mia E., Farah J. Griffin, Martha S. Jones, and Barbara D. Savage, eds. *Toward an Intellectual History of Black Women*. Chapel Hill: University of North Carolina Press, 2015.

Berger, Jane. A. "'A Lot Closer to What It Ought To Be': Black Women and Public Sector Employment in Baltimore, 1950–1970." In *Life and Labor in the New New South*, edited by Robert Zieger. Gainesville: University of Florida Press, 2012.

Berger, Jane A. "When Hard Work Doesn't Pay: Gender and the Urban Crisis in Baltimore, 1945–1985." PhD diss., Ohio State University, 2007.

Berger, Jane A. *A New Working Class: The Legacies of Public-Sector Employment in the Civil Rights Movement*. Philadelphia: University of Pennsylvania Press, 2021.

Bennett, William S. *New Careers and Urban Schools: A Sociological Study of Teacher and Teacher Aide Roles*. New York: Holt, Rinehart and Winston, 1970.

Benson, Richard D., II, *Fighting for Our Place in the Sun: Malcolm X and the Radicalization of the Black Student Movement, 1965–1974*. New York: Peter Lang, 2015.

Biondi, Martha. *To Stand and Fight: The Struggle for Civil Rights in Postwar New York City*. Cambridge, MA: Harvard University Press, 2003.

Biondi, Martha. *The Black Revolution on Campus*. Berkeley: University of California Press, 2012.

Bisht, Biraj, Zachary LeClair, Susanna Loeb, and Min Sun. "Paraeducators: Growth, Diversity and a Dearth of Professional Supports." *EdWorkingPaper*: 21–490 (2021). Retrieved from Annenberg Institute at Brown University: https://doi.org/10.26300/nk1z-c164.

Blanc, Paul Le, and Michael D. Yates. *A Freedom Budget for All Americans: Recapturing the Promise of the Civil Rights Movement in the Struggle for Economic Justice Today*. New York: Monthly Review Press, 2013.

Bonastia, Christopher. *The Battle Nearer to Home: The Persistence of School Segregation in New York City*. Stanford, CA: Stanford University Press, 2022.

Boris, Eileen, and Jennifer Klein. *Caring for America: Home Health Workers in the Shadow of the Welfare State*. New York: Oxford University Press, 2012.

Bowman, Garda W., and Gordon John Klopf. *New Careers and Roles in the American School*. New York: Bank Street College, 1968.

Bowman, Garda W., and Gordon John Klopf. *New Partners in the Educational Enterprise: Report of Phase One of a Study of Auxiliary Personnel in Education*. New York: Bank Street College of Education, 1967.

Bradley, Stefan. "'Gym Crow Must Go!': Black Student Activism at Columbia University, 1967–1968." *Journal of African American History* 88, no. 2 (Spring 2003): 163–81.

Brickell, Henry M., et al. *An In-Depth Study of Paraprofessionals in District Decentralized ESEA Title I and New York State Urban Education Projects in the New York City Schools*. New York: Institute for Educational Development, 1971.

Brilliant, Mark. *The Color of America Has Changed: How Racial Diversity Shaped*

Civil Rights Reform in California, 1941–1978. New York: Oxford University Press, 2009.

Brown-Nagin, Tomiko. *Courage to Dissent: Atlanta and the Long History of the Civil Rights Movement*. Oxford, UK: Oxford University Press, 2011.

Bundy, McGeorge, ed. *Reconnection for Learning: A Community School System for New York City*. New York: Mayor's Advisory Panel on the Decentralization of Schools, 1967.

Carmichael, Stokely, and Charles V. Hamilton. *Black Power: The Politics of Liberation*. New York: Random House, 1967.

Carroll, Tamar W. *Mobilizing New York: AIDS, Antipoverty, and Feminist Activism*. Chapel Hill: University of North Carolina Press, 2015.

Casey, Leo. *The Teacher Insurgency: A Strategic and Organizing Perspective*. Cambridge, MA: Harvard Education Press, 2020.

Cazenave, Noel E. *Impossible Democracy: The Unlikely Success of the War on Poverty Community Action Program*. Albany: State University of New York Press, 2007.

Certeau, Michel de. *The Practice of Everyday Life*. Translated by Steven F. Rendall. Berkeley: University of California Press, 2011.

Chaney, Mahasan. "Discipline for the 'Educationally Deprived': ESEA and the Punitive Function of Federal Education Policy 1965–1998." PhD diss., University of California, 2019.

Chappell, Marisa. *The War on Welfare: Family, Poverty, and Politics in Modern America*. Philadelphia: University of Pennsylvania Press, 2011.

Chowkwanyun, Merlin. *All Health Politics Is Local: Community Battles for Medical Care and Environmental Health*. Chapel Hill: University of North Carolina Press, 2022.

Clark, Kenneth. *Dark Ghetto: Dilemmas of Social Power*. New York: Harper & Row, 1965.

Coad, James Robert. "A Descriptive Survey of Teacher Aide Programs in Selected Cook County, Illinois, Elementary School Districts." Ed.D. diss., Indiana University, 1970.

Cohen, David K., and Susan L. Moffitt. *The Ordeal of Equality: Did Federal Regulation Fix the Schools?* Cambridge, MA: Harvard University Press, 2009.

Cohen, Miriam. "Reconsidering Schools and the American Welfare State." *History of Education Quarterly* 45, no. 4 (Winter 2005).

Coleman, LeShawna, and Gemayel Keyes. "Recruiting the Talent Within: Philadelphia's Paraprofessional-to-Teacher Pipeline." *American Educator* (Winter 2022–2023). https://www.aft.org/ae/winter2022-2023/coleman_keyes.

Collins, Christina. *"Ethnically Qualified": Race, Merit, and the Selection of Urban Teachers, 1920–1980*. New York: Teachers College Press, 2011.

Collins, Patricia Hill. *Black Feminist Thought: Knowledge, Consciousness and the Politics of Empowerment*. New York: Routledge, 1991.

Connor, David J., and Beth A. Ferri, "Introduction to DSQ Special Issue: 'Why Is There Learning Disabilities?'—Revisiting Christine Sleeter's Socio-Political

Construction of Disability Two Decades On." *Disability Studies Quarterly* 30, no. 2 (April 9, 2010), https://doi.org/10.18061/dsq.v30i2.1229.

Cowie, Jefferson R. *Stayin' Alive: The 1970s and the Last Days of the Working Class*. New York: The New Press, 2012.

Cutler, William W. *Parents and Schools: The 150-Year Struggle for Control in American Education*. Chicago: University of Chicago Press, 2000.

D'Amico, Diana. "Claiming Profession: The Dynamic Struggle for Teacher Professionalism in the Twentieth Century." PhD diss., New York University, 2010.

D'Amico, Diana. "Teachers' Rights Versus Students' Rights: Race and Professional Authority in the New York City Public Schools, 1960–1986." *American Educational Research Journal* 53, no. 3 (June 1, 2016): 541–72.

Decade of Experiment: The Fund for the Advancement of Education, 1951–61. New York: The Ford Foundation, 1961.

Delmont, Matthew F. *Why Busing Failed: Race, Media, and the National Resistance to School Desegregation*. Oakland: University of California Press, 2016.

Denning, Michael. *The Cultural Front: The Laboring of American Culture in the Twentieth Century*. New York: Verso, 1997.

Devine, John. *Maximum Security: The Culture of Violence in Inner-City Schools*. Chicago: University of Chicago Press, 1997.

Dougherty, Jack, and contributors. *On The Line: How Schooling, Housing, and Civil Rights Shaped Hartford and Its Suburbs*. Amherst: Amherst College Press, 2017. Digital book in progress, accessed March 13, 2017. http://ontheline.trincoll.edu.

Dougherty, Jack. *More Than One Struggle: The Evolution of Black School Reform in Milwaukee*. Chapel Hill: University of North Carolina Press, 2004.

Dunning, Claire. "New Careers for the Poor: Human Services and the Post-Industrial City." *Journal of Urban History* 44, no. 4 (July 2018).

Erickson, Ansley T. *Making the Unequal Metropolis: School Desegregation and Its Limits*. Chicago: University of Chicago Press, 2016.

Erickson, Ansley T., and Ernest Morrell, eds. *Educating Harlem: A Century of Schooling and Resistance in a Black Community*. New York: Columbia University Press, 2019.

Farmer, Ashley D. "'All the Progress to Be Made Will Be Made by Maladjusted Negroes': Mae Mallory, Black Women's Activism, and the Making of the Black Radical Tradition." *Journal of Social History* 53, no. 2 (November 2019).

Fernandez, Johanna. "The Young Lords and the Postwar City: Notes on the Geographical and Structural Reconfigurations of Contemporary Urban Life." In *African American Urban History Since World War II*, edited by Kenneth L. Kusmer and Joe W. Trotter. 60–82. Chicago: University of Chicago Press, 2009.

Fink, Leon, and Brian Greenberg. *Upheaval in the Quiet Zone: 1199SEIU and the Politics of Health Care Unionism*. 2nd ed. Urbana: University of Illinois Press, 2009.

Flamm, Michael W. *In the Heat of the Summer: The New York Riots of 1964 and the War on Crime*. Philadelphia: University of Pennsylvania Press, 2016.

Foley, Michael Stewart. *Front Porch Politics: The Forgotten Heyday of American Activism in the 1970s and 1980s*. New York: Hill and Wang, 2014.

Fraser, Nancy. "Contradictions of Capital and Care." *New Left Review* no. 100 (August 1, 2016). https://newleftreview.org/issues/ii100/articles/nancy-fraser -contradictions-of-capital-and-care.

Freeman, Joshua Benjamin. *Working-Class New York: Life and Labor since World War II*. New York: The New Press, 2000.

French-Marcelin, Megan, and Sarah Hinger. *Bullies in Blue: The Origins and Consequences of School Policing*. New York: American Civil Liberties Union, 2017.

Friesema, H. Paul. "Black Control of Central Cities: The Hollow Prize." *Journal of the American Institute of Planners* 35, no. 2 (March 1, 1969): 75–79.

Frymer, Paul. *Black and Blue: African Americans, the Labor Movement, and the Decline of the Democratic Party*. Princeton, NJ: Princeton University Press, 2009.

Gaddis, Jennifer E. *The Labor of Lunch: Why We Need Real Food and Real Jobs in American Public Schools*. Berkeley: University of California Press, 2019.

Gartner, Alan. *Paraprofessionals and Their Performance: A Survey of Education, Health, and Social Service Programs*. New York: Praeger, 1971.

Gartner, Alan, and Frank Riessman. "The Paraprofessional Movement in Perspective." *The Personnel and Guidance Journal* 53, no. 4 (December 1, 1974): 253–56.

Gartner, Alan, Frank Riessman, and Russell Nixon. *Public Service Employment: An Analysis of Its History, Problems, and Prospects*. New York: Praeger, 1973.

Gartner, Alan, Frank Riessman, and Vivian Carter Jackson. *Paraprofessionals Today: Volume I: Education*. New York: Human Sciences Press, 1977.

Gartner, Audrey J. "Biography of Frank Riessman." *The Journal of Applied Behavioral Science* 29, no. 2 (June 1, 1993): 148–50.

Gilkes, Cheryl Townsend. "Going Up for the Oppressed: The Career Mobility of Black Women Community Workers." *Journal of Social Issues* 39, no. 3 (Fall 1983): 115–39.

Gilkes, Cheryl Townsend. "Successful Rebellious Professionals: The Black Woman's Professional Identity and Community Commitment." *Psychology of Women Quarterly* 6, no. 3 (Spring 1982): 289.

Gilmore, Stephanie, ed. *Feminist Coalitions: Historical Perspectives on Second-Wave Feminism in the United States*. Urbana: University of Illinois Press, 2008.

Givan, Rebecca Kolins, and Amy Schrager Lang, eds. *Strike for the Common Good: Fighting for the Future of Public Education*. Ann Arbor: University of Michigan Press, 2021.

Glass, Michael R. "From Sword to Shield to Myth: Facing the Facts of De Facto School Segregation." *Journal of Urban History* (November 9, 2016).

Glass, Michael R. "Schooling Suburbia: The Politics of School Finance in Postwar Long Island." PhD diss., Princeton University, 2020.

Glenn, Evelyn Nakano. *Forced to Care: Coercion and Caregiving in America*. Cambridge, MA: Harvard University Press, 2010.

Gold, Roberta. *When Tenants Claimed the City: The Struggle for Citizenship in New York City Housing*. Urbana: University of Illinois Press, 2014.

Goldenback, Gary Dale. "Teaching Career Aspirations of Monolingual and Bilingual Paraprofessionals in the New York City School System." PhD diss., Hofstra University, 1985.

Gooding Jr., Frederick W., and Eric S. Yellin, eds. *Public Workers in Service of America: A Reader.* Urbana: University of Illinois Press, 2022.

Gregory, Stephen. *Black Corona: Race and the Politics of Place in an Urban Community.* Princeton, NJ: Princeton University Press, 1999.

Hall, Burton, ed. *Autocracy and Insurgency in Organized Labor.* New Brunswick, NJ: Transaction Books, 1972.

Hall, Stuart. *Cultural Studies 1983: A Theoretical History.* Durham, NC: Duke University Press, 2016.

Hall, Stuart. "Gramsci's Relevance for the Study of Race and Ethnicity." *Journal of Communication Inquiry* 10 (1986).

Harvey, David. *Rebel Cities: From the Right to the City to the Urban Revolution.* New York: Verso, 2013.

Highsmith, Andrew R. *Demolition Means Progress: Flint, Michigan, and the Fate of the American Metropolis.* Chicago: University of Chicago Press, 2015.

Highsmith, Andrew, and Ansley Erickson. "Segregation as Splitting and Joining: Schools, Housing, and the Many Modes of Jim Crow." *American Journal of Education* (August 2015).

Hill, Norman, and Velma Murphy Hill. *Climbing the Rough Side of the Mountain: The Extraordinary Story of Love, Civil Rights, and Labor Activism.* New York: Regalo Press: 2023.

Hinton, Elizabeth. *From the War on Poverty to the War on Crime: The Making of Mass Incarceration in America.* Cambridge, MA: Harvard University Press, 2016.

Hoffnung-Garskof, Jesse. *A Tale of Two Cities: Santo Domingo and New York After 1950.* Princeton, NJ: Princeton University Press, 2007.

Honey, Michael K. *Going Down Jericho Road: The Memphis Strike, Martin Luther King's Last Campaign.* New York: W. W. Norton, 2008.

Hong, Soo. *A Cord of Three Strands: A New Approach to Parent Engagement in Schools.* Cambridge, MA: Harvard Education Press, 2011.

Issacs, Charles S. *Inside Ocean Hill–Brownsville: A Teachers' Education, 1968–69.* New York: SUNY Press Excelsior Editions, 2014.

Jaffe, Sarah. *Work Won't Love You Back: How Devotion to Our Jobs Keeps Us Exploited, Exhausted, and Alone.* New York: Bold Type Books, 2021.

Johnson, Lauri. "A Generation of Women Activists: African-American Female Educators in Harlem, 1930–1950." *Journal of African-American History* 89, no. 3 (Summer 2004): 223–40.

Jones, William P. *The March on Washington: Jobs, Freedom, and the Forgotten History of Civil Rights.* New York: W. W. Norton & Company, 2014.

Juravich, Nick. "Reclaiming the Promise: Union Advocacy for Paraprofessional-to-Teacher Pathways." *American Educator* (Winter 2022–2023).

Kafka, Judith. *The History of "Zero Tolerance" in American Public Schooling.* New York: Palgrave Studies in Urban Education, 2011.

Kahlenberg, Richard D. *Tough Liberal: Albert Shanker and the Battles over Schools, Unions, Race, and Democracy.* New York: Columbia University Press, 2007.

Kantor, Harvey. "Education, Social Reform, and the State: ESEA and Federal

Education Policy in the 1960s." *American Journal of Education* 100, no. 1 (November 1, 1991): 47–83.

Kantor, Harvey, and Robert Lowe. "Class, Race, and the Emergence of Federal Education Policy: From the New Deal to the Great Society." *Educational Researcher* 24, no. 3 (April 1, 1995): 4–21.

Kaplan, George R. *From Aide to Teacher: The Story of the Career Opportunities Program.* Washington, DC: U.S. Government Printing Office, 1977.

Kaplan, Laura J. "P.S. 25, South Bronx: Bilingual Education and Community Control." PhD diss, 2018.

Katz, Michael B. *Reconstructing American Education.* Cambridge, MA: Harvard University Press, 1987.

Katz, Michael B. *The Undeserving Poor: America's Enduring Confrontation with Poverty: Fully Updated and Revised.* New York: Oxford University Press, 2013.

Katz, Michael B., ed. *The "Underclass" Debate: Views from History.* Princeton, NJ: Princeton University Press, 1993.

Katz, Michael B., and Mark J. Stern. "The New African-American Inequality." *Journal of American History* (June 2005).

Katznelson, Ira. *City Trenches: Urban Politics and the Patterning of Class in the United States.* Chicago: University of Chicago Press, 1982.

Katznelson, Ira, and Margaret Weir. *Schooling for All: Class, Race, and the Decline of the Democratic Ideal.* New York: Basic Books, 1985.

Katznelson, Ira. "Was the Great Society a Lost Opportunity?" in Steve Fraser and Gary Gerstle, eds., *The Rise and Fall of the New Deal Order, 1930–1980.* Princeton, NJ: Princeton University Press, 1989.

Kautz, Matthew B. "From Segregation to Suspension: The Solidification of the Contemporary School-Prison Nexus in Boston, 1963–1985." *Journal of Urban History* 49, no. 5 (September 2023).

Kerner Commission. *Report of the National Advisory Commission on Civil Disorders.* New York: Bantam Books, 1968.

Kornbluh, Felicia Ann. *The Battle for Welfare Rights: Politics and Poverty in Modern America.* Philadelphia: University of Pennsylvania Press, 2007.

Labaree, David F. "The Winning Ways of a Losing Strategy: Educationalizing Social Problems in the United States." *Educational Theory* 58, no. 4 (November 1, 2008): 447–60.

Lachman, Seymour P., and Robert Polner, *The Man Who Saved New York: Hugh Carey and the Great Fiscal Crisis of 1975.* Albany: State University of New York Press, 2010.

Lee, Sonia Song-Ha. *Building a Latino Civil Rights Movement: Puerto Ricans, African Americans, and the Pursuit of Racial Justice in New York City.* Chapel Hill: University of North Carolina Press, 2014.

Levine, Daniel. *Bayard Rustin and the Civil Rights Movement.* New Brunswick, NJ: Rutgers University Press, 2000.

Lewis, Heather. *New York City Public Schools from Brownsville to Bloomberg: Community Control and Its Legacy.* New York: Teachers College Press, 2013.

Lissy, Rachel E. "From Rehabilitation to Punishment: The Institutionalization of Suspension Policies in Post–World War II New York City Schools." PhD diss., University of California, 2015.

MacLean, Nancy. *Freedom Is Not Enough: The Opening of the American Workplace.* Cambridge, MA: Harvard/Russell Sage, 2008.

Maier, Mark. *City Unions: Managing Discontent in New York City.* New Brunswick, NJ: Rutgers University Press, 1987.

Marable, Manning, and Elizabeth Kai Hinton, eds. *The New Black History: Revisiting the Second Reconstruction.* New York: Palgrave Macmillan, 2011.

Mark, Jorie Lester. *Paraprofessionals in Education: A Study of the Training and Utilization of Paraprofessionals in U.S. Public School Systems Enrolling 5,000 or More Pupils.* New York: Bank Street College of Education, 1976.

Markowitz, Gerald, and David Rosner. *Children, Race, and Power: Kenneth and Mamie Clark's Northside Center.* New York: Routledge, 1999.

McCartin, Joseph A. *Collision Course: Ronald Reagan, the Air Traffic Controllers, and the Strike That Changed America.* New York: Oxford University Press, 2013.

McGuinn, Patrick J. *No Child Left Behind and the Transformation of Federal Education Policy, 1965–2005.* Lawrence: University Press of Kansas, 2006.

Moynihan, Daniel Patrick. *Maximum Feasible Misunderstanding: Community Action in the War on Poverty.* New York: The Free Press, 1969.

Moynihan, Daniel Patrick. *The Negro Family: A Case for National Action.* Washington, DC: Department of Labor, 1965.

Murch, Donna. *Living for the City: Migration, Education, and the Rise of the Black Panther Party in Oakland, California.* Chapel Hill: University of North Carolina Press, 2010.

Murphy, Marjorie. *Blackboard Unions: The AFT and the NEA, 1900–1980.* Ithaca, NY: Cornell University Press, 1990.

Nadasen, Premilla. *Household Workers Unite: The Untold Story of African American Women Who Built a Movement.* Reprint edition. Boston: Beacon Press, 2016.

Nadasen, Premilla. "Rethinking Care Work: (Dis)Affection and the Politics of Caring." *Feminist Formations* 33, no. 1 (2021).

Nadasen, Premilla. *Welfare Warriors: The Welfare Rights Movement in the United States.* New York: Routledge, 2005.

Naples, Nancy A. *Grassroots Warriors: Activist Mothering, Community Work, and the War on Poverty.* New York: Routledge, 1998.

Nelson, Adam R. *The Elusive Ideal: Equal Educational Opportunity and the Federal Role in Boston's Public Schools, 1950–1985.* Chicago: University of Chicago Press, 2005.

O'Connor, Alice. *Poverty Knowledge: Social Science, Social Policy, and the Poor in Twentieth-Century U.S. History.* Princeton, NJ: Princeton University Press, 2001.

Ohlin, Lloyd, and Richard A. Cloward. *Delinquency and Opportunity: A Study of Delinquent Gangs.* New York: Routledge, 1961.

Orleck, Annelise. *Storming Caesars Palace: How Black Mothers Fought Their Own War on Poverty.* Boston: Beacon Press, 2005.

Orleck, Annelise, and Lisa Gayle Hazirjian, eds. *The War on Poverty: A New Grassroots History, 1964–1980*. Athens: University of Georgia Press, 2011.

Park, Charles B. "The Bay City Experiment . . . As Seen by the Director." *Journal of Teacher Education* 7, no. 2 (June 1, 1956): 101–10.

Pawlewicz, Diana D'Amico. *Blaming Teachers: Professionalization Policies and the Failure of Reform in American History*. New Brunswick, NJ: Rutgers University Press, 2020.

Pawlewicz, Diana D'Amico, ed. *Walkout! Teacher Militancy, Activism, and School Reform*. Charlotte, NC: Information Age Publishing, 2022.

Payne, Charles M., and Adam Green, eds. *Time Longer than Rope: A Century of African American Activism, 1850–1950*. New York: New York University Press, 2003.

Payne, Charles M., and Carol Sills Strickland, eds. *Teach Freedom: Education for Liberation in the African-American Tradition*. New York: Teachers College Press, 2008.

Pearl, Arthur, and Frank Riessman. *New Careers for the Poor: The Nonprofessional in Human Service*. New York: Free Press, 1965.

Perks, Robert, and Alistair Thompson, eds. *The Oral History Reader*. 2nd ed. New York: Routledge, 2006.

Perlstein, Daniel Hiram. *Justice, Justice: School Politics and the Eclipse of Liberalism*. New York: Peter Lang, 2004.

Perlstein, Rick. *Nixonland: The Rise of a President and the Fracturing of America*. New York: Scribner, 2009.

Perrillo, Jonna. *Uncivil Rights: Teachers, Unions, and Race in the Battle for School Equity*. Chicago: University of Chicago Press, 2012.

Phillips-Fein, Kim. *Fear City: New York's Fiscal Crisis and the Rise of Austerity Politics*. New York: Metropolitan Books, 2017.

Piven, Frances Fox, and Richard Cloward. *Poor People's Movements: How They Succeed, Why They Fail*. New York: Vintage, 1978.

Podair, Jerald E. *Bayard Rustin: American Dreamer*. Blue Ridge Summit, PA: Rowman & Littlefield Publishers, 2008.

Podair, Jerald E. *The Strike That Changed New York: Blacks, Whites, and the Ocean Hill–Brownsville Crisis*. New Haven, CT: Yale University Press, 2002.

Pritchett, Wendell. *Brownsville, Brooklyn: Blacks, Jews, and the Changing Face of the Ghetto*. Chicago: University of Chicago Press, 2003.

Purnell, Brian. *Fighting Jim Crow in the County of Kings: The Congress of Racial Equality in Brooklyn*. Lexington: University Press of Kentucky, 2014.

Quinn, Johanna S. "Unequal Work in Unequal Schools: Working in NYC Middle Schools in an Era of Accountability." PhD diss., University of Wisconsin, 2017.

Quinn, Johanna S., and Myra Marx Ferree. "Schools as Workplaces: Intersectional Regimes of Inequality." *Gender, Work & Organization* 26, no. 12 (2019).

Ransby, Barbara. *Ella Baker and the Black Freedom Movement*. Chapel Hill: University of North Carolina Press, 2003.

Ravitch, Diane. *The Great Schools Wars: New York City 1805–1973*. New York: Basic Books, 1973.

Remnick, Noah. "'The Police State in Franklin K. Lane': Desegregation, Student Resistance, and the Carceral Turn at a New York City High School." *Journal of Urban History* 49, no. 5 (September 2023).

Rickford, Russell. *We Are an African People: Independent Education, Black Power, and the Radical Imagination.* New York: Oxford University Press, 2016.

Riessman, Frank. *Mental Health of the Poor: New Treatment Approaches for Low Income People.* New York: Free Press of Glencoe, 1964.

Riessman, Frank. *The Culturally Deprived Child.* New York: Harper, 1962.

Riessman, Frank. "Workers' Attitudes toward Participation and Leadership." PhD diss., Columbia University, 1955.

Riessman, Frank, and Hermine I. Popper, eds. *Up from Poverty: New Career Ladders for Nonprofessionals.* New York: Harper & Row, 1968.

Roderick, Tom. *A School of Our Own: Parents, Power, and Community at the East Harlem Block Schools.* New York: Teachers College Press, 2001.

Rodgers, Daniel T. *Age of Fracture.* Cambridge, MA: Harvard University Press, 2011.

Rogers, Bethany. "'Better' People, Better Teaching: The Vision of the National Teacher Corps, 1965–1968." *History of Education Quarterly,* Vol. 49, No. 3 (August 2009).

Rogers, Ibram H. *The Black Campus Movement: Black Students and the Racial Reconstitution of Higher Education, 1965–1972.* Albany: State University of New York Press, 2012.

Roosevelt, Grace G. *Creating a College That Works: Audrey Cohen and Metropolitan College of New York.* Albany: State University of New York Press, 2015.

Rustin, Bayard. *Down the Line: The Collected Writings of Bayard Rustin.* Chicago: Quadrangle Books, 1971.

Rustin, Bayard. "From Protest to Politics: The Future of the Civil Rights Movement." *Commentary Magazine,* February 1, 1965.

Sanders, Crystal R. *A Chance for Change: Head Start and Mississippi's Black Freedom Struggle.* Chapel Hill: University of North Carolina Press, 2016.

Selden, David. *The Teacher Rebellion.* Washington, DC: Howard University Press, 1985.

Self, Robert O. *American Babylon: Race and the Struggle for Postwar Oakland.* Princeton, NJ: Princeton University Press, 2005.

Shelton, Jon K. "Against the Public: The Pittsburgh Teachers Strike of 1975–1976 and the Crisis of the Labor-Liberal Coalition." *Labor* 10, no. 2 (June 20, 2013): 55–75.

Shelton, Jon K. *Teacher Strike! Public Education and the Making of a New American Political Order.* Urbana: University of Illinois Press, 2017.

Singh, Nikhil Pal. *Black Is a Country: Race and the Unfinished Struggle for Democracy.* Cambridge, MA: Harvard University Press, 2005.

Slater, Joseph. *Public Workers: Government Employee Unions, the Law, and the State, 1900–1962.* Ithaca, NY: Cornell University Press, 2004.

Sleeter, Christine. "Learning Disabilities: The Social Construction of a Special Education Category." *Exceptional Children* 53, no. 1 (1986).

Sleeter, Christine. "Why Is There Learning Disabilities? A Critical Analysis of the Birth of the Field in Its Social Context." *Disability Studies Quarterly* 30, no. 2 (June 1, 2010). https://doi.org/10.18061/dsq.v30i2.1261.

Snyder, Robert W. *Crossing Broadway: Washington Heights and the Promise of New York City*. Ithaca, NY: Cornell University Press, 2014.

Soffer, Jonathan. *Ed Koch and the Rebuilding of New York City*. New York: Columbia University Press, 2010.

Sokol, Jason. *All Eyes Are Upon Us: Race and Politics from Boston to Brooklyn*. New York: Basic Books, 2014.

Spear, Michael. "In the Shadows of the 1970s Fiscal Crisis: New York City's Municipal Unions in the Twenty-First Century." *WorkingUSA: The Journal of Labor and Society* 13 (September 2010): 351–66.

Stein, David P. "Fearing Inflation, Inflating Fears: The End of Full Employment and the Rise of the Carceral State." PhD diss., University of Southern California, 2014.

Stein, David P. "'This Nation Has Never Honestly Dealt with the Question of a Peacetime Economy': Coretta Scott King and the Struggle for a Nonviolent Economy in the 1970s." *Souls* 18, no. 1 (March 14, 2016): 80–105.

Stein, Judith. *Pivotal Decade: How the United States Traded Factories for Finance in the Seventies*. New Haven, CT: Yale University Press, 2010.

Straus, Emily. "Unequal Pieces of a Shrinking Pie: The Struggle between African Americans and Latinos over Education, Employment, and Empowerment in Compton, California." *History of Education Quarterly* 49 (November 2009).

Sugrue, Thomas J. *The Origins of the Urban Crisis: Race and Inequality in Postwar Detroit*. Princeton, NJ: Princeton University Press, 1995.

Taylor, Clarence, ed. *Civil Rights in New York City: From World War II to the Giuliani Era*. New York: Fordham University Press, 2011.

Taylor, Clarence. *Knocking at Our Own Door: Milton A. Galamison and the Struggle to Integrate New York City Schools*. New York: Columbia University Press, 1997.

Taylor, Clarence. *Reds at the Blackboard: Communism, Civil Rights, and the New York City Teachers Union*. New York: Columbia University Press, 2011.

Theoharis, Jeanne, and Komozi Woodard, *Groundwork: Local Black Freedom Movements in America*. New York: New York University Press, 2005.

Thompson, E. P. *The Making of the English Working Class*. New York: Vintage, 1966.

Todd-Breland, Elizabeth. *A Political Education: Black Politics and Education Reform in Chicago since the 1960s*. Chapel Hill: University of North Carolina Press, 2018.

Urban, Wayne J. *Gender, Race and the National Education Association: Professionalism and Its Limitations*. New York: Routledge, 2000.

Walker, Vanessa Siddle. *Their Highest Potential: An African American School Community in the Segregated South*. Chapel Hill: University of North Carolina Press, 1996.

Weiner, Lois. *The Future of Our Schools: Teachers Unions and Social Justice*. Chicago: Haymarket Books, 2012.

Weir, Margaret. *Politics and Jobs: The Boundaries of Employment Policy in the United States.* Princeton, NJ: Princeton University Press, 1992.

Wilcox, Preston. "Parental Decision-Making: An Educational Necessity." *Theory into Practice* 11, no. 3 (1972): 178–82.

Wilkerson, Jessica. *To Live Here, You Have to Fight: How Women Led Appalachian Movements for Social Justice.* Urbana: University of Illinois Press, 2019.

Will, Madeline. "Paraprofessionals: As the 'Backbones' of the Classroom, They Get Low Pay, Little Support." *Education Week*, June 15, 2022. https://www.edweek.org/leadership/paraprofessionals-as-the-backbones-of-the-classroom-they-get-low-pay-little-support/2022/06.

Williams, Rhonda Y. *Concrete Demands: The Search for Black Power in the 20th Century.* New York: Routledge, 2014.

Williams, Rhonda Y. *The Politics of Public Housing: Black Women's Struggles against Urban Inequality.* New York: Oxford University Press, 2005.

Winant, Gabriel. *The Next Shift: The Fall of Industry and the Rise of Health Care in Rust Belt America.* Cambridge, MA: Harvard University Press, 2021.

Woodsworth, Michael. *Battle for Bed-Stuy: The Long War on Poverty in New York City.* Cambridge, MA: Harvard University Press, 2016.

Yale-Fairfield Study of Elementary Teaching. *Teacher Assistants: An Abridged Report.* Prepared by John H. Howell. New Haven, CT: Yale University Press, 1959.

Index

49, 63, 64; Preston Wilcox and, 33;
Women's Talent Corps and, 49, 64,
99–100; *Youth in the Ghetto* and,
37–38, 41, 63
Pittsburgh Courier, 32
Piven, Francis Fox, 211–12, 239, 304n110
Popper, Hermine: *Up from Poverty*
(with Riessman), 194–95
Portalatin, Maria, 175, 176
Powell, Adam Clayton, Jr., 33
Powell, James, 44
PRESS (Paraprofessionals Retrained
for Employment as School Secretar-
ies), 243–44
Professional Air Traffic Controllers
Organization (PATCO) strike, 242
professionalism of teachers: appren-
ticeship model of paraprofessionalism and, 106, 119; decoupling of
professional instruction from social-
reproductive work, 8–9; postwar
redefinition of, 8; unionization and,
8, 9, 14
Project Follow Through. *See* Follow
Through
Project Head Start. *See* Head Start
Public Education Association, 103
pull-out model of pedagogy, 39–40

Quinones, Anna, 76

Randolph, A. Philip: A. Philip Randolph Institute (APRI) and, 47–48,
88, 180–81, 297n99; civil rights and
paraprofessional organizing, 137, 163,
172, 180–81; "Freedom Budget for All
Americans" (with Rustin), 4, 47–48,
180, 195, 299n20; "march on conventions" movement, 87; Ocean Hill-
Brownsville crisis and, 88–89
Rauner, Bruce, 252
Reagan, Ronald, 211, 227, 242
Reconnection for Learning (Bundy),
44–45, 93
*Regents of the University of California v.
Bakke*, 184
Riessman, Frank, 193–96; background,
41, 187–88; Career Opportunities Program and, 131–32, 145, 188,

288n32 (*see also* Career Opportunities Program); *The Culturally
Deprived Child*, 194; full-employment
advocacy, 207–8, 211, 218; National
Paraprofessionals Conference and,
177; New Careers Development
Center, New York University, 45–46,
66, 105, 159, 188, 193–96, 213; *New
Careers for the Poor* (with Pearl),
41–43, 45, 62–63, 92, 143, 184–85,
187, 191, 193–95; New Careers Train-
ing Laboratory (NCTL), Queens
College, CUNY, 173, 188–93, 197–99,
213, 220–21; "new human services
paradigm" and, 41–43; *Public Service
Employment* (with Gartner and
Nixon), 211–12; *Up from Poverty*
(with Popper), 194–95; work with
Mobilization for Youth, 34, 35, 46,
186, 211–12
Robbins, Larry, 117
Roberts, Lillian, 104, 108
Robinson, Isaiah, 128, 229
Rockefeller, Nelson, 211
Rodgers, Julia, 110
Rose, Marion E., 156–57
Roth, Gladys: as UFT paraprofessional
field organizer, 93, 94, 95–96, 101–3,
106, 111, 169; UFT survey of teachers
and paraprofessionals, 59, 111, 143
Rustin, Bayard: at A. Philip Randolph
Institute (APRI), 47–48, 88, 180–81,
297n99; Black Power movement
and, 47–48, 87–88, 203; civil rights
and paraprofessional organiz-
ing, 137, 163, 172, 174, 179–82, 184;
"Freedom Budget for All Americans"
(with Randolph), 4, 47–48, 180, 195,
299n20; full-employment advocacy and, 4, 48, 179–81, 194, 207–8;
March on Washington for Jobs and
Freedom, 43; national organization of paras and, 160; Ocean Hill-
Brownsville crisis and, 88–89; para
contract of 1970 as the "Triumph of
the Paraprofessionals," 1, 2, 4, 156;
Socialist Party of America/Social
Democrats USA and, 180; support for
AFT paraprofessional unionization,

NICK JURAVICH is an assistant professor of history and labor studies and the associate director of the Labor Resource Center at UMass Boston.

The University of Illinois Press
is a founding member of the
Association of University Presses.

University of Illinois Press
1325 South Oak Street
Champaign, IL 61820-6903
www.press.uillinois.edu